Keeping Faith, Losing Faith

Keeping Faith, Losing Faith: Religious Belief and Political Economy

Annual Supplement to Volume 40
History of Political Economy

Edited by Bradley Bateman and H. Spencer Banzhaf

Duke University Press
Durham and London 2008

Printed in the United States of America
on acid-free paper. ISBN 978-0-8223-6702-4.
This is the 2008 supplement to
History of Political Economy, ISSN 0018-2702.

To my father, Harry B. Banzhaf,
my first economics teacher
—HSB

To the memory of my first son, Brad,
who taught me much in a short life
—BWB

Contents

Keeping Faith, Losing Faith: An Introduction

Bradley Bateman and H. Spencer Banzhaf

Although some of the early efforts of Western social and political theorists were made in opposition to religious interpretations of the world, religious belief held sway throughout the early modern period as the dominant means to interpret human experience.[1] Sometime in the nineteenth century, however, economics and the other social sciences began to develop analytical models that were completely severed from theology and religious belief. For example, in the late eighteenth century, Thomas Robert Malthus's famous *Essay on the Principle of Population* (1798) was animated by his religious beliefs, but by the late nineteenth century, Henry Sidgwick and Alfred Marshall were each working to develop an analytical apparatus that, while still focused heavily on social ethics, was completely secular.

Viewed from the perspective of the sociology of religion, as it first was being contemporaneously developed by Émile Durkheim and Max Weber, this secularization of economics would appear to be nothing more than

We thank Duke University Press and the Lilly Endowment for generous financial support for the preparation of this book and for the conference on which it is based. We also thank the editors of *HOPE*, Craufurd Goodwin, Neil De Marchi, and Roy Weintraub, and the Department of Economics at Duke University for giving us the opportunity to hold the event and for their thoughtful comments throughout the process.

1. Albert O. Hirschman's *Passions and the Interests: Political Arguments for Capitalism before Its Triumph* (1977) may be the most well-known and accessible guide to the early efforts to create social and political thought not based in religious self-understanding.

History of Political Economy 40 (annual suppl.) DOI 10.1215/00182702-2007-057

a specific instance of the broader secularization of developing societies, in which the increasingly specialized roles for social institutions increasingly marginalized religion, which they believed eventually would die out. Indeed, reflecting on the institution of his own Cambridge tradition in economics, John Maynard Keynes viewed this process as having been completed by roughly 1863, when Marshall started his career at Cambridge University. "Marshall's Cambridge career came just at the date which will," Keynes ([1933] 1972, 168) wrote, "be regarded by the historians of opinion as the critical moment at which Christian dogma fell away from the serious philosophical world of England, or at any rate of Cambridge."

Of course, as events in recent decades have made clear—from the rise of Hindu fundamentalists in India to the Iranian revolution, from the Solidarity movement in Poland to the rise of evangelical Protestantism in the "new right" of the United States—religion and religious engagement with the polis is not going away any time soon. Accordingly, the recent trend in sociology has been to abandon the secularization hypothesis. But what then do we do with the fact that economics today clearly looks much more secular than it did in 1800? José Casanova (1994) has provided a particularly nuanced and helpful account of secularization. Casanova affirms that the increasing differentiation of social institutions has helped shape a world in which religious belief no longer informs the modern understanding of how economic and political institutions function. Consequently, even believers do not view religious understanding as a prerequisite for expertise in these arenas. On the other hand, religious belief has not declined in the modern world. Nor has religious engagement with the state and with broader networks of social relations declined. Thus, even while believing that the economy *functions* in theologically neutral ways, modern citizens have not abandoned their religious commitments when it comes to evaluating economic outcomes and behaviors.

Casanova also reminds us that all of these generalizations are historically contingent; some specific times and places will fit them well, others will not. In this vein, Robert Wuthnow (1992) has pointed out that the eruptions of religion into the public square during the 1980s were hardly unprecedented even if they did serve as a wake-up call to social scientists. In the United States, the 1970s saw the election of a "born again" president, the Jesus movement, and experimentation with Eastern religions. In the 1960s, it was the religiously inspired civil rights movement. The presence of so many revivals on so regular a basis suggests that religion has been a regular visitor to the public square in America, whether or not social scientists have noted it.

If social scientists are now noticing the continuing salience of religion in politics and society in recent history,[2] might we, as historians of social science, also take note? Might it not be possible that *social scientists themselves* have developed their ideas in harmony, or in tension, with their religious beliefs and commitments?

Religious belief and economic reasoning have had a long and intimate history, and there is a substantial literature in the history of economic thought on these connections in premodern eras.[3] But with some exceptions, historians have implicitly agreed with Keynes, writing as if such connections were of no importance in modern times. Yet the period from the middle of the nineteenth to the middle of the twentieth century did not involve a sudden transition, or even a steady progression, to a secular economics.

Some historians of economics have begun to rediscover and reemphasize the importance of religion in the history of modern economics. For example, A. M. C. Waterman (1991) has argued that attempts to read the "economic" and the "theological" portions of Malthus's *Essay* separately are misguided; the two are a coherent whole. In an ongoing project that includes a contribution to this volume, António Almodovar and Pedro Teixeira have shown how, in Catholic Europe, the "labor question" that arose in the last decades of the nineteenth century as a result of the Second Industrial Revolution posed problems that forced many economic theorists back to their religious beliefs. Some of this work was in dialogue with the official teachings of the church, as exemplified in the papal encyclicals *Rerum Novarum* and *Quadragesimo Anno*, which attempted to articulate a humane, Christian understanding of how to live in a seemingly inhuman capitalism. And one of us has recently emphasized how, at the same time in the United States, economists returning from their German graduate studies included many dedicated to Christian socialism and the Social Gospel. Like their European counterparts in the Catholic Church, these American Protestants felt that their religious beliefs were an indispensable part of their understanding of why it was necessary to

2. We have already discussed the case of sociology. We discuss such discovery in economics in some detail below. For an example from political science, see Philpott 2002. Philpott argues that if the events of the 1980s were not enough to awaken scholars to the fact that religious motives are as relevant for international relations as material ones, then the events of 9/11 certainly should.

3. See, for example, Gordon 1989 and Lowry and Gordon 1998.

ameliorate the social ills caused as millions of workers were drawn into factory work by rapid industrialization (Bateman 1998, 1999, 2001).

These examples are natural, even obvious, places to start an inquiry into economists' engagement with religion. (Malthus was, after all, an ordained Anglican minister.) When we began talking about the project that led to the volume in your hands, we started from the idea that the time was right to begin broadening this project of exploring the role of religion in economics.

The 2007 Duke *History of Political Economy* Conference

The opportunity to seize that moment came in the form of a small conference hosted by Duke University Press and Duke's Department of Economics in April 2007, with generous support from the Lilly Endowment. We suggested a conference that would explore the complex history of the relationship(s) between religious and economic thinking in Europe and North America from the early nineteenth century to 1950. We were interested in describing, contextualizing, and interpreting the work of economists who were animated by their religious faith as well as those who had helped bring about the rupture between their discipline and theology. We were primarily interested in the work of those who could be considered professional economists (understanding the meaning of that concept to have changed over our period), rather than the social writings of theologians and religious leaders, except insofar as the latter have a direct bearing on the former.[4]

When we made the original call for papers, we suggested that proposals might address some of the following questions:

- Who were economists whose work was animated by a desire to keep religious perspectives in political economy? How did their work differ—in methodology, motivation, narrative, and area of inquiry—from the work of other contemporary economists and social theorists?
- What differences existed between these patterns in Europe and North America?

4. Such theological writings, of course, have a long and uninterrupted history. For a recent example of a theological critique of market behavior, see, for example, Stephen Long's *Divine Economy* (2000).

- Were there significant differences in the efforts of people from different religious traditions to keep religious perspectives in political economy?
- Did religious economists work together in formal or informal networks to integrate their faith and study, and if so, what was their form and how did they shape the history of economics?
- To what extent were the political economists who tried to keep religious perspectives in their work successful or unsuccessful at influencing public policy?
- How did the nature of the efforts to keep religious perspectives in political economy change through the period 1800–1950? Were these changes in response to clearly discernible events?
- How did secularization finally overtake mainstream economic analysis? Did this take place differently in different contexts? Was European secularization significantly different than North American secularization?

Two topics that we specifically were *not* interested in were the economic study of religion or religious organizations and economics per se as religion. The first of these approaches is surveyed nicely in Laurence Iannaccone's (1998) review essay; the second is well represented by Robert Nelson (2001). Both of these approaches make valid rhetorical points, but the points are different than those we wish to explore in this volume. In practice, the former ignores the fact that religious belief and economic reasoning have a long and intimate history, focusing instead on how the tools of traditional (secular) neoclassical economics can be used to analyze religious institutions. The latter, while recognizing the buried history of connections between economics and religious belief, focuses its analysis on the idea that economics *itself* is a religion.

The response to our call for papers was gratifying, affirming our intuition that the time was ripe for considering the *historical* relationship between religious and economic thought. We received nearly fifty proposals for the twelve to fifteen slots available for presentations. At least half of the proposals were of a very high quality, so we easily could have accepted twice the number of papers or held a second conference. It is our hope that this supply will be met by an equal or greater demand for more such work. This seems likely, for the essays in this volume, even when taken as a whole, are only a beginning. They lay out some of the most compelling chapters in the history of religious belief and economic analysis, and they go a long way toward sketching out the parameters of that history. Nevertheless, many questions remain.

Some of those questions are raised by the essays in this volume; others were already apparent, but we excluded them in our planning to keep the project manageable; still others we had hoped to see addressed but by chance were not taken up. We purposely made the call for proposals for the conference as inclusive as possible, given our own ignorance about the set of potential topics. We specifically did not call for papers on Christianity and economics because we did not want to close the door to economics and other religion(s). That said, we understood that by restricting the geographic and temporal coverage of the conference to Europe and North America in the nineteenth and twentieth centuries, the proposals would be skewed to the Christian tradition, simply because those countries have had majority Christian populations. Still, we had hoped that we might receive proposals, for example, that would give us a window on the connections that emerged in the early twentieth century when Jews began to enter the economics profession in the United States, but none appeared.[5] In fact, nearly all the proposals we received, and all we accepted, were about Christians or people primarily operating within Christian traditions.

We did, however, receive proposals representing a broad geographic spread, including Continental Europe, Britain, and North America. One proposal we did not accept for the conference dealt with connections between Spain and Latin America but fell outside the time frame we had set; another one discussed Canada but did not obviously fit with the other proposals. We received numerous proposals about individual nineteenth-century European Catholic writers.

The proposals we accepted fell into three broad categories in the Christian tradition: Continental European Catholicism, British Protestantism, and American Protestantism. This diversity allows for some interesting comparisons and contrasts. As mentioned above, for instance, it is easy to see that the Second Industrial Revolution and the economies of scale that it wrought led to a religious response among economists in both Continental Europe and the United States, although it was largely a Catholic response in Europe and largely Protestant in America. And these responses varied greatly not only in the theological self-understanding of the econo-

5. David Hollinger's (2001) essay on secularization in the American academy is one of the few references we have to the early-twentieth-century entrance of Jews into the discipline of economics in America.

mists but in the ways that theory ultimately developed and the forms that economic analysis took. For instance, the Catholic economists in Europe were largely opposed to utilitarian analysis, while the Protestant economists in America introduced utilitarian analysis to American economics.[6]

Although pleased by this diversity, we are nevertheless aware of several holes in this volume's coverage. One of the obvious potential topics for the conference, never proposed, is the connection between Northern European Protestantism and economic analysis. There are clear possibilities in Sweden, Norway, Denmark, Germany, and the Netherlands to see how leading economists were animated by their Protestant beliefs. There was some irony in this lacuna, since we first formed the idea of the conference after attending a session together at the 2004 History of Economics Society meetings in Toronto, in which we heard a paper on the influence of Protestant social thought in Danish economics (Kaegard 2004).

Nor did we receive any proposals on economists' involvement in the different strains of the Christian Democratic parties emerging in Europe in the twentieth century and their late-nineteenth-century antecedents such as the Dutch Anti Revolutionary Party (primarily Reformed) and Germany's Center Party (primary Catholic). Nor, with the exception of a few passing references in the essay on France by Gilbert Faccarello and Philippe Steiner, did we receive any proposals about Continental European Protestantism in any other country, about the religious influences on the German historical school (except at one remove in Don Frey's paper on the American economist Richard T. Ely), or about Spanish Catholicism in the period 1850–1950.

One of the biggest lacunas is undoubtedly the absence of a full treatment of the effects of Marxism on the secularism of European thought, in general, and of economics, in particular. Marx's work in economics fits into a larger Continental tradition that includes Friedrich Nietzsche and Durkheim and that saw social analysis as a part of an inevitable secularization of society and human knowledge. The nature of that secularization effort and its impact across European economics is an important story that still needs to be explored. Almodovar and Teixeira's essay on European Catholicism (this volume) touches on some of the reaction against Marx among Catholic thinkers, but the main story about Marx and his influence on the relationship(s) between religious belief and economic analysis remains to be told.

6. See note 8 for references to the American side of this story.

Among the proposals we received about British economists and British economics, none directly addressed the work of Marshall or A. C. Pigou, two men who had been intensely religious when they were young but whose economics was secular. How and why these two great theorists evolved away from religious belief, and how that evolution affected their work as economists, is another untold story.

In the American case, everything we received dealt with American Protestantism. There was nothing on the Catholic Church in America and nothing, for instance, on Father John Ryan or on the formation of the Catholic Economics Association (now the Association for Social Economists) in 1941.[7]

All of this is by way of repeating that while this collection is the first attempt to deal with the history of the relationship between economic analysis and religious belief transnationally, it is only a beginning. There is much more ground still to be covered, and many stories waiting to be told.

These holes notwithstanding, the essays collected here raise several important themes, two of which in particular arise repeatedly: (1) the tension between Christianity and utilitarianism; and (2) secularization. Because of their prominence, we discuss these in the next two sections.

Christianity versus Utilitarianism

The antagonism between Christianity and utilitarianism is immediately apparent in the opening essay by Faccarello and Steiner, on the debates in early-nineteenth-century French economics following the Revolution, and in the final essay, by Ross Emmett, on the work of the great American neoclassicist Frank Knight. Almost everywhere one looks at the fissures between religious belief and the emergence of modern economic theory, there is a tension between the principles of Christian faith and the utilitarian underpinnings of modern economics. This tension is evident in descriptive and normative accounts of human behavior. Unlike utilitarianism, Christian thought would never reduce the *description* of human behavior to simply utility maximization. Likewise, the normative *prescription* of Christians that humans should love one another is a far cry from utilitarianism's insistence that good actions are necessarily those that maximize material well-being or individual preference.

7. Elsewhere, Kevin Schmiesing (2004) has provided a valuable start to this inquiry.

In Europe in the eighteenth and nineteenth centuries, this tension was mirrored in the often explicit tensions between liberalism and the ancien régime or between modernity and tradition. As the Roman Catholic Church began to lose its authority, and as markets began to shape everyday life more and more, European social theorists realized the inherent tensions between the materialistic, individualistic ethic of the market and the religious, traditional ethic of the old order. In practice, as Almodovar and Teixeira's essay shows, this tension came to be expressed for many European economists in a battle between Catholic belief and utilitarian ideals. Catholics joined the battle at numerous points, but we note only two of them here. At the Catholic University of Louvain, Charles Périn (1815–1905) argued that liberal economics encouraged excessive self-gratification, to the point of being socially detrimental, a tendency that could be tempered only by the Christian virtue of charity and the discipline of renouncement. Second, as discussed by Daniela Parisi, at the Catholic University of Milan the economist Francesco Vito developed an economic theory centered on the concept of personalism, which had its fullest expression in *Rerum Novarum* and *Quadragesimo Anno*. Thus, even while bringing English blueprints such as the Beveridge Report to Italian welfare reform, Vito tried to reshape those blueprints into more holistic, humanitarian endeavors.

One finds this same tension in Britain. Harro Maas tells a story primarily about why Richard Jones and William Whewell objected to Ricardian-style deductive economics. Such an approach, they believed, led scientists to substitute their own axioms for God, in contrast to a humble discovery of God's laws as he reveals them in nature. Even within this broader methodological debate, however, it was the particular axiom of utilitarianism that was most in dispute. As Steven Medema shows, a generation later, Sidgwick adopted utilitarian imperatives while arguing that individuals' self-interested pursuit of their desires would not, in fact, produce the greatest good for society. On the other hand, Roger Backhouse tells the story of a group of early-twentieth-century welfare economists who rejected the utilitarian welfare economics that was emerging from the tradition of Sidgwick and was being further developed by Marshall and Pigou. R. H. Tawney, J. A. Hobson, and Sir Henry Clay all sought an alternative ethic to utilitarianism. They believed that there was more to human welfare than the mere acquisition of material goods or, for that matter, the fulfillment of any individual desire.

In the American case, Stewart Davenport explains how Francis Wayland and others commonly referred to as "the clerical economists" reinterpreted faculty psychology so that self-interest was part of one's moral sense (or conscience) rather than a passion. Only by bestowing self-interest with this virtue could they prepare the ground in which political economy could take root in America. This ground would appear to have been one receptive to utilitarianism. This was borne out in the closing decades of the nineteenth century by the leading young American economists being schooled in Germany, the most prominent among them being John Bates Clark and Ely. Studying in Heidelberg under Karl Knies, one of the leaders of the older German historical school, they learned the rudiments of marginal utility analysis as well as a deep-seated suspicion of the applicability of utility analysis to *all* economic problems. Returning home, they introduced utility analysis to American economics, but they also kept it closely cosseted within a larger ethical context that included Christian principles and national values. Following the First World War, when their work was supplanted in the push to remove the Christian influence from American social science, the cosseting fell away, and the influence of logical positivism and scientism led to a stripped-down and straight-up utilitarianism that would underpin the dominance of modern neoclassicism after the Great Depression.[8]

Secularization

The relationship between economics and religious belief is inevitably tied up with the general question of the extent and nature of the secularization of Western societies, and this points to some of the difficulties in trying to explain the disentanglement of political economy from religious belief. For example, as historians of economics, we must be wary of comparing across time a supposedly fixed subject matter, which is in fact constituted differently in different times. Thus, if we compare economics in the twentieth century to economics in the eighteenth century, the former appears much more secular. But, of course, the twentieth-century meaning of political economy is much more narrowly focused on academic economics than was the contemporaneous meaning of political economy in the eighteenth century. If we were to use a broader definition of political economy

8. For more on what Clark and Ely learned from Knies, see Bateman 2004. For a discussion of how logical positivism filled the vacuum created when Protestant Christianity was purged from American social science after the First World War, see Bateman 2008.

in the twentieth century that included the economic writings of contemporary theologians, priests, and rabbis, economics in the twentieth century would undoubtedly appear more religious. But that would be beside the point, for the narrowing of the definition is itself a manifestation of the kind of institutional differentiation that is the hallmark of secularization. Thus the story of the secularization of economics is inevitably tied up with the broader story of the secularization of the research university (see, e.g., Marsden 1994 and Reuben 1996), and the stories in this volume all follow the trajectory of the professionalization of economics and its evolution into a discipline inseparable from the academy.

As we have noted previously, such institutional differentiation plays a key role in the work of Casanova (1994). Casanova points out that in the nineteenth-century arguments about secularization, several components were conflated and confused. One component was the argument that as social institutions (e.g., the state, the economy, science) became more highly differentiated, specialization allowed people to understand how the institutions functioned without recourse to religious explanations. But attached to this part of the early social-scientific theories of secularization was one of two additional assumptions: either (1) that religious belief itself would wither away and disappear as people came to understand the world without reference to religious explanations of how it functioned, or (2) that religion would become greatly diminished and reduced to no more than a set of private beliefs for people who remained too superstitious or too weak to accept the nonreligious understanding of the modern world.

Those who look primarily at the European experience often argue that secularization, understood in one of these two ways, has indeed taken place, while those who look at the United States and much of the rest of the world often argue that the secularization predicted in the nineteenth century has not happened.[9] If we mean by secularization whether or not people believe in a god (or gods), then it seems clear that Europe is the only place in which widespread secularization has taken place; everywhere else in the world, religious belief permeates individual and social life.

As a matter of generalization, then, religious belief certainly has not withered away and died. Nor has it become a purely private sphere of

9. At the extremes in the debate over secularization would be Steve Bruce (2002), who insists that religious belief has declined everywhere in modernity, and Rodney Stark and William Bainbridge (1985), who insist that religious belief flourishes in modernity and will continue to do so.

human experience. Religiously based ethics and morals still anchor arguments about wealth, liberty, and policy in many places in the world. Religious institutions enter the public square to make such arguments. Yet, as Casanova points out, over the last two hundred years, many institutions have become autonomous spheres clearly differentiated from religious ones. Thus, "like modern science, capitalist markets and modern state bureaucracies manage to function 'as if' God would not exist" (Casanova 1994, 40). In this way, a fundamentalist Christian in the United States might have strong views about the ethics of personal business conduct and about the morality of the distribution of income, yet think that either Ben Bernanke or Alan Greenspan (neither of whom are Christian) could make an excellent chair of the Federal Reserve.

The title of our volume, *Keeping Faith, Losing Faith: Religious Belief and Political Economy*, reflects the general pattern of secularization in both economics and the academy. But because we felt that historians and social scientists have often overemphasized the "losing faith" side of this coupling and uncritically accepted the story of secularization, we were especially interested in the discontinuities in the story and in people who had held on to their religious beliefs as a part of their work as economists. Of course, we also hoped that these stories would shed new light on the trend toward secularization (understood as differentiation within these two important social institutions) between the middle of the nineteenth century and the middle of the twentieth. Several of them do so. In Medema's account of Sidgwick, for example, we see how the psychological crisis of a personal loss of Christian faith, and the quest for a new faith, could drive an economist's agenda—and help shape the future of economics. But the theme of secularization appears in some surprising, indeed ironic, places as well. For example, Faccarello and Steiner tell the story of social theorists who saw in the French Revolution the social evil of wiping away the moderating forces of religion. But by attempting to create new secular civil religions, one might argue that they contributed to marginalizing the Catholic faith in France by differentiating what it had to offer from what was needed in the public sphere. On the other hand, Neil Skaggs tells the story of Henry Thornton, a man who in belief was as orthodox, and who in life was as devoted, as any considered in this volume. Yet Thornton viewed monetary economics, his area of specialty, as purely a technical subject requiring no reference to Christianity or any religious principles. In this way, Thornton, a man of deep faith, also helped differentiate economics from the world of faith.

Casanova's understanding of secularization raises interesting questions about the nature of the story explored in this volume. Has the disentanglement of economics from religion followed from a gradual change in our understanding of how the world works? Is it the case that as the general population came to understand how markets function as an essentially human enterprise, economists followed suit in their own analytic explanations? If rather than disappear altogether or become a purely private matter, religion has maintained its public position, then why has the discipline of economics remained largely based in utilitarianism with little or no explicit acknowledgment of people's religious beliefs in its models of human behavior?[10] As the modern project of forcing a dualism between fact and value loses its force in a postmodern age, will the basis for disentangling social science from religion and (more broadly) ethics erode?

Contemporary Valences and Historical Questions

It seems the answers to these questions may be just as relevant for understanding contemporary economics as for understanding its history. Several trends in economics today resonate with the themes of the following essays.

For example, economists who view their religious commitments as integral to their understanding of what it means to be a good economist have formed and continue to form mutual societies to facilitate interaction and mutual encouragement. We mentioned earlier the Association for Social Economists, organized largely by Catholic economists in 1941, and that group still thrives and publishes a well-respected journal, the *Review of Social Economics*. Although that association no longer has a strictly Christian identity, a new Society of Catholic Social Scientists was born in 1995. The Acton Institute, another group of Catholic economists begun the same year, is more Austrian and libertarian in orientation, but publishes the journal *Markets and Morality*, which covers

10. In his well-known survey of "religion and economics," Laurence Iannaccone (1998) argues that he is interested only in surveying how economists can use their tools to analyze religious behavior, not in analyzing how religious belief might shape economic behavior.

a range of perspectives. Articles often stress the humanist themes of personalism and a suspicion of hard-core utilitarianism.[11]

Groups of evangelical economists have also formed in both the United States (1982) and Britain (1980) under the same name: the Association of Christian Economists. Both groups also publish their own journals, *Faith and Economics* and the *ACE Journal*, respectively. The U.S. group has over three hundred members. It has two stated goals, the first simply to "promote interaction and communication among Christian economists." At this level, it serves as a kind of fellowship group among Christians who happen to be economists. The other goal is "to encourage Christian scholars to explore and communicate the relationship between their faith and the discipline of economics." The understanding of what this relationship entails is itself a matter of discussion within the group. At the mundane end of the spectrum, it may mean the virtue of performing services that are not well rewarded professionally, such as a referee report or preparation in teaching. Or it may mean applying the tools of economics, taken on their own terms, to the biblical commandment to love the poor. At the more radical end, it may mean questioning the utilitarian basis of neoclassical economics.

The question of the role of utilitarianism in economics, one of the most important for the relationship between economics and religion that emerged from the conference, may also be the one that resonates most strongly with contemporary trends in economics. As noted above, some religious economists have begun to question its consonance with their religious beliefs. Moreover, and perhaps more surprisingly, there is important work now being done in economics by people who declare no explicit religious intent but whose work nonetheless opens the possibility for the kind of serious ethical reflection that many people could ground only in their religious belief.

Consider recent work in neuro-economics. Douglas Bernheim and Antonio Rangel (2004) have recently argued that people may not be very good at choosing that which makes them happy, a point that Backhouse's essay notes was also made by J. A. Hobson early in the last century. The failure to choose what makes one most happy is not only a failure of will but a failure of memory. Drawing on modern neuroscience, Bernheim

11. According to the journal's Web page, its purpose is to promote "intellectual exploration of the relationship between economics and morality from both social science and theological perspectives. It seeks to bring together theologians, philosophers, economists, and other scholars for dialogue concerning the morality of the marketplace."

and Rangel show, for example, that addicts' memories systematically overestimate the actual pleasure they received in the past from using alcohol, nicotine, or other substances. As a consequence, when they indulge their addictions, they are systematically disappointed.

Other examples come from work in experimental economics and its connections to game theory and behavioral economics. As these research agendas have arisen and flourished over the last two decades, they have begun to demonstrate the fallacy of assuming that people are simple utility maximizers. As economists have tried to bring the insights of psychology into their modeling and testing of human decision making, they have discovered that people's decisions are not easily explained by utility maximization.

Consider, for example, the case of the dictator game or the ultimatum game. In the latter, two players are given a pot of money (or other reward) to divide. Player 1 proposes a division; Player 2 can accept it or veto it, in which case neither gets anything. Standard theory would predict that Player 1 would propose taking nearly all the pie and that Player 2 would accept (something being better than nothing). But experimental and field evidence has shown neither player acts in this way: Player 1 is often much more generous, and if not, Player 2 will often sacrifice the (smaller) share to penalize Player 1. Moreover, in the simpler dictator game, the second player doesn't even have the veto option, yet the first player often proposes a fair division. James Andreoni and John Miller (2002) have shown that players are consistent across different forms of these games, so the explanation cannot be that people are confused or irrational. Moreover, the second player never punishes a first mover who is *more* than fair, so the explanation cannot be *simply* over preferences for *equity* in distributing the resource. Rather, preferences must be over players' behaviors and norms as well as over the actual distribution of the resource.[12] Matthew Rabin (1993), for instance, shows that people care about mutual kindness, which he models as a joint function of the generosity of each player.[13] This is

12. Amartya Sen (1977), using the terms *sympathy* and *commitment*, offers the following story to illustrate the distinction we have in mind. Two boys are about to share two apples, one bigger than the other. Boy A, going first, chooses the larger apple. Boy B objects, suggesting A did not act fairly. A asks, "Well, which one would you have chosen?" B replies, "The smaller one, of course." To which A replies, "Then what are you complaining about? That's the one you got!"

13. For a bibliography of Rabin's work and an interview with Rabin about how his work has created openings for others to question the models of simple utility maximization, see Colander, Holt, and Rosser 2004.

exactly the kind of opening that people of faith, many of whom would argue for the importance of values other than just utility maximization, need to reenter the debates about economic welfare.

The importance of such norms for explaining observed outcomes are not only important in such micro behaviors, they are becoming increasingly important at macro levels as well. The "new institutional" economics associated with Douglas North and others has given renewed emphasis to the importance of social norms like trust and integrity to support exchange. Although it is a theme that dates to at least Weber, the importance of a social system that organically supports these norms is increasingly being emphasized as a prerequisite for successful economic development (see, e.g., Platteau 2000).

Just as economists have discovered that ethical considerations play a role in shaping individual behavior and in economic outcomes, so too have they begun to acknowledge that such considerations must play a role in policy proposals. Working from the premise that inequity in distributing immaterial goods and "spiritual assets," more than inequity in distributing resources, lies at the heart of social problems in the United States, Robert Fogel (2000) calls for a program of education that would inculcate the needed virtues (sense of purpose, self-discipline, etc.). Although he recognizes the importance of the private formation of these virtues, his public policy proposals look very similar to the kind of civil, secular religion discussed by Faccarello and Steiner. While agreeing with the broad premise that these virtues support prosperity, Deirdre McCloskey (2006) has recently reversed directions as well, defending capitalist organization of economies on the grounds that they can encourage virtuous living.[14]

Finally, such findings as those by Bernheim and Rangel in neuroeconomics have motivated economists to reconsider their approaches to policy evaluation (so-called welfare economics). In fact, the specific issue they raise of the addict making poor choices was a problem foreseen some one hundred years ago by the architects of modern utilitarian welfare economics. Sidgwick, Marshall, and Pigou all discussed the distinction between the motive force of desire and the actually experienced satisfaction, but in the end most such inconsistencies were ruled minor exceptions or inscrutable. Apparently, not all economists are still willing to dismiss the distinction. Consider two recent papers that both accept the premise

14. See also Novak 1982 for an earlier defense of this claim.

that individuals do not necessarily make consistent choices. The authors of both papers, when confronted with this dilemma, argue that normative economics should continue to be based on choice rather than realized or objective measures of utility. But if choices are not consistent, the question for the welfare economist is which of the individual's many preference orderings to regard as prescriptive. Bernheim and Rangel (2007) argue that when individual behavior is different under different choice contexts, so welfare economists should restrict their attention to a subset of preference orderings that have a claim for being more rational. Robert Sugden (2007) takes the opposite approach, arguing that economists should defer to the preferences in play at the moment of choice.

Closing Thoughts

This recent renaissance of interest in looking at economic behavior through the prism of religious belief, and the openings for economists of faith created by experimental and behavioral economics, still leaves unanswered the question of how economics and religion became largely disentangled by 1950. And to tell that history, one must not be anachronistic. The contemporary manifestations of public religion, which Casanova has so nicely explained, do not provide an answer to the local and contingent stories that characterize the earlier period explored in this volume. And we know that this earlier story was predominantly one of disentanglement. We also know from the work in this volume and elsewhere that disentangling religion from most academic disciplines was not a simple story of people gradually discovering that they did not need religion to understand the institutions of modernity. Some scholars, such as Jon Roberts and James Turner (2000), have told a story of a slow, almost accidental, severing of religious outlooks from modern academic disciplines, and that interpretation would be very compatible with the idea that the secularization of economics simply reflected the secularization taking place as people came to understand human institutions without a necessary reference to religious understandings of the world. But the facts of the story in the social sciences do not bear out this interpretation. Those who built analytic models that removed religious perspectives from economics, for instance, did so deliberately.[15] Likewise, the story in America is

15. For a fuller treatment of the effort among American economists to remove religious perspectives from their work, see Bateman 2008.

the same in sociology and political science. And those who tried to hold on to their religious understandings of the world in their economic analysis also did so deliberately, although they ultimately were not successful, for by the mid-twentieth century, neoclassical economics, drawing heavily from the tenets of logical positivism, had swept the boards. And the elegant models of utility maximization at the heart of neoclassical economics had no place for religious belief or any other ethical or metaphysical framework.

With this volume, we take a step toward looking at the long history that preceded the rise and triumph of a secular neoclassical economics at the middle of the last century. It is an uneven story, and its outcome was by no means certain. But it will never be understood until the many separate pieces in many different countries are put together so that we can begin to see the larger picture. The essays we have collected here should help fill out the story of what happened in economics as a matter of historical fact, rather than as we might see that story theoretically or hypothetically.

References

Andreoni, James, and John Miller. 2002. Giving according to GARP: An Experimental Test of the Consistency of Preferences for Altruism. *Econometrica* 70:737–53.

Bateman, Bradley W. 1998. Clearing the Ground: The Demise of the Social Gospel Movement and the Rise of Neoclassicism in American Economics. In *From Interwar Pluralism to Postwar Neoclassicism*, edited by Mary S. Morgan and Malcolm Rutherford. *HOPE* 30 (supplement): 29–52.

———. 1999. Born Again in 1904: John R. Commons and the Social Gospel. In *Perspectives on the Social Gospel: Papers from the Inaugural Social Gospel Conference at Colgate Rochester Divinity School*, edited by Christopher H. Evans. Lewiston, N.Y.: Mellen.

———. 2001. Making a Righteous Number: Social Surveys, the Men and Religion Forward Movement, and Quantification in American Economics. In *The Age of Economic Measurement*, edited by Judy L. Klein and Mary S. Morgan. *HOPE* 33 (supplement): 57–85.

———. 2004. Why Institutional Economics Matters as a Category of Historical Analysis. *Research in the History of Economic Thought and Methodology.* 22A:193–201.

———. 2008. Reflections on the Secularization of American Economics. *Journal of the History of Economic Thought* 30.1:1–20.

Bernheim, B. Douglas, and Antonio Rangel. 2004. Addiction and Cue-Triggered Decision Processes. *American Economic Review* 94.5:1558–90.

———. 2007. Toward Choice-Theoretic Foundations for Behavioral Welfare Economics. Paper presented at the Resources for the Future conference, "The Frontiers of Environmental Economics," Washington, D.C., April. http://www.rff.org/rff/Events/loader.cfm?url=/commonspot/security/getfile.cfm&PageID=28011.

Bruce, Steve. 2002. *God Is Dead: Secularization in the West.* Oxford: Blackwell.
Casanova, José. 1994. *Public Religions in the Modern World.* Chicago: University of Chicago Press.
Colander, David, Richard P. F. Holt, and J. Barkley Rosser Jr. 2004. *The Changing Face of Economics: Conversations with Cutting Edge Economists.* Ann Arbor: University of Michigan Press.
Fogel, Robert William. 2000. *The Fourth Great Awakening and the Future of Egalitarianism.* Chicago: University of Chicago Press.
Gordon, Barry. 1989. *The Economic Problem in Biblical and Patristic Thought.* New York: Brill.
Hollinger, David A. 2001. The "Secularization" Question and the United States in the Twentieth Century. *Church History* 70.1:132–43.
Iannaccone, Laurence. 1998. An Introduction to the Economics of Religion. *Journal of Economic Literature* 36:1465–95.
Kaegard, Niels. 2004. Debates between Economists and Theologians about Economic Justice. Paper presented at the annual meeting of the History of Economics Society, Toronto.
Keynes, John Maynard. [1933] 1972. *Essays in Biography.* Vol. 10 of *The Collected Writings of John Maynard Keynes*, edited by Elizabeth Johnson and Donald Moggridge. London: Macmillan.
Long, D. Stephen. 2000. *Divine Economy: Theology and the Market.* London: Routledge.
Lowry, S. Todd, and Barry Gordon. 1998. *Ancient and Medieval Economic Ideas and Concepts of Social Justice.* New York: Brill.
Marsden, George M. 1994. *The Soul of the American University: From Protestant Establishment to Established Nonbelief.* New York: Oxford University Press.
McCloskey, Deirdre N. 2006. *The Bourgeois Virtues: Ethics for an Age of Commerce.* Chicago: University of Chicago Press.
Nelson, Robert H. 2001. *Economics as Religion: From Samuelson to Chicago and Beyond.* University Park: Pennsylvania State University Press.
Novak, Michael. 1982. *The Spirit of Democratic Capitalism.* Washington, D.C.: American Enterprise Institute.
Philpott, Daniel. 2002. The Challenge of September 11 to Secularism in International Relations. *World Politics* 55:65–95.
Platteau, Jean-Philippe. 2000. *Institutions, Social Norms, and Economic Development.* Amsterdam: Harwood.
Rabin, Matthew. 1993. Incorporating Fairness into Game Theory and Economics. *American Economic Review* 83:1281–302.
Reuben, Julie A. 1996. *The Making of the Modern University: Intellectual Transformation and the Marginalization of Morality.* Chicago: University of Chicago Press.
Roberts, Jon, and James Turner. 2000. *The Sacred and Secular University.* Princeton, N.J.: Princeton University Press.
Schmiesing, Kevin E. 2004. *Within the Market Strife.* Lanham, Md.: Lexington.
Sen, Amartya. 1977. Rational Fools: A Critique of the Behavioral Foundations of Economic Theory. *Philosophy and Public Affairs* 6.4:317–44.

Stark, Rodney, and William Sims Bainbridge. 1985. *The Future of Religion: Secularization, Revival, and Cult Formation*. Berkeley: University of California Press.

Sugden, Robert. 2007. Cost-Benefit Analysis as Market Simulation. Paper presented at the Resources for the Future conference, "The Frontiers of Environmental Economics," Washington, D.C., April. http://www.rff.org/rff/Documents/RFF-DP-07–28–REV.pdf.

Waterman, A. M. C. 1991. *Revolution, Economics, and Religion: Christian Political Economy, 1798–1833*. Cambridge: Cambridge University Press.

Wuthnow, Robert. 1992. *Rediscovering the Sacred: Perspectives on Religion in Contemporary Society*. Grand Rapids, Mich.: Eerdmans.

Part 1
Continental Europe

Continental Europe: Introduction

In many ways, it seems logical to begin this volume on the historical relationship between political economy and religion by looking first at Continental Europe. For if economics as we know it today sprang from European roots, then the most obvious roots of the connections between political economy and religion would spring from the traditional place of the Roman Catholic Church in European society.

Although Adam Smith's work does not mark the beginning of modern economic analysis, it is still worth noting that after he lays out his theoretical apparatus in the first two books of the *Wealth of Nations*, he turns in the third book to show how that apparatus can explain the demise of feudalism and the emergence of the market economy in Europe. For this more than anything else was for Smith the major historical fact that needed to be explained: how were the ancien régime and the feudal system being displaced by market life? Smith knew that this transformation was not finished, but he felt that he could begin to explain what was happening in contemporary Europe.

The changes that Smith sought to explain were to accelerate less than twenty years after the publication of the *Wealth of Nations*, with the French Revolution. The economic changes that Smith saw represented the results of the deliberate actions of many individuals, but the demise of the ancien régime and of feudalism was an unintended consequence of those actions. With the French Revolution, the attack on the ancien régime

History of Political Economy 40 (annual suppl.) DOI 10.1215/00182702-2007-058

became deliberate, not accidental. Those who led the French Revolution meant to unseat the authority of the church in French life, and they were successful.

Gilbert Faccarello and Philippe Steiner's essay in this section explains the debate that emerged among French economists in the wake of the Revolution in the early nineteenth century about what the proper role of religion should be in society and in economic life. The debate among the figures they examine was, in essence, to ask, "Are political economy and religion necessarily in conflict? Or are they rather complementary, and if so, what was the nature of that complementarity?" As Faccarello and Steiner point out, the work of Jean-Baptiste Say, which was based on self-interested behavior and utilitarianism, became the *a-religious* basis for many French economists in the wake of the Revolution, making an explicit appeal that it was able to avoid the errors of religious thinking. But this a-religious viewpoint was challenged by others, such as Germaine Necker de Staël-Holstein and Henri-Benjamin Constant de Rebeque. Both Staël and Constant believed that religion played an important and necessary role in society without, however, believing that the Roman Catholic Church was the correct religion. Faccarello and Steiner finish their essay by looking at other economists who explored the possible relationship that might best suit the new industrial society that was emerging in the post-Revolutionary period. They look first at the work of Claude-Henri Saint-Simon, who advocated the need for a new Christianity, and finish by looking at several figures, like Frédéric Bastiat and Charles Dunoyer, who pushed French political economy back toward a more orthodox position and who saw traditional Christianity as amenable with political economy.

António Almodovar and Pedro Teixeira examine the rise and fall of Catholic economic thought in Europe after the Roman Catholic Church began to recover from the shock of the French Revolution and the emergence of modernity in Europe. Faced with the reality that a new economic and political order was arising in Europe that would not, after all, be underpinned by explicit fealty to the church, Catholic thinkers began to search for ways to offer a rigorous ethical critique of economic life in an industrial, market-based system. Almodovar and Teixeira survey 120 years of this Catholic tradition. Their essay begins with the work of François Xavier Joseph Droz and Alban de Villeneuve-Bargemont, the first of the Catholics to try to forge the new Catholic ethical frame for considering modern economic life. Almodovar and Teixeira's narrative then turns to a nuanced and complex story as a Catholic school began to emerge across continental Europe that included the subsequent emergence of a more traditional, market-oriented school, led by comte Charles de Coux, as well as a school more focused on the possibilities of ameliorating the harm of the new system, led by the Jesuits Luigi Taparelli d'Azeglio and Matteo Liberatore, who helped found the journal *Civiltà Cattolica*.

The reemergence of Catholic universities in the mid-nineteenth century further spurred the Catholic tradition of economic analysis, especially in the work of Victor Brants and Charles Périn. Almodovar and Teixeira then describe a "golden age" of Catholic economic thought that began in 1891 with the publication of the papal encyclical *Rerum Novarum* by Leo XIII. The fruit of this golden age was corporatism, a "Catholic third way" that was seen as the means to manage the new industrial system in such a way as both to respect private property and to encourage a system of redistribution that respected the dignity of laborers. The fate of this stream of Catholic thought was sealed when corporatism was adopted by the fascists; when the fascists were defeated, so too was corporatism, and with it a tradition of Catholic economic thought that had been evolving for over one hundred years.

The essay by Daniela Parisi that concludes this section points to another legacy of Catholicism in the history of economic thought. While the tradition that Almodovar and Teixeira describe may have fallen because of its unfortunate association with fascism, there were nonetheless other Catholic economists whose work was shaped by their beliefs. Parisi looks at one of these economists who was educated in Italy and studied around the world in the 1930s, Francesco Vito. At the forefront internationally of business cycle theory and theories of employment, unemployment, and the welfare state, Vito insisted that economics recognize the inherent dignity of every human being. Parisi makes a compelling argument that Vito, who was actively involved in the Roman Catholic Church, represents a tendency that can be seen in many postwar Catholic economists to abandon the utilitarian calculus of neoclassical welfare economics and to critique market models while putting their positive energies into development economics, cycle theory, and theories of employment.

Religion and Political Economy in Early-Nineteenth-Century France

Gilbert Faccarello and Philippe Steiner

There was in early-nineteenth-century France a widespread revival of religious sentiment, after the turmoil of the Revolution and the intellectual onslaught on religion so central to the French Enlightenment. Simultaneously, political economy became more prominent among "publicists"—educated people or theoreticians writing as journalists—and political elites. These two developments greatly influenced those who sought to further a modern, postrevolutionary society, and who in their different ways expressed a new approach to economics and politics known as *industrialisme*. These writers put forward several versions of the links that should exist in industrial society between political economy and religion. Are political economy and religion necessarily in conflict? Or are they complementary, and if so, how are they complementary? This article examines the issues at stake and responses to them. Our analysis entails the following steps.

We first note that a truly a-religious political economy based on self-interested behavior and utilitarianism, such as the one presented in Jean-Baptiste Say's *Traité d'économie politique* and in his *Catéchisme d'économie politique*,[1] gained acceptance and became the point of reference

We would like to thank the participants for helpful comments and discussions. Discussions and correspondence with Anthony Waterman are gratefully acknowledged.

1. Catechisms are books in which a doctrine—usually a religious doctrine—is set out as a series of questions and answers; these were common among the writers with whom we are dealing: Claude-Henri Saint-Simon and Auguste Comte together wrote a *Catéchisme des industriels*; Comte wrote a lengthy *Catéchisme positiviste* directed to the diffusion of his new religion.

History of Political Economy 40 (annual suppl.) DOI 10.1215/00182702-2007-059

for most people interested in the "new" science—a form of political economy belonging to what we have called *philosophie économique* (Faccarello and Steiner 2004, 2008). From the 1820s onward this approach was also developed by Charles Comte and Charles Dunoyer. In the following, we emphasize how deeply political economy and utilitarianism merged in Say's works—especially when he broadened the field of his inquiry in the opening pages of the *Cours complet d'économie politique pratique*. This point of departure is important not only because Say's thought became a major reference for the different conceptions of *industrialisme* but also because it provided a utilitarian evaluation of religious institutions and feelings.

Next, we note that some conceptions of *industrialisme*—criticizing various aspects of the *industrialisme* of Say and his followers—can be found in the writings of the leading members of two distinct schools of thought, very active and influential in France either during Say's lifetime or immediately after his death: first, the Groupe de Coppet, with Germaine de Staël and Benjamin Constant; second, the less homogeneous group formed by Claude-Henri Saint-Simon, the Saint-Simonians, and Auguste Comte. Both approaches presumed that self-interest was incapable of uniting the social body, and emphasized religious feelings to explain how societies could function harmoniously.[2]

Religion was thus once again thought to be a central institution in a modern society. It is important, however, to distinguish carefully the position of Staël, Constant, Saint-Simon, and Auguste Comte from that of the reactionary or traditionalist philosophers of the time like Joseph de Maistre, Louis de Bonald, and Pierre-Simon Ballanche. For these latter writers the return to religious values meant revoking almost all the philosophical ideas of the Enlightenment[3] and, at the institutional level, either restoring a prerevolutionary political order and the traditional power of the Catholic Church or establishing a kind of theocracy in which the Catholic Church and the pope would have played a prominent role.[4] In contrast, our authors claimed a strong attachment to the tradition of the philosophes and felt deeply committed to the main progressive ideas developed

2. Later on, a similar problem was raised in the United States, but the answers involved different possible links between interest, reason, and the passions (see Davenport, this volume).

3. In particular the emancipation of the human mind and the ability of human beings to think and to freely organize the economic and political society they are living in.

4. These authors also took into account some economic problems in order to reassess the supremacy of religion over material wealth (Bonald [1819] 1845, 584–96; see also Epsztein 1966, 105–12).

by their predecessors—first and foremost the marquis de Condorcet. They considered themselves to be in some respects their heirs, whose task was to develop their legacy as a social and political philosophy for a new society, following the sometimes unhappy and terrible events of the Revolution.

But while our authors regarded religion as fundamental to modern society, the way in which they reintroduced it differed greatly from case to case, as did their understanding of the links between religion and political economy.[5]

Here we first examine how Staël and Constant dealt with these issues and how, while they accept the principle of competition in economic activity, their conception of the specific nature of liberty in a modern society led them to a critique of utilitarianism and morals based on interest, and also to the idea that the harmonious functioning of industrial society requires a morality based on religion.

We then study how *industrialisme* was modified to fit the views of modern society held by Saint-Simon, the Saint-Simonians, and Auguste Comte. Political and civil liberty was not a central matter for these writers. Instead, they favored the creation of economic and political organizations capable of regulating a chaotic social order, and in this perspective new forms of religion were given a prominent place, specifically formed to suit the industrial social order and based on philanthropy or altruism:[6] the new Christianity of Saint Simon and the religion of humanity of Comte.

Finally, we cannot neglect the fact that, after all such criticism, some leading liberal economists during the 1840s and 1850s reacted in defense of political economy and developed their own conceptions of the links between economics and religion. In particular they rejected the idea of the necessity of a new religion and insisted instead on traditional Catholic ideas. But then political economy and religion were conceived as two pillars of a conservative order following the rise of socialist ideas. In the conclusion we briefly summarize how this reaction was reflected in the ideas of Dunoyer, Frédéric Bastiat, and Michel Chevalier.

5. We focus here on the industrialist current of thought and thus neglect some other authors like, for example, Alban de Villeneuve-Bargemont and his *Économie politique chrétienne* (1834). On Villeneuve-Bargemont and some other Catholic writers of the period, see Almodovar and Teixeira, this volume.

6. The debate on political economy and religion thus assumed in Great Britain a totally different aspect during the same period (see Waterman, this volume, and 1991).

1. Say and the Sayards: Utility and Political Economy against Religious Error

Jean-Baptiste Say

Utilitarianism developed in eighteenth-century France with a strong anti-religious sentiment (Helvétius 1773, [1758] 1988; d'Holbach [1770] 1993, [1773] 1994). During the French Revolution, as a consequence of the political problems associated with natural law, utilitarianism became prominent in the work of the *idéologues*. Among them was Say, who wrote as follows to Pierre-Samuel Dupont de Nemours:

> For some time I have been of the opinion that men, by engaging with society, renounce one part of their rights to secure the other; following this, I was of the opinion that the social condition lent them greater rights; now I am no longer so certain that they have rights and I recognize only facts: I can see rights only where there is an effective pleasure. (Say 1814)

The high esteem in which Say held Jeremy Bentham's thought never altered, and the utilitarian approach remained central for Say's political economy. This is demonstrated by two episodes where morals and religion are confronted with utilitarianism and political economy.[7]

The first episode concerns Say's 1817 book on morals and sociability: *Petit volume contenant quelques aperçus des hommes et de la société*, in which he asserted the importance of utilitarianism for the conduct of life in modern industrial society. Other forms of conduct supposedly resulted from vanity, error, or sheer ignorance of the true principles ruling social life. Vanity appeared to him the most dangerous:

> Moral philosophers seem to believe that self-love, interest, directs the actions of men more than self-importance, or vanity. I believe, on the contrary, that vanity has more power over them, generally speaking, than self-love. It suffices to observe how many times men act out of vanity in a way that is contrary to their interests. (83)

The correct response to such a situation is consistent self-interested behavior: "You complain that each pays attention only to his own interest; I am

7. In a note dedicated to his wife and children about what should be done with his papers after his death, Say explained that besides a book on politics (*Essais de politique pratique*) and a book on morals (*Essais de morale pratique*), he had planned a book on religion (*Traité de l'utilité morale des religions*) (Say n.d., MS F379–1).

afflicted with the opposite. To know one's true interests is the beginning of wisdom; having the courage to follow them is the complement" (84).

The second episode relates to the composition of the book written on the basis of the lectures Say gave at the Conservatoire royal des arts et métiers from 1819 to the end of his life. He asked his friend Dumont to write a piece on utilitarianism for an appendix to the last volume of the *Cours complet d'économie politique pratique*. This was an unusual move from an author who neither wrote nor printed anything jointly: what might explain this request? Say tried to write the piece by himself—two lectures given in 1819 in the Athénée royal, a private teaching institution, were the basis for his draft chapter, but he was not satisfied with the result (Say 1829). Yet this does confirm that Say considered utilitarianism to be the real foundation of his political economy. An undated manuscript states quite clearly:

> Write a little book entitled *On the Principle of Utility*, or simply *On Utility*. First of all I will define utility in its most extensive sense, *its capacity to serve man*. Many examples. I will show that for men, caring for themselves, everything that does not have utility as an aim is ignorance, ill-conceived interest, insanity. That to lead men back to the principle of utility is to bring them back to healthy use of their reason and to their greater happiness. Application to politics, political economy, to all sciences and arts. To publish only after my other works. It will be the key. (Say n.d., MS G385)

In this light the Say-Dumont correspondence is most helpful in understanding how, and by whom, *philosophie économique* was attacked:

> Utility has no other foes than the two troops of sophistries that Bentham unites under the banners of *asceticism* and the *arbitrary* or *sentiment*; and it seems to me possible to render intelligible in one of these categories all the objections that are today raised against an eminently beneficial and social principle. . . . the attacks are vague, verbal, lost in periodicals and not specialized works. Without having read all of Benjamin Constant's book on religions, I have seen there attacks of this kind. And in the work of Madam de Staël on Germany. And in *Corinne* by the same author, book V, chapter 1 and in book IX, chapter 5 ("Oh! How *I love uselessness*! etc"). . . . Necker, in chapter 1 of his *Opinions religieuses*, does not directly attack the principle of utility; but he believes that it has no practical application, and that man can only be constrained by force to act for the good of society, or by hell, which is another species of force. (Say to Dumont, 10 May 1829, in Say 1833, 366–67)

Dumont finally wrote to Say that he did not feel himself capable of the complex work of refutation necessary to answer the statements of the growing anti-utilitarian movement (Dumont to Say, 21 July 1829, in Say 1833, 372), and Say's essay on utilitarianism was published posthumously by Charles Comte (Say 1833, 406–55; now in Say 2003b, 130–54).

However, a previous response to a critique that favored religious argument makes clear that Say did not wish to leave such criticism unanswered. This appeared in the first volume of the *Cours complet* where Say answered Jean-Denis Lanjuinais's assertion that political economy, because of its orientation toward material well-being, prevented men from considering their salvation. Say pointed out that political economy as a science had precise boundaries and could not be accused of neglecting the next life (Say 1828–29, 1:99). But he also emphasized that political economy did not limit itself to material wealth and that in his book he was broadening his definition of the science precisely so that he might deal with the entire social system (1:7). As soon as men endow goods, services, institutions, or virtues with exchange value, Say argued, they can be supposed to fall within the province of political economy (1:100). The same issue recurs in his personal papers, expressed with some heat, for Say suggested religious institutions might be subjected to utilitarian evaluation.

> But, some assert, political economy regards the costs of worship to be a mistaken expenditure. . . . Listen: yes, if worship is false, if it does not give to man the benefits that it promises him. But if because of religion all men live as brothers, if they never wrong one another, if they do not torment themselves with the spirit of proselytism, if they are not subjected to dogmas or practices which degrade the soundness of their minds, their well-being, then in truth, political economy informs them of the disadvantage in subscribing to a harmful institution as if it were useful, but does not prescribe anything; on the contrary, it counsels them to make all necessary sacrifice to build good institutions, just as it counsels them to be just, equitable, and benevolent toward each and all, and to respect the rights and properties of each, for their own interest directs them to do so. Its counsel is thus extremely favorable to the good of humanity, and states nothing contrary to hopes that go beyond this life. (Say n.d., MS F378–103)

Say was being ironic: he did not believe that any religion could be considered free from dogmatism, proselytism, persecution, and so forth. Furthermore, the manuscripts show that he was inclined to utilitarian assessment of religion: whatever their doctrinal content, the truth of a religion lay, for him, in the manner in which it promoted peaceful social life. Finally, in some unpublished notes that form the first steps of a chapter on the political usefulness of religions (Say 2003a, 515–32), Say acknowledged the existence of a religious sentiment specific to human beings (515–16); however, contrary to Constant, he asserted that this sentiment resulted from the intellectual faculty of generalization: when this faculty was pushed too far, then men were prone to believe there to be a general cause motivating the whole world. This feeling was nothing but the mark of the limitation of the human mind, to which Say added the effects derived from natural propensities such as fear, love, sociability, the habits of subordination, and a credulous belief in fantastical and marvelous stories.

Charles Comte

Say died in November 1832, three years after the publication of the last volume of the *Cours complet*. Was his perspective also passing away, or was there still life in it? Generally speaking, the French liberal school was not convinced of the merits of Bentham's thought, principally because utilitarianism considered property to be a political outcome—that is, an institution that could be modified according to the utilitarian principle—and not a natural right with which government should never interfere. Nevertheless, a small number of economists and writers endorsed the utilitarian principle, as Say had done in his own time. Central here were Charles Comte and Dunoyer,[8] since they were both personally acquainted with Say, and because Dunoyer became an important author, to whom we return in the conclusion.

In 1826, Comte published a book in four volumes on legislation in which he sought to implement in the science of legislation what had already been done in political economy—to discover the laws according to which nations improve or decay. His approach ran counter to speculative legislation such as that of natural jurisprudence and Jean-Jacques Rousseau's writings. Adopting the principle of utility, Comte (1826, 1:41) also criticized those religious thinkers and philosophers who relied on sentiments such as Constant. Here he closely followed Say's approach, that men should be

8. Charles Comte (1782–1837) and Charles Dunoyer (1786–1864) were liberal publicists and lawyers; they edited together *Le censeur* (1814–15) and *Le censeur européen* (1816–19). Comte was Say's son-in-law.

driven by their interest,[9] provided that this interest is well understood (*intérêt bien entendu*) or self-love (1:102) enlightened by the truth established by social science.

Comte contrasted the religious and the utilitarian approaches with regard to the legislation they tended to promote. He did not mince words; although he stated cautiously that his comments concerned all religions but one—the true one—he rejected religion as a sound basis for legislation. The reason was plain: if there were an authority superior to law, such as religious beliefs represented, then nothing could be altered without prior change to this authority, an alteration to which the clergy would be opposed (1:218–19, 223–27). This would induce a stationary state, and the forces promoting national progress would dissipate (1:128). Comte added that, in many instances, the link between religion and legislation was even more perverse, since the same people who were prepared to allow that the precepts of their religion were false nevertheless argued that the people had need of a set of beliefs so that they might remain docile and respectful.

The contrast with the principle of utility—that is, the calculation of pleasure and pain for all individuals whose situation was affected by a given legislative measure (1:245)—was straightforward. Comte most emphatically emphasized the role of genuine science and national enlightenment.

> Considerable dissemination of enlightenment is the only way of effecting legislation and securing the morality of progress. It is necessary that the people become sufficiently enlightened, so that those invested with power, who place some individual interests above general utility, and who do not believe in another world, at least find their hell in this one. (1:259–60 n. 1)

This argument was central for him, and it was the basis of the critique he made of Constant each time this writer was suspected of favoring religious sentiment at the cost of disseminating a truth derived from the science of legislation (1:249–51, 257).[10]

The increased role that Say and his immediate followers claimed for political economy and utilitarianism was not uncontested, as were also

9. This point was elaborated further in a special chapter (bk. 2, chap. 4), in which Comte (1826, 1:353–62) gave his understanding of the utilitarian view of sensationism.

10. A similar point was elaborated by Dunoyer (1825; 1845, vol. 3) when emphasizing the importance of human capital, that is, the capital provided by an able and healthy body and a well-educated mind, the latter being the result of education, religious belief, and social morality.

their ideas on religion. An important debate began, involving very different viewpoints. Say mentioned in his letter to Dumont of 10 May 1829 some of those who were known to him: Staël and Constant.[11] These authors are now to be examined. But there are also others with whom Say was familiar, whom we discuss in due course: Saint-Simon and in particular Auguste Comte.[12]

2. Staël and Constant: Religion and the Liberal Strand of Industrialism

The writings of Germaine Necker de Staël-Holstein and Henri-Benjamin Constant de Rebecque are first and foremost political: they seek to found and develop a political science for commercial society in a postrevolutionary context.[13] Their ideas are of material importance here because of the specific criticism they direct to *philosophie économique*. In particular, they emphasize the necessary and positive role played by religion in social life, and the manner in which they do so marks a significant departure from the thinking of the majority of eighteenth-century French philosophers.

Although criticizing the liberal creed of Say, Charles Comte, and Dunoyer, Staël and Constant are themselves genuine liberal thinkers—Constant's thought is of the greatest importance for liberal political philosophy—despite the many pages in which they set forth ideas usually attributed to antiliberal writers. This makes their position all the more interesting.

11. We have considered the connection between Say and the Groupe de Coppet in greater detail in a previous paper (Steiner 2003).

12. Say was among those who assisted Saint-Simon financially (Gouhier 1964, 3:220); he also sent him a copy of his *Catéchisme d'économie politique* with a long letter arguing that Saint-Simon's plan for peace was close to his own views (Say to Saint Simon, Bibliothèque Nationale de France, MS NAF 24605, folio no. 54). Furthermore, Say, Dunoyer, and Charles Comte, the editors of *Le censeur européen*, and Saint-Simon and his assistants, Augustin Thierry and Auguste Comte, would have regularly met each other, since *L'industrie* was run from the same building (Gouhier 1964, 3:152). Finally, in his autobiography John Stuart Mill (1993, 75) mentioned that he had met Saint-Simon in Say's salon.

13. Germaine de Staël (1766–1817) was the daughter of Jacques Necker, the celebrated Swiss banker and finance minister of Louis XVI. Together with Benjamin Constant (1767–1830) she was at the center of a major intellectual group known as the Groupe de Coppet—named after one of her estates, Coppet, in Switzerland. This group included, among others, Jean-Charles-Léonard Simonde de Sismondi. On Staël, see, for example, Balayé 1979; on Constant, Holmes 1984.

For present purposes their approach can be restated as follows. First, they direct their analysis to the new social order at the heart of modern society, and they emphasize the fundamental role that a new form of liberty plays. Second, they strongly disagree with generalizing the so-called principle of utility to the social order and criticize the widespread belief that, in a modern society, morals should be based on interest. Third, they explain why "religious sentiment" and ideas have a leading role to play in the new liberal order.

The Fundamental Feature of the New Society: The "Liberty of the Moderns"

What are the foundations of the new social order? An opposition between the ancients and the moderns is heavily emphasized, between two kinds of society involving two very different attitudes on the part of citizens with respect to political activity and the state.

Staël writes in her *Des circonstances actuelles qui peuvent terminer la Révolution* that in ancient societies, in the times of the Greek cities and the Roman republic, for example, those who were citizens—free men—were deeply involved in politics and in discussing and managing public activities. This "liberty of ancient times" (Staël [1799] 1906, 95) involved deep and far-reaching commitment—generally facilitated by the small size of the republic—up to and including the sacrifice of one's wealth and life, if the republic's law or safety so demanded. Political organization bound its members tightly and imposed particular habits and behaviors on all activities of the citizen.

In modern times, however, things are quite different. The "liberty of our times" (94) consists of the possibility, for citizens, to accumulate wealth, to live a private life in total independence of the state—"private" being understood extensively, including professional activities.

> The liberty of present times consists of everything that guarantees the independence of the citizens from government. The liberty of ancient times consists of everything that guarantees to the citizens the greatest part in the exercise of power. (94–95)

What the modern citizen seeks is total freedom to earn a revenue in whatever activity he or she wishes, and the enjoyment of his or her wealth and life without taking up arms or being disturbed by other citizens, or by political turmoil. Modern citizens are "peaceful egoists"

(92). "Agriculture, commerce, public debt, taxes, peace and war—all this concerns [the mass of citizens] for it only has a single desire: ease and tranquillity" (90).

The modern legislator must not forget that, as a consequence, people will usually display a particular indifference to politics (94)—"Political activity: of no use since individual happiness" (310), notes Staël—even concerning the form of government. "The nation wants only results and is not concerned about the means. In one era the Republic is thought most favorable to its ease, in another monarchy" (91).

These form the basis of the modern social contract: the state's role is purely negative, in the sense that the objective of law and public institutions is merely to secure the autonomy and safety of individuals (198; see also Staël [1810] 1968, 2:192).

Staël declares, moreover, this historical evolution of societies to be irreversible. A reversion to ancient times is now clearly impossible: the mind of today is totally different, and countries are so extensive and densely populated that the direct participation of citizens in political life is simply out of the question—only a representative government is feasible (13), thus increasing the inherent tendency of citizens to concentrate on their own private lives (93).

Moreover, even if such a small state were still to exist with such a political constitution, it could not endure because of the inexorable tendency for states to grow in size (Staël 1796, 110). It is also obvious that, following the great philosophical developments of the eighteenth century and the social and political earthquake caused by the Revolution, it is not even possible—contrary to the assertions of traditionalists—to go back to a form of prerevolutionary society. The law of the "perfectibility of the human mind" and the recent impressive progress of the sciences—including moral and political sciences—prevent it. There is no way out: we cannot but accept how things stand and infer from this the best way to organize the political life of the country.

Constant ([1806] 1997, 357–81; 1814, 182–95) made extensive use of this polarity, but his most celebrated text remains his 1819 address in the Athénée royal: "De la liberté des anciens comparée à celle des modernes." There he sums up the distinction between the ancients and the moderns in a striking way:

> [In Rome] mores are ruled by laws, and just as mores apply to all, so there is nothing left ungoverned by law. In ancient society, while the

> individual was nearly always supreme in public affairs, he was enslaved in all private relations. By contrast, in the modern world the individual, independent in private life, is only apparently supreme even in the freest of states. (Constant 1819, 496)

The "individual liberty"—the "civil liberty"—of the moderns rests on "guarantees conferred by institutions" (502) to private enjoyments.

Does this mean that, in a modern society, political freedom is neither practiced nor necessary? If this were the case, Staël's and Constant's positions would perfectly exemplify Isaiah Berlin's idea of "negative liberty." But it is not so. Constant is fully aware that the tendency to neglect or give up political freedom is "the danger presented by modern liberty" (512). Citizens must resist this temptation and be careful not to surrender political liberty—reconceived and adapted to the new society—since it nonetheless remains necessary. It is the guarantee and safeguard of civil liberty. "Far from opposing one freedom to another, it is necessary to present the first as guarantee of the second" (Constant [1806] 1997, 373; cf. 1819, 509).

Opposition to the Principle of Utility and the Morals of Interest

Say (1803, 2:262–64, 455–62) also alluded to the difference between the ancients and moderns. But he differs from Staël and Constant in that his appreciation of the consequences of modern liberty in a commercial society is unambiguously positive. Staël and Constant, on the contrary, are of the opinion that these consequences can be extremely negative. This is where the critique of *philosophie économique* begins. Here we can find the foundation for a positive role of religion.

According to Staël, if people are left to pursue freely their private activities, even within the "negative" rules of police and justice dictated by the state, society unavoidably goes to ruin: people will act in an entirely selfish way and destroy all social bonds. A dramatic choice is proposed: civilization or moral depravity. "But today . . . if no motivation for emulation is provided to talent, the taste for money will take its place. . . . There will be soulless corruption, and that is the lowest level to which the human species can fall" (Staël [1818] 1861, 333). "Exaltation of self-interest" leads only to moral and economic violence (Staël [1799] 1906, 227).

These negative consequences follow from the fact that people behave solely according to the principle of utility, basing their morals on interest. In her celebrated novel *Corinne ou l'Italie*, Staël ([1807] 1985, 118, 122–23, 142) is strongly negative when she speaks of economic self-interest and avidity—Say complained, in his "Essai sur le principe d'utilité," that she could write of "this arid principle of utility which fertilises so many corners of the earth, rendering sterile the vast domain of sentiment and thought" (Staël [1807] 1985; Say 2003b, 144). But *Corinne* is just a novel. In *De l'Allemagne* ([1810] 1968) her views are more developed.

There we can find a vigorous critique of morals based on self-interest and its philosophical underpinning: sensationist philosophy. It is the success of sensationist ideas in the eighteenth century that explains both the decay of religious sentiment during the Enlightenment and the success of the "morality founded upon self-interest." This philosophy, reasoning in terms of pleasure and pain, did in fact emphasize self-love and induced human beings to devote all their time and effort to the pursuit of material well-being (Staël [1810] 1968, 2:116). At this point, Staël strikingly remarks, "Enlighteners became arsonists" (108).

In this system, where all elements of the will are derived externally through sensations, true morals are necessarily destroyed: anyone can justify any conduct, simply claiming that it was caused by external circumstances. A general system of irresponsibility is thus likely to emerge, denying any free will.

Moreover, this system is dangerous for the peace and happiness of citizen and state. Morals based on individual interest do indeed generate the idea that, at the collective level, prudence in the conduct of the state follows from a collective or national interest—and this would have two negative consequences. In the first place, this would unfortunately be likely to justify injustice and crime (190). In the second place, this would also complete the destruction of true morality in the mind of the citizen.

In the end, the proof of the spirituality of the soul cannot be found in the realm of sensations, and true religious sentiment is thus destroyed (183). In this system of thought, "man will be no more than a mechanism within the great mechanism of the universe: his faculties no more than clockwork, his morals a calculation, and his worship success" (101). Corrupted men hence equate the just and the unjust, or rather consider them to be part of a game played well or ill. For the sensationist philosophers, "there is in the conduct of life only skilful schemes and unskilful schemes" (182). Staël argues against consequentialism:

> If calculation rules everything, the actions of men are judged following success: the man whose good intentions have caused suffering will be properly blamed; the perverted but skilful man will be justly applauded. Finally, individuals will come to consider themselves no more than obstacles or instruments; they will loathe each other as obstacles, and regard each as no more than means. (185)

At first sight, Constant's opinion of modern society appears to be different and much more in line with the ideas of Say, Charles Comte, or Dunoyer. And he does suggest two very positive points in favor of modern society. He insists on the positive progress achieved by modern commercial society and *industrie* with respect to the society it replaces: the Old Regime. This progress is, of course, material, but also moral. The system of the Old Regime, based on "privilege" and favors, created a society of beggars of dubious morality. By contrast, the industrial system allows to human beings their dignity and liberty (Constant 1825, 667).

Constant also endorses the view that self-interested behavior and freedom lead to a politically valuable result in terms of efficiency. In the preface he wrote to his *Mélanges de littérature et de politique* (1829), he is emphatic:

> I have defended the same principle for forty years: complete liberty, in philosophy, in literature, in industry, in politics. And I mean by liberty the triumph of individuality, in respect both to authority, which seeks to govern through despotism, and to the masses, who arrogate the right to subordinate the minority to the majority. (Constant 1829b, 520)

In his book of commentaries on Gaetano Filangieri, we can read a sentence that could also have been written by a follower of *philosophie économique*: "Leave egoism to itself: private egoisms will struggle among themselves; the one will cancel out the other" (Constant [1822–24] 2004, 320). He concludes the book with these unambiguous words: "For thought, for education, for industry, the slogan of government must be: *Laissez faire et laissez passer*" (332; see also [1806] 1997, 317–18).

But it is also Constant's view that the progress generated by *industrie* and the efficient role of self-interest are not without problems. While self-interested behaviors can neutralize each other, in some circumstances, this neutralization can fail.

> The public spirit is only perverted by egoism if poor government combines all egoism in opposition to the ideas of justice; nature, which

> has endowed man with love of himself for his personal preservation, has also given him sympathy, generosity, pity, so that he does not sacrifice his fellow men. Egoism only becomes destructive if this counterweight is destroyed. (Constant 1822–24, 320)

Thus the naked competition of self-interest in markets is not enough for the attainment of harmony. Self-interest is supposed to be checked by some positive virtues: sympathy, generosity, and pity. The problem is that, for Constant, in a modern society this equilibrium between self-interest and virtue can be destroyed to the benefit of the former, and not only because of state intervention: these virtues are likely to disappear for a more fundamental and structural reason.

The negative aspect of modernity is best developed in his 1826 review of Dunoyer's *L'industrie et la morale* (Constant 1826b), later republished under the title "De M. Dunoyer, et de quelques-uns de ses ouvrages," with the addition of some pages criticizing Bentham and the principle of utility (Constant 1829a).[14]

The material success of modern society, based as it is on *industrie* and on the enjoyment of civil liberty and privacy, unavoidably leads to moral lethargy and apathy: to moral decay. Citizens, living in a state of material wealth, tend to accept any compromise to preserve their wealth and well-being, endangering domestic political liberty and even the independence of the country (Constant 1826b, 420–21). This process of compromise also naturally entails a deterioration in the moral position of human beings, who now appear to be no more than animals: "This state of civilization tends toward . . . good order, rather than moral virtue. However, good order . . . is rather a means than an end. If, in maintaining it, one sacrifices all generous emotion, men are reduced to a condition little different from that of some industrious animals, for well-ordered hives and artistically constructed huts cannot represent an ideal for the human species" (421; Constant [1824–31] 1999, 29–34).

Constant also champions the notion of natural rights against the desire of Bentham to replace it with the concept of utility. It is true, he admits, that a natural right is sometimes imprecise and can be interpreted in many ways. But the concept of utility is worse in this respect: it can be interpreted in many contradictory ways, and it involves an important subjective and arbitrary element.

14. Staël also alludes to Bentham and Dumont in a long footnote in *De l'Allemagne* (see Staël [1810] 1968, 2:185–86).

> The principle of utility has a greater danger than that of law, since it arouses in the mind of man hope of profit, and not the sentiment of duty. But the appraisal of profit is arbitrary; it is the imagination that decides; but neither its error nor its caprice is capable of altering the notion of duty. (Constant 1829a, 552)

Natural rights, the sentiment of duty, are causes, and independent of any calculation. Utility is just a result, a consequence. And the principle of utility, as Constant, like Staël, emphasizes, inducing everybody to calculate in terms of pleasures and pains, destroys morality (554). Constant naturally states that it is always possible to redefine the concept of utility so that one might infer from it the same rules as those following from natural law and justice. But this would be vain and dangerous:

> The word *utility*, following common usage, puts us in mind of a different idea than that of justice, or of law. Insofar as usage and common sense attach a specific meaning to a word, it is dangerous to alter this meaning; one vainly explains subsequently what one wished to say; the word remains, the explanation forgotten. (551–52)

The same argument is advanced with respect to morals based on interest and the notion of interest well understood. Constant remarks that if many authors can maintain that actions based on self-interest always coincide with sound morality and justice, this is because the notion of self-interest is used in a much broader and philosophical way than usually understood. Political economists such as Say, for example, emphasize the fact that this self-interest must be enlightened. Men, Say (2003b, 142) writes, must always follow "a self-interest that one has good reason to regard as superior to passing and risky advantage" resulting from satisfying a more immediate self-interest. From this perspective, good laws are "*monitors that constantly turn each man away from sacrificing a LASTING interest to a MOMENTARY interest—the latter seeming vivacious, the former less lively, but all the same, superior*" (142). Constant disagrees and questions this kind of argument. This acceptance of the word *self-interest*, he states, might be true of the best philosophy, and a man should of course avoid an action that will hurt others' interests in order to bring him an immediate pleasure, but that will also later bring him lasting pain. But people simply do not understand this way of thinking, and, as far as they are concerned, self-interest only entails an immediate and restrictive meaning. As a consequence, "When you say to them [the people] that they must govern according to their self-interest, they hear that they have to sacrifice to their interest all opposing or rival interests" (Constant 1829a, 548). We have come back to the most negative effects of the liberty associated with the moderns.

Religion and the Liberal Sociopolitical Order

In sum, for Constant as for Staël, the analysis of modern society reveals a worrying situation. The liberty of the moderns, the morality based on self-interest and the principle of utility, strictly separates "the logical and rational part of man" from his "noble and elevated part"—the realm of sentiments—retaining the first and rejecting the second. Constant (1829a, 550) thought it high time to react against this state of affairs. But how can this be done? Next comes the fundamental role of genuine morals and of religion.

> All systems can be reduced to two only. One gives self-interest as its guide, and well-being as its end. The other proposes that the end is perfection, guided by intimate sentiment, the abnegation of self and the faculty of sacrifice. (Constant [1824–31] 1999, 33)

Staël's conviction is not different. The true understanding of human beings, the true philosophical system, lies not in "experimental philosophy," that is, sensationism, or in "speculative philosophy": it is equally nonsensical to blindly trust the sensations or to reject their evidence. Both philosophies are unacceptably one-sided and cannot grasp the complexity and truth of the moral world. Both sides are necessary: reason and sentiment, each having its own field, must support each other.[15] Each field is legitimate, provided however that the soul, the religious sentiment, and morals have the last word (Staël [1810] 1968, 2:95).

At all levels of society—individual as well as collective—morals are necessary to counteract the corrosive effects of the form of liberty espoused by the Moderns. The very recent example of the darkest moments of the French Revolution, where all moral bonds were suppressed, forms a negative and illuminating illustration of this proposition (Staël [1799] 1906, 298–99).

15. This is why Staël so warmly welcomed the ideas of Immanuel Kant, who marked out "les limites des deux empires, des sens et de l'âme, de la nature extérieure et de la nature intellectuelle" ([1810] 1968, 2:129).

At the individual level, each person is greatly helped in his or her choices by a kind of moral code received in childhood. This code generates feelings and habits before a human being is able to think carefully and to calculate (Staël [1800] 1991, 378). Morals are also necessary at the collective level. They form an effective protection against the "métaphysique du vague," false deductions and fanaticism. The legislator must rely on philosophy, and philosophy "has to rest on two foundations, morality and calculation." Morals are thus a powerful and necessary check on the legislator's action; one should never depart from the principle that "every time that calculation fails to coincide with morals, it is calculation which is wrong" (374).

But where do morals originate? "Religion is the true foundation of morality" (Staël [1810] 1968, 2:199). Of course some people will always contest the religious origin of moral ideas. But in vain: the best proof that morals come from God is that those who deny this fact are obliged to deify morality itself! (Staël [1800] 1991, 380). At both individual and collective levels, only religion provides human beings with a complete and basic moral code that permits social pacts.

> Morality, and morality bound into religious opinion, gives the sole complete code for all life's actions, a code that brings men back together through a kind of pact of the spirit, an indispensable preliminary for any social contract. (Staël [1799] 1906, 214)

Most of the time, people practice virtue impulsively. The origin of these impulses cannot be found in reflection but in something different, higher, and prior to all reasoning. First come the habits that religion creates in human beings, for it is part of their education (Staël [1800] 1991, 378). But this of course cannot be the main reason. Something more is needed to explain why a virtuous human being often sacrifices some earthly pleasure or material interest in order to adopt a moral attitude. The real point is the very nature of religious feeling: a "sentiment of the infinite."[16] "All sacrifices of personal interest come from this need to place oneself in harmony with this sentiment of the infinite, whose attraction is fully experienced, even if it cannot be expressed" (239). Only this "sentiment of the infinite" can provoke strong, lasting, and "sublime emotions," and only these sentiments, or religious emotion, can induce people to fight against and defeat negative passions (272).

16. See also Staël's ([1810] 1968, 2:248) reference to Friedrich Schleiermacher's ideas.

As for Constant, it is his opinion that the very nature of the human being is to evolve and constantly develop, bettering his mind together with his intellectual and moral abilities. This is the work of civilization. With modern society, succeeding the Old Regime, civilization took a large step forward: but, as outlined above, it is still imperfect. Constant is convinced, however, that these defects can be cured. The unique solution consists in arousing and maintaining "the most that is possible, noble and disinterested sentiments" (421).

The practice of political liberty can help, and this is a reason why Constant (1819, 513) warns against its neglect. But this practice alone cannot be conclusive. Moral sentiments depend in fact on religion. Morals and religious sentiment—defined rather loosely and not susceptible to rational discourse (Constant [1806] 1997, 142; 1826a, 528)—have the same origin, God. "Morals are the work of God, as the religious sentiment itself; they come from the same source. Morality is similar in its lack of origin, and independence. Its rule is placed in every heart" (Constant [1824–31] 1999, 513). Everything therefore comes from a kind of universal and intimate revelation that everybody can freely feel, independently of any intercession on the part of any other human being—priests—and thus of any dogma.

> Yes, without doubt there was a revelation, but this revelation is universal, it is permanent, it has its source in the human heart. Man need only listen to himself, he need only listen to a nature that speaks to him with a thousand voices to be carried invincibly into religion. There is also no doubt that external objects have an influence upon beliefs; but they modify the forms, they do not create the inner sentiment that forms their basis. (43–44)

In addition, Constant is also eager to show that the broad diffusion of morals and religion is not at all counterproductive materially and economically—contrary to what some followers of *philosophie économique* might have thought. This is the reason why he emphasized that the countries in which religious sentiment is the most widespread, namely, England and the United States, are also the most successful in economic matters and development.

> Look around you. Intolerance did what it could to make religion odious. Incredulity did what it could to make it ridiculous, yet religious feeling is everywhere. Look at England, this crowd of sects that make it the object of their most lively ardor and of their assiduous medita-

> tions. England is, however, first among European countries for work, production, industry. Look at America. . . . America covers the seas with its flag; it devotes itself, more than any other people, to the exploitation of physical nature; yet such is the degree of religious feeling in this region, that often just one family is divided into several sects, without this divergence disturbing the peace or domestic affection, because the members of this family come together in the worship of a just and beneficial providence, coming together like travellers at a destination that they have reached by different paths. (Constant 1825, 672–73)

This leads us to a last important point. When they speak of religious sentiment, are Staël and Constant indifferent to the kind of religion that can produce this sentiment, are they favoring any specific institutionalized faith, or are they suggesting the creation of a new religion? Their position cannot be elaborated any further here, but it can be summarized briefly as follows.[17] First, they accept the basic teaching of the Christian faith that, they say, is in accordance with the principles of liberty and equality. Second, religious sentiment is a highly personal feeling, independent of institutionalized churches. The institutionalization of religion and the existence of a clergy is considered to be a negative point that can prevent the full development of this sentiment, and even kill it off. One of the best expressions of genuine faith, according to Staël, is Rousseau's celebrated "Profession de foi du vicaire savoyard."[18] Third, if an institutionalized church had to be selected, this would obviously not be the Catholic Church but some modernized version of the Protestant Church. Fourth, while they are hostile to the clergy, they are all the more opposed to any combination of religion and politics, and thus against any theocracy. Religious freedom is the only just political standpoint for a state, the only one, moreover, capable of preserving religious sentiment, and even of favoring its diffusion.

All these points are not only essential for an understanding of the positions taken by Staël and Constant but also for distinguishing their ideas from those of the other schools of thought dealt with in this article.

17. Staël's ideas are scattered in almost all her writings—she also acknowledged her debt to the ideas developed by her father in *De l'importance des opinions religieuses* (Necker 1788). Constant more specifically developed his position in his *Principes de politique* ([1806] 1997), his article "Du développement progressif des idées religieuses" (1826b), and, of course, his grand opus on this subject, *De la religion* ([1824–31] 1999).

18. Inserted in his philosophical novel, *Émile ou de l'éducation* (1762).

For example, while Say was a-religious, the Traditionalists—in fact another target of Constant and Staël—were Catholic,[19] and so were later the various authors who, from the 1840s on, defended political economy (see sec. 4). On the contrary, the Saint-Simonians and Auguste Comte, to whom we turn now, rejected Christian faith in the modern age and are in favor of creating a new religion and, moreover, of a theocracy. These different positions are, as we can see, rather sharply differentiated.

3. Saint-Simon, the Saint-Simonians, and Auguste Comte: The Organizational Strand of Industrialism

Claude-Henri Saint-Simon

After the fall of Napoleon's regime, publicists interested in the social sciences felt free to publish again and to address the public. Say immediately published an updated second edition of his *Traité d'économie politique* (1814), soon followed by the third (1817) and the fourth (1819). The book was a success, and the managers of the Athénée royal asked Say to give a series of lectures on political economy during the winter of 1815–16; these lectures were also successful, and Say lectured again in 1816–17 and 1819.[20] Claude-Henri Saint-Simon attended the first series of these lectures and was very impressed (Gouhier 1964, vol. 3, chaps. 2–3).[21] This much seems plain when we read Saint-Simon's works, published with the help of Augustin Thierry in the first few volumes of *L'industrie*.

In this short-lived periodical Saint-Simon praised political economy and considered this science to be the bedrock of the new politics he was

19. These Traditionalists—we employ the term used by French historians—were those political philosophers like Bonald or Maistre (see sec. 1), and the politicians who would have liked to annihilate the political conquests of the French Revolution. A celebrated assertion by Bonald illustrates this trend of thought rather well, when he states that men cannot give any constitution to the religious or political society, just as they cannot give gravity to bodies or extension to matter. For what concerns the Catholic economists proper, the "first generation: 1829–34" (Almodovar and Teixeira, this volume), in fact started publishing after Staël's death and just before Constant's.

20. The manuscripts of the last series of these lectures were among Say's papers; they are now published in Say's *Leçons d'économie politique* (2003a).

21. There is a handwritten note about Say's second lecture in which Saint-Simon emphasized the necessity of spreading good principles in order to build sound public opinion. He added that the leading bankers and manufacturers should have attended Say's opening lecture (Say n.d., MS NAF 24605, folio no. 33).

seeking, to bring peace to France and Europe.[22] What was the reason for such an enthusiastic perspective? Basically, it came from Saint-Simon's endorsement of the logic of interest:

> There is an order of interests felt by all men, interests that nourish life and well-being. This order of interests is the only one upon which all men need agree, the only one where they have to deliberate, to act jointly, thus the only one around which politics can be pursued and which has to be taken as the sole standard for criticism of all institutions and all social matters. Politics is thus, in sum, the *science of production*, that is, the science that has as its aim the order of the things most favorable to all forms of production. (Saint-Simon and Thierry [1817] 1966, 1:188)

At that time Saint-Simon was clearly on the side of *philosophie économique*. As a consequence of the role given to political economy, morals suited to the new social system (industrialism) were grounded in concrete interest: "The era of positive ideas now begins: one cannot give to morals anything but palpable, certain, and present interest" (2:38). But two years later, when he began working with Auguste Comte after Thierry's departure, Saint-Simon's view on morals and interests changed radically (Steiner 2006a, 2006b). From then on right to the end, he claimed that societies rested on two pillars: interests and common moral ideas, because men needed both material and spiritual bonds to live together.

> A society cannot exist without common moral ideas; and this commonality is as necessary to the spiritual as well as the temporal community of interest. However, these ideas cannot be shared in common if they lack a basis in a philosophical doctrine that is universally taken into the social edifice; this doctrine is the keystone of the arch, the link that unites and consolidates all parts. (Saint-Simon and Comte [1821] 1966, 51)

It is important to notice that common values (*idées morales communes*) are equal in importance to self-interest and are considered to be the central element presently lacking in the social sciences and industrial society. What explains the emphasis put on values?

22. Contrary to Say's cautious efforts to distance politics from his political economy, Saint-Simon exhorted him to fully grasp the political content and consequences of his science (Saint-Simon and Thierry [1817] 1866, 1:186).

According to Saint-Simon and Comte, industrialism was threatened by its own motivating force: by material interest, a dynamizing element that has a name in the science of morals: egoism, or selfishness. Egoism endangered industrialism because it meant that people acted in isolation, thus severely weakening social bonds. Both writers considered that this situation demanded a new moral element, which they called philanthropy. They described the major issue facing industrial society in "Adresse aux philanthropes":

> Cupidity has been a national sentiment and has only been experienced by citizens in a collective manner [during conquests]; greed becomes a dominant sentiment in all citizens; egoism, which is the moral gangrene of the human race, catches hold on the political body and becomes a sickness common to all classes of society. (90)

Morals became in this way central to stabilizing the new social system: without common moral beliefs, the economic wellspring of action would block all collective achievement, and personal interest would prevail at the cost of the social or general interest. Here lies the moral illness of the industrial system; here is the social meaning Saint-Simon and Comte attached to *égoïsme*.

For a brief period they considered the Christian moral code to be the best possible moral code (Saint-Simon and Comte [1823–24] 1966, 4:200–201), but in his last book Saint-Simon ([1825] 1966) expressed the view that a *new* Christianity should take the place of the outmoded and exhausted version.[23] He praised Christian faith because of the universality of its message: "Men must behave toward one another as brothers" (108). Perfectly suited to the Middle Ages, the Christian faith now lagged behind the needs of the present not only because the modern division of religion from politics was no longer capable of coordinating the social system but also because of scientific progress. Saint-Simon's new Christianity gave prominence to the new industrial elites, seeking to find a new relationship between scientific knowledge and morals, the latter being the foundation for the science of social organization (187). This would permit the eradication of poverty and the enhancement of well-being for the entire society:

23. Such a move was not limited to the French social thought; for example, as Steve Medema (this volume) shows, with Henry Sidgwick the search for a new form of religion became for a while an issue in England as well.

> Those who must found the new Christianity and who will become the heads of the new church are those men most capable of contributing through their work to the enhanced well-being of the poorest class. The functions of the clergy will be reduced to teaching the new Christian doctrine, on the perfection of which the heads of the church will unceasingly labor. (117)

The new faith was intended to put an end to present political weakness and ills, that is to say, to the egoism that plagued those efforts made by all useful, industrious persons (185).

The Saint-Simonians

After Saint-Simon's death in 1825, his thought was taken up by a group of young men,[24] many of whom were former students of the École polytechnique (Picon 2002, 102–12), an exclusive institution recognized for the high level of mathematics and physics required and taught. They were considered to be a sect, even a dangerous sect because of their stance as proselytizers for Saint-Simon's thought (Bazard and Enfantin 1829, 1830). They expounded the ideas of their master in a systematic way while introducing modifications and lending religion a much more prominent place.

Their presentation of the doctrine was founded on Saint-Simon's historical approach, according to which understanding of an institution required comparison with similar institutions in the past, even going back to antiquity. As a consequence, they minted a famous formulation, stating the need to move from men exploiting men to men exploiting the globe (Bazard and Enfantin 1829, 24). They linked the first type of exploitation and, more generally, contemporary political and social instability to the duality at the root of human agency:

> In two words, *calculation* or reasoning, science, applied to *material interests*, is not the sole factor motivating human action; we also act out of *sympathy*, which fine arts arouse, and favor; we are *reasoners*, but also *impassioned*, we are *self-interested*, but nonetheless we know how to *devote* ourselves to the most general. (27, 396)

24. On the history and doctrines of this famous sect, see Sébastien Charléty's ([1931] 1964) and Antoine Picon's (2002) studies.

The commitment to the well-being of other people, other-oriented action, was then assigned to religion, and the historical method finally emerged as a powerful tool to explain how religion could once more take its place in industrial society. Following Saint-Simon, they explained history as a succession of organic and critical periods: organic periods are characterized by a clear definition of a social goal and, thus, by a convergence between reason, feelings, and actions (79, 360), between spiritual and material principles, as was the case before the Hellenistic period and from the foundation of the Christian Church to the fifteenth century. In contrast, critical periods are those in which these two principles conflict, and reason, feelings, and acts diverge. This was the case from the sixteenth century to the present, and particularly during the Enlightenment, when science and philosophy attacked those religious and political institutions that shackled industrial classes. Does this mean that religious feelings and institutions were losing their importance as the industrialist classes rose to prominence?

That, they argued, would be a misleading view of history. The authors of the *Doctrine de Saint-Simon* explained that critical periods had two different phases. The first is the destructive phase, in which there is still a collective goal and a collective impetus aiming at destroying the previous social system; during such phases atheism and egoism reign and irreligion flourishes (360, 413): this is a state of anarchy (79). The second phase is characterized by a different task: destruction is no longer on the agenda, since a new social system has to be built; this is not easy because anarchy, albeit less violent, is deeply rooted in the mind and behavior of the various classes, as was the case in France and Europe at that time. The authors of the *Doctrine de Saint-Simon* illustrated these points, noting that there was no longer any collective effort directed to ending anarchy and egoism in science and in industry (85–92): scientists worked in isolation, hurriedly seeking to establish their discoveries before other scientists did so. The Saint-Simonians acknowledged the progress already made in the industrial domain, but they thought that it could be achieved more rapidly.

What was the rationale behind such a judgment? Industrial effort was made in isolation, and egoism prevailed as a consequence of the slogan *laissez-faire, laissez-passer*. Every "industrial" sought to achieve his goal according to his own personal interest, without taking a collective interest into account; he relied on personal knowledge and judgment, which were neither systematic nor comprehensive.[25] Does competition really offer a social mechanism capable of transforming self-interested behavior into a socially beneficial outcome, as the economists claimed? According to the Saint-Simonians, the answer was in the negative, as commercial crises plainly showed. The slogan to which economists were so deeply attached takes for granted a harmony between personal and collective interest that did not in fact exist. For example, it is not enough to state, as Say did, that the invention of printing machines had created an enormous industry compared with that existing in the era of handwritten manuscripts, because there is a time lag involving unemployment, between the introduction of new machines and the creation of a new and broader market (91–92).

Accordingly, the Saint-Simonians felt the need to promote "enthusiasm for collective life [*vie commune*]" and to spread a "love of the universal family of man" (104). They sought to achieve this in the final lectures of the first series, devoted to the religious future of the industrial system. Pointing to their historical approach to the religious past of humanity, they claimed that religion was not fading. There was no doubt that the Christian faith had lost its power over humanity, for this set of beliefs was no longer suited to the contemporary industrial situation (344). In contradistinction to fetishism and polytheism, monotheism—whether Judaism or Christianity—was praised because one unique God was responsible for creation. And Christianity was progressive in comparison with Judaism because the message of love was universal, and not restricted to a single nation (420–21).

> By proclaiming that religion is destined once more to reclaim its rule over societies, we are undoubtedly far from claiming that it is necessary to restore any one religious institution from the past. . . . We are proclaiming a new moral condition, a new political condition; and thus also a very new religious condition; because, for us, *religion*, *politics*, *morals* are only different names for the same thing. This problem . . . is no less likely to be posed and solved in terms at once simple and clear. (415)

25. It is likely that the Saint-Simonians were under the influence of Jean-Charles-Léonard Simonde de Sismondi's ([1819] 1971, 245–60) view of the entrepreneur confronting the world market and, hence, confronting that market uncertainty which fostered commercial crisis and, they argued, egoism.

The second series of lectures (Bazard and Enfantin 1830) dealt almost entirely with the religious issue. The aim of the book was to provide the basis for the new religion. The principal instrument is the idea of progress. Christianity was an improvement over previous religions because of its doctrines of monotheism and universalism. Yet this progress was marred by those political circumstances that engendered the serious divide between politics and religion, on the one hand (24–26), and a serious neglect of the industrial and material dimension of life, on the other (76–80). What had now to be achieved goes beyond this divide, because of the emancipation of industry from the fetters of previous systems, organized as they were around man's exploitation of man. We are thus led from the religious to the political aspect of this perspective—but both aspects were consistently thought to be equivalent (107–8, 114, 122, 161).

What were the leading principles of this theocracy? The Saint-Simonians explained that politics involved three dimensions: morals (or love), science (or intelligence), and industry (or strength), each of them having a specific structure or hierarchy. The priests of the new religion would be in charge of the connections between the three dimensions, including their hierarchy, and in charge of the link between humanity and God (115).

At this point, the authors came back to an important point from the earlier volume, explaining that the priests would have to act on sentiments, not on reason. Why? According to them, sentiments were losing their grip on the industrial population, but this did not mean that reason was growing in importance, since the void created by the weakening of the sentiments was being filled with egoistic feelings and behaviors (117). Consequently, the priests of the new religion would have to act on the sentiment of sympathy, which was at the root of the organic phase of the industrial system.

The priests' duty would also be to coordinate hierarchically the efforts of scientists and "industrials" (123). This coordination implied that the organization of scientific endeavors would be based on public funds instead of wealthy individuals or through the market for scientific books (135–37). On the industrial side, this implied that competition would be excluded in favor of a different coordination device: a priest whose business it was to link production and distribution. The priests would "classify [industrial people] according to their capacities and he will distribute according to their work [*oeuvres*]" (160). Thus the priests would be devoted to the work of hierarchical coordination in science and in industry, linking what had remained separate in the older form of the best religion, Christian Catholicism.

Auguste Comte

An inclination toward religion was also present in Comte's ([1851–54] 1893, [1853] 1922) writings published at the end of our period, when he advocated the need for a new religion and for a new theocracy. This was, however, linked to his severe criticism of political economy. We should not forget that when Comte became his secretary, Saint-Simon gave the young and brilliant former *polytechnicien* the task of reforming political economy (Gouhier 1964, 3:189).

The first instance of this critique appeared in a lengthy paper published soon after Saint-Simon's death, on the spiritual bond in industrial society and with the unsatisfactory nature of social solidarity as conceived in the economists' account of the division of labor (Comte [1826] 1893). The point of departure was close to that of the Saint-Simonians: society was characterized in terms of self-interest and anarchy following the decay of spiritual power and a consequent absence of any common system of legitimate general ideas; a lack of public morality, for which the rise of utilitarianism was a good indicator; prominence given to the material dimension of life; and, finally, the increasing centralization of political power in government (184–87). However, Comte argued that spiritual and political powers were different and should be carefully distinguished, since spiritual power could not do its regulative work if it were involved in those activities specific to government (181, 193, 204). Accordingly, spiritual power should be limited to the great task of education—the government of opinion (193)—at the national and also the European level.

According to Comte—and here his critique of political economy began—social organization based on the division of labor inevitably involves a weakening of social bonds, because individuals consider only their personal interest. As a consequence, spiritual and political powers were needed to lend these individuals a common foundation, to remind them of the existence of the general interest (199). That is why this approach was in conflict with political economy as a political discourse. Comte did not believe in the existence of beneficial unintended consequences of self-interested behavior, because individuals were unable to perform the calculation attributed to them (209). This critique was expanded in a lecture in his *Cours de philosophie positive*

(Comte 1837–42, 2:80–99),[26] so that he might discard political economy as a "premature attempt to construct the social sciences," as he said.

He returned to these issues in his *Système de politique positive*. In this book, he modified his philosophy so that he might bring together the objective and subjective viewpoints. The objective point of view was dealt with in his assessment of the scientific process (Comte 1837–42), and the subjective viewpoint meant the full development of the views exposed in the essay on spiritual power (Comte [1826] 1893), which dealt in terms of a religion of the *Grand Être*, or Humanity. Comte acknowledged the positive role of self-interest and markets in producing the material elements for social life; however, he was more insistent than ever on the necessity of coordinating human behaviors through sentiments and, thus, through elaborating a common set of moral ideas belonging to the province of theology.[27] How could sentiments and the altruistic dimension of human nature have an influence on human agency? According to him, the altruistic dimension, however weak it might be, gains a great part of its strength from harmony within the social body, that is, the harmony between the different dimensions of social life ([1826] 1893, 23–24)—what he called the *consensus* (Comte [1837–42] 1988, 2:118). Furthermore, the altruistic dimension receives the assistance of love, which seemed to him to be the superior good:

> However, the fortune of being loved can never be free of an egoistic inversion: how can we not be pleased at having gained the fondness of the person whom we prefer before all others? If, therefore, to love is the most satisfying thing for us, that confirms the natural superiority of affections entirely disinterested. Our radical inability consists above all in their being instinctively much less powerful than our egoistic inclinations, which are essential to our preservation. But once excited, even for initially quite personal reasons, they tend to increasingly develop, by virtue of their own gentleness. . . . Once freed from theological oppression and metaphysical aridity, our heart easily senses that real happiness, as much private as public, consists in the greatest development of sociability and in according to oneself only the necessary satisfactions, as inevitable infirmities. (Comte [1851–54] 1893, 1:222)

26. We have dealt with this issue in other work (Steiner 2005, chap. 7, and Steiner 2008).

27. Note that here Comte used the old meaning of economy, designating a harmony within the body, or within the nation, or within the social body (see Faccarello and Steiner 2008).

He explained the superiority of his own religion by the way that it eliminated the egoistic element present within Catholic worship. Instead of asking and expecting something when worshiping God, positive worship was free from any personal interest: the purpose was the unification of the *Grand Être*, that is, the succession of human generations, past, present, and future. In the positive view of religion, the Great Being is Humanity (334–35), and the goal is extending individual life through subjective (religion) and objective (division of labor) participation in this collective, and thereby real, being:

> To exist in others is a very real mode of existence since it fulfills itself, fundamentally the best part of our existence. . . . This faculty of freely prolonging our life into the past and into the future so that we might develop the best in the present, is a necessary compensation for the puerile illusions which we have lost irrevocably. Finally come to maturity, the same science that destroys these subjective consolations constructs today the objective base of a compensation previously thought impossible, while allowing each to hope for incorporation into the Great Being and revealing its laws both static and dynamic. (346–47)

The important role given to the succession of human generations was then emphasized in Comte's examination of life's material dimension. From his religious viewpoint, the so-called science of economists (2:156) missed the point where the formation of capital was concerned: they failed to understand the importance of generational succession, which meant that a given generation received the greatest part of its capital from former generations and had a duty to convey a larger stock of capital to the next. This meant that the economic issue was not limited to the increase in the volume of available capital but also involved considering how wealth is transmitted from generation to generation—that is the Comtian *Grand Être*. Pushing this idiosyncratic view of the organization of the material dimension of life farther, Comte explained that goods could be transferred through gifts, (market) exchanges, bequests, and conquest (2:156). But these four social techniques should be reduced to two: bequests and gift on the altruistic side, exchange and conquest on the egoistic one (2:158). The "great human issue," or the prominence of altruism over egoism, could be resolved thanks to the superiority of the social dimension of economic life over self-interest (1:372; 2:173).

4. Conclusion: Political Economy in an Age of Religious Revival

Was political economy transformed as a result of these debates about the importance and role of religion in social life? The answer is of course negative, but religion nevertheless became an integral part of the liberal view of political economy, then considered to be fundamentally aligned with Catholicism.[28] The apologetic dimension of political economy-cum-religion assumed different forms and can be briefly illustrated in the work of three important authors: Frédéric Bastiat, member of the parliament and well known for his position in favor of free trade; Michel Chevalier, a former member of the Saint-Simonian group who became an atypical liberal economist, then teaching political economy in the Collège de France; and Charles Dunoyer, member of the Conseil d'État, the most consistent proponent of a catallactic order within the French liberal school.

While Dunoyer fully endorsed and radicalized the utilitarian stance of Say's work, he proposed a new and broader definition of political economy, giving a new role to education, religion, and the state in the formation of industrial man, without allowing for any administrative or political regulation of the market system. He rejected the accusation that the new social system would unilaterally favor self-interest and thus the lure of gain: on the contrary, he said, competitive industrialism was a wonderful institution for tempering and regulating the lure of gain through the competitive process. If the moral vices referred to by these accusations still existed, it was because competition had not been systematically introduced (Dunoyer 1845, vol. 1, chaps. 9–10)—the real connecting link of industrial society. Furthermore, Dunoyer devoted a full volume to the moral components of human capital. A good education, he stated, was necessary to moral education, and he had no doubt that moral education could be directed toward social prosperity as its fundamental goal. Religion was also enrolled in this economization of social life, and priests were conceived as contributors to morality (3:275). He rejected the idea that new religions should be created, such as the one established by the Saint-Simonians (3:308–9)—provided that the old forms of religion were practiced in a way that did not impede the progress of arts, mores, and social relations. Dunoyer acknowledged the existence of religious sentiment, but he added that this sentiment should be enlightened and regu-

28. For a general presentation of the evolution of Catholic economic thought, see Almodovar and Teixeira, this volume.

lated, as any other sentiment, so that it could produce those good consequences that could be expected of it (3:293).

Bastiat's *Harmonies économiques* opened with an address to the youth of France, in which harmony lay precisely at the juncture of religion and political economy:

> Young people, you will find the title of this work rather ambitious: HARMONIES ÉCONOMIQUES! Would I pretend to reveal the plan of Providence in social order, and the mechanism of all forces destined for humanity to realise progress? Certainly not; but I would like to place you on the path to this truth: *all legitimate interests are harmonious*. This is the leading idea of this essay. And it is impossible to overlook its importance. (Bastiat 1851, 1–2)

Against the socialists and the reformers, against the Catholics condemning self-interest,[29] Bastiat explained that self-interest was nothing but the fundamental wellspring of action placed by God within men (631), and if it could not be flushed out as some reformers thought to do (633), it could be transformed.

As for Chevalier, he followed on from Bastiat, and when he mentioned religion, this was no longer the Saint-Simonian form that he had in mind but the Catholic faith. However, Chevalier had a more optimistic view of the industrial system, and the Leibnizian element—so instrumental in explaining that social suffering was a necessary component of social organization—cannot be found in his writings.

In the three opening lectures at the Collège de France, Chevalier (1850, 1851, 1852) aimed to put on the same footing not only morals and political economy but religion as well. According to him, social bonds meant that three kinds of duty constituted the very stuff of social life: duty toward oneself (self-interest), duty toward one's relatives and citizens (association), and duty toward the Creator (brotherhood). This explained why he stated so forcefully that political economy had a spiritual dimension (Chevalier 1850, 211) and why he made such a strong link between political economy and religion—both sharing the principles of freedom and justice (213–15).

And Chevalier explained that it would be impossible to found political economy *solely* on self-interest, that all attempts in that direction should

29. On the divisions among the liberal and conservative Catholic thinkers of that period, see Weill [1909] 1979.

be considered exceptional and short-lived mistakes, since political economy concerned the common interest (222). In the following lectures, Chevalier added to these statements the idea according to which the desire of well-being was legitimate—which could have been an echo of Bastiat's reference to Jacques-Bénigne Bossuet—and, he concluded, "in this sense, progress is a Divine institution" (Chevalier 1851, 125).

References

Balayé, Simone. 1979. *Madame de Staël: Lumières et liberté.* Paris: Klincksieck.

Bastiat, Frédéric. [1851] 1881. *Harmonies économiques.* Vol. 6 of *Oeuvres complètes de Frédéric Bastiat.* Paris: Guillaumin.

Bazard, Saint-Amand, and Prosper Enfantin. 1829. *Exposition de la doctrine de Saint-Simon: Première année.* Paris: Bureau de l'organisateur.

———. 1830. *Exposition de la doctrine de Saint-Simon: Deuxième année.* Paris: Bureau de l'organisateur.

Bonald, Louis de. [1819] 1845. *Mélanges littéraires, politiques et philosophiques.* Vol. 7 of *Oeuvres de M. de Bonald.* Brussels: Société nationale pour la propagation des bons livres.

Charléty, Sébastien. [1931] 1964. *Histoire du saint-simonisme (1825–1864).* Paris: Gonthiers.

Chevalier, Michel. 1850. Accord de l'économie politique et de la morale: Discours d'ouverture du cours d'économie politique au Collège de France. *Journal des économistes* 25.3:209–27.

———. 1851. Le désir du bien-être est légitime, il peut obtenir satisfaction, mais sous quelles conditions: Discours d'ouverture du cours d'économie politique au Collège de France. *Journal des économistes* 28.2:113–31.

———. 1852. Du progrès: Discours prononcé à l'ouverture de son cours au Collège de France. *Journal des économistes* 31.1:29–49.

Comte, Auguste. [1826] 1893. Considérations sur le pouvoir spirituel. In vol. 4 of *Système de politique positive ou traité de sociologie instituant la religion de l'humanité.* Paris: Larousse.

———. [1851–54] 1893. *Système de politique positive ou traité de sociologie instituant la religion de l'humanité.* Paris: Larousse.

———. [1853] 1922. *Catéchisme positiviste ou sommaire exposition de la religion universelle.* Paris: Garnier.

———. [1837–42] 1988. *Cours de philosophie positive.* Paris: Hermann.

Comte, Charles. 1826. *Traité de législation ou expositions des lois générales suivant lesquelles les peuples prospèrent, dépérissent ou restent stationnaires.* Paris: Sautelet.

Constant, Benjamin. 1814. *De l'esprit de conquête et de l'usurpation dans leurs rapports avec la civilisation européenne.* In Constant 1980.

———. 1819. *De la liberté des anciens comparée à celle des modernes.* In Constant 1980.

——. 1825. Coup d'oeil sur la tendance générale des esprits dans le dix-neuvième siècle. *Revue encyclopédique* (December): 661–74.
——. 1826a. *Du développement progressif des idées religieuses*. In Constant 1980.
——. 1826b. Review of Ch. Dunoyer, *L'industrie et la morale considérés dans leur rapport avec la liberté*. *Revue encyclopédique* (February): 416–35.
——. 1829a. *De M. Dunoyer, et de quelques-uns de ses ouvrages*. In Constant 1980.
——. 1829b. *Mélanges de littérature et de politique*. In Constant 1980.
——. 1980. *De la liberté chez les modernes: Écrits politiques*. Paris: Le livre de poche "Pluriel."
——. [1806] 1997. *Principes de politique, applicables à tous les gouvernements*. Paris: Hachette.
——. [1824–31] 1999. *De la religion considérée dans sa source, ses formes et ses développements*. Arles: Actes Sud.
——. [1822–24] 2004. *Commentaire sur l'ouvrage de Filangieri*. Paris: Les Belles Lettres.
Dunoyer, Charles. 1825. *L'industrie et la morale considérées dans leur rapport avec la liberté*. Paris: Sautelet.
——. 1827. Esquisse historique des doctrines auxquelles on a donné le nom d'industrialisme, c'est-à-dire des doctrines qui fondent la société sur l'industrie. *Revue encyclopédique* 29:416–35.
——. 1845. *De la liberté du travail ou simple exposé des conditions dans lesquelles les forces humaines s'exercent avec le plus de puissance*. Paris: Guillaumin.
Epsztein, Léon. 1966. *L'économie et la morale aux débuts du capitalisme industriel en France et en Grande-Bretagne*. Paris: Armand Colin.
Faccarello, Gilbert, and Philippe Steiner. 2004. *Philosophie économique* and Money in France, 1750–1776: The Stakes of a Transformation. In *Money and Enlightenment*, edited by Daniel Carey and Christopher Finlay. Oxford: The Voltaire Foundation.
——. 2008. Interest, Sensationism, and the Science of the Legislator: French *Philosophie économique* (1690–1830). *European Journal of the History of Economic Thought* 15.1:1–23.
Gouhier, Henri. 1964. *La jeunesse d'Auguste Comte et la formation du positivisme*. 2nd ed. Paris: Vrin.
Helvétius, Claude-Adrien. [1758] 1988. *De l'esprit*. Paris: Fayard.
——. [1773] 1989. *De l'homme, de ses facultés intellectuelles, et de son éducation*. Paris: Fayard.
Holbach, Paul Thiry, baron d'. [1770] 1993. *Le système de la nature*. Paris: Fayard.
——. [1773] 1994. *Système social ou principes naturels de la morale et de la politique avec un examen de l'influence du gouvernement sur les moeurs*. Paris: Fayard.
Holmes, Stephen. 1984. *Benjamin Constant and the Making of Modern Liberalism*. New Haven, Conn.: Yale University Press.
Mill, John Stuart. 1993. *Autobiographie*. Translated by Guillaume Villeneuve. Paris: Aubier.
Necker, Jacques. 1788. *De l'importance des opinions religieuses*. Liège: Plomteux.

Picon, Antoine. 2002. *Les Saint-Simoniens: Raison, imaginaire, et utopie*. Paris: Belin.

Saint-Simon, Henri. [1825] 1966. *Le nouveau christianisme*. In vol. 3 of *Oeuvres de Claude-Henri de Saint-Simon*. Paris: Anthropos.

Saint-Simon, Henri, and Auguste Comte. [1821] 1966. *Du système industriel*. In vol. 3 of *Oeuvres de Claude-Henri de Saint-Simon*. Paris: Anthropos.

———. [1823–24] 1966. *Catéchisme des industriels*. Vols. 4–5 of *Oeuvres de Claude-Henri de Saint-Simon*. Paris: Anthropos.

Saint-Simon, Henri, and Augustin Thierry. [1817] 1966. *L'industrie*. Vols. 1–2 in *Oeuvres de Claude-Henri de Saint-Simon*. Paris: Anthropos.

Say, Jean-Baptiste. n.d. *J.-B. Say's Manuscripts*. Paris: Bibliothèque Nationale de France.

———. 1803. *Traité d'économie politique*. Paris: Déterville.

———. 1814. Letter to Pierre-Samuel Dupont de Nemours, June 23. Eleutherian Mills Historical Library (Greenville, Del.), W2-4131.

———. 1817. *Petit volume contenant quelques aperçus des hommes et de la société*. Paris: Déterville.

———. 1828–29. *Cours complet d'économie politique pratique*. Paris: Rapilly.

———. 1829. Letter to Dumont, March 5. In Say 1833.

———. 1833. *Mélanges et correspondance d'économie politique*. Paris: Chamerot.

———. 2003a. *Essais de politique pratique*. In vol. 5 of *Oeuvres économiques complètes de J.-B. Say*. Paris: Economica.

———. 2003b. *Leçons d'économie politique*. In vol. 4 of *Oeuvres économiques complètes de J.-B. Say*. Paris: Economica.

Sismondi, Jean-Charles-Léonard, Simonde de. [1819] 1971. *Nouveaux principes d'économie politique*. Paris: Calmann-Levy.

Staël, Germaine Necker de. 1788. *Lettres sur les écrits et le caractère de J. J. Rousseau*. In vol. 1 of Staël 1871.

———. 1796. *De l'influence des passions sur le bonheur des individus et des nations*. In vol. 1 of Staël 1871.

———. [1818] 1861. *Considérations sur les principaux événements de la Révolution française*. In *Oeuvres posthumes de Madame la baronne de Staël-Holstein*. Paris: Firmin Didot.

———. 1871. *Oeuvres complètes de madame la baronne de Staël-Holstein*. 2 vols. Paris: Firmin Didot.

———. [1799] 1906. *Des circonstances actuelles qui peuvent terminer la Révolution, et des principes qui doivent fonder la république en France*. Paris: Librairie Fischbacher.

———. [1810] 1968. *De l'Allemagne*. Paris: Flammarion.

———. [1807] 1985. *Corinne ou l'Italie*. Paris: Gallimard.

———. [1800] 1991. *De la littérature considérée dans ses rapports avec les institutions sociales*. 2nd ed. Paris: Flammarion.

Steiner, Philippe. 2003. Say, les Idéologues, et le groupe de Coppet: La société industrielle comme système politique. *Revue française d'histoire des idées politiques* 18:331–53.

——. 2005. *L'école durkheimienne et l'économie: Sociologie, religion et connaissance*. Geneva: Droz.

——. 2006a. French Political Economy, Industrialism, and Social Change (1815–30). In *Economic Development and Social Change: A Historical Approach*, edited by Y. Sthatakis and G. Vaggi. London: Routledge.

——. 2006b. La science de l'économie politique et les sciences sociales en France (1750–1840). *Revue d'histoire des sciences humaines* 15:15–42.

——. 2008. La tradition française de critique sociologique de l'économie. *Revue d'histoire des sciences humaines* 18:64–83.

Waterman, A. M. C. 1991. *Revolution, Economics, and Religion: Christian Political Economy, 1798–1833*. Cambridge: Cambridge University Press.

Weill, Georges. [1909] 1979. *Histoire du catholicisme libéral en France, 1828–1908*. Geneva: Droz.

The Ascent and Decline of Catholic Economic Thought, 1830–1950s

António Almodovar and Pedro Teixeira

Although the emergence of Catholic economic thought in the late nineteenth century was preceded by attempts to deal with some crucial moral issues arising out of economic activity,[1] as a rule economic questions did not rank high in the church's concerns until the second half of the nineteenth century. Several causes stirred the change, including the French Revolution, the emergence of liberalism, and the overthrow of monarchic regimes, the traditional support of the altar (see Faccarello and Steiner, this volume). In addition, there were social and economic changes driven by the growing use of machinery, the opening of new markets, and the development of industry and commerce, fueled by and fueling rapid urbanization and a rural exodus by significant portions of the European population.

In this article we analyze the impact of those transformations on the reconstruction of Catholic economic ideas and their evolution during the nineteenth century and the first half of the twentieth century. Our primary focus is on the efforts to develop a network—or a Catholic school of economic thought—with a specific agenda of research and of social

1. The earlier scholarly attempts to organize an explicit and meaningful set of theological principles for economic problems was performed in the sixteenth century by authors belonging to the Salamanca school (see Grice-Hutchinson 1978, 1993; Camacho 1998).

History of Political Economy 40 (annual suppl.) DOI 10.1215/00182702-2007-060

and economic transformation.[2] We limit our discussion to the development of this network within France, Belgium, Germany, and Italy.[3]

We consider Catholic economic thought as synonymous with a set of ideas originating in different hierarchical streams, but always and permanently subject to the church's verdict about its exactness. Catholic economic thought is therefore to be found in two different sets of documents. The first includes authorized documents by the church hierarchy;[4] the second, documents produced by Catholics in an attempt to develop and apply the church's social teaching. The analysis of the second set of documents, which may be subsequently discarded by the hierarchy, is obviously indispensable if one wishes to fully capture the historical expressions that were assumed by Catholic economic thought.

The present article's first section depicts the emergence and evolution of Catholic economic thought previous to the *Rerum Novarum*, by analyzing the work of the first political economists bearing a Catholic viewpoint and the intellectual networks that emerged within several continental European Catholic countries in the second half of the nineteenth

2. Although there is an extensive literature on the emergence and subsequent evolution of the church's social doctrines, not to mention the numerous studies on the emergence of Christian Democracy, corporatism, and other particular themes related to Catholic political and social thought, there is no systematic study of the economic ideas put forward by a series of authors who strived to establish a Catholic approach to political economy in the nineteenth century. A study of these ideas should take into account the development of this network at least into Eastern Europe and England, as well as the Americas and Canada. On these matters, see the articles in this volume, particularly those by Waterman, Davenport, and Backhouse.

3. The articles in this volume by Faccarello and Steiner and by Parisi provide specific examples of these efforts in early-nineteenth-century France and early-twentieth-century Italy, respectively.

4. Following a traditional methodological approach to the Catholic social doctrine, we may define Catholic economic thought as the set of authorized attempts to appraise the livelihood of people and its underlying philosophical and anthropological tenets from an ethical and theological perspective. In its more evolved forms, Catholic economic thought is inevitably led to include in its assessment of economic life some of the findings of political economy, and later of economics. The economic propositions in the church documents are offered as part of the church's social doctrine, usually through theological and philosophical propositions about the nature of humanity and society, which define an overall desirable socioeconomic framework (see also Parisi, this volume). As it happens with the social doctrine, the production (and universal validation) of Catholic economic thought is subject to a hierarchical structure where the pope's ex cathedra statements (together with those by the bishops gathered either in a council or in a synod) occupy the highest authoritative rank (see Massaro and Shannon 2002; Curran 2002). The encyclicals and other major documents are therefore proposed as universal documents where the church offers essential guidelines to be further developed and specified in order to be locally applied by both church officials and laypeople.

century. The second section covers the mature period of the Catholic school of economic thought, which had its heyday in the first decades of the twentieth century. In the third section we highlight the main reasons for the waning of the concept of a Catholic school of economic thought in the postwar years.[5]

The Emergence of Catholic Economic Thought in the Mid-Nineteenth Century

One of the most alarming nineteenth-century social and economic issues was the so-called social question.[6] If the humanitarian aspects of this issue could naturally appeal to Catholics, the fact is that the political aspects were also important for the church effort to recover its ethical preeminence within the modern industrial world. As a consequence, a substantial part of the initial Catholic approach to the social question was an attempt to prove that peace and social harmony were the trademark of Catholicism throughout human history. In entering this debate, the church was confronted with political economy. Although new, this science was influential enough to cause the church to perceive it as a sort of threatening Magna Carta of modernity, not only because its doctrines packed together most of the aforementioned new political and philosophical ideas but also because its unveiled materialistic emphasis had won a frightening doctrinal supremacy over the traditional values supported by Catholic ethics, philosophy, and natural law (similar debates were occurring among other Christian traditions—for the case of the United States, see Davenport, this volume).

At this new social, political, and economic juncture, the church recognized that the basic Catholic principles for social and ethical teaching present in the Gospels and in the patristic literature were not enough to counteract the growing materialist ethos. As such, the church adopted a two-step strategy: first, a serious effort was made to recover the systematic

5. Although the most recent decades have produced fascinating and relevant material on this topic, in this article we restrict our analysis to the period up to the 1950s, in order to keep to the historical boundaries defined in the collective volume. Moreover, the recent decades have not brought a revival of the type of approach to Catholic economic thought as the one we address here.

6. An interesting analysis of the French nineteenth-century debates about the social question may be found in Smith 1997 and Gueslin 1998.

theology of Aquinas, which was instrumental for establishing a coherent, logical, and clear metaphysical picture of the material and spiritual worlds;[7] second, the neo-Thomist matrix was meticulously applied to an extensive assessment of political economy's philosophical tenets and teachings. This strategy required a substantial philosophical investment; thus, the emergence of a distinctive and mature Catholic alternative to political economy took some time to develop and would become more visible only in the last decades of the nineteenth century.

Until the first official church statement, Catholic economic thought was mainly the outcome of individual attempts to discuss the social question, which did not always follow a similar line of reasoning. This heterogeneity is a natural outcome of the aforementioned complex transformations that stimulated a Catholic reaction and also of the fact that a Catholic approach had to find its own identity in the face of existing schools of economic thought—the liberal and the socialist. Since the contextual identity of a Catholic approach was not easy to establish and to convey solely by a reference to the Gospels, the initial wavering led to the emergence of two trends that managed to survive up to the twilight of this school.

The First Generation (1829–34)

The scholarly acknowledgment of the emergence of a Catholic approach to political economy was relatively swift in France, especially through the work of such authors as François Xavier Joseph Droz (1773–1850) and Alban de Villeneuve-Bargemont (1784–1850). The existence of Catholic relief organizations (like the Société des amis de l'enfance established in 1838 or the Société de Saint Vincent de Paul established in 1839) and of Catholic societies and newspapers (like the Société d'économie charitable established in 1846 and the *Annales de la charité* established in 1845) was probably helpful for the initial acknowledgment of a Catholic variety of economic thought. Outside France, there was also some acknowledgment of this school, which in several cases was somewhat less than sympathetic. In the United Kingdom, the native soil of classical

7. This revival of Aquinas is sometimes labeled as the "third scholasticism" (see Nichols 2002, 136–39). On the details of this process, see Rosa 2004 and Dante 1990, 78–86; 2004.

political economy, the reception of the Catholic approach was particularly reserved (see Waterman 1991, 2004).[8]

The first of these early authors, Droz, was a member of the Académie française (1824) and of the Académie des sciences morales et politiques, having joined those two societies in 1833. In his youth he was a follower of the *idéologues*, but he changed into a committed Catholic in his later years. His interest in political economy preceded his conversion. His 1801 work, *Des lois relatives aux progrès de l'industrie*, focused on the links between freedom and prosperity. Being noticeably influenced by Adam Smith, Droz unsurprisingly concluded that there was only one system able to provide people with their utmost cherished goods—civil liberty and wealth growth. As it happens in other countries, the reflections on industry by Jean-Antoine Chaptal are also present in Droz's reasoning. As a result, his final proposal highlights the need for a careful and gradual transition from the existing prohibitive system to Smith's "ideal" system. However standard this work may be, it is important to notice that the need for a better distribution of wealth was already one of Droz's explicit recommendations.

Another work is the 1829 *Économie politique ou principes de la science des richesses*. Here we find evidence of an adhesion to the optimistic views of classical political economy, namely, the possibility of a better future distribution of wealth. Although acknowledging the utmost importance of moral values as an irreplaceable basis for human society, Droz thought that the new science of political economy had in fact proved a powerful aid for human moral and material betterment. His major admonitions, which appear throughout the book, were directed against some economists who seemed to believe "que les produits ne sont pas faits pour les hommes, et que les hommes son faits pour les produits" ["that products are not made by men, and that men are made by products"] (Droz 1829, 1:76). His social concerns also led him to criticize David Ricardo's aloofness and to stand unequivocally for a better distribution

8. In 1838 Jérôme-Adolphe Blanqui ([1837] 1860, 2:210–30) already mentions Droz and Villeneuve-Bargemont as belonging to a subgroup—the *Christian* economists—within the new generation of French social economists. In the *Dictionnaire des sciences politiques et sociales*, Auguste Ott (1854, 2:296) mentions the so-called *économie charitable* as being a special branch of economic studies, one specifically concerned with the study of the social and economic consequences of moral decay. Some years later, even if Droz's and Villeneuve-Bargemont's works still deserved a mention in McCulloch's 1845 overview of the literature of political economy, they were no longer classified as belonging to the same school of thought or even as writers pertaining to a same department of political economy.

of wealth. Droz's main recipe for amending the problems of contemporary society—poverty included—was therefore mostly based on an effort to enlighten people, both in the sense of making clear to them the lessons of political economy and in the sense of enhancing their moral values, so that they could effectively turn their labor into wealth and thus achieve a decent standard of living.

The social concern present in Droz's work was only an indirectly Catholic one—at least in that it was more centered on happiness than on justice and was not founded on a meaningful appeal to charity or to other Gospel values. Besides, most of his solutions relied on developing industry and enhancing education, not on public or private poor relief. Even so, his concerns with the destitute and his forewarning to entrepreneurs about their *patronage* duties toward workers were noticeable. To those political economists engaged in securing political economy from moral and political judgments, Droz was therefore to be blamed for a failure to distinguish, with sufficient exactness, moral from economic precepts (*Palgrave's Dictionary* 1925, 1:641).

Of the authors mentioned as Catholic or Christian economists in this period, the vicomte Alban de Villeneuve-Bargemont is probably the most well known today. He entered an administrative career as subprefect and always showed a significant concern—in both doctrine and practice—for the poor and destitute. Contrary to Droz, who embraced classical political economy with only some minor restrictions, moral criticism and the willingness to find an alternative to the status quo played an important role in Villeneuve-Bargemont's approach. The existence of a difference in the overall approach to the same kind of problems (pauperism) is immediately perceptible in the preface of the *Économie politique chrétienne*, for Villeneuve-Bargemont (1834, 24) is quite aloof toward the foundations of the existing liberal system. The ultimate consequences of such a system are described in an almost apocalyptic tone, since Villeneuve-Bargemont thought that the coexistence of mass poverty and moral decay with extreme wealth was thrusting Europe into an unsustainable social and political situation (25).

The legal and institutional reform that Villeneuve-Bargemont had in mind relied heavily on Christian values. It was not a conventional moral appeal to individual consciences; it was a proposal for the voluntary establishment of a different social and economic system. The ultimate consequence of Villeneuve-Bargemont's negative assessment of the existing economic system was therefore the inescapable need for a meaningful revision of the philosophical foundations of classical political economy. His system pointed out the need to establish a fair distribution of wealth, fair wages, agricultural development, and a general reorganization of industry to prevent the kind of excessive concentration of wealth that had already taken place in England. Villeneuve-Bargemont was also quite clear about the need for effective moral regeneration, and he favored the insertion of essential Christian values—not just charity—within the framework of both institutions and laws, that is, within the basic framework of the contemporary state.

The less-known comte Charles de Coux (1787–1864) worked along with Droz and Villeneuve-Bargemont in the Société d'économie charitable (Battini 1995, 148) and was a collaborator of Felicité de Lamennais at the newspaper *L'Avenir* (Kothen 1945, 94–96). In addition, Coux took charge of the first chair of political economy at the Catholic University of Louvain (1834–45), where he was subsequently replaced by a disciple and an admirer, Charles Périn (Fallon [1924] 1935, 481). Unfortunately, Coux's published work on political economy is quite incomplete, for we have only the first two of a series of twenty-six essays that he had planned to write on the subject.[9]

Although associated with the group of so-called liberal Catholics gathered around Lamennais (Kothen 1945, 95, 143), Coux was nevertheless quite critical of liberal political economy. His approach to the history of economic doctrines is illustrative of this critical stance toward the excessive materialism of Smith, Jean-Baptiste Say, and Say's disciples, for all political economists (the critics like Sismondi and the Saint-Simonians included) are held responsible by Coux (1832, 50) for the emergence of pauperism and the ensuing social question. However harsh it may seem, the fact is that Coux's criticism was not synonymous with a complete denial of political economy's relevance for the modern world.

As a Christian political economist, his major goal was to reinstate the importance of Catholicism not just within contemporary society but also within the legitimate concerns of political economists. Accordingly, Coux was interested in bridging the gap between political economy and religion, not in enlarging it. His approach would therefore lead political econ-

9. These two essays—*Discours prononcé à l'ouverture d'un cours d'économie politique* and *Des richesses morales et des richesses matérielles*—were published in 1832 in a small book titled *Essais d'économie politique*. For a contemporary reaction to this work, which is labeled as "une nouvelle doctrine d'économie politique" belonging to the "école catholique" of *L'Avenir*, see the *Revue des deux mondes*, 2nd ser., 2:372–80.

omy to enlarge its scope in order to embrace the study of the fundamental laws of social organization. According to this perspective, political economists had the professional duty to examine all doctrines and moral systems in order to assess their consequences for developing both wealth and social welfare. By doing this, Coux believed that they could not but acknowledge that Catholicism ought to be considered as part of the philosophical roots of political economy. At this earlier stage, the identity of the network of Catholic political economists was still under construction. Droz was more confident about the benefits of an overall orientation in favor of growth by means of freedom; the other two were more prone to believe that the excessively materialistic and individualistic orientations of political economy doctrines were not only wrong but also responsible for the deadlock of the ongoing status quo.[10] However, their overall position on political economy at this early stage is still nonconfrontational, if nothing else because some political economists did share analogous philanthropic concerns with the poor and were ready to accept the need for some improvement in the distribution of wealth. As a whole, their views may still be considered as somewhat marginal to political economy, not as an organized attempt to change its core tenets.

Even so, their identity was being built under the influence of two types of forces. On the one hand, all the aforementioned authors share several concerns. Although in different degrees, they all feel sorry for the situation of the poor, all of them are seriously concerned with the social and political proportions that the poor question may acquire and believe that charity and other Catholic religious principles may help ameliorate this upcoming threat. On the other hand, they were being brought together by the criticisms of their opponents, namely, by the liberal political economists who accused them of being unable to keep science apart from morals.

The Second Generation (1850–90)

The second half of the nineteenth century witnessed not only the growing criticisms of socialism against political economy but also the development of an explicit Catholic approach to the existing social and economic problems, both at a practical level (Catholic organizations) and at

10. This was somehow different from the kind of methodological concerns raised among other Christian circles in England (see Maas, this volume).

a doctrinal level. At this stage, the network of Catholic economists—among whom we must mention Luigi Taparelli d'Azeglio (1793–1862), Charles Périn (1815–1905), Victor Brants (1856–1917), and Matteo Liberatore (1810–1892)—began to spread within continental Europe Catholic countries and gradually become more structured. As this network grew in importance and in visibility, its protagonists became aware of some differences among themselves. It was also at this stage that the church began to more closely inspect and supervise this network.[11] Périn and Brants correspond to the Catholic perspective that emerged gradually in the context of the nineteenth-century restoration and development of the Catholic universities.[12] They may be considered as belonging to the path opened by Droz and Coux and as the immediate forerunners of the so-called conservative tendency that was later formally organized around the Angers school. The Jesuits Taparelli and Liberatore represent a second trend, centered on the journal *Civiltà Cattolica* (founded in 1850 by Jesuit priests to spread the views of the Catholic Church), and they were therefore closer to the ongoing neo-Thomist doctrinal effort that would eventually lead to the *Rerum Novarum*. They may be considered as precursors of the so-called progressive tendency, later embodied by the Fribourg Union and the Liège school.

Economic Thought in the Catholic University: Périn and Brants

As soon as the nineteenth-century restoration of the Catholic universities took place, political economy was established within their curricula. Coux was in charge of this chair in Louvain from 1834 to 1845 and was replaced by Périn, who stood in charge until he was replaced in 1881 by Brants. Among these authors, Périn must be considered as the pivotal figure in developing the intellectual path followed in Louvain regarding a Catholic approach to political economy.

Périn's approach to economic life was twofold. First, he tried to prove that contrary to what its enemies said, Catholicism was not an obstacle to the progress of wealth. In the first book he published—with the appropri-

11. This is also the period where the church made its first statements on the proper Catholic orientation in the face of both socialism and liberalism (Pius IX 1876); conversely, this is also the period when Leo XIII (1879) formally reinstated the importance of Aquinas.

12. Louvain was the first to be restored; the University of Notre Dame (Indiana) was founded in 1842, and the University of Laval (Quebec) was founded in 1852. In France, the restoration took place only after 1875.

ate title *De la richesse dans les sociétés chrétiennes*—there is a meticulous demonstration that Catholicism was closely associated with the historical progress of wealth. Nevertheless, Périn's approach added a new element, for he wanted to prove that the only possible way for modern society to keep on developing was by reinstating the social (and political) authority of the Catholic Church (Périn [1861] 1868, 1:424–25).

Périn was not entirely opposed to the doctrines of political economy. Like Coux, his major criticisms were addressed to a series of philosophical and methodological errors in which Smith and his followers had incurred by pushing too far the relative independence of the spiritual and material aspects of life and by relying excessively on the powers of abstraction alone. Any *excess* of individualism, which would emerge whenever the virtue of renouncement was forgotten and individuals were left to act solely in accordance with a narrow and greedy disposition, was viewed by him as unacceptable. But whenever individualism and freedom were properly understood, and particularly whenever the self-interested actions were curbed by a sense of justice and of charity, they could not but set up valuable forces for the progress of the commonwealth.

According to Périn (1895, x), the sole way to carry on the "catholic restoration of political economy"—without either falling into the "aberrations of socialism" or becoming as "powerless" as the liberal economists were in the face of the ongoing social problems—was to "take in the first principles of political economy as Catholics may find them by meditating upon the Gospels." Périn considered the two principles of renouncement and of Christian charity as the essential basis to build a truly Catholic approach to political economy. The first was instrumental in curbing the excesses of the individual search for wealth and craving for material pleasures that had been unleashed by liberalism; the second would lessen the excessive existing inequalities between men up to a *natural* (and therefore unavoidable) level. Through their joint action, these principles would steer the adoption of a responsible attitude of the rich and powerful toward the workers, namely, by means of patronage (Périn [1861] 1868, 2:569–60).

Brants, Périn's disciple and successor in Louvain's chair of political economy, approached this same problem in a short introduction to his course on political economy. In this 1883 book, Brants's purpose was to survey the existing schools of economic thought according to a four-level scheme of analysis: the autonomy of political economy in the face of morals, the perspectives on the nature and existence of economic laws, the economic role allotted to the state, and the role of deduction and induction. According to this method of classification, Brants (1883, vi) could condense the considerable array of schools of economic thought into two major trends—one followed by the *science libérale* and the other followed by the *science morale*.

As a consequence of this taxonomy, it was easier to perceive the existence of resemblances than to discern the specific identity of each particular school that emerged as a reaction to the doctrines of the *liberal* science, which was precisely what Brants wanted to achieve. Brants describes the four main contemporary schools belonging to the *moral* science: the Ketteler school (also called the Mayence school), the Périn school, the Le Play school (also known as the observation school), and the Roscher school (also called the historical-ethical school). Since they were all supposed to share a common moral concern, their differences were necessarily to be established on the basis of the degree in which they would define the autonomy of political economy, the nature and existence of its laws, the need for state intervention, and the role to be performed by deduction. Being less intransigent than Périn, Brants (1883, 90) was therefore less disposed to view the existence of some variation as a threat to Catholic economists.

According to Brants (1883, 8–13), besides the religious, positive moral that was known through revelation and the tradition embedded in the Catholic Church, there was also a natural moral, whose importance should not be completely dismissed. Bearing this in mind, the Christian economist, while knowing beyond any doubt that truth is in Christ, should demonstrate and explain that only the Christian political economy is perfect and that, as long as it aims only at a purely worldly order, every economy is in fact workable in a less than perfect way. The distinctive task of a Christian economist would therefore be to sponsor indirectly the moral truth by providing evidence of its social effects—thus facilitating the eventual convergence between the natural and the religious moral.

Economic Thought at the *Civiltà Cattolica*: Taparelli and Liberatore

Although missing the authoritative character of the church's formal statements, the journal *Civiltà Cattolica* must nevertheless be considered as one of the most important nineteenth-century informal channels for spreading the church's views on contemporary issues. This journal, which was sponsored by Pope Pius IX and subsequently by Leo XIII, was edited by a well-organized group of nine Jesuits, some of whom had already played an important role in reviving neo-Thomist philosophy within the Catholic Church. The journal's success was indisputable, since ten years after its launch in 1850 it had already managed to sell more than ten thousand copies per number. As a consequence, its approach to the social question and to political economy surely had a considerable impact on Catholic opinion.

The first meaningful essay on political economy—*Le due économie*—was written by Taparelli in 1856.[13] Its purpose was twofold: on the one hand, Taparelli wanted to link the principles behind *heterodox*—that is, liberal—political economy to a series of observable evils experienced by contemporary societies; on the other hand, he did not want Catholics to entirely reject the science of political economy, for he wanted them to acknowledge its importance once it was adequately inspired by Catholic principles. For Taparelli (1943, 35), the aim was to replace the "utilitarian and atheist" ethos currently used by political economists by the Christian belief that "l'homme et la société dépendent absolument de Dieu." For Taparelli, only a Catholic anthropology could inspire an exact political economy (59).

The fact that the church had the leading role in spreading this anthropology was not tantamount to saying that everyone else—both individuals and governments—could relinquish their own responsibilities. Hence the government's function was to regulate the use of things by individuals so that they would do no harm to each other and to collect the quality and quantity of wealth necessary to ensure the common good. This principle had a double consequence. On the one hand, it distinguished between the conventional political economy embraced by the liberals and the social economics that should be enacted by Catholics. On the other hand, this principle implied that the state had the duty to intervene in favor of the weak and destitute, not in favor of the rich and powerful.[14]

Taparelli's views, which to a certain extent were at odds with those voiced by Périn and Brants, rely little on a direct appeal to Catholic principles like charity or renouncement. Their foundation is to be found in the concepts of justice, hierarchy, and order as explained in the context of neo-Thomism. These same views were subsequently refined and developed by Liberatore between 1872 and 1891. In this author we may witness the same perspective on the need for state intervention in economic life. Liberatore did not care to conceal the distance he had about the alleged

13. The charge of addressing economic questions and of assessing political economy was sequentially taken by Taparelli, Liberatore, and Valentino Steccanella.

14. This is clearly different from (and beyond) what was advocated on the other side of the channel by political economists with ethical and moral concerns such as Sidgwick (see Medema, this volume).

virtues of both competition and liberalism. Hence the criticism voiced by Périn and echoed by Brants on the dangerous similitude between some Catholic writers and the socialists.

The state's generic duty to intervene in order to ensure the existence of a well-ordered society, which had been explained by Taparelli, was now depicted with much more detail by Liberatore. The state was inescapably bound to intervene to regulate children's work, to establish limits to the working day of women, to institute Sunday's rest, and to set up a maximum of working hours for the adult industrial laborer. Although Périn believed that every attempt to enforce by law a minimum wage was socialism and some would argue that the state should not interfere in freely established agreements, the fact was that on more than one occasion the worker's consent was disturbingly like the acquiescence of a victim faced with a menacing assailant (Liberatore [1881] 1990, 257). Given such disturbing situations, Liberatore was absolutely persuaded that state intervention was indispensable and in absolute accordance with justice.

Catholic economists like Taparelli and Liberatore did in fact believe that the social question was a phenomenon that could not be solved by traditional means (charity), as its causes were built into the modern social and economic organization. Modern poverty and modern social unrest were the consequences of erroneous philosophical notions embedded in political economy and in the overall liberal ethos, as well as in modern institutions. Thus the changes necessary to achieve an acceptable distribution of wealth according to justice and to the due respect for the human person—meaning that labor should no longer be considered as a mere commodity to be bought and sold in the market—were out of the reach of the church alone. To replace the ongoing selfishness and utilitarianism by a sounder perspective of mutual need and mutually beneficial collaboration, some coordination between the church and the state was necessary to design new institutional arrangements. Corporations, once properly adapted to the modern world, were one example of a feasible institutional solution for achieving that goal.

Besides this obvious penchant for a more meaningful involvement of the state in social and economic welfare, the other important characteristic of Liberatore's economic thought was the emphasis on the fact that labor was not a commodity. Taparelli had already stressed that according to Christian values, humanity should be considered as an end, not as a means. The incorporation of this idea into Catholic economic thought led to another divergence with the views of liberal political economists.

The Golden Period of Catholic Economic Thought (1891–1950s)

On the eve of the *Rerum Novarum*, Catholic movements were already considerably organized. Thanks to local initiatives, they had not only developed a doctrinal corpus but also established charitable organizations, Catholic trade unions, and several other institutional arrangements to help and guide the poor. The network of Catholic economists was also considerably developed before the *Rerum Novarum*. There was a growing awareness of the importance of the social question, and there was a common will to Christianize political economy. In addition, there was also room for some divergence between sensibilities about the proper role of the state.

The Social Encyclicals: *Rerum Novarum* and *Quadragesimo Anno*

Throughout the nineteenth century there were various signs of the difficulty on the part of the Catholic Church to understand, let alone accept, modernity and the consequences of an ever-expanding market system. Eventually, the Catholic hierarchy decided to address the church's contemporary economic and social role more articulately with Leo XIII's encyclical *Rerum Novarum* (15 May 1891).[15] The innovative nature of this encyclical was twofold. It offered a set of general guiding principles, properly articulated into a global vision, on the proper way to deal with the new socioeconomic realities of industrialization. It also was a recognition that the church had to keep up with the new subjects of moral reflection engendered by a changing social and economic reality.

The central issue of *Rerum Novarum* was the analysis of the condition of workers, especially of industrial workers, the complexity of their condition, and the moral and material risks of their current degrading situation. Leo XIII made clear from the outset that the major problem to be tackled was liberalism in its political and economic dimensions. The *Rerum Novarum* blamed the political and economic transformations of the previous hundred years, which had destroyed or seriously damaged traditional social structures that protected its members, such as the long-established medieval corporations, and had secularized the legal and

15. On the inception of this encyclical, see Gaspieri 1931, Misner 1991, and Rosa 2004.

political framework, which undermined the church's moral influence. With its support for political secularization and economic nonintervention, liberalism created a social vacuum in which prospered an unregulated competition, greediness, usury, and a substantive concentration of wealth and power. The latter eventually promoted an unbalanced distribution of privileges that made possible the utter exploitation of the workers by the all-mighty owners of capital. Liberalism was also to blame for the increasing popularity of socialism as the solution to overthrow an entrenched and hard-hearted minority of plutocrats.

To restore the rotten industrial relations the church proposed a new relationship between workers and capitalists. Instead of deliberately damaging the interests of the capitalists, the workers should opt for nonviolent ways to solve labor disputes, thereby avoiding those perfidious voices that called for social upheaval. Foremost among the workers' duties was the obligation to perform faithfully and completely the tasks allocated to them. Likewise, paramount among the capitalists' duties was to acknowledge and respect the human dignity of the workers. This meant respecting the workers' physical and intellectual limitations, namely, those concerning female and youth labor, as well as paying a fair wage. Although the church accepted the inequality of property, it also cared for those poorest members of society, knowing that, unless these were actively supported, society could place them in a state of quasi-serfdom, risking a drift toward social disorder.

Although not always strictly embraced by all the Catholic economists, these views nevertheless embodied the church's official position on economic and social matters. They prevailed as the unavoidable benchmark for all Catholic economists until Pius XI's 1931 *Quadragesimo Anno*. According to this encyclical, capitalism per se was not an evil system: the problem was its excessive development in recent decades, which led to what the pope called economic despotism, that is, the concentration of wealth that gave to a few members of society the power to influence and subjugate governments and countries. The subjugation of the state to the interests of a wealthy minority, whose power was nurtured by the social triumph of ambition, greed, and speculative behavior, constituted a vilification of the state and of humanity and fostered social disorder.

Although the church accepted and supported a social system based on private property, it also underlined the dual nature of property (individual and social) and the difference between property ownership and property usage. Hence the capitalistic system had to be reorganized according to Christian principles. Pius XI saw labor as a source of wealth, although he rejected the idea that labor was the sole creator of wealth. He also criticized the excesses of capital that, by promoting inequality, would foster the risks of social disruption, or even a socialist revolution. According to him, labor and capital did have common interests that the productive process did consubstantiate, and this communality of efforts and purposes called for both to share the responsibility for the productive process and for the wealth created, including the resulting profits. Commutative justice would be insufficient; thus, he stressed the need to complement it with social justice.

Despite acknowledging the important role of the state, Pius XI advocated the principle of subsidarity, according to which the state should not intervene when intermediate levels of society (associations, local community, family) could have an effective action. Social harmony ought therefore to be built on the contribution of intermediate communities and groups, through multiple forms. This strengthening of the social bonds required the state to regulate competition, which had eroded those bonds, subordinating competition to the higher values of justice and Christian charity. Hence promoting a Christian social order required reconstructing the social fabric, which had been ruined by unlimited competition and the concentration of wealth, by rebalancing social power in order to promote the common good. Rather unsurprisingly, Pius XI explicitly referred to the advantages and risks of the contemporary emerging corporatist organization (in Italy and elsewhere). The pope saw the establishment of the corporative system as a step in the right direction of a Christian socioeconomic order, namely, by its contribution to a harmonious society and its emphasis on the pursuit of the common good.

Charles Antoine's Course on Social Economics

One of the main outcomes of the *Rerum Novarum* was a significant amount of literature conveying the renewed Catholic social and economic awareness for the use of both ministers and Catholic activists. A first stream of Catholic literature tried to deal comprehensively and pedagogically with economic subjects. As a rule, these books did the most to explain and apply to economics a social philosophy that allegedly could secure a coherent and global project of society based on Christian values

(Galindo 1996, 143). These works, many of which were authored by Jesuits and bore titles like "Principles" or "Courses on Social Economics," did ask for a complex scholarly analysis aimed at fulfilling a set of several difficult tasks: they had to explain (classical) political economy to the members of the church and to the laity engaged in social action; they had to introduce and explain the criticisms addressed by the pope to the philosophical tenets underlying classical political economy; they had to deal with socialism to make sure that this doctrine would not be seen as a possible alternative to liberalism's shortcomings; and finally they had to highlight the proper course of Catholic action to be followed in order to amend the contemporary existing evils.

The 1896 *Course on Social Economics* by Father Charles Antoine is a nice example of this trend. We select this book not just on account of its success but also because it may be considered as a direct offspring of the agenda set by *Rerum Novarum*. In the first section of part 1, the reader is introduced little by little to the proper views about the foundations of society and its natural purpose, to the inescapable problem of power and the origins of the state and its functions, to the general aspects of social organization, to the links between justice and charity, and finally to the important role to be performed by the church. As for the second section, the ongoing controversies about the character and the way out of the social question are discussed by appraising the principles endorsed by three different schools—the liberal, the socialist, and the Catholic. In the book's second part, there is an unsurprising presence of certain topics like just price, usury and speculation, just salary, and several other expressions of concern with justice and the situation of the poor. This singular structure, quite dissimilar from that of an orthodox manual on political economy, was not accidental. The first part, fundamentally rooted in the natural law tradition, was in fact instrumental to fully understand the criticisms addressed by the church to the conceptual errors of both liberalism and its laissez-faire political economy—for the errors coupled with liberalism and political economy were nothing but an unavoidable consequence of more deep-rooted, philosophical misconceptions about human nature.

This concern with elucidating the appropriate type of connections that should be established between theology, natural law, and political economy is omnipresent in Antoine's *Course*. And, since the social question was in fact the major issue in the late nineteenth century, it was only natural for Antoine to try to scrutinize and organize as thoroughly as possible the several different issues under debate within the workings of the labor market. A first and lengthy chapter deals with the *rational* theory of wages, not only by criticizing several different political economy theories about the workings of the labor market but also by establishing the concept of wages as a price agreed on between the employer and the worker for a certain amount of work, therefore rejecting the supply and demand approach on the basis that human work could not be considered as a merchandise—that is, as a material thing whose property rights could be entirely transferred. Consequently, the real objective of a labor contract was the leasing of the worker's productive powers, consisting not only of material and physical vigor but also of the worker's capacity to act as "a moral person, a free and intelligent cause, meant to fulfil a spiritual and supernatural purpose" (Antoine [1896] 1921, 2:78–79).

Predictably, the ultimate consequence of this analysis about the meaning of the employer-employee bond was the conclusion that the approach of social economics was in fact quite different from that of political economy, because "the laws of social economics are not, as the classic school would like, about *what is*, but instead about what *ought to be*, meaning what is in agreement with the natural order of things" (2:86). Hence the obvious need to go beyond the defective and incomplete theories of wages put forward by several different schools of political economy and delve into the concept of just wages—inquiring about the influence of wages on the material and moral situation of the workers and their families, and also trying to figure out the possible ways to raise wages.

In accordance with the views previously developed, Antoine considers that a wage may be defined as just whenever it is in accordance with justice, that is, whenever there is a real "equivalence between the things that are exchanged" or when "the labour exerted is equal to the price that is paid" (2:458). And since "the theory of natural wages contained in the Encyclical is entirely different from the economist's notion of a natural law of wages" (2:468), it was quite possible for the current minimum wage to be quite below the wage level commanded by the natural rules of justice. A just wage should therefore be enough for the worker to meet not only basic expenses for food, lodging, tidiness, firewood, and light but also some other ordinary expenses related to "honest recreation" and "religious festivities." Desirably, this wage would also allow the worker to save some money to lessen the ever-possible evils of disease, unemployment, incapacity, and aging.

The Semaines Sociales

A second stream of early-twentieth-century Catholic economic literature had its origins in Catholic organizations like the Semaines sociales de France.[16] This movement, which started in 1904 in Lyon, was intended by its founders as an "itinerant university of social Catholicism" aimed at the "spread of a teaching that would help the practice of an appropriate social action" (*Chronique* 1931, 2, 4). Since their motto was "science for action," the configuration of the Semaines sociales was largely based on a series of conferences by invited experts on the "historical, geographical, juridical, psycho-physiological, and statistical data" relevant for establishing the facts. However, contrary to the practice commonly followed by "sociologists and economists," these experts would not look at social and economic problems solely with "the spirit and the methods that apply to the inert or unconscious nature of physics and the natural sciences" (3); they would also tackle the normative aspects. As one would expect whenever economic problems were selected for these conferences, they were approached in accordance with the basic tenets established by the previous generations of Catholic economists. Consequently, the characteristic refusal to accept the separateness of political economy from morals and the concomitant sponsorship of a Catholic approach to political economy was embraced by most of the invited speakers.

Although the organizers did their best to arrange a balanced presence of the representatives of the main Catholic sensibilities and avoid extreme views, a statistical analysis of the speakers points out the relative importance assumed by those related to the Liège school (see Fouilloux 2006, 119–32). As a consequence, it was justice—not just charity—that was assumed to be the fundamental criterion for analyzing social and economic relations; in addition, the more interventionist vein of the Liège school was also present.[17]

16. This type of organization was replicated in Italy, Spain, Portugal, and several other Catholic countries. In 1890 the Unione cattolica per gli studi sociali had already expressed the goal of establishing a school and a journal for the study of social questions. The first number of the *Rivista internazionale di scienze sociali* was eventually published in 1893. Among the authors who participated in this project is the economist Giuseppe Toniolo (see Parisi 1996, 497–500).

17. This interventionist penchant shocked some of the sympathizers of the Angers school (see Fouilloux 2006, 125; also Poulat 2006, 460); assuming that the organizers were trying to be neutral about the existing sensibilities, this predominance of the Liège school may confirm their closeness to the church views as expressed in the *Rerum Novarum*.

A fine surrogate example of the intended overall orientation of these meetings may be found in the work of Eugène Duthoit (1869–1944), dean of the Catholic law faculty of Lille and president of the Semaines sociales between 1919 and 1944. In a book published in 1932, Duthoit, following a path analogous to the one embraced by Brants in 1901, criticizes liberal political economy by pointing out a crucial methodological misconception about the object of economic science: the focus on things rather than on humans in their individual and social dimensions. This emphasis on the human side of all economic activity was obviously instrumental for establishing a specifically Catholic notion of political economy as an alternative both to the liberal views and to the socialist views (Duthoit 1932, 9).

As with Taparelli and Liberatore, Duthoit was therefore led to believe that the changes necessary to eradicate the cause of the social question were out of the church's reach. The state was therefore to be considered as indispensable in fostering a new social order—one where materialism and unbridled competition would be tamed by embedding Christian values in individual consciences, in the social practices, and in the legal framework. Although Duthoit was perfectly aware of the fact that any appeal to state intervention was likely to engender several types of opposition, from both liberals and some Catholics, he firmly believed that the close link between liberal political economy and the existing economic order could—and should—in fact be replaced by another duo, now matching a Catholic political economy with a Catholic economic order.

Corporatism and the Third Way

Besides these two important streams of Catholic economic literature, this period witnessed the emergence of a still more voluminous stream, which may be considered as the logical offspring of the former two. This third stream was focused on the defense of corporatism as the symbolic cornerstone of a Catholic third way between liberalism and socialism, and its emergence in the 1930s may be considered as a last step in the development of a Catholic political economy and a Catholic social and economic order taking place since the 1830s. The standard view on the conception of a neocorporative Catholic system usually starts with the doctrines of Wilhelm von Ketteler and Karl von Vogelsang and their influence on Albert de Mun and René de La Tour du Pin, then moves to the further developments made under the auspices of the Liège school, which were eventually accepted, if not warmly supported, by the *Quadragesimo Anno*. However, it should be stressed that a certain fascination for medieval corporations was almost always present in the analysis of the several Catholic economic writers whom we have analyzed in this article. Therefore, even if the most representative supporters of a corporative solution for the social question are the above-mentioned authors, we must not forget that their ideas were not likely to be deemed eccentric by other Catholic economic thinkers.[18]

Consequently, the real novelty of corporations is the fact that they began to be considered not merely as a solution for a particular (albeit important) problem but as an iconic foundation for a fully alternative system to both the capitalist and the socialist ones. The emergence of a full-fledged Catholic alternative to competing systems may be considered as a result of the action of three different causes: the appeal of a mythic medieval order, the resistance from modern society to the Catholic attempts to bring forth a moral piecemeal amendment, and a growing belief that the close link between liberal political economy and the existing economic order could—and should—in fact be replaced by a Catholic political economy matched with a Catholic economic order. Once these forces coalesced in the mainstream of Catholic economic thought, the idea of a corporative order became a likely proposition.

A scholarly example of this stream of thought may be found in the massive *Lehrbuch der nationalökonomie* written by the German Jesuit Heinrich Pesch (1854–1926), who was appropriately considered by Abram Harris (1958, 311) as "the catholic writer who has given the most systematic exposition of the corporate state as an ideal of social reform." The main intention of Pesch's work was to establish the analytic foundations of a "*social system of human industry* as an economic system which emanates from the *solidaristic notion of a moral organism*" (Pesch [1905–26] 2002–3, 1.2.242). This system was therefore based on the concept of solidarity, which Pesch defined as "the orderly amalgamation of all efforts by forces which are supposed to or do in fact bind society together with reference to a morally required common good" (1.2.201). As Pesch cares to explain, this notion of solidarity was based on natural law, not on mere mutual interdependence based on the division of labor (Smith), on the

18. We must bear in mind that even non-Catholic economists did not dismiss the likelihood of corporatism as a possible third way. For a more detailed analysis of the early-twentieth-century debate about the feasibility of corporatism, see Almodovar and Cardoso 2005.

organicist exaggerations of nineteenth-century sociology (Comte, Fourier, Proudhon), or even on the cooperative solidarism of Charles Gide (Pesch [1905–26] 2002–3, 1.2:197–98). By being based on natural law, the concept of solidarity supported by Pesch was considerably more demanding both at the individual level and at the social level.

The social system supported by Pesch was in fact intended as an alternative to both capitalist and socialist systems. This system was sometimes labeled as a third way, because it was supposed "to *avoid the fallacies* which are contained in both the individualistic and the socialist system, while trying *to retain what is right* in both of them" (1.2:228; emphasis added). He tried to explain the uniqueness of the solidaristic system while offering an answer to many of the objections raised by its opponents. Contrary to socialism, this system would keep private property and a meaningful respect for individual initiative; contrary to capitalism, it would check egotism and would restore a series of social and moral bonds between individuals. Finally, this system would secure the state in its natural role, not as a night watchman or as an overwhelming power but as an indispensable guardian of the common good.

One important characteristic of Pesch's views stems from the fact that he tried to recollect and organize into an articulate and comprehensive proposal several ideas already found in the writings of previous Catholic economists. The care that Pesch showed in merging the ideas advocated by different Catholic sensibilities is in fact a quality that might explain the similarity between his views and the line of reasoning that prevailed in *Quadragesimo Anno*. His work is a first-rate example of the historical and analytic climax reached by the Catholic school of social and economic thought in the early decades of the twentieth century.

The Waning of Catholic Economic Thought in the Postwar Years

Things started to change significantly after World War II. Corporatism was by then inextricably connected with the defeated authoritarian regimes and had therefore become a politically unsustainable proposal. The idea that the church was not to sponsor any particular economic system and that the Gospels did not offer a specific economic doctrine gained support. This new emerging mood, which was to put an end to the nineteenth-century prospect of a Christian or Catholic political economy, took some time to find its way into Catholic circles.

In 1950 Achille Dauphin-Meunier would still try to sponsor the idea that the Catholic Church had an economic doctrine—not an economic theory—that could be found in the encyclicals, and in pontifical speeches and messages, which was subsequently commented on and explained in works sponsored by the hierarchy. Therefore, no matter their merit, the works by single authors—either Catholic economists or theologians—should be considered as representing only their authors' views (Dauphin-Meunier 1950, 9).[19]

But less than ten years later, Jean-Yves Calvez and Jacques Perrin would make clear that the social doctrine of the church was essentially a statement about the social implications of a religious belief, not an economic doctrine or an outline of a social system (Calvez and Perrin 1959, 11). The views expressed by the post–World War II Catholic authors become therefore ever more distant from the nineteenth-century efforts to find an alternative to liberal (and socialist) political economy. As a consequence, the church's authority over all the religious and philosophical aspects of human life—including those pertaining to economic activity—was no longer to be considered as a direct or indirect challenge to the scientific findings of economics.

After the 1950s Catholic economic and social thought would pursue very different paths from the ones analyzed in this essay. Many of the changes would be fostered by the transformations that the Catholic Church underwent, particularly epitomized by the Second Vatican Council (1962–65), especially concerning the role of the laity and the dialogue between different churches. Moreover, Catholic theology would also change significantly in the following decades, with the demise of Thomism, the theological and philosophical basis of the earlier social doctrine of the church. The subsequent encyclicals would inaugurate a new methodological approach in ethical theology, emphasizing the scriptures and minimizing to some extent the previous role of natural law methodology. Moreover, with the beginning of the Cold War, the church also ceased the previous search for its own third way, and socialism and communism became the targets of the church's criticisms. Thus, in the second half of the twentieth century, Catholic economic thought would be deeply transformed and a new chapter would start that would steer the church clearly away from the attempts analyzed here to develop an autonomous school of economic thought.

19. For a good example of these individual efforts, see Parisi, this volume.

References

Almodovar, António, and José Luís Cardoso. 2005. Corporatism and the Economic Role of Government. In *The Role of Government in the History of Economic Thought*, edited by Steven G. Medema and Peter Boettke. *HOPE* 37 (supplement): 333–54.

Antoine, Charles. [1896] 1921. *Cours d'économie sociale*. 6th ed. Paris: Félix Alcan.

Battini, Michele. 1995. *L'ordine della gerarchia: I contributi reazionari e progressisti alle crisi della democrazia in Francia, 1789–1914*. Turin: Bollati Boringhieri.

Blanqui, Jérôme-Adolphe. [1837] 1860. *Histoire de l'économie politique depuis les anciens jusqu'à nos jours: Suivie d'une bibliographie raisonnée de l'économie politique*. Paris: Guillaumin et Cie.

Brants, Victor. 1883. *Lois et méthode de l'économie politique: Précis des leçons d'introduction au cours d'économie politique*. Louvain: Ch. Peeters.

———. 1901. Les grandes lignes de l'économie politique. Louvain: Ch. Peeters.

Calvez, Jean-Yves, and Jacques Perrin. 1959. *Église et société économique: L'enseignement social des Papes de Léon XIII à Pie XII*. Paris: Éditions Montaigne.

Camacho, Francisco Gómez. 1998. *Economia y filosofia moral: La formación del pensamiento económico europeo en la Escolástica española*. Madrid: Editorial Sintesis.

Chronique sociale de France. 1931. No. 5, May.

Coux, Charles de. 1832. *Essais d'économie politique*. Paris: Sauvignet et Cie.

Curran, Charles E. 2002. *Catholic Social Teaching, 1891–Present: A Historical, Theological, and Ethical Analysis*. Washington, D.C.: Georgetown University Press.

Dante, Francesco. 1990. *Storia della Civiltà Cattolica (1850–1891): Il laboratorio del Papa*. Rome: Edizioni Studium.

———. 2004. "La Civiltà Cattolica" e la "Rerum Novarum": Cattolici intransigenti nell'Europa del XIX secolo. Milan: Edizioni Unicopli.

Dauphin-Meunier, Achille. 1950. *La doctrine économique de l'église*. Paris: Nouvelles Éditions Latines.

Droz, Joseph. 1826–29. *Oeuvres*. 3 vols. Paris: Renouard.

Duthoit, Eugène. 1932. *L'économie au service de l'homme*. Paris: Flammarion.

Fallon, Valère. [1924] 1935. *Principes d'économie sociale*. Namur: Ad. Wesmael-Charlier.

Fouilloux, Étienne. 2006. Les professeurs des Semaines sociales: Portrait de groupe. In *Les Semaines sociales de France (1904–2004)*, edited by Jean-Dominique Durand. Paris: Éditions Parole et Silence.

Galindo, Angel. 1996. *Moral socioeconómica*. Madrid: Biblioteca de Autores Cristianos.

Gaspieri, A. de. 1931. *I tempi e gli uomini che prepararono la "Rerum Novarum."* Milan: Vita e Pensiero.

Grice-Hutchinson, Marjorie. 1978. *Early Economic Thought in Spain, 1177–1740*. London: Allen and Unwin.

——. 1993. *Ensayos sobre el pensamiento económico en España*. Madrid: Alianza Universidad.

Gueslin, André. 1998. *L'invention de l'économie sociale: Idées, pratiques et imaginaires coopératifs et mutualistes dans la France du XIXe siècle*. Paris: Economica.

Harris, Abram L. 1958. *Economics and Social Reform*. New York: Harper and Brothers.

Kothen, Robert. 1945. *La pensée et l'action sociales des catholiques (1789–1944)*. Louvain: Em. Warny.

La Tour du Pin, Réne de. 1929. *Vers un ordre social Chrétien: Jalons de Route, 1882–1907.* Paris: Gabriel Beauchesne.

Leo XIII. 1879. *Aeternis Patris*. http://www.vatican.va/holy_father/.

——. 1891. *Rerum Novarum*, On Capital and Labour. http://www.vatican.va/holy_father/.

Liberatore, Matteo. [1889] 1990. Dell'economia politica. In *Storia della Civiltà Cattolica (1850–1891): Il laboratorio del Papa*, edited by Francesco Dante. Rome: Edizioni Studium.

——. [1891] 1990. Dell'intervenzione governativa nel regolamento del lavoro. In *Storia della Civiltà Cattolica (1850–1891): Il laboratorio del Papa*, edited by Francesco Dante. Rome: Edizioni Studium.

Massaro, Thomas J., and Thomas A. Shannon, eds. 2002. *American Catholic Social Teaching*. Collegeville, Minn.: Order of St. Benedict.

McCulloch, John R. [1845] 1991. *The Literature of Political Economy: A Classified Catalogue of Select Publications in the Different Departments of That Science with Historical, Critical, and Biographical Notices*. Fairfield, N.J.: Kelley.

Misner, Paul. 1991. *Social Catholicism in Europe: From the Onset of Industrialization to the First World War.* New York: Crossroad.

Nichols, Aidan. 2002. *Discovering Aquinas: An Introduction to His Life, Work, and Influence*. London: Darton, Longman and Todd.

Ott, Auguste. 1854. *Dictionnaire des sciences politiques et sociales*. Paris: J.-P. Migne.

Palgrave's Dictionary of Political Economy. 1925. Edited by Henry Higgs. London: Macmillan.

Parisi, Daniela. 1996. La "Rivista Internazionale di Scienze Sociali e Discipline Ausiliare": La divulgazione di una dottrina morale dei fatti sociale (1893–1900). In *Le reviste di economia in Italia (1700–1900)*, edited by Massimo Augello, Marco Bianchini, and Marco Guidi. Milan: Franco Angeli.

Périn, Charles. [1861] 1868. *De la richesse dans les sociétés chrétiennes*. 2nd ed. 2 vols. Paris: J. Lecoffre & Guillaumin.

——. 1895. *Premiers principes d'économie politique*. 2 vols. Paris: Librairie Victor Lecoffre.

Pesch, Heinrich. [1905–26] 2002–3. *Lehrbuch der nationalökonomie* [*Teaching Guide to Economics*]. 5 vols. Translated by Rupert J. Ederer. Lewiston, N.Y.: Mellen.

Pius IX. 1876. *Syllabus*.

Pius XI. 1931. *Quadragesimo Anno*, On Reconstruction of the Social Order. http://www.vatican.va/holy_father/.

Poulat, Emile. 2006. La grande aventure des Semaines sociales de France. In *Les Semaines sociales de France (1904–2004)*, edited by Jean-Dominique Durand. Paris: Éditions Parole et Silence.

Rosa, Gabriele de. 2004. *I tempi della "Rerum Novarum."* Rome: Rubbettino/Istituto Luigi Sturzo.

Smith, Timothy B. 1997. The Ideology of Charity, the Image of the English Poor Law, and Debates over the Right to Assistance in France, 1830–1905. *Historical Journal* 40:997–1032.

Taparelli d'Azeglio, Luigi. 1943. *Essai sur les principes philosophiques de l'économie politique: Recueil d'articles publiés dans la Civiltà Cattolica de 1856 à 1862.* Edited and translated by Robert Jacquin. Paris: P. Lethielleux.

Villeneuve-Bargemont, Alban de. 1834. *Économie politique chrétienne, ou recherches sur la nature et les causes du paupérisme, en France et en Europe, et sur les moyens de le soulager et de le prévenir.* 3 vols. Paris: Paulin.

Waterman, A. M. C. 1991. *Revolution, Economics, and Religion: Christian Political Economy, 1798–1833.* Cambridge: Cambridge University Press.

———. 2004. *Political Economy and Christian Theology since the Enlightenment.* Basingstoke, U.K.: Palgrave Macmillan.

Revealing the Connection between the Gospel and History: The Definition of "Economics at the Service of Humankind" in the Analysis of Francesco Vito

Daniela Parisi

This essay focuses on Francesco Vito (1902–1968), one of the most important Italian economists and a contributor to a thorough debate in Catholic social thinking in an effort to turn into action the mediation between the Gospel and history suggested by that thinking.

The most relevant and authoritative milestones in Catholic social thinking are the magisterial documents, that is, the documents issued by the *magister. Magisterium* is here intended as the authoritative teaching function of the pastors of the church, the corpus of declarations on Christian faith that took shape with the councils and matured from generation to generation—as written in the *Catechism of the Catholic Church* (*Cathechismus Romanus* 1992, pt. 3, sec. 1, chap. 3, article 3.1), "under the aegis and vigilance of the pastors"—popes, bishops, Episcopal conference of the continents and of every single state—forming a common patrimony and "deposit of Christian moral teaching."

The documents of the official social Magisterium reflect on human activity, contemplate changing reality, and scrutinize people's behavior not so much to acquire specific knowledge but to show the moral consequences of these acts or behaviors on human beings in light of values coming from a source beyond objective and subjective reality.

The publication of each document of the Magisterium is preceded, accompanied, and followed by the work of experts with a theological background and by debate and comment from specialists in the different

History of Political Economy 40 (annual suppl.) DOI 10.1215/00182702-2007-061

disciplines. All these elements constitute, then, *social knowledge* that matures in meetings and cultural milieus.

Notably, all these different sources have to cooperate, since the Magisterium does not intend to ossify the theological-moral analysis of the world in a stiff, unalterable, and unhistorical vision from which the model of a new kind of society may be derived;[1] on the contrary, it wishes to receive inputs from society and provide individuals and governments with guidelines for reflection and action, entrusting its historical realization to the free and responsible action of the faithful laypersons,[2] of those who have the true good of humanity at heart and accept the responsibility of our common journey and destiny.

In turn, scientists know that the economic system has its own operative laws that must be examined with science and its tools in full autonomy; they also know that along this path they must keep an open mind and never think themselves capable of reaching definitive knowledge. In this sense, scientific inquiry is essential for the church's social doctrine, as the "understanding of faith, especially faith leading to practical action, is structured by reason and makes use of every contribution that reason has to offer. Social doctrine too, insofar as it is a knowledge applied to the circumstantial and historical aspects of praxis, brings *fides et ratio* together and is an eloquent expression of that rich relationship" (*Cathechismus Romanus* 2005, chap. 2, article 74); however, this dialogue among disciplines "also challenges the sciences to grasp the perspectives of meaning, value and commitment that the Church's social doctrine reveals and to open themselves to a broader horizon" (article 78).

In this way, the Magisterium is not intended to provide solutions for difficulties arising from social intercourse; instead, the church should create instruments of evangelization, a *deposit* of moral teaching. It is evident that, in general, the Magisterium does not seem to cite the work done by economists explicitly in its documents. However, I think that a unity of

1. A lively debate on the formulation of a "third way" model, an alternative to both capitalism and socialism, characterized twentieth-century Italian Catholicism, especially after the publication of *Quadragesimo Anno* (1931).

2. The term *laity* is understood to mean "all the faithful except those in holy orders and those in the state of religious life. . . . What specifically characterizes the laity is their secular nature. . . . the laity, by their very vocation, seek the kingdom of God by engaging in temporal affairs and by ordering them according to the plan of God. They live in the world, that is, in each and in all of the secular professions and occupations. They live in the ordinary circumstances of family and social life, from which the very web of their assistance is woven" (Second Vatican Ecumenical Council 1964, chap. 4, article 31).

purpose can be detected in the sensibility that both the Magisterium and some economists display—obviously according to their own specific profile, the moral and the scientific, respectively—in dealing with economic themes.

The Magisterium has accepted certain realities and aspects of behavior as morally relevant, has pinpointed definite criteria on which human conduct must base itself, and has shown the boundaries within which men of faith can accept and share economic choices. In some cases economic science seems to have "accompanied," so to speak, the preparation of documents, in the sense that the messages by the pope appear intent on taking root not only in the biblical revelation, in the Christian and Catholic tradition, in the social reflection and systematization carried out by the church itself in the past, but also in the reference to scientific thought. In this sense, if the declarations of the Magisterium are to be the result of a humble and not unilateral request for expert advice, then it should be interesting for the historian of economic thought to examine and elaborate again on this aspect of the compilation of documents of the social teaching, with careful research into their sources.[3]

On the other hand, historical studies show that economists have been stimulated by Catholic social thinking on two levels at least: when they came to define the boundaries of their discipline, and when they chose to orientate their research toward certain specific themes. Economists were driven to follow this direction under the influence of what can be regarded as the last stage of a tradition already present in the culture surrounding economic matters and behavior and in the Western Catholic social movement; it was the continuation of an interest that had been previously expressed as a vigilant preoccupation on the part of Catholic intellectuals and politicians for the novelty of "modern times" phenomena. It was a continuation yet, of course, a renewed one.[4]

The history of economic thought undoubtedly proves that some economists have accepted to be spurred not only by the contents of the documents of the Magisterium but also by current wide-ranging reflection and debate on their drafting, contents, future implications, issues posed, and

3. G. Crepaldi—secretary of the Pontifical Council for Justice and Peace—has published much on interdisciplinarity and social doctrine of the church. See the 2006 interview given to the Catholic newswire online (www.zenit.org). On the relationships between economic science (as a subject matter and as a method, that is, positive analysis) and religion (as spirituality, morality, theology), see Brennan and Waterman 1994, Wilson [1997] 2003, and the debate on the different editions of Amintore Fanfani (1933, 1934, [1935] 2003) in Parisi 2004.

4. See the introduction in Pontifical Council for Justice and Peace 2004.

matters left unsolved, that is, by the general invitation to see, judge, and act as economists within a moral perspective, in an effort to blend transcendental and historicist perspectives.[5]

This is indeed the perspective of this essay on Vito, as he helped pave the way that in the twentieth century led to accepting that autonomy of earthly reality so well expressed in the pastoral constitution *Gaudium et Spes* of the Second Vatican Ecumenical Council (1965), where "the social teaching of the Church asks economic science to provide an ever more profound knowledge of the complex and interdependent economic realities" and where social teaching provides an interpretive framework and indicates concepts of humankind and society on which to base operational interventions.

Italian Criticism on Classical and Socialist Economic Thought between the Nineteenth and Twentieth Centuries: Giuseppe Toniolo

Discussion about Francesco Vito needs to be contextualized within the Italian background in which he grew, as a lay Catholic, at the beginning of the twentieth century.

In the second half of the nineteenth century, Catholicism in Italy went through a complex phase because of the so-called Roman issue that divided Catholics into factions: those hoping for a fall of the Italian state, effected even by means of mass actions, and those, a minority, hoping for church-state agreements.

This division was reflected in the economic orientations of Catholics who in this period mainly embraced classical liberal theories—the most popular in the Italian cultural milieus—that showed little sensibility toward social issues and overlooked the problem of effective economic order equity.

However, in those years, a new economic orientation was also emerging in the European and North American Christian world that wished to overcome the welfare state logic, focusing instead on the social question as a structural problem. This strand of social and economic theory had arisen in the first half of the nineteenth century, mainly thanks to the experiences of Social Catholicism in Belgium, France, and Germany and the works of Charles de Coux (1778–1864), Alban de Villeneuve-Bargemont

5. The conceptual distance between this formulation and Almodovar and Teixeira's (this volume) legitimate stance is evident.

(1784–1850), the Leuven group,[6] Victor Leopold J. L. Brants (1856–1917), and Viktor Cathrein (1845–1931), and also by North American Protestants who realized that they were living in an era of new economic opportunities and moral perils.[7] The focus of these authors lay in their attempt to emphasize the epistemological "false bases" of classical economics and their impact on actual conduct: selfish behavior generates alienating situations, individuals' control of others, supremacy of capital, class struggle.

This trend reached Italy in the last decades of the nineteenth century through Giuseppe Toniolo (1845–1918), whose sensibility toward Catholic social-cultural issues was particularly acute. Until then, the most authoritative stance in Italian Catholic social thinking had been expressed by the group connected to the Jesuit journal *La civiltà cattolica*; among those representatives, the Jesuit Matteo Liberatore (1810–1892), an expert in economic ethics, was commissioned by Pope Leo XIII to write, along with the Dominican cardinal Tommaso M. Zigliara (1833–1893), the first version of the 1891 encyclical *Rerum Novarum*.[8]

In theorizing Italian Catholic social action, Toniolo assigned supremacy to reflexive rather than operative steps, thus emphasizing cultural qualification and maturity for Catholics as necessary in political and social action. This point of view was legitimized in the *Rerum Novarum*, which determined that the church was to address social questions more as "an observer" for analyses and evaluations, rather than as "the active builder" of the new society; the latter was instead to be the sphere of laypersons and their active commitment, and of political and social bodies.

Toniolo, a professor of political economy in Padua, Venice, and—in the years of his maturity, that is, from 1883—at the university of Pisa, was convinced of the necessity of giving scientific roots to his dissent against a system that commercialized human existence, turning profit into an absolute value, and he grounded his position in the principles of Catholicism. He realized his ideas by contributing to the foundation of the Unione cattolica per gli studi sociali in Italia and of the *Rivista internazionale di scienze sociali e discipline ausiliarie* (1893) that has been the journal of economic studies of the Catholic University of the Sacred Heart of Milan since 1927 (Parisi 1996).

6. See Faccarello and Steiner, this volume.
7. See Davenport, this volume.
8. See Almodovar and Teixeira, this volume; Misner 1991.

The cultural stance expressed by Toniolo rested on three pillars. First is its reference to historicism, that is, the background within which he had received his economic education in Padua. In his opinion this philosophical approach could properly define social and economic growth as the result of the general history of a people and of its institutions.

Second, he founded his scientific activity on a critique of classical economic science as relying on analytical assumptions, neither explicit nor neutral, connected with a materialistic conception of humanity and an individualistic conception of society.[9] In his opinion, in the second half of the nineteenth century these notions, because of biological, historical, and psychological positivism, were undergoing evolutionary steps that might have devastating consequences for human existence.

Third, Toniolo opposed socialism, as in his opinion it justified class struggle, denied property rights, and avoided clarifying the relation between property and work rights. In fairness, however, it must be noted that Toniolo's critique of classical and socialist thought did not prevent him from assessing the value of the former as a scientific approach that provided theoretical tools for analyzing the new forms of production, and of the latter as capable of highlighting direct and indirect connections between economic conditions and phenomena in social life (Pecorari 1997).

In Toniolo's opinion, the scientific path consisted of a historicist approach to accomplishing the "synthesis of a oneness with multiplicity, of absolute with relative [that is, the transcendental and material nature of humankind]" and "to find[ing] the result of human freedom and Divine Providence in history" (Toniolo, quoted in Pecorari 1997, 18). He maintained that the faithful professed science as any other scientists but that they should avoid the risk of both identifying their object of study with the totality of the Being and of turning the abstract hypothesis of *homo economicus* into a model of humankind. According to Toniolo, only by putting humankind at the center of its reflection could science explain the system's contradictions and suggest solutions for the diffused uneasiness and malcontent of the poorest among agricultural and factory workers, the new realities of late-nineteenth-century Italy. Toniolo left it then to politicians the specific task of choosing, among these theoretical frameworks, the solution closer to their ideological inspiration and to the necessities of the system.

9. After all, even Toniolo's historicism dissented from the absolutization of methodological relativism and of political totalitarianism proposed by some German economists.

The key to approaching the relation between economic science and faith, and between economic science and ethics, was thus not to introduce ethics into economics but to acknowledge that ethical considerations are intrinsic in economics. Economics, autonomous in terms of tools, models, and forecasts, is not, however, free from ethics, and this directly depends on its object of study, that is, the system in which humans express not necessarily material needs, choose according to individual criteria, and rank their satisfaction in connection with the quality of their and their offsprings' lives.

Thus Toniolo proceeded along that slow and fatiguing path aimed at the overcoming of aversion and fear of science on the part of Catholics, a process that had already made a notable step forward in the second half of the nineteenth century as the First Vatican Council (1869–70, sess. 3, chap. 4) qualified the connection between supernatural and natural order along a definition that spurred Catholics to cultivate knowledge both through faith and through human and physical sciences.

In the decades between the two centuries, this led some economists—among them Toniolo himself—to historicizing the notion of economic science and to relativizing the general and universal features of economic laws through a "cultural avant-garde operation." In Catholic milieus this resulted in the spread of a scientific program that pervaded the cultural background of several Italian intellectuals and social workers, albeit not directly attracting scholars into what historiography would consider a "valuable and highly reputed" group until the 1920s, when the echo of Toniolo's teaching and his civil and social initiative resounded in the founding of the Catholic University of the Sacred Heart in Milan, and of its laboratories and scientific departments, including the Department of Economics directed by Vito since the mid-1930s.

Toniolo was a layman, a faithful lay, and an economist who prophetically contributed to shape the notion of the church as a pilgrim people having to operate within temporal realities, a notion that would find its first full expression by the Magisterium with the Second Vatican Council. This is exactly my perspective here: it is through the lens of Vatican II that I am attempting to explain the implications of Catholic economic thought.

Toniolo's legacy was acknowledged by one of his major followers, Vito, who recognized Toniolo as the source of his own commitment to the immense task of reevaluating the history of economic thought in light of an integral vision of economics as the manifestation of people, their culture, and their civilization.

Francesco Vito

Francesco Vito graduated in law (1925), in economic, political, and social sciences (1926), and in philosophy (1928) at the University of Naples. In 1929 he moved to the Catholic University of Milan with a grant to specialize in economic studies in the economics department, at that time directed by Angelo Mauri, and then to Munich and Berlin with a Humboldt Stiftung prize. Under Alfred Weber's supervision, in Munich he studied trusts, syndicates, cartels, and increasing technical progress, extending his study stay thanks to a von Humboldt grant (1 April 1931). In Berlin he began his long and fruitful collaboration with Edgar Salin (1892–1974), cemented by a common interest in the history of economic thought.

He qualified as a university professor in 1932, spending two years in North American universities with a Rockefeller Foundation grant. Before sailing to the United States, he had been registered as a research student at the London School of Economics and Political Science, under the supervision of Friedrich von Hayek in the second half of the Lent term and the summer term of the 1931–32 session.[10] No doubt Vito attended the Robbins seminar run by Hayek: "Since Robbins had already asked Hayek to join him in running the seminar he (Robbins) suggested that, as the [LSE] Calendar duly announced, 'During the session 1931–32 the seminar will be chiefly conducted by Dr Hayek and will be devoted to informal discussions on the Theory of Production with special reference to Capital and Interest.' Hayek provided a syllabus and a reading list which appear in the Calendar" (Howson 2005, 10).[11] Having met Lionel Robbins at LSE and, given his academic and philosophical background, Vito's deepest involvement in the cultural climate of these milieus was certainly coalescing around the debate on defining social science versus social sciences, and economics (Dahrendorf 1995).[12]

10. See ASUC n.d.a, box 1, folder 7.

11. I am grateful to Susan Howson for the precise information she gave me recently on Hayek at LSE.

12. Vito was eyewitness to Robbins's role in "the teaching of economics" problem at LSE (Dahrendorf 1995, chaps. 3, 4), and in the following months he realized how influential was Robbins's *Essay on the Nature and Significance of Economic Science* (1932), the various editions of which Vito would have reviewed in the *Rivista internazionale* in 1932, 1935, and 1936. Both in the first and in the second review Vito criticized the *Essay* while approving, however, of the logical demonstration the author gave of the inadequacy of a pure concept of economic science (1932), and adding that Robbins (1936) clearly stated the validity and applicability limits of the results of pure theory. This essay had a long-lasting impact on European methodological debate, involving economists and philosophers in interdisciplinary research.

From material collected at the Catholic University Historical Archives and from the *Columbia University Bulletin of Information*,[13] we know that in the 1932–33 winter session at Columbia University in New York Vito was registered in the seminars of H. P. Willis on banking and of W. C. Mitchell on business cycles, and in the spring session he attended five courses: Economic Aspects of Industrial Relations (L. Wolman), Current Types of Economic Theory (W. C. Mitchell), Money and Currency (H. P. Willis), Special Problems in the History of Sciences (F. Barry), and Modern Social Problems (A. A. Tenney).[14]

Vito was keeping up-to-date with historical and economic studies on the origins of capitalism. This was a prominent research issue at the Catholic University in the wake of Italian and German literature of the first decades of the twentieth century, within which conflicting positions, by Max Weber, Werner Sombart, and the Italian Amintore Fanfani (1930, 1933, 1934, [1935] 2003), just to mention a few, coexisted. On Easter Day 1933, Vito wrote a letter to Jacopo Mazzei in which he expressed his astonishment at the "wide reaction of American economists against traditional methods" (Archivio Privato Mazzei 1933): his orientation toward the new, as it was taking shape in different and distant milieus, is thus revealing.

He had undoubtedly absorbed the message of R. G. Tugwell and of the authors of *The Trend of Economics*: "Man can change society in very nearly any respect he cares to; he has only to will it persistently and strongly enough, to formulate his ideals distinctly enough to present determinants in transforming his environment into the ideal" (Tugwell 1924a, 391). This interest demanded an open mind toward a much more fruitful future, which would impact Vito himself, the academic milieu in which he worked until 1968, and his numerous students, for whom, in the second

13. See the documents signed by Willis (17 May 1933) and Mitchell (16 May 1933) and the records sent to Milan by the administrative offices of Columbia University (ASUC n.d.a). Handwritten notes of lectures given by Mitchell and materials related to the London period are in ASUC n.d.b, box 3, folder 2; box 15, folders 2, 4, 5; box 16, folder 1. The typewritten text "Lectures on types of economic theory, professor Wesley C. Mitchell, Columbia University, vol. II, Summer session, New edition 1931" is in ASUC n.d.a, box 7, folder 5. On Vito's specialization abroad, see Quadrio Curzio and Rotondi 2004, 371–83.

14. Books by North American economists, on North American economists and economic policies, were regularly reviewed in the *Rivista internazionale* of the Catholic University of Milan in the early thirties; the university library hosted several volumes on U.S. economic thinking: Homan [1928] 1933, Pirou 1935–43, Surany-Unger 1931, Teilhac [1931] 1936, and Tugwell 1924b.

postwar period, studying and researching abroad (in education and specialization curricula) would become the norm.

During the 1933 autumn quarter, under the supervision of Frank Knight,[15] he was a visiting doctor in the economics department of the University of Chicago. Even though this experience has been unfortunately left untraced in archives in Milan, Chicago, and at the Rockefeller Archives Center, Vito must have realized the importance of being in contact with Knight's acute critical intelligence (Knight 1924; Buchanan 1991).[16]

Naples, Milan, Munich, Berlin, London, New York, Chicago, brief sojourns in New Orleans, Cambridge, Yale:[17] all these experiences broadened Vito's research perspective in the thirties, but he never lost sight of the most profound and significant root of his education, that is, the notion of economics as a human and social science, never neutral toward ethics.

In 1935 he returned to Italy and finally settled down as a professor of political economy on the faculty of political sciences at the Catholic University in Milan. His university lessons were collected in volumes and published in seventeen editions.

He was directly involved in the life of his university: he was the director of the Department of Economics, of the *Rivista internazionale di scienze sociali* (since 1945), of the *Studi di sociologia* (since 1963), of the series Problemi economici d'oggi; he was appointed as prorector (1943–45), then rector, of the Catholic University (1959–65). In these years he also completed and directed the founding of the new faculty of medicine at the Catholic University of Rome. In 1940 he began teaching permanently on the faculty of engineering and on the faculty of architecture at the Politecnico in Milan, and he occasionally taught in several European and North American universities, too.

15. Reports written and signed by Knight and Mitchell are among the documents related to the second Rockefeller Foundation grant Vito received on 20 May 1936: he stayed in Geneva where he established relationships with Ludwig von Mises and in Vienna where he met Oskar Morgenstern (see the report dated 7 May 1937 in ASUC n.d.a, box 1, folder 7).

16. In a phase in which some economists "attempted to integrate advances in psychology into economic theory . . . Knight agrees that the use of introspection prevents economics from becoming a rigorous science like physics. However, . . . Knight suggests that economics should not try to emulate physics, for it studies inherently different subject matter for which the (logical positivist) scientific approach is inappropriate" (Lewin 1996).

17. Thanks to a further Rockefeller Foundation grant, Vito spent four months (July–October 1938) at the University of Stockholm.

Vito's numerous official appointments prove his national and international fame: he was president of the Associazione italiana di scienze politiche, member of the Union International d'Etude Sociales, vice president of the International Political Science Association (1958–64), member of the United Nations Educational, Scientific and Cultural Organization (UNESCO) Italian Commission, and member of the first board of the Società italiana degli economisti (1951–54). He coupled his scientific activity with a rich series of institutional appointments and outstanding experiences in the Catholic world: serving as president of the International Federation of the Catholic Universities and attending the Second Vatican Council as a lay observer.

His life was thus permeated by constant scientific commitment in light of a notion of economic science as "leading to action," and by continuous teaching service in universities and in Catholic organizations of cultural, civil, and political action, which contributed to spreading his notions. These different sides of his activity as an economist were cohesively sustained throughout his life, marked as it was by such historical events as the economic crisis of the thirties, war economy, reconstruction, European economic integration process, phases of increased development, and employment policies. He died in Milan in 1968, during a meeting of the board of the Catholic University.

Vito's scientific activity was intense, as proved by his extensive bibliography of about five hundred titles, several of which have been translated into foreign languages. His work develops along some major thematic strands: investigation of the noncompeting market forms that result from technological innovation and structural changes in enterprises, with the consequent need for market control interventions (Vito 1930, 1933, 1939, 1943, 1967, [1931] 1998); the analysis of cyclical fluctuations because of enterprise self-funding (Vito 1934, 1944a);[18] his 1950s and 1960s analyses of world hunger and economic, not to mention social and institutional, underdevelopment (Vito 1954, 1956b, 1957; UNESCO Italian Commission 1960), with a renewed focus on the sociocultural factors affecting development and the reduction of territorial disparities.

These brief biographical data prove, then, that Vito's early analytical interests coalesced around a research project—never abandoned—which consisted in investigating noncompetitive market structure, aimed at

18. Subsequent editions of this book were published under a different title until 1954.

explaining the reason why the market does not accomplish its scarce resources allocation function spontaneously and has, consequently, to be regulated.

Economics and Philosophy in the 1930s: Vito and Personalism

After his sojourn in London and in North America, Vito experienced the vigorous reemergence of his legal and philosophical background; he focused now both on the dichotomy between theoretical thought and action and on issues related to the notions of "human agent" and "society" that economists use to guide and inspire their research. Analytical and ethical perspectives, together with deep commitment in actual policies, proceeded jointly in Vito's life, and his commitment to a theoretical approach to economic problems was incessantly tied to his interest in the ethical impact of socioeconomic issues.

For Vito, no theoretical economic system could hold without reference to real data from the actual system, and to a philosophical and anthropological framework. He was convinced that economic analysis could be scientifically grounded even without assuming "ethically valid" hypothesis, yet it needed to be based on clearly ethical principles to achieve chosen social goals. The results of scientific research could be a guide to action only if economists connected chosen goals with economic tools. Vito's work clearly demonstrates that he adopted a philosophical horizon that referred to personalism, that is, a "philosophy which takes the person as a fundamental reality and yardstick of value" (Heseltine and Harvey 1969), at that time authoritatively embodied in France by Jacques Maritain (1882–1973), Emmanuel Mounier (1905–1950), and the group of the periodical *Esprit*.

Vito had kept informed on current philosophical debate ever since his degree in philosophy in Naples, among other things, by reading *Esprit* and the publications by the French personalists in the library of the Catholic University of Milan, as well as by keeping in contact with the Semaines sociales group established in France. He was well acquainted with this strand of thought in philosophical literature,[19] which was in turn well

19. Each issue of the *Rivista internazionale* devoted specific sections to events and publications by worldwide Catholic groups.

known in Europe in those years as personalism and was fueling the interests of many Catholics working on issues of freedom and social commitment. Notably, let me briefly mention a remarkable event during Vito's sojourn in Chicago in 1933: the university was hosting vivid debate on Maritain's ideas and on conflicting stances by Knight and John U. Nef;[20] Maritain himself lectured there that year, and I believe it was a unique opportunity for Vito.

Among the different positions expressed by personalists, Vito was especially close to the theoretical stances of Mounier's community personalism, with which he shared his commitment to analyze the depersonalizing character of modern capitalistic society and to give birth to a movement directed toward realizing moral values in order to accomplish people's "insertion in the social world" through "a number of levels of organization, culminating in an integrated community, where a person's potential could be most fully realized" without indulging in excessive collectivism.

In this perspective the "human person was conceived as a free centre of initiative, but distinguished from the abstract individual by its roots in natural, social, and spiritual dimensions. The person was characterized by his/her *incarnation*, combining both material and spiritual existence; *communication*, combining both autonomous and social existence; and *vocation*, combining both immanence and transcendence. The fulfilment of the person could only be envisaged in a dynamic balance among these dimensions, and depended on the natural, social, and spiritual process of which the person was part."[21]

This approach embodied the dawning of a new era that emphasized the purpose of human—and economic—activity in terms of conservation, development, and improvement of every person, a purpose not spontaneously attained by individual action. This notion, derived from Mounier's work (1935, 1936, 1946), originated in particularly lively years for economists, in which the definition of economic science was being reexamined

20. See Hammond 2007; Emmett, this volume.

21. "Personalism was strongly articulated in the debates of the *Second Vatican Council* (1962–1964), . . . and the 'human person' largely supplanted the 'soul' as the focus of Catholic social thinking." These ideas spun off in Europe, North and West Africa, Southeast Asia, and Latin America. They flourished at Boston University; the main theologian of Boston personalism was Borden Parker Bowne. Martin Luther King Jr. is said to have been influenced by personalism in his studies at Boston; Pope John Paul II was influenced by personalism as well, especially in his explanation of the origin of moral norms (see, in particular, *Person and Act*, also translated as *The Acting Person*).

in light of both shrinking trust in market system automatism and the establishment of controlled economic systems.

Mounier was elaborating on how the main goal of "individual calling" might be reached within the "imperfect communities" that characterize social convivence. He concluded that the realization of the individual must avoid depersonalization, that is, the individual must be protected from experiencing a split between herself or himself and the community that she or he belongs to; in turn, this can be accomplished only by avoiding abuses of the right to freedom in society.

In light of this notion, the economic system was to be evaluated in terms of personal freedom and in terms of its congruity with the social goals to be reached, that is, by principles that could assess whether the economic system respected individual calling. In these terms, then, when analyzing the relation between available means and individual and social goals to be attained, economists were to consider the findings of other sciences, too, such as ethics, law, and philosophy in particular.

Against the background of the crisis in which economic science lay, facing the dilemma between classic orthodoxy and fascist corporativism, these issues were debated also in Italy, in an attempt to revise the principles of human action in the economic field. Scholars considered whether acknowledging superior ethical principles, which comprise vaster political, juridical, and economic values, legitimized state intervention in the social system. Vito was among the protagonists of this debate, which culminated in the exchange of argumentations published in the *Revue d'économie politique* in the years 1935–37.

Vito maintained that the relation between means and goals could not be examined by focusing on the former; there was a prior issue to be tackled: Can economic laws be formulated without ethical principles? Can economic laws ignore economic goals, that is, the "spiritual and material well-being of human agent and collectivity"? (Vito 1936a, 1936b, 1937, 1938, 1944b, 1945a, 1953, 1956a).

In 1938 he proposed that economic science should aim at depicting the economic life of the collectivity: "The economic system operates in order to guarantee the most compatible attainment of social goals against the particular conditions of the system itself, so that the level of importance of the employed means corresponds to the level of importance of the social goals" (Vito 1938, 376). Indeed, the core of the issue lay again in coordinating social and individual goals while pursuing a system of justice in which, as Vito lucidly explained, attained goals are neither the sum of individual goals nor their equal attainment.

Therefore Vito's notion departed from the utilitarian concept of "welfare" and revolved around the goal of developing humans "as a whole"—as spiritual and material beings—within the institutional system. The aim was clearly laden with ethical implications, as it evolved from a notion of the relation between particular societies and their members in the social context, and from a belief in the supernatural dignity of humankind. In this sense, the ethical element was inherently pertinent to economic discourse, since it was indissolubly tied to the actual contents of economic science; the scientific process had thus to be grounded in ideas or hypotheses from "a set of values explicitly and consciously derived from society as an ethical notion" (Vito 1953) and was therefore not a merely logic-formal construction to be applied to any typology of society. Thus economics served human well-being, intended as the conservation, development, and improvement of humans, with a strong belief in the supernatural dignity of humankind; this aim was accomplished insofar as different and differently ranked goals were attained by limited and unspecialized means.

In light of this, the relevance that Vito attached to the notion of "person" was also reflected in the role of "person" as the responsible subject and receiver of reforms that tackle actual "social issues" and define policies to solve them; in this respect, Vito's support for establishing social services and programs of education and professional training in post–World War II years certainly deserves mention.

Vito and the Social Aims of the Economic System: A Central Role for Work and Social Justice

Vito's theoretical consideration of ethical values in social life was at times the result of accurate and patient internal criticism; at other times, it was the result of the urging by contemporary events to engage in the eager, laborious, and often turbulent search for new ways that set demanding and not postponable tasks to economic theory.

To Vito the question was how, that is, by which theoretical activity and model creation, economists could shape tools to intervene in the economic system and improve general welfare. In effect, interaction between theoretical approach and political commitment has always preoccupied

Italian economic thought (Augello and Guidi 2007)[22] and has prompted several studies aimed at defining the notion of welfare in terms that go beyond the so-called values-assessment obsession that characterizes the mainstream in economics.

The inevitable need to refer to a balanced view of knowledge and of the relations between facts and principles, and between tools and facts, oriented Vito's scientific activity toward the search for the optimal conditions for realizing detected values. In his opinion, values of reference for both theoretical research and economic policy had to derive from the Christian tradition, itself founded on an anthropology that respects the dignity, integrity, and uniqueness of each human being and that promotes the common destiny of humankind, intended as generations of people characterized by indissolubly linked individual and social features.

For Vito, the choice of the Christian framework of reference was inevitable, as it was the only option respectful of human nature in its entirety. In light of this perspective, according to Vito, economists were not to translate the provisions of the official documents of the Magisterium into economic theory. Rather, they had to consider theoretical research at the service of humankind, follow insights from their experience of faith, and be guided by the work of philosophers belonging to the Christian tradition and committed, in turn, to elaborating social and economic thinking illuminated by Christianity and by "expert" debate within the church.[23] This was, indeed, in Vito's opinion, the only way to provide both economists and economic politicians with a correct ethical orientation, that is, with guidelines tendentially respectful of the true human nature, otherwise diminished, devalued, and alienated by moral and material poverty.

In time, Vito became increasingly attracted by the analysis of poverty, whose root causes were being increasingly identified with unfair distribution of wealth. This was countered by a growing conviction that the general conditions of unfair distribution of income, which affected people's lives while representing the situation in which the systems operated, could be rectified without radically overturning the natural distribution mechanism among classes. The remedy would be achieved by introducing policies for job maintenance and for prevention both of mass unemployment and of yearly individual unemployment. Unfair distribution

22. As widely agreed on by historiography.

23. Vito's reference to personalism is here explicit.

was considered the condition of the system that made it impossible to abolish need; it was described as the lack of sufficient income to meet one's responsibilities that could hit any citizen wishing to work to the extent of his or her abilities, at any time.

Thus social justice and work emerged as key issues in Vito's mature thought and in his notion of diffused social welfare. The idea that there were direct, mechanistically consequential implications in interpersonal confrontations between utility and social welfare was being gradually and widely abandoned; in the new theoretical perspective, the possibility to intervene in the system through fiscal and redistributive policies was gaining momentum in Italy, too.

Evaluation of this new theoretical stance must, however, be set within a wider new trend in economic thought, which had become evident in Italy since the first decades of the nineteenth century. This essay can only briefly mention some symptoms of novelty in Italian thought, which surely deserve more discussion. Think, for example, of the tormented intellectual biography of Vilfredo Pareto (1935) who—as is well known—had turned away from economics to seek in sociology the foundation to satisfying terminological formulation of issues on the relations between individual and social welfare. Think of the development of the typically Italian trend in public finance that became one of the most widely known contributions of the twentieth-century Italian tradition.[24] Think of the set of issues posed by considering labor in economic theory: traditional analysis was evidently not up to the task, while scholars were beginning to emphasize market imperfections, dynamic relations between variation, and effects of technical progress; there emerged the need to integrate analysis with the understanding of extra-economic elements. Think, finally, of the theory of imperfect markets discussed in Piero Sraffa's (1925, 1926) early writ-

24. One of the first formulations of this stance is by Buggeri and Sundelson 1938, then by Buchanan 1960; the most recent are by Meacci 1998, Fausto and De Bonis 2003, Kayaalp 2004, and Wagner 2007 with ample bibliography. Maffeo Pantaleoni is considered the founder of the modern Italian "public finance" tradition: "In the analysis of distribution of public costs, published in 1883, he employed the criteria that Jevons and Walras had used to explain individual determination of the distribution of economic means between present and future goods. . . . he prepared a comprehensive analysis of the effect of taxes on labor and savings. . . . he referred to a collective judgement expressed through the lawmaking body. He emphasized the importance of the decision of the State in evaluating the marginal utility of the public expenditure and of the taxpayer's sacrifice, neither of which can be judged by the individual. These political judgements, he insisted, are always based upon logical economic choices" (Buggeri and Sundelson 1938, 252–53). Mazzola, de Viti de Marco, Puviani, Murray, and Tangorra have also stressed the elements in their theory of public finance.

ings, of the critique of market economy and of the analysis of market economy failure along with the problematic reception of Keynesian thought (Pasinetti and Schefold 1999).

The latter stance in particular was especially common among economists with a Catholic background, and after World War II it accompanied the elaboration of a project for a "different society" aimed at attaining social justice goals that could coincide with improving life conditions for the proletariat, that is, with the defense of the personality of workers and of their dignity as human beings.

Among Vito's most original works in this respect, one clearly expresses a renewed cultural project, insofar as it states that "the attempt to shape an economic science which would be 'neutral' towards the notion of society is illusory at this point; any interpretation of civil life aims always takes part, although surreptitiously, in the scientific construction of any discipline that deals with human action. It is evident that, to proceed correctly and successfully, one has to define preliminarily the notion of social justice according to which economics is to be considered" (Vito 1944b). In these terms, I believe that Vito intended to renew economics, to make it a science oriented toward the principle of serving humankind, that is, a discipline from which to derive economic policy tools aimed at establishing a society that could realize divine indications in historical time. Social goals "are realized in time depending on the historical moment, and are oriented towards common welfare or social justice," so that price alone does not exert a directive function of the volume and the trend of production (Vito 1945a, 83–84). In this perspective, the main goal of the system seems to be identified with workers' spiritual and social—including economic—improvement.

Immediately after World War II the development of insurances was seen by Vito as a means to grant workers the fulfillment of their primary needs. This is the notion proposed by the "Beveridge Plan," a particularly wide-ranging project that aimed at improving workers' living and working conditions, and that considered "all human beings in the national community, independently from their job, risk and profit, in order to provide for basic needs, that, were they unfulfilled, could lead citizens to a serious state of necessity" (156).

The investigation of this project highlights a risk that, in the long run, the sense of workers' responsibility, and employees' initiative and enterprise spirit, might shrink; it also alerts one to the fact that one could lose sight of the economic criterion of management in enterprises and of the defense of private initiative. Yet, all in all, the project displays the "capacity to neutralize workers' spiritual depression and improve their whole personality"; moreover, the "irreplaceable function in altering the distribution of wealth exerted by social insurance" (158–59) is therein positively assessed.

Consequently, society becomes a "site" for the betterment of human beings; to be so, it must sustain individual and social rights, along with those of intermediate bodies. In this perspective, the state, with its central and decentralized organization, should be assigned a modern significance within a society that requires individuals to express themselves as a whole—no aspect excluded—through work.

As Vito would later write, social reform consisted in reforming the whole economic system. One should not pursue single initiatives aimed at claiming rights and guarantees. The legislator should instead be required to intervene through far-reaching reforms, not limited to ensuring a fairer distribution of wealth but capable of enforcing a change in the "leading criteria" and in the "headquarters" of economics.

Although Vito's works (1945b, 1946) mark the acceptance and the beginning of the diffusion of W. H. Beveridge's ideas on social welfare in Italy, some steps on this path had already been taken immediately prior to the publication of the reports. The stages of this initial acquaintance are fundamental to reconstructing the complete picture of the influence that Beveridge exerted in Italy, both in the debate among economists on welfare and labor issues, and in the economic policy projects being elaborated for reconstructing the national social-economic system.

Although Vito undoubtedly realized the importance of Beveridge's work also in lessons attended in New York and Chicago, the historical analysis of this complex cultural phenomenon that affected Italian economic policy so deeply is aided also by the investigation of the documents that testify to the first reception of Beveridge's work in non-English-speaking countries. By the thirties, Beveridge was known in detail in Italy, thanks to W. C. Mitchell's translation of the first five sections of *Business Cycles* (1932); furthermore, his books of the 1930s were "available" at the Catholic University Library and had been reviewed in the *Rivista internazionale* since 1931.

In years of intense elaboration on system reconstruction issues, debate on Beveridge's work in major scientific journals enlivened the ongoing acclimation to analyzing social welfare and the possibilities of economic welfare policies applicable to the Italian case. As noted, economists considered employment issues indissoluble from welfare issues, placing them at the core of any welfare policy and setting the consideration of labor and laborers within the wider project of full employment of available resources in society.[25]

In this perspective, the convention held by M. Shapiro—representative of the United Nations Relief and Rehabilitation Administration—and Vito in Tremezzo in September and October 1946, in view of the reorganization of social services, was one of the outstanding results of this intellectual elaboration and marked the start of policies aimed at establishing a social welfare system. The contextualization of the notion of the welfare state shaped on that occasion is particularly relevant for the present analysis: social assistance projects were set within a general wealth-redistribution program in a society in which, with no egalitarianism and without overlooking the efficiency criterion, individual access to overall wealth ought to be at least enough to grant adequate existence.

The picture sketched thus far, however, should not lead to the conclusion that scientists and representatives in institutions operating in Italy were unanimous: as examined in both general and particular studies, confrontations among "advanced posts" committed to spurring economic recovery and to tackling unemployment are well known. Differences were present even among Catholic scholars involved in economic research or in active civil life, in whose background were the philosophical systems of August Joseph Alphonse Gratry, Maritain, and Mounier, major reference points for the notions of humanity and society; the permanent model of Gospel parables as explicit premises to any discourse; and the reference to the authoritativeness of papal pronunciations on social issues.

By these paths English-world literature and debates fully penetrated the spectrum of sources and experiences of the group of economists at the Catholic University. I believe that the main feature of this group lay in its focus on the theoretical analysis of labor, employment and unemployment, alienation—at internal and international levels—including investigations into a wider notion of well-being that does not imply the activation of the state as an instrument to repair damages inflicted on laborers by the

25. The worldwide Christmas radio appeals by Pius XII (1941, 1942, 1944, 1945) in the first half of the forties was a strong call and a stimulus for Christians already committed to peace projects and reconstructing political and economic systems devastated by the war and by the economic crisis.

competitive system considered to be inviolable, and is guided by the fear of a fall in productivity or even by humanitarian and charitable motives. In the opinion of these scholars, the new social policy had to start from the positive plan of elevating laborers in economic, social, hierarchical, political, and cultural terms, and required the full transformation of the economic system and its rerouting toward this aim. Economic theory could support this process by showing how effectively the economic system could work when freed from the automatism of competition and governed for the attainment of common welfare.

Although following their own research paths, Vito's students kept his teachings alive and considered them a common point of reference: economics is a science at the service of humankind; as such, it relates to the anthropological notion that grounds both Christian theological thought and the church's social thinking, which in turn center on the indications by the Magisterium. In light of this perspective, as I approach the conclusion of the present article, I would like to mention, briefly and with no pretension of reconstructing biographical and bibliographical sources, one of the leading figures among the scholars of the Department of Economics at the Catholic University of Milan: Luigi L. Pasinetti.

Vito's legacy to Pasinetti is evident in the latter's path of research (1965, 2002) and in explicit declarations (2003). Vito's influence on his disciple's scientific personality is moreover both direct and indirect: direct ever since Pasinetti's early studies, as proved by the topic of his final dissertation, "Modelli econometrici e loro applicazione allo studio dei cicli economici" (1954; "Econometric Models and Their Application to the Study of Economic Cycles"); indirect, for their common framework of reference and inspiration in economic analysis.

As far as Vito's direct impact on Pasinetti is concerned, Vito himself analyzed economic cycles in his scientific itinerary, and the Department of Economics he directed was also oriented toward the study of the new frontiers of econometrics, under the leadership of Siro Lombardini in particular. Working and interacting within this scientific milieu, Pasinetti naturally absorbed, used, and confirmed these hints as key elements of his analysis.

However, it is Vito's indirect impact on Pasinetti's scientific biography that becomes especially noteworthy, and that Pasinetti himself, when accepting the invitation to reflect on his own research experience, has recently revealed to be his framework of reference. On this occasion, he compared his own theoretical work with one of Vito's most fruitful insights, that is, clarifying the goals of economics as "at the service of mankind" and the relevance of "permanent human learning, in terms of production of new technologies, new products, new consumption models and new spare time use patterns, which have become available in the meantime" (Pasinetti 2003, 251–52). Focusing on this phenomenon, which is an aspect of modern economies, theory is able not only to show how this principle grounds labor division and the disproportionate growth of productivity and of different productive sectors, but also to illustrate a series of issues emerging from this process and the multiple countermeasures that might be adopted to solve them.

As Pasinetti (2003, 252) concludes, this research path is rich in indications and "encouraging, as it fosters hope of further debate on *what* 'economics at the service of mankind' should mean and, above all, on *how* it might be established in real life situations," and that undoubtedly is the terrain in which his research has been rooted. The *what* indicates the phenomena occurring simultaneously that make the system natural, a set of natural economic magnitudes possessing a series of remarkable normative properties through which this natural system becomes the site of conditions respectful of human dignity. The *how* indicates both how those natural magnitudes can actually be achieved and (in terms of behavioral and organizational choices) how the problems they bring to the surface can be solved at the institutional level (Pasinetti 1994).

Thus Pasinetti's system has evolved in a continuous process of revision and complementation that, nonetheless, neither invalidates the original definition of economics as action-oriented research aimed at goal attainment (Pasinetti 2003, 236–37) nor prevents the free, autonomous growth of the single elements of the theoretical system under elaboration. Rather, his theoretical work seems to have given a new boost to the history of economic thought, assigning unquestionable theoretical rigor to the original definition.

As proven by discussion in the present article, the common ground shared by both Vito and Pasinetti lies in their reference to Christian faith as embodied in the Word, in Tradition, and in the social thinking elaborated by the church, God's people. Supported by their commitment to study and reflect on documents, and by their common reference to faith, to lay intellect, and to science, both master and student have thus effectively researched the role of "labor" in a system aimed at realizing a pattern of justice in terms of distributing resources among individuals, social groups, and nations.

References

Archivio Privato Mazzei (APM). 1933. Folder 32. Fonte Rutoli, Siena, Italy.

Archivio Storico Università Cattolica (ASUC). n.d.a. *Carte Personali Francesco Vito*, box 1, folder 7; box 3, folder 2; box 15, folders 2, 4, 5; box 16, folder 1. Largo Gemelli 1, Milan, Italy.

———. n.d.b. *Archivio Professor Vito*, box 16, folders 3, 5. Largo Gemelli 1, Milan, Italy.

Augello, M., and M. E. L. Guidi. 2007. Italy: Economics. In *The New Palgrave Dictionary of Economics*, edited by S. Durlauf and L. Blume. 2nd ed. London: Palgrave-Macmillan.

Brennan, H. G., and A. M. C. Waterman. 1994. *Economics and Religion: Are They Distinct?* Boston: Kluwer Academic Publishers.

Buchanan, J. M. 1960. "La scienza delle finanze": The Italian Tradition. In *Fiscal Theory and Political Economy: Selected Essays*. Chapel Hill: University of North Carolina Press.

———. 1991. Frank H. Knight, 1885–1972. In *Remembering the University of Chicago*, edited by E. Shils. Chicago: University of Chicago Press.

Buggeri, M. L., and J. W. Sundelson. 1938. Italian Theories of Fiscal Science. *Political Science Quarterly* 2:249–67.

Cathechismus Romanus. 1992. Pt. 3, sec. 1, chap. 3, article 3.I.

———. 2005. 2nd ed. Rome: Libreria Editrice Vaticana.

Columbia University Bulletin of Information. 1933. Thirty-third Series, 26 (History, Economics, Public Law, and Social Science. Courses offered by the Faculty of Political Science for winter and spring session 1933–34), 25 March.

Crepaldi, G. 2006. Social Doctrine: Not Just for Catholics. Interview, 13 February. Catholic newswire online, 15 February. www. zenit.org.

Dahrendorf, R. 1995. *LSE: A History of the London School of Economics and Political Science, 1895–1995*. Oxford: Oxford University Press.

Fanfani, A. 1930. Riforma e capitalismo moderno nella recente letteratura. *Rivista internazionale di scienze sociali* 1:358–65.

———. 1933. *Le origini dello spirito capitalistico in Italia*. Milan: Vita e Pensiero.

———. 1934. *Cattolicesimo e Protestantesimo nella formazione storica del capitalismo*. Milan: Vita e Pensiero.

———. [1935] 2003. *Catholicism, Protestantism, and Capitalism*. Norfolk, Va.: IHS.

Fausto, D., and V. De Bonis, eds. 2003. *The Theory of Public Finance in Italy from the Origins to the 1940s*. Pisa: IEPI.

First Vatican Council. 1869–70. www.vatican.va.

Hammond, J. D. 2007. *Transcendental Commitments of Economists: Friedman, Night, and Nef.* Unpublished draft.

Heseltine, J. E., and P. Harvey. 1969. *The Oxford Companion to French Literature*. Oxford: Clarendon Press.

Homan, P. T. [1928] 1933. *Essay sur la pensée économique contemporaine des Anglo-Américains-contemporary economic thought*. Translated by Emile James. Paris: Librairie du Recueil Sirey.

Howson, S. 2005. The Robbins Seminar. Paper presented at the session "LSE and English Economics" at the History of Economics Society (HES) meeting, Tacoma, Wash., 24–27 June.

Kayaalp, O. 2004. *The National Element in the Development of Fiscal Theory.* New York: Palgrave-Macmillan.

Knight, F. 1924. The Limitation of Scientific Method in Economics. In Tugwell 1924a, 229–67.

Leo XIII. 1891. *Rerum Novarum.* 15 May. www.vatican.va.

Lewin, S. B. 1996. Economics and Psychology: Lessons for Our Own Day from the Early Twentieth Century. *Journal of Economic Literature* 3:1293–323.

Meacci, F., ed. 1998. *Italian Economists of the Twentieth Century.* Cheltenham, U.K.: Elgar.

Misner, P. 1991. The Predecessors of Rerum Novarum within Catholicism. *Review of Social Economy* 4:444–64.

Mounier, E. 1935. *Révolution personnaliste et communautaire.* Paris: F. Aubier.

———. 1936. *De la propriété capitaliste à la propriété humaine.* Paris: Desclée de Brouwer.

———. 1946. *Liberté sous conditions.* Paris: Edition de Seuil.

Pareto, V. 1935. *The Mind and Society: A Treatise on General Sociology.* New York: Harcourt, Brace.

Parisi, D. 1996. La "Rivista internazionale di scienze sociali" (1893–1900). In *Le riviste di economia in Italia (1700–1900)*, edited by M. M. Augello, M. Bianchini, and M. E. L. Guidi. Milan: Franco Angeli.

———. 2004. Is a Good Catholic Necessarily a Capitalist? Comments on a New American Edition of Fanfani's Work on the Origins of Capitalism. *Storia del pensiero economico* 2:185–90.

Pasinetti, L. L. 1965. A New Approach to the Problems of Economic Growth. In *Pontificae Academia Scientiarum, Scripta Varia*, no. 28. Amsterdam: North Holland.

———. 1994. Economic Theory and Institutions. In *The Political Economy of Diversity: Evolutionary Perspectives on Economic Order and Disorder*, edited by R. Delorme and K. Dopfer. Cheltenham, U.K.: Elgar.

———. 2002. Due modi diversi di fare teoria economica. In *Le vie della storia in economia*, edited by P. Ciocca. Bologna: Il Mulino.

———. 2003. Una teoria per una economia a servizio dell'uomo. In *Francesco Vito: Attualità di un economista politico*, edited by D. Parisi and C. Rotondi. Milano: V&P-Università.

Pasinetti, L. L., and B. Schefold, eds. 1999. *The Impact of Keynes on Economics in the Twentieth Century.* Cheltenham, U.K.: Elgar.

Pecorari, P. 1997. Ethics and Economics in Giuseppe Toniolo. In *Ethics and Economics: Catholic Thinkers in the Twentieth Century*, edited by G. Gaburro. Heidelberg: Physica Verlag.

Pirou, G. 1935–43. *Les nouveaux courants de la théorie économique aux Etats-Unis.* 4 vols. Paris: Les éditions Domat-Montchrestien F. Loviton.

Pius XII. 1941. Nell'alba e nella luce: Auspici di pace giusta e duratura. 24 December. www.vatican.va/holy_father/pius_xii/speeches/documents.
——. 1942. Con sempre nuova freschezza: Il santo Natale e l'umanità dolorante. 24 December. www.vatican.va/holy_father/pius_xii/speeches/documents.
——. 1944. Oggi al compiersi del quinto anno dello scoppio della guerra. 1 September.
——. 1945. Ecco alfine terminata: La fine della guerra in Europa. 24 December. www.vatican.va/holy_father/pius_xii/speeches/documents.
Pontifical Council for Justice and Peace. 2004. *Compendium of the Social Doctrine of the Church.* Città del Vaticano: Libreria Editrice Vaticana. www.vatican.va/roman_curia/pontifical_councils/justpeace/documents.
Quadrio Curzio, A., and C. Rotondi. 2004. Sulle ricerche di economia politica in Cattolica: Proiezioni specialistiche e internazionali. In *La formazione degli economisti in Italia*, edited by G. Garofano and A. Graziani. Bologna: Il Mulino.
Robbins, L. 1932. *An Essay on the Nature and Significance of Economic Science.* London: Macmillan.
——. 1936. *An Essay on the Nature and Significance of Economic Science.* 3rd ed. London: Macmillan.
Second Vatican Ecumenical Council. 1964. *Dogmatic Constitution (Lumen Gentium).* 21 November. www.vatican.va.
——. 1965. *Pastoral Constitution on the Church in the Modern World (Gaudium et Spes).* 7 December. www.vatican.va.
Shapiro, M. 1946. Convegno di studi di assistenza sociale. *I problemi dell'assistenza sociale* 5–6:247.
Sraffa, P. 1925. Sulla relazione tra costo e quantità prodotta. *Annali di economia* 2:277–328.
——. 1926. The Laws of Return under Competitive Conditions. *Economic Journal*, December, 535–50.
Surany-Unger, T. 1931. *Economics in the Twentieth Century: The History of Its International Development.* Edited by E. R. A. Seligman, translated by N. D. Moulton. London: Allen and Unwin.
Teilhac, E. [1931] 1936. *Pioneers of American Economic Thought in the Nineteenth Century.* Translated by E. A. J. Johnson. New York: Macmillan.
Tugwell, R. G. 1924a. Experimental Economics. In Tugwell 1924b.
——, ed. 1924b. *The Trend of Economics.* New York: Knopf.
UNESCO Commissione Nazionale Italiana (UNESCO Italian Commission). 1960. *Gli aspetti sociali dello sviluppo economico.* Milan: Vita e Pensiero.
Vito, F. 1930. *I sindacati industriali: Consorzi e gruppi.* Milan: Vita e Pensiero.
——. 1933. La tendenza monopolistica dei sindacati industriali. *Rivista internazionale di scienze sociali* 4:815–19.
——. 1934. Il risparmio forzato e la teoria dei cicli economici. *Rivista internazionale di scienze sociali* 5:3–46.
——. 1936a. Alcune osservazioni attorno ai rapporti tra economia corporativa ed etica. In *Studi in onore di Riccardo Dalla Volta.* Vol. 2. Florence: Cya.

——. 1936b. Economia ed etica. *Rivista internazionale di scienze sociali* 7:254–71.
——. 1937. Morale et économie. *Revue d'économie politique*, January–February, 42–49.
——. 1938. Economia e Filosofia. *Rivista di filosofia neoscolastica*, July, 367–86.
——. 1939. Die Kartellregelung in der korporativen Wirtschaft. *Kartell-Rundschau Monatsschrift für Kartell und Korzernwesen*, November, 553–64.
——. 1943. Di un criterio direttivo del piano economico: La giustizia sociale. *Rivista internazionale di scienze sociali* 2:32–41.
——. 1944a. *Le fluttuazioni cicliche*. Milan: Vita e Pensiero.
——. 1944b. *I nuovi orientamenti della politica economica e sociale: Appunti delle lezioni di politica economica e finanziaria*. Milan: Vita e Pensiero.
——. 1945a. *L'economia a servizio dell'uomo: I nuovi orientamenti della politica economica e sociale*. Milan: Vita e Pensiero.
——. 1945b. I piani per la sicurezza sociale: I limiti di applicabilità e le condizioni di successo. *Rivista internazionale di scienze sociali* 2:1–10; 4:189–98.
——. 1946. Schema di classificazione dei programmi di socializzazione. *Rivista internazionale di scienze sociali* 1:44–51.
——. 1953. La posizione dell'uomo nel pensiero sociale contemporaneo. *Giornale degli economisti e annali di economia* 5:510–26.
——. 1954. Osservazioni preliminari sul problema della aree arretrate e delle aree depresse. *Rivista internazionale di scienze sociali* 3:255–61.
——. 1956a. Pensiero economico, attività economica e ordine morale. *Rivista internazionale di scienze sociali* 5:381–96.
——. 1956b. Popolazione e sviluppo economico. In *I problemi dello sviluppo economico con particolare riguardo alle aree arretrate*. Milan: Vita e Pensiero.
——. 1957. Gli aspetti politici dello sviluppo delle aree arretrate. *Rivista internazionale di scienze sociali* 6:491–509.
——. 1967. L'economia di mercato, le sue deficienze, e i suoi correttivi secondo la dottrina sociale cattolica. In *Nuovi saggi sulla pacem in terris*. Milan: Vita e Pensiero.
——. [1931] 1998. Economic Theory and Industrial Syndicates. In vol. 3 of *Italian Economic Papers*, edited by L. Pasinetti. Bologna: Il Mulino–Oxford University Press.
Wagner, R. E. 2007. *Fiscal Sociology and the Theory of Public Finance: An Explanatory Essay*. Cheltenham, U.K.: Elgar.
Wilson, R. [1997] 2003. *Economics, Ethics, and Religion: Jewish, Christian, and Muslim Economic Thought*. New York: Palgrave.

Part 2
The United Kingdom

The United Kingdom: Introduction

Our second section, on British political economy, parallels the section on Catholic Europe quite nicely. It begins with an essay by A. M. C. Waterman, who points out that the Protestant—particularly Anglican—and Roman branches of Christianity had more commonalities than differences. The shared Christian culture made Britain a receptive environment to developments in French political economy during the late seventeenth and early eighteenth centuries, particularly for the economics of Pierre de Boisguilbert.

Waterman emphasizes three themes in particular. First, Boisguilbert picked up on a stream of Jansenist theodicy, in which our self-love, itself an expression of sin, by God's providence remedied some of the evil effects of sin, serving as a foundation for the social interactions that ensure our survival. Second, Boisguilbert identified this providential system with "Nature." This move is particularly significant because the laws of Nature, although God's laws, can be known by natural philosophy, without the aid of revelation. If we may impose the language of sociology that we used in our introductory essay, this then was a critical step in disentangling or differentiating political economy from theology. Boisguilbert's third theme was on understanding the unintended consequences of self-love not only in terms of Augustinian "harmony" but also according to the mechanical analogy of "equilibrium." All these themes are of course perfectly consistent with the Newtonian natural theology that Britain had already embraced.

History of Political Economy 40 (annual suppl.) DOI 10.1215/00182702-2007-062

But if these moves in France led eventually to the action of the Revolution, then in Britain we find Newton's equal and opposite reaction. Part of this reaction included Thomas Robert Malthus's *Essay on Population*, which emphasized the problem of scarcity created by population pressures. As later developed by William Paley, John Bird Sumner, and Richard Whately, these population pressures played a central role in a theodicy in which God subjected us to them so that they would discipline us. This line of thought continued to disentangle political economy, understood as the scientific study of Nature, from theology, but at the same time emphasized that such study also pointed the way to God. For those who stood on this ground, the rug later would be pulled out beneath them when Darwin removed the creator from nature.

The next chapter in this section, by Harro Maas, picks up midway through Waterman's narrative. Maas presents the perspective of Richard Jones and William Whewell, two critics of the Malthus-Paley-Whately tradition in political economy. They particularly rejected the "dismal" message of the first edition of Malthus's *Essay on Population.* They viewed it as a challenge to God's Providence, by introducing, in Jones's words, "an apparent inconsistency between the permanence of human happiness, and the natural action of the laws established by Providence." As Waterman has shown, this was precisely the kind of problem that Paley had also recognized and had tried to shore up.

But Maas shows that Jones and Whewell were not convinced. If Paley's revision and Whately's were more coherent logically, Jones and Whewell argued that they erred *methodologically.* Moreover, their methodological critique was based on theological concerns. In particular, Whewell feared their deductive method would encourage a kind of hubris that would lead one to "substitute for the Deity certain axioms and first principles, as the cause of all," "thrusting some mechanic cause into the place of God." In elevating self-interest to a law, they felt that Paley and Whately, although perhaps well intentioned, committed the same sin as Ricardo and Jeremy Bentham. Rather than reason from a speculative theory of self-interest to the virtues of laissez-faire, the more humble approach was to look at the facts as God had provided them in history. Jones, for example, argued that, contrary to the deductive conclusions of Bentham's system, an examination of the facts showed that usury laws protected the poor.

Our next two chapters take up the stories of two individuals, each of which illustrates the growing separation between political economy and religion, but in quite distinct ways. The first of these is Neil Skaggs's discussion of Henry Thornton. Thornton was one of the most brilliant students of money and banking in the nineteenth century, both as a practitioner and as a theorist. He also, as is well known, was a thoroughly devout Christian, by all accounts inwardly and certainly outwardly. Along with other members of the "Clapham sect" he helped lead the campaign against the slave trade, organized Christian missions to Africa and India, and even wrote Sunday school materials. In short, Thornton was an energetic "doer of the Gospel." Skaggs shows how Thornton's work in banking could be construed as an extension of this zeal, both in service to the poor generally and as a personal service to colleagues. Yet Thornton has left no trace of having ever considered the theological basis or the theological implication of any of this work. Thornton appears to have found it perfectly obvious that political economy was a distinct enterprise from theology.

An almost perfect mirror-image of this narrative is found in the life of another Henry, Henry Sidgwick, told in the next article by Steven Medema. Whereas Thornton was a faithful believer who saw no apparent connection between his faith and his economics, Sidgwick lost his early faith and struggled mightily with the implications for society and for political economy of losing a Christian foundation. (In Keynes's well-known summary, Sidgwick "never did anything but wonder whether Christianity was true and prove that it wasn't and hope that it was.") Sidgwick deeply desired an ethical basis around which to organize society. As he struggled with his crisis of faith, he substituted a utilitarian ethical system for the Christian one, emphasizing the general happiness of society. One tradition in Franco-Anglo political economy, as we have seen, was to believe that a benevolent God established in nature the rule that the pursuit of self-interest would promote the commonweal. Sidgwick inherited that tradition, but in removing the hand of God he also removed the comforting outcome: he could no longer believe that individual self-interest was in harmony with the social interest. Breaking the connection between utilitarianism and laissez-faire economics, Sidgwick therefore emphasized the importance of the visible hand of the state in promoting social welfare.

The final chapter in this section is a Christian reaction to Sidgwick's welfare economics, as it was developed later by Marshall and Pigou. Roger Backhouse describes an alternative welfare economics, advocated by Henry Clay, J. A. Hobson, and R. H. Tawney. All three drew on a common Oxford intellectual context, but otherwise were quite different: Tawney was a socialist and a committed Anglican, Hobson a Liberal and agnostic humanist. But all three created a space for normative considerations at least consistent with, and in Tawney's case explicitly based on, religious principles. In their critique of the Cambridge tradition in welfare economics, Clay and Hobson emphasized that people often pursued the "artificial" wants instilled in them by marketing, that they did not always know what was good for them, and that even if they did they might be too weak to choose it. Tawney went farther, arguing that social welfare must be based on shared community purposes, not on the sum of individual wants; that behavior had to be judged by moral principles as well as the materialistic consequences; and that God ultimately judges "value." Although they are not well known among mainstream economists today, Backhouse shows that these individuals were well respected in their time. Their books were prominently reviewed in such outlets as the *Journal of Political Economy*, and it was their work that American institutionalists such as Walton Hamilton and Wesley Clair Mitchell referred to when they spoke of "welfare economics." As we commented in our introductory essay, their views continue to have salience today, especially in the findings of neuro- and behavioral economics that individuals may not be good at choosing what they truly want.

The Changing Theological Context of Economic Analysis since the Eighteenth Century

A. M. C. Waterman

Economists, like other human beings, pursue their inquiries in light of the presuppositions held by all the learned of their own time and place. Some of these are implicit, and almost invisible at the time. Among those that are explicit, some are recognized as an orthodoxy from which it may be possible to dissent. But what counts as dissent is as much a part of the intellectual context as is orthodoxy.

What with hindsight we now recognize as economic analysis first appeared circa 1700 in ancien régime France, in the work of Pierre de Boisguilbert. Intellectual culture in France and indeed throughout Europe was then almost entirely determined by the implicit and explicit presuppositions of Western Christianity. Although formal and jurisdictional differences existed between the Roman Catholic and Protestant branches of this religion, theological differences were less important for political—and even scientific—culture than is often supposed. This is partly because of the large body of Christian doctrine shared by all and partly because the range of theological opinion existing within each branch often made it possible for substantial agreement between at least some Catholic and some Protestant (especially Anglican) theologians. In 1686, at the instigation of the great Bishop Bossuet, the Synod of St. Germain formally communicated its thanks and appreciation to the Anglican bishop George Bull for his *Defensio Fidei Nicaenae* (Cross 1958, 206).

I am grateful for helpful comments from Gilbert Faccarello, Paul Oslington, Philippe Steiner, and Donald Winch; all remaining errors and infelicities are mine.

History of Political Economy 40 (annual suppl.) DOI 10.1215/00182702-2007-063

Although as late as the middle of the twentieth century it was still possible in some countries to speak of a "Christian society" (e.g., Eliot 1939) and even to debate the proper approach to economic policy in such a society (e.g., Temple 1942; Munby 1956), the reality had largely disappeared by the end of the nineteenth. Theological considerations, once at the heart of scientific discourse in the European world, had ceased to be of professional interest to any but theologians. A half century later, Christian theology is hardly a memory among most scholars and scientists born since the Second World War.

Although the transformation of an officially sacral society to an officially secular one was long and gradual, it is possible to identify a few sharp discontinuities in the theological context, and in some measure to correlate these with changing approaches to economic analysis. In what follows, I attempt to exhibit these discontinuities and some of their effects. The story begins in France, which until the end of the eighteenth century occupied a position in Western civilization comparable to that of Britain in the nineteenth century or the United States in the twentieth, and in which what we now call economics had its origin. However, between the *Wealth of Nations* and Paul Samuelson's *Foundations*, the chief focus of attention in the new science shifted to Britain, and much of this essay, including what is said of nonanglophone authors, is written from an English (indeed at times a narrowly "Cambridge") point of view.

In section 1, which is based largely on the work of Gilbert Faccarello (1999), I report the evidence for supposing that the origin of the central economic-theoretic conception of spontaneous order may be found in the Augustinian theodicy of the Jansenists Pierre Nicole and Jean Domat.

Section 2 reports a slightly later and very different tradition: the natural theology of Sir Isaac Newton's *Principia*, which dominated anglophone theology for much of the eighteenth century and was also influential among the philosophes in France.

In section 3, based on my own work on Christian political economy (Waterman 1991), I report the response of economists and theologians to Thomas Robert Malthus's novel version of the perennial "problem of evil." In this case, the change in theological context was brought about by changes in economic analysis itself.

Section 4 considers the drastic effect on the intellectual underpinning of Victorian Christianity of Charles Darwin's theory of organic evolution first published in 1859, and the consequent divorce of science from theology.

Section 5 contains a brief epilogue.

Jansenism, Boisguilbert, and Spontaneous Order

In the seventh decade of the long reign (1643–1715) of Louis XIV, there appeared in Paris a posthumous work by one of the most celebrated theologians of that period, Jacques-Bénigne Bossuet (1627–1704), tutor to the dauphin and bishop of Meaux. *Politiques tirée des propres paroles de l'écriture sainte* (1709), based on Bossuet's lessons to his princely pupil thirty years before, establishes at length the divine (i.e., scriptural) authority of the sovereign and his laws.

> Ministers of princes . . . will find in his word lessons which only God could give them. It is a part of Christian morality to form the magistrature by his laws: God wills to decide everything . . . to give decisions for all states; and more especially for that on which all others depend. (Bossuet 1990, 2)

There is obvious congruence between this view and the political theology of Restoration England, made luminous for all in the powerful rhetoric of the Book of Common Prayer (Waterman 2004, chaps. 3, 4).

Bossuet supplied a theological rationale of the absolutist state. Jean-Baptiste Colbert, the king's minister of finance, presided over its economy from 1665 to 1683, paying off the national debt and fostering French industry by a variety of mercantilist expedients. France was to be run for profit as the private estate of *le roi soleil.* Antoyne de Montchrétien's *Traicté de l'oeconomie politique* (1615)—which employed the term newly minted by Montchrétien's fellow Huguenot Louis de Mayerne-Turquet four years earlier—provided an economic rationale. In so doing, Montchrétien inaugurated an intellectual tradition that has continued, through many mutations, to the present day (Waterman 2004, chap. 14). Throughout the seventeenth century, therefore, political economy dealt with the top-down administration of the absolutist state by such as Colbert. Not until the very end of that century did the first signs appear of the attention to unintended consequences that characterizes modern economics. They emerged circa 1670 within the Jansenist tradition in the French church, a slightly detached and eventually persecuted enclave that had its home in the Benedictine community of Port Royal. They were first formulated by Boisguilbert in *Le détail de la France* ([1695] 1966, 2.591–661).

Boisguilbert (1966, 1:132–34) had been a student in his teens at the Petits Ecoles of Port Royal, subsequently reading law in Paris. He was undoubtedly familiar with the teachings of the widely influential moralist

Pierre Nicole (1625–1695) and the eminent jurist Jean Domat (1625–1696). Although less rigorous and more influenced by Thomism than some Jansenists such as Martin de Barcos and Blaise Pascal, these authors' theology was more purely Augustinian, and therefore more nearly Calvinist, than was usual among Romanists at that time. Acutely conscious of the pervasiveness of human sin, they were forced to construct a theodicy of civil life. Why does God allow humans, created in his own image defaced by original sin, to be as selfish, power hungry, predatory, and cruel as we continually observe our species to be? St. Augustine himself had taught that the state, private property, marriage, and slavery, although indeed self-inflicted *punishment* for sin, were willed by God to become *remedies* for sin. For these institutions harness the self-regarding acts of sinful men and women to produce unintended consequences that are socially benign (Waterman 1991, 76–77; 2004, 101). The Jansenists were the first to perform a similar exercise for the market economy.

> When travelling . . . we find men ready to serve those who pass by and who have lodgings to receive them almost everywhere. We dispose of their services as we wish. We command them; they obey. . . . What could be more admirable than these people if they were acting from charity? It is cupidity which induces them to act. . . . Think what charity would be required to build an entire house for another man, furnish it, carpet it and hand him the key. Cupidity does this quite joyfully. (Nicole, quoted in Faccarello 1999, 28)

We are reminded of Sir Dennis Robertson's (1956, 154) famous question: "What is it that economists economize? . . . love, the scarcest and most precious of all resources."

Faccarello (1999, 26–32) cites a range of cognate passages from both Nicole and Domat to illustrate the general, Augustinian, position summarized by Domat:

> From so evil a passion as our self-love, and from a poison so contrary to the mutual love which ought to be the foundation of society, God created one of the remedies which enable it to survive; for from the principle of division He constructed a link which unites all men in a thousand ways and which maintains most agreements. (Domat, quoted in Faccarello 1999, 27)

Another passage from Domat is cited that illustrates the conception of "Providence" that Boisguilbert shared with Nicole and Domat, and which is obviously proleptic of Adam Smith. Under Providence, there is a "secret conducting" of society by an omnipresent God (Faccarello 1999, 32), which in the next century becomes Samuel Johnson's ([1753] 1998, vol. 4, no. 67; Winch 1996, 57–59) "secret concatenation of society." As did Smith in *Wealth of Nations* (Waterman 2004, chap. 6), Boisguilbert ([1704] 2000, 29) explicitly identified Providence with Nature. But he went beyond Nicole and Domat in understanding that the way Providence = Nature operates in a market society is through the unintended consequence of the competition of agents, each motivated by self-love: a state of "harmony" or "equilibrium." Herein lies Boisguilbert's originality.

Although Boisguilbert was himself an absolutist on theological grounds, his radically new conception of an economy governed by Nature, beneficently coordinating the self-love of individuals through relative market prices, brought him into a head-on collision with authority. His published works on economic matters were violently polemical, attacking all mercantilist policy and above all its folly in confusing money with wealth. The king's interest would be better served by setting the French economy free. The bureaucracy was predictably scandalized by this outrageous suggestion. Boisguilbert was exiled for a time, and some of his works suppressed (Cadet 1887, 80–90; Roberts 1935, 81–93).

Yet an edition, albeit incomplete, of Boisguilbert's writings was possible by 1712 (Roberts 1935, 96–97). These continued to be read throughout the eighteenth century and appear to have deeply influenced Richard Cantillon and the physiocrats. Not only can the real definition of wealth, the allocative function of relative prices, the general equilibrium of many markets, and the beneficence of free trade be traced to Boisguilbert, but so can that fingerprint of preclassical analysis: a macroeconomic conception of the general level of activity sustained by reciprocal demand in a two-sector—"town" and "country"—economy (Waterman 2001). It is hard to disagree with Eugène Daire's (1843, 168–69) admiring view of Boisguilbert as "the Christopher Columbus of the economic world" (cited in Faccarello 1999, 148).

Although Boisguilbert was a true pioneer in his vision of a self-regulating economy, his central conception—the benign consequences of self-love—can be correlated with certain features of the Jansenist theology expounded by Nicole and Domat. But whether this conception has its only, or even primary, source in those authors is problematic and has been contested (e.g., Christensen 2003, 102). Faccarello (1999, 11) asserts that "the fundamental idea of the efficiency of 'free trade' . . . originates in one of the most austere versions of the Catholic religion." But he has not proved the filiation, since there is little or nothing in Boisguilbert's own writings (aside from a marked stylistic resemblance to those of Nicole) to sustain it. All the evidence is circumstantial. And apart from Cadet (1887), no other author has noted the possible significance of the years at Port Royal. In general it would seem that all ideas—in the eighteenth century at any rate—are overdetermined. Epicurean and Stoic sources may be relevant, as Christensen argues; Cartesian sources may be, too, as Joseph Spengler (1984, 73) conjectured. What we may say with certainty, however, is that Christian theology was part, perhaps the most important part, of the intellectual context in late-seventeenth-century France and that in the case of Boisguilbert this was in particular the Augustinian theodicy of Port Royal.

Newtonian Natural Theology and Related Matters

Nature, and Nature's Laws lay hid in Night:
God said, *Let NEWTON be*: and all was Light!

This epitaph by Alexander Pope, engraved on the pedestal of Newton's statue in the chapel of Trinity College, Cambridge, captures the profound reverence of the learned throughout eighteenth-century Europe for the triumphant success of natural philosophy.

"Enlightenment" was to be had by extending Newton's method into all possible lines of human inquiry. However, the pursuit of this enterprise in Britain was quite different from that in France. In the latter, Cartesian physics continued to be preferred to Newtonian until the middle of the century. This is partly because the metaphysical assumption of gravity—intangible, unobservable, and unknowable save through its putative effects—seemed to undermine the orthodox mechanical philosophy. Moreover, as Willem 's Gravesande had noted as early as 1717, the heuristic success of Newtonian philosophy rested on the arbitrary axiom of the uniformity of nature (Cassirer 1955, 61). Perhaps as important, the natural theology associated with Newton's cosmology was feared by authority in France down to the Revolution as tending to deism (Brockliss 1987, 360, 455). Voltaire's widely influential mythopoea (Epstein 1979) can only have confirmed the worst fears of the French hierarchy. For in papist France—it was imagined in Scotland, at any rate—the church "discourages inquiries into nature, lest, by having our views enlarged, we may escape from her bonds" (Maclaurin [1748] 1775, 3, 5). But in Protestant Britain where freedom of thought was usually tolerated, establishment thinkers quickly grasped the apologetic importance of natural theology, and Newton was made not an enemy but an ally.

Newton himself was a devoted student of scripture, and no deist but a clandestine Socinian (Keynes 1972, 368; Snobelen 2005). He therefore kept his scriptural exegesis to himself but published *Philosophiae Naturalis Principia Mathematica*, he later said, "with an eye upon such Principles as might work with considering Men for the belief of a Deity" (Newton 1756, 1). Some of the earliest Newtonians such as John Toland, Anthony Collins, and Samuel Clarke were thinly veiled deists (Brooke 1991, 167–71). But the well-known ability of establishment culture to digest or co-opt the most unpalatable intrusions soon harnessed Newtonian science to the cause of orthodoxy. *An Account of Sir Isaac Newton's Philosophical Discoveries*, Colin Maclaurin's ([1748] 1775) long-lived textbook, showed that Newton's cosmology not only demonstrates the existence and attributes of God—as Newton himself believed—but also leads to a belief in an afterlife and a view of this life as a state of probation, which thus prepares us for the study of scripture (3–5, 401–11). The book immediately became required reading at Cambridge and in the Scottish universities. Smith read it soon after publication (Ross 1995, 100) and presumably made use of it in his own lectures on natural theology in the 1750s (Stewart [1793] 1980, 274). Both William Paley, "the first of the Cambridge economists" (Keynes 1972, 79 n. 2), and Malthus read Newton with the aid of Maclaurin for the tripos examinations and as a prolegomenon to their theological studies. By the end of the century the Cambridge-educated, impeccably orthodox layman William Wilberforce (1797, 39–40, 467) could enroll Newton, along with Locke, as an exemplar of Christian belief.

Newtonian natural theology powerfully reinforced two Boisguilbertian—or at any rate French—ideas among anglophone economic thinkers: that of Providence or Nature, and that of equilibrium. A third French idea, the crucial concept of self-love with which Boisguilbert's story began, belonged as much to "revealed" as to "natural" theology and was taken far beyond the Jansenists' disapproving pietism by the mighty Bishop Butler.

Boisguilbert's economic thought had passed by way of Cantillon to the "French oeconomists," called "physiocrats" by Pierre-Samuel Du Pont de Nemours because of their insistence on the rule of Nature in economic affairs. For François Quesnay ([1765] 1969, 371–77) and his colleagues, the laws of Nature were announced to have been ordained by *l'Auteur de la Nature* who is *l'Etre Suprême*, and Joseph Schumpeter (1954, 228–29) judged that Quesnay's theories were "nothing but reformulations of scholastic doctrine." It is obvious that for Newton, too, and for all who followed him, the laws of Nature are indeed the laws of God. But these are known by means of natural philosophy (the formulation of theoretical models that can be tested by observation) and not by metaphysics. David Hume and Smith learned much in France, possibly from Cantillon's unpublished manuscript that circulated privately from the mid-1730s, certainly by friendship with Quesnay, Turgot, and their circle. However, Hume's and Smith's view of Nature was Newtonian, not Scholastic. The crucial importance of this move is that it allows the natural sciences to be recruited as *allies*, not *subjects*, of theology. And because the scientific method is accessible to all, natural theology seemed to offer an irenic escape from the religious strife that had plagued Europe for much of the previous century. Nature might unite us as scripture seemingly had not. This at any rate appears to have been the belief of Adam Smith, although not, it is generally supposed, of Hume. Smith's most famous book, I have argued, can be read—and may conceivably have been so read by some in the half century after its publication—as a contribution to natural theology (Waterman 2004, chap. 6). Smith's fellow club member Edmund Burke, who held that the *Wealth of Nations* was "probably the most important book ever written" (O'Brien 1993, 144 n. 1), maintained that "the laws of commerce, which are the laws of nature, [are] consequently the laws of God" (Burke 1981–2000, 9.125).

The concept of equilibrium, which Boisguilbert was the first to apply to market processes, is obviously congruent with Newtonian mechanics. It is no surprise that Smith ([1776] 1976, 72–77) used the powerful Newtonian metaphor of gravitation to describe disequilibrium adjustment of market prices, although we have recently been warned against too easy a passage from that undoubted fact to present-day general equilibrium theory (Montes 2006). Two generations later, Edward Copleston (1819, 61–62) observed that "profit is in mercantile dealings, what *gravitation* is in the system of the universe." But by far the most sophisticated and—for economic analysis—far-reaching application of the Newtonian concept of equilibrium was Hume's ([1752] 1994) essay "Of the Balance of Trade." Hume constructed an equilibrium model of international monetary adjustment, the stability of which depends on the assumption that the domestic price level is an increasing function of the domestic share of the world's stock of gold. Malthus, who probably owed more to Hume than any other economic thinker of his time (Winch 1996, 370–71), employed a mathematically isomorphic model of stable equilibrium in his population dynamics (Waterman 1988).

The third and most important strand in the theological context of eighteenth-century anglophone economic thought, inherited from the French, was the possibly social beneficence of self-love. There is no obvious relation in this case to Newtonian ideas, although by the end of the century Malthus ([1798] 1966, 175, 207, 286, 370) could refer to self-love as "the main-spring of the great machine." What seems to have happened in Britain is that Mandeville's provocative argument, collaterally derived from the Jansenists (Hundert 1994, 23, 31–35; Faccarello 1999, 58, 174 n. 2), that "private vice" is "public benefit" was met with a powerful rebuttal from Joseph Butler ([1726] 1969). Butler's Rolls sermons were preached in the immediate aftermath of the public outcry aroused by the 1723 edition of *The Fable of the Bees*. As against the influential doctrine of Lord Shaftesbury's *Characteristicks* (1711), these sermons showed that the ends of private and public good coincide, that "self-love is one chief security of our right behaviour towards society," and that "under Providence there is seldom any inconsistency between what is called our duty and what is called our interest." Sermons 11 and 12 recognize that self-love is a duty commanded by Christ himself (Butler [1726] 1969, 32, 36, 37–38, 67, 164–202). Hume ([1739–40] 1888, xxi) acknowledged both Mandeville and Butler as one of those "who have begun to put the science of man on a new footing" and sent a copy of his *Treatise* to the latter. Josiah Tucker, who had been Bishop Butler's chaplain in Bristol and was a correspondent and friend of Hume, fully digested both Butler's argument and Boisguilbert's advocacy of laissez-faire, which it rationalized:

> Let the Legislature but take care not to make *bad Laws*, and then as to *good ones*, they will make themselves: That is, the Self-Love and Self-Interest of each Individual will prompt him to seek such Ways of Gain, Trade and Occupations of Life, as by serving himself, will promote the public Welfare at the same Time. (Tucker [1753–65] 1993, 3:48)

Smith had Tucker's economic writings in his own library (Mizuta 1996) and would have known of him through their mutual friends Hume and Lord Kames. There are many traces of Tucker's Butlerian view of the human condition in the *Theory of Moral Sentiments* (Smith [1759] 1982), which appeared four years after Tucker's *Elements of Commerce and Taxes* and immediately became the most influential of all the many attempts to counter Mandeville's assumption that self-love must be regarded as vice.

Resource Scarcity and the Divine Attributes

Seventeen years after the *Theory of Moral Sentiments*, Smith's *Wealth of Nations* codified the existing body of economic knowledge and became the point of departure for the English school of political economy in the next generation (Waterman 2007). Like all his contemporaries, Smith advocated economic growth to improve the condition of the lower orders. For Smith, the chief cause of growth was the accumulation of capital, driven by "parsimony" of the masters. The chief constraint on growth was therefore any tendency among masters to spend their revenue "unproductively" rather than to plough it back into their firms. Smith's argument depended on the continuing possibility of a rate of population growth equal (in dynamic equilibrium) to the rate of accumulation. Although aware of land scarcity, Smith did not incorporate it in his analysis. Those few contemporaries who did—Sir James Steuart (1767), Turgot ([1768] 1970), and James Anderson ([1777] 1968)—were ignored by Smith. All this changed dramatically in 1798 with the first (anonymous) appearance of *An Essay on the Principle of Population* (Malthus [1798] 1966).

Although the idea of diminishing returns implicit in the first *Essay* was not fully explicated until 1815 (Malthus 1815; West 1815; Ricardo 1815), its consequences for living standards in a growing economy, contradicting Smith's optimism about economic growth, were immediately perceived and were deeply shocking. Deliberately exaggerating his conclusions for polemical purposes, Malthus ([1798] 1966, 140–41, for example) had announced that human fecundity in a world of finite resources must doom our race either to "misery" or to "vice." As a highly educated Cambridge cleric, Malthus realized of course that this must call into question the coexistence of the divine attributes and devoted the last two chapters of his *Essay* to an attempt at theodicy. But his attempt was a failure (Waterman 1991, 106–12), and he and his work were greeted with howls of execration, in which hatred for his seeming blasphemy was mingled with hatred for his highly successful demolition of revolutionary doctrine. Robert Southey's (1803) vitriolic review of the second *Essay* was the first blast in what Arnold Toynbee later called "the bitter argument between economists and human beings" (Winch 1996, 6), an "argument" that recruited Coleridge, Wordsworth, Carlyle, Dickens, Kingsley, Ruskin, Morris, and many another Romantic to the cause of "human beings" (Levy 2001), and that a recent historian has described as "one of the enduring fault-lines in British cultural debate" (Winch 1996, 402, 418). Pamphlets denounced Malthus for "his impious and blasphemous assertion, *that the Almighty brings more beings into the world than he prepares nourishment for*" (*A Summons* 1807; see also James 1979, 116–21; Pyle 1994). By 1832, political economy as a whole was detested by many. It was claimed that the writings of Malthus and David Ricardo had "tended to lead the public away from the true path of inquiry" and to make of political economy "a hideous chain of paradoxes at apparent war with religion and humanity" (*Eclectic Review* 1832, 9).

The first theologian to offer an orthodox alternative to Malthus's flawed theodicy was his Cambridge tutor's own tutor, Archdeacon Paley, who was converted from optimistic populationism by Malthus's argument, but who saw that the supporting theology was in need of reworking. In his last work, Paley (1802) argued that the evil produced by population pressure could be reconciled with Butler's account of human life as a "state of discipline and trial" (which Malthus had rejected in 1798) and could therefore be incorporated into his general teleological argument for the existence of God. Paley's brief sketch was greatly expanded and refined by John Bird Sumner in a two-volume, prize-winning essay *Treatise on the Records of the Creation* (1816), which made political economy respectable in evangelical circles and which led to Sumner's eventual enthronement as the ninety-first archbishop of Canterbury. Malthus (1817, 3:423) acknowledged Sumner's "masterly developement and completion" of his views; Ricardo judged the *Treatise* a "clever book"; and J. R. McCulloch called it "an excellent work" (cited in Waterman 2007). For the time being, political economy was exonerated from the charge of being "hostile to religion" (see Waterman 1991, chaps. 3 and 4, for the full story).

However, the good effects of Sumner's work were soon called into question by the activities of the Philosophic Radicals (Halévy 1928), a small but vocal group of Benthamites who sought to hijack political economy for their blatantly godless attack on the establishment in church and state. The *Westminster Review*, launched in 1824 to propagate the Radicals' unique and unpalatable mixture of Jeremy Bentham's utilitarianism, Ricardo's economics, and James Mill's depreciation of the arts

(Thomas 1979), was viewed with alarm by influential Oxford Tories and the struggling new science of political economy tainted by association. Despite Sumner's valiant efforts seven years before, it seemed once again that political economy was indeed at war with the Christian presuppositions of Anglican culture (Waterman 1991, 196–204).

As Sumner had reassured Whiggish, Newtonian, and evangelical Cambridge, so Richard Whately (1787–1863) sought to reassure Tory, Aristotelian, and high-church Oxford. In 1825 he engineered the election of his former pupil, Nassau Senior, as the first Drummond Professor of Political Economy in the hope that this would confer respectability on the new discipline. In 1831 he accepted the chair himself and delivered his *Introductory Lectures* (1831), which showed that political economy is a *scientific* enterprise that affords "secular" knowledge, or knowledge of Nature, whereas theology is a *religious* enterprise that affords "sacred" knowledge, or knowledge of God. The two inquiries are distinct save to the extent that scientific knowledge of Nature can throw light on Nature's God and therefore contribute to natural theology, and they are noncompeting.

> That Political-Economy should have been complained of as hostile to Religion, will probably be regarded a century hence . . . with the same wonder, almost approaching to incredulity, with which we at the present day hear of men's having sincerely opposed, on religious grounds, the Copernican system. (Whately 1831, 18)

As an unintended consequence of his apologia, Whately established that methodology of economic analysis that has remained orthodox to the present day (Waterman 2004, chap. 8; see also Maas, this volume).

Although economic analysis was often unpopular with authority in eighteenth-century France because it exposed the folly of attempting to control the French economy from Versailles, no one ever suggested or even hinted either in France or in Britain that political economy was incompatible with Christian theology, whether "revealed" or "natural." It is important to emphasize that in this case, and perhaps in this case only, it was a sudden mutation in economic analysis, triggered by Malthus's first *Essay*, which brought about large changes in the theological context, not the other way round. The first change was Sumner's comprehensive reconciliation of Paley's natural theology with the new, biblical and evangelical theology that had become dominant in England and Scotland after the French Revolution sent the British upper classes scurrying back to their church and their bibles. The second was more radical and far-reaching, and more permanent. Whately's demarcation of "science" from "theology" marked the beginning of a sea change in the theological context of scientific and scholarly thinking. Although it was necessarily implicit in eighteenth-century natural theology—else how could science be recruited as independent evidence for a deity?—it was only implicit. By the middle of the nineteenth century, however, England's intellectual culture, at any rate, although still Christian, was a world away from the biblical literalism of Bishop Bossuet's *Politiques*.

In France, where Newtonian and Paleyesque natural theology had never played an important part in buttressing orthodoxy, Christian theology seems to have faded from the intellectual context of scientific thought after the Revolution save among Romanists nostalgic for the ancien régime such as Alban de Villeneuve-Bargemont (1834, 1:20), whose *Économie politique chrétienne* was a vast but unsuccessful attempt to construct an "alternative" political economy *à l'aide . . . du phare lumineux du christianisme*. This heterodox undercurrent survived, however, in nineteenth-century papal social doctrine (Waterman 2004, 185–86; Almodovar and Teixeira, this volume) and merged with the incipient Christian socialism of the Swiss Protestant aristocrat J.-C.-L. Simonde de Sismondi. The epoch-making contributions to orthodox economic analysis of Antoine Augustin Cournot (1838) and Jules Dupuit ([1844] 1952) were composed in the theologically sterile atmosphere of Comtean positivism. As late as 1850, however, Frédéric Bastiat (converted from infidelity to Christianity very late in life) could press more or less orthodox political economy into the service of natural theology in his unfinished *Harmonies économiques* (1850). Faccarello and Steiner (this volume) report postrevolutionary discussions in France of the question: Are political economy and religion necessarily in conflict?

In Germany, where economic analysis was rare before the 1870s, the totally neglected outlier, Herman Heinrich Gossen (1854), constructed his now-famous book within a framework of religious rhetoric strongly reminiscent of eighteenth-century natural theology (Steiner 2007).

Darwin and the Collapse of Paley's Teleology

British intellectual culture did not remain Christian for long. The decade of the 1860s, Lord Keynes (1972, 168) believed, "was the critical moment at which Christian dogma fell away from the serious philosophical world of England, or at any rate of Cambridge." Although many social and cultural changes had prepared the ground (Brooke 1991, 219–25), two coincidental and unconnected causes would seem to have produced this debacle.

J. S. Mill's (1865) attack on Henry Mansel's Bampton lectures of 1858 undermined their Kantian foundations and challenged their theodicy as morally obnoxious (see Raeder 2002, 162). Mansel's lectures, Keynes believed—no doubt reflecting the opinions of his father's circle in Cambridge during the 1870s and later—were "the last attempt to found Christian dogma on an intellectual basis."

More fundamentally, the appearance of *On the Origin of Species* in 1859 followed closely by Herbert Spencer's *First Principles* (1862) appeared to torpedo Paley's teleology on which the entire intellectual structure of Victorian Christianity rested. Paley's influence, which had remained dominant in Britain and America for seventy-five years (Haddow 1939, 67), suddenly collapsed, and his books were no longer reprinted. Nearly a century before, Hume (1779) had demonstrated that since *cause* may not be inferred from *observation*, nothing can be known of the watchmaker from the watch. But Hume's Scotch metaphysics had merely bored the pragmatic English public, and his arguments were ignored. Paley referred to Hume in *Natural Theology* and was thought to have dealt with his objections (McLean 2003). But something tangible and visible was a different matter. Science, which for nearly two centuries had taught the learned that religious belief rested on sure foundations, suddenly changed its tune. Evolution is blind and purposeless and, even if Hume's objection is set aside, can tell us nothing (it seemed to many at the time) about any putative Creator. The effect on the educated in Britain was immediate and drastic. "Metaphysical agnosticism, Evolutionary progress, and—the one remnant still left of the intellectual inheritance of the previous generation—Utilitarian ethics joined to propel the youthful mind in a new direction" (Keynes 1972, 170).

Among the "youthful" that Keynes had in mind were several Cambridge dons influential in transforming political economy—still to a large extent an avocation of gifted amateurs and Whig politicians (Waterman 2007)—into the professional and internationalized economics of the present day. In 1867, when Millicent Garret married the professor of political economy Henry Fawcett MP, she was twenty and he thirty-four. Henry Sidgwick was twenty-nine, Alfred Marshall twenty-five, Herbert Foxwell eighteen, and Neville Keynes fifteen. All had been brought up Christian. Marshall and Sidgwick had been destined for holy orders, and Sidgwick—

brother-in-law of the archbishop of Canterbury—subscribed to the Thirty-nine Articles in 1863 on becoming a fellow of Trinity. Marshall's wife, Mary Paley, was great-granddaughter of the illustrious archdeacon. Foxwell was raised a Wesleyan Methodist. But by 1872, with the possible exception of the young Neville, "none of these could have been called Christians" (Keynes 1972, 168, 232, 79, 273–74).

Yet none evinced any hostility to Christianity or to religion in general, and Millicent Fawcett at any rate returned to the Church of England in later years. Marshall "sympathised with Christian morals and Christian ideals and Christian incentives" (168). Sidgwick was sometimes regarded as "saintly" (Schultz 2004, 157; see also Medema, this volume; Backhouse, this volume). In general, Cambridge economists of the first agnostic generation seem to have regarded their studies of economics as a secularized extension of their former Christianity, and their scientific work as a means—perhaps the best means—of loving their neighbor. The influence of J. S. Mill was still powerful among them, and Mill had publicly identified "the ethics of utilitarianism" with "the golden rule of Jesus" (Raeder 2002, 17, 20, 55, 86, 251; Levy 2001, 52–54).

Not all Cambridge economists were agnostic. William Cunningham (1849–1919), who lectured in the university until 1891, was a cleric and archdeacon of Ely. J. Shield Nicholson (1850–1927), a tutor at Cambridge until becoming professor of political economy in Edinburgh, concluded the third volume of his widely used *Principles of Political Economy* (1893–1901) with a chapter on the relation of political economy to morality and Christianity, which opened with the affirmation "Credo in Unum Deum" (Nicholson 1893–1901, 3:427).

Oxford was more resistant to the new religious ideas than Cambridge, and two of its most distinguished economists, Whately and W. F. Lloyd (1794–1852), had been clerics. W. J. Ashley (1860–1927) "for the whole of his life . . . remained an active churchgoer." Edwin Cannan (1861–1935), son of a Presbyterian elder, read devotional books as an undergraduate (Kadish 1982, 2, 7, 10). By the end of the nineteenth century about two-thirds of all Oxford undergraduates belonged to the mildly socialist Christian Social Union.

Although all British economists in this period, including the Irishmen Cliffe Leslie (1827–1882) and J. E. Cairnes (1823–1875), tended to prefer the "fruit" that economics promised to afford rather than the "light," there appears to be more than a slight correlation between religion and method. Cunningham at Cambridge, and the leading Oxford figures, favored the historical and inductive methods advocated in the previous generation by William Whewell (1794–1866) and Richard Jones (1790–1855; see Maas, this volume). Neville Keynes's classic *Scope and Method of Political Economy* (1891) was written to resolve the *Methodenstreit* between Oxford and Cambridge, and although Schumpeter (1954, 824) judged that Keynes "settled most of these methodological issues . . . to the satisfaction of the profession," this is history written by the victors. The *Economic Review* was founded in 1891 by the Oxford Economic Society and the Christian Social Union as a historicist alternative to the Marshallian *Economic Journal* (see Backhouse, this volume). Two decades later the Anglo-Catholic Oxonian R. H. Tawney (1880–1962) confided to his *Commonplace Book* that "there is no such thing as a science of economics, and Marshall's talk as to the need for social problems to be studied 'by the same order of mind which tests the stability of a battleship in bad weather' is twaddle" (Tawney 1972, 72). It would seem probable that Nicholson's (1893–1901, 3:427) concluding chapter, written to oppose the view that "the study of political economy leads to intellectual agnosticism and moral pessimism," was a last attempt to bridge the widening gap between the profession (such as it was) and dissident Christian socialists such as Tawney.

The picture that emerges of this sharpest of all mutations in the theological context of economic theorizing is of economists'—in Britain, at any rate—beginning to go their separate religious or irreligious ways. Sixty years before, Sumner's success in demonstrating the consistency of economic analysis with the most orthodox variety of English Christianity had been of vital importance to the formerly Jewish, subsequently Unitarian Ricardo and his ex-Presbyterian disciple M'Culloch. But by the 1880s religion had become actually, although not yet officially, privatized in Britain. It was no longer part of the professional duty of economists to reconcile their findings with Christian theology.

Epilogue: Economics and Christian Theology in a Secular Society

The divorce of science from theology adumbrated by Whately was complete by the end of the nineteenth century. For those economists who wished to remain Christian, Whately's demarcation of scientific from religious knowledge became the only intellectually defensible theological position for all save the few such as Tawney—marginalized by Marshall's intellectual dominance of the profession—who denied that economics was or could be science, Philip Wicksteed who is sui generis (Steedman 1994), and metaphysical absolutists such as those of the Dooyerweerdian neo-Calvinist school who continue to assert that theology is *Regina Scientiae* (Tiemstra 1999).

Although most economists since Marshall regard theology as irrelevant to analysis, some of those who share his morally instrumental view of economics have regarded analysis as a means of implementing Christian social goals. When Archbishop William Temple submitted the proofs of *Christianity and Social Order* (1942) to the agnostic John Maynard Keynes for his critical scrutiny, Keynes went out of his way to reassure Temple as to "the right of the Church to interfere [Temple's own phrase] in what is essentially a branch of ethics" (Iremonger 1948, 438–39). The Oxford economist Denys Munby (1956) was influential in propounding this view. Perhaps an extreme example of this strategy is the work of the French Jesuit Maurice Potron (1872–1942), who in the spirit of Francesco Vito (Parisi, this volume) constructed elaborate linear models—decades before Wassily Leontief—to formalize and test papal social teaching (Bidard, Erreygers, and Parys 2006). Meanwhile, in Germany at the same time and a little later, Christian economists opposed to Hitler and his ideology—Alfred Müller-Armack, Wilhelm Röpke, Walter Eucken—envisaged a secular social order enlightened by Christian doctrine and fostered by humane public policy informed by economic analysis (Wagner 1994). By 1991 the ideas of the Ordo liberals, as they were called, had begun to affect papal social doctrine (Waterman 2004, 200 n. 41).

Among those economists who take theology to be irrelevant to analysis, which is the vast majority (including the author of this survey), perhaps most attempt to abstract as much as possible from values of any kind, whether or not given by religion. Whately's pupil Senior (1836) had maintained that an economist's analytic conclusions, being strictly positive, "do not authorize him in adding a single syllable of advice"; a doctrine followed by Cairnes, criticized by McCulloch and Sidgwick (Waterman 2007), canonized by Lionel Robbins (1932), and now orthodox although seldom heeded.

References

Anderson, James. [1777] 1968. *Observations on the means of exciting a spirit of National Industry; chiefly intended to promote the Agriculture, Commerce, Manufactures and Fisheries of Scotland*. New York: Kelley.

Bastiat, Frédéric. 1850. *Harmonies économiques*. Paris: Guillaumin.

Bidard, C., G. Erreyegers, and W. Parys. 2006. Review of *Les oeuvres economiques de l'Abbé Potron*, edited by G. Abraham-Frois and E. Lendjel. *European Journal of the History of Economic Thought* 13.1:163–67.

Boisguilbert, Pierre de. [1695] 1966. *Pierre de Boisguilbert ou la naissance de l'économie politique*. 2 vols. Paris: Institut National d'Études Démographiques.

———. [1704] 2000. *A Treatise on the Nature of Wealth, Money, and Taxation. . . .* Translated and edited by Peter Groenewegen. Sydney: University of Sydney, Centre for the Study of the History of Economic Thought.

Bossuet, J.-B. 1709. *Politiques tirée des propres paroles de l'écriture sainte*. Paris: Pierre Cot.

———. 1990. *Politics Drawn from the Very Words of Holy Scripture*. Translated and edited by Patrick Riley. Cambridge: Cambridge University Press.

Brennan, H. Geoffrey, and A. M. C. Waterman, eds. 1994. *Economics and Religion: Are They Distinct?* Boston: Kluwer.

Brockliss, L. W. B. 1987. *French Higher Education in the Seventeenth and Eighteenth Centuries: A Cultural History*. Oxford: Clarendon.

Brooke, J. H. 1991. *Science and Religion: Some Historical Perspectives*. Cambridge: Cambridge University Press.

Burke, Edmund. 1981–2000. *The Writings and Speeches of Edmund Burke, 1759–1797*. 9 vols. Edited by P. K. Langford et al. Oxford: Clarendon.

Butler, Joseph. [1726] 1969. *Fifteen Sermons Preached at the Rolls Chapel and a Dissertation upon the Nature of Virtue*. Edited by W. R. Matthews. London: Bell.

Cadet, Félix. 1870. *Pierre de Boisguilbert: Précurseur des économistes, 1646–1714*. Paris: Guillaumin.

———. 1887. *L'éducation à Port-Royal*. Paris: Hachette.

Cassirer, Ernst von. 1955. *The Philosophy of the Enlightenment*. Translated by F. C. A. Koelln and J. P. Pettegrove. Boston: Deacon.

Christensen, Paul P. 2003. Epicurean and Stoic Sources for Boisguilbert's Physiological and Hippocratic Vision of Nature and Economics. In *Oeconomies in the Age of Newton*, edited by Margaret Schabas and Neil De Marchi. *HOPE* 35 (supplement): 101–28.

[Copleston, Edward]. 1819. *A Letter to the Right Hon. Robert Peel, MP for the University of Oxford, on the Pernicious Effects of a Variable Standard of Value. . . .* Oxford: Murray.

Cournot, Augustin. 1838. *Recherches sur les principes mathématiques de la théorie des richesses*. Paris: L. Hachette.

Cross, F. L., ed. 1958. *The Oxford Dictionary of the Christian Church*. London: Oxford University Press.

Daire, Eugène. 1843. Notice historique à la réédition des oeuvres de Boisguilbert. In *Économistes financiers du XVIIIe siècle*. Paris: Guillaumin.

Darwin, Charles. 1859. *On the Origin of Species by Means of Natural Selection. . . .* London: John Murray.

Dean, J. M., and A. M. C. Waterman, eds. 1999. *Religion and Economics: Normative Social Theory*. Boston: Kluwer.

Dupuit, Jules. [1844] 1952. On the Measurement of the Utility of Public Works. In *International Economic Papers* 2, translated by R. H. Barback.

Eclectic Review. 1832. January.

Eliot, T. S. 1939. *The Idea of a Christian Society*. London: Faber.

Epstein, Julia L. 1979. Voltaire's Myth of Newton. *Pacific Coast Philology* 14:27–33.

Faccarello, Gilbert. 1999. *The Foundations of Laissez-Faire: The Economics of Pierre de Boisguilbert*. London: Routledge.

Gossen, H. H. 1854. *Entwickelung der Gesetze des menschlichen Verkehrs. . . .* Braunschweig: Vieweg.

Haddow, A. 1939. *Political Science in American Colleges and Universities, 1636–1900*. New York: Appleton-Century.

Halévy, Elie. 1928. *The Growth of Philosophic Radicalism*. Translated by M. Morris. London: Faber and Gwyer.

Hume, David. 1779. *Dialogues Concerning Natural Religion*. London.

———. [1739–40] 1888. *A Treatise of Human Nature*. Edited by L. A. Selby-Bigge. 2 vols. Oxford: Clarendon.

———. [1752] 1994. Of the Balance of Trade. In *Political Essays*, edited by K. Haakonssen. Cambridge: Cambridge University Press.

Hundert, E. J. 1994. *The Enlightenment's Fable: Bernard Mandeville and the Discovery of Society*. Cambridge: Cambridge University Press.

Iremonger, F. A. 1948. *William Temple Archbishop of Canterbury: His Life and Letters*. London: Oxford University Press.

James, Patricia. 1979. *Population Malthus: His Life and Times*. London: Routledge.

Johnson, Samuel. [1753] 1998. *The Works of Samuel Johnson*. 16 vols. Seattle: World Wide School.

Keynes, John Maynard. 1972. *Essays in Biography*. Vol. 10 of *The Collected Writings of John Maynard Keynes*. Edited by E. Johnson and D. Moggeridge. London: Macmillan.

Kadish, Alon. 1982. *The Oxford Economists in the Late Nineteenth Century*. Oxford: Clarendon.

Levy, David. 2001. *How the Dismal Science Got Its Name: Classical Economics and the Ur-Text of Racial Politics*. Ann Arbor: University of Michigan Press.

Maclaurin, Colin. [1748] 1775. *An Account of Sir Isaac Newton's Philosophical Discoveries*. 3rd ed. London: Nourse.

Malthus, T. R. 1815. *An Essay on the Nature and Progress of Rent*. London.

———. 1817. *An Essay on the Principle of Population, or, A View of Its Past and Present Effects on Human Happiness. . . .* 3 vols. London: Murray.

———. [1798] 1966. *An Essay on the Principle of Population as It Affects the Future Improvement of Society. . . .* Facsimile reprint for the Royal Economic Society. London: Macmillan.

McLean, M. R. 2003. Did Paley Ignore Hume on the Argument from Design? In *Faith, Reason, and Economics: Essays in Honour of Anthony Waterman*, edited by Derek Hum. Winnipeg: St. John's College Press.

Mill, J. S. 1865. *An Examination of Sir William Hamilton's Philosophy. . . .* London: Longman, Green.

Mizuta, H. 1996. *Adam Smith's Library: A Catalogue*. Oxford: Clarendon.

Montes, Leonidas. 2006. On Adam Smith's Newtonianism and General Equilibrium Economic Theory. In *New Voices on Adam Smith*, edited by Leonidas Montes and Eric Schliesser. Abingdon, U.K.: Routledge.

Munby, D. L. 1956. *Christianity and Economic Problems*. London: Macmillan.

Newton, Isaac. 1756. *Four Letters from Sir Isaac Newton to Dr Bentley containing some Arguments in Proof of a Deity*. London: Dodsley.

Nicholson, J. Shield. 1893–1901. *Principles of Political Economy*. 3 vols. London: Black.

O'Brien, C. C. 1993. *The Great Melody*. London: Minerva.

Paley, William. 1802. *Natural Theology*. London: Wilkes and Taylor.

Pyle, A., ed. 1994. *Population: Contemporary Responses to Thomas Malthus*. Bristol, U.K.: Thoemmes.

Quesnay, François. [1765] 1969. *Traité de droit natural*. In *Oeuvres économiques et philosophiques*. New York: Franklin.

Raeder, Linda C. 2002. *John Stuart Mill and the Religion of Humanity*. Columbia: University of Missouri Press.

Ricardo, David. 1815. *An Essay on the Influence of a Low Price of Corn on the Profit of Stock; Shewing the Inexpediency of Restrictions on Importation; with Remarks on Mr. Malthus*. London.

Robbins, L. 1932. *An Essay on the Nature and Significance of Economic Science*. London: Macmillan.

Roberts, Hazel van Dyke. 1935. *Boisguilbert: Economist of the Reign of Louis XIV*. New York: Columbia University Press.

Robertson, D. H. 1956. *Economic Commentaries*. London: Staples.

Ross, I. S. 1995. *The Life of Adam Smith*. Oxford: Clarendon.

Schultz, B. 2004. The Methods of J. B. Schneewind. *Utilitas* 16:146–67.

Schumpeter, Joseph A. 1954. *History of Economic Analysis*. London: Allen and Unwin.

Senior, Nassau W. 1836. *An Outline of the Science of Political Economy*. London: Clowes.

Shaftesbury, Anthony Ashley Cooper, Earl of. 1711. *Characteristicks of Men, Manners, Opinions, Times*. London.

Smith, Adam. [1776] 1976. *An Inquiry into the Nature and Causes of the Wealth of Nations*. Edited by R. H. Campbell, A. S. Skinner, and W. B. Todd. 2 vols. Oxford: Clarendon.

———. [1759] 1982. *The Theory of Moral Sentiments*. Edited by E. G. West. Indianapolis: Liberty Classics.

Snobelen, Stephen Davis. 2005. Newton Reconsidered. http://www.galilean-library.org/snobelen.html.

[Southey, Robert.] 1803. Malthus's Essay on Population. *Annual Review*, 292–301.

Spencer, Herbert. 1862. *First Principles*. London: Williams and Norgate.

Spengler, J. J. 1984. Boisguilbert's Economic Views vis-à-vis Those of Contemporary *Réformateurs*. *HOPE* 16.1:69–88.

Steedman, Ian. 1994. Wicksteed: Economist and Prophet. In Brennan and Waterman 1994.

Steiner, Philippe. 2007. The Economic Theology of Herman Heinrich Gossen: The Creator, Human Conduct, and the Maximization of Utility. Unpublished paper.

Steuart, James. 1767. *An Inquiry into the Principles of Political Oeconomy. . . .* London: Millar and Cadell.

Stewart, Dugald. [1793] 1980. *Account of the Life and Writings of Adam Smith, LLD.* In *Essays on Philosophical Subjects [by Adam Smith]*, edited by W. P. D. Wightman, J. C. Bryce, and I. S. Ross. Oxford: Oxford University Press.

A Summons of Awakening, or, the Evil Tendency and Danger of Speculative Philosophy. 1807. Hawick.

Sumner, John Bird. 1816. *A Treatise on the Records of the Creation: with Particular Reference to . . . the Consistency of the Principle of Population with the Wisdom and Goodness of the Deity.* 2 vols. London: Hatchard.

Tawney, R. H. 1972. *R. H. Tawney's Commonplace Book.* Edited by J. M. Winter and D. M. Joslin. New York: Cambridge University Press.

Temple, William. 1942. *Christianity and Social Order.* London: Penguin.

Thomas, W. 1979. *The Philosophic Radicals: Nine Studies in Theory and Practice, 1817–1841.* Oxford: Clarendon.

Tiemstra, John P. 1999. Every Square Inch: Kuyperian Social Theory and Economics. In Dean and Waterman 1999.

Tucker, Josiah. [1753–65] 1993. *The Collected Works of Josiah Tucker.* With a new introduction by Jeffrey Stern. London: Routledge/Thoemmes.

Turgot, A. R. J. [1768] 1970. *Observations sur le mémoire de M. de Saint-Péravy en faveur de l'Impôt indirect.* In *Écrits économiques*, edited by B. Cazes. Paris: Calman-Lévy.

Villeneuve-Bargemont, Alban de. 1834. *Économie politiques chrétienne, ou recherches sur la nature et les causes du paupérisme, en France et en Europe, et sur les moyens de le soulager et de le prévenir.* 3 vols. Paris: Paulin.

Wagner, Richard E. 1994. *ORDO* Liberalism and the Social Market Economy. In Brennan and Waterman 1994.

Waterman, A. M. C. 1988. Hume, Malthus, and the Stability of Equilibrium. *HOPE* 20.1:85–94.

———. 1991. *Revolution, Economics, and Religion: Christian Political Economy, 1798–1833.* Cambridge: Cambridge University Press.

———. 2001. Notes towards an Un-Canonical, Pre-Classical Model of Political Oeconomy. In *Reflections on the Classical Canon in Economics*, edited by E. Forget and S. Peart. London: Routledge.

———. 2004. *Political Economy and Christian Theology since the Enlightenment: Essays in Intellectual History.* Basingstoke, U.K.: Palgrave Macmillan.

———. 2007. English School of Political Economy, 1798–1909. In *The New Palgrave: A Dictionary of Economics.* Edited by Steven N. Durlauf and Lawrence E. Blume. 2nd ed. London: Macmillan.

[West, E.] 1815. *Essay on the Application of Capital to Land; with Observation Shewing the Impolicy of Any Great Restrictions on the Importation of Corn, by a Fellow of University College Oxford.* London: Underwood.

Whately, Richard. 1831. *Introductory Lectures in Political Economy.* London: Fellowes.

Wilberforce, William. 1797. *A Practical View of the Prevailing Religious System of Professed Christians. . . .* London: Cadell.

Winch, D. N. 1996. *Riches and Poverty: An Intellectual History of Political Economy in Britain, 1750–1834.* Cambridge: Cambridge University Press.

"A Hard Battle to Fight": Natural Theology and the Dismal Science, 1820–50

Harro Maas

Il est plus facile d'élever un temple que
d'y faire descendre l'objet du culte.
—Samuel Beckett, *L'innommable*

On 15 March 1832 the Reverend Richard Jones wrote to his friend of study William Whewell, at the time Knightsbridge professor of mineralogy at Cambridge University and fellow of Trinity College, about the political economy professorship at King's College, London. There was some guarded excitement in the letter. Nassau Senior had just resigned from the professorship to become chair of the Poor Law Reform Committee, and Jones had been sounded out by Herbert Mayo, professor of anatomy at King's, about the job. Jones, serving as a vicar in Sussex, was interested, but he had reason to believe that Edward Copleston "and the Seniorites" might oppose his appointment, and so he was soliciting Whewell's advice on how to respond to Mayo's offer (Jones 1932a).

Copleston, provost of Oriel College at Oxford and Richard Whately's former tutor at Oriel, was one of the most powerful men in the Oxford

I would like to thank Brad Bateman, Spencer Banzhaf, Marcel Boumans, John Davis, Mary Morgan, Paul Oslington, and Anthony Waterman for comments on an earlier draft of this article. Thanks also to the participants of the 2007 *HOPE* conference and to the anonymous referees of this journal for their suggestions for improvement. I also would like to thank the master and fellows of Trinity College, Cambridge, for permission to quote from the Whewell papers. All faults and flaws of course are mine.

History of Political Economy 40 (annual suppl.) DOI 10.1215/00182702-2007-064

circuit. Whately, better known as archbishop of Dublin, was Drummond professor in political economy, a position first held by Senior. All three were part of the so-called Oriel Noetics (after the Greek *noèticos*—intellectual power), a group of speculative inquirers who vigorously used the Oriel Common Room to question "nearly every conceivable practice of church and state" so that the place, as Ralph Pomeroy (1985, xiv) quotes a contemporary observer, "*stunk* of logic." Neither Whewell nor Jones scorned debate, but the Noetics' logical speculative approach to political economy was really quite alien to their views on the proper method of the sciences, including political economy. As I show in this article, these different views were motivated by different consequences drawn at Oxford and Cambridge from the natural theology tradition as it emerged in the beginning of the nineteenth century in Great Britain.

Asked by Whewell for more information on the reasons for Senior's resignation and on the precise nature of the offer made, Jones wrote an explanatory note, adding that the chair would provide a great opportunity to further an alternative to the political economy of the Oxford school. Referring to the pressing issue of tithe-conversion, he wrote that he would not be willing to "act as an 'ecclesiastical puppet' against 'tithe-haters.'"

> [I would oppose] Whatelys and Senior's projects about tithes if I was forced to grapple with the subject in as much as with the needless dogmatism which disfigures all they say or do. They have got a new-fangled system of their own ready cut & dried which they would like to force down the throat of England & Ireland on their authority & without the slightest regard to local difficulties reasonable modifications or any ones views or experience but their own. (Jones 1832b)

One month later it had become clear to Jones that his initial fears about Oxford opposition had been well warranted: all proposed him "*except Copleston* who *opposed* stating there was philosophy in my book which was not Oxford philosophy or to that effect *not that he had read it but was told so*." So this clearly meant that to alter anything in the way in which political economy was practiced and perceived in England, Jones and Whewell had "a hard battle to fight" (Jones 1832c).

The book Jones referred to was his *Essay on the Distribution of Wealth and on the Sources of Taxation* published one year before (1831). The message to be drawn from it was that the Ricardians presented their theory of distribution as a natural and general law in the first place. In contrast, Jones argued, to correctly understand the rules of distribution one had to study the social and institutional order in all its complexity, rather than to present something as natural that was inherently social. As a consequence, political economy could not start from speculative "axioms" and random definitions that were claimed to be universally true; it had to proceed inductively on the basis of sound observations. Once it was seen that this other route to political economy was the appropriate one, it was also clear that this should have consequences for political economists' claims to knowledge and for questions of politics.

Given Jones's and Whewell's opposition to Ricardianism, it was more than unfortunate that the Oriel school of political economy happened to share sides with the Ricardians. Just before his book appeared, Jones discovered to his surprise and annoyance that the Oriel school, Whately and Senior in particular, fundamentally agreed with the Ricardians on questions of method (Corsi 1987; Snyder 2006). It was easy to accuse the Ricardians of a faulty method and a blind spot for God's hand in nature and society, but it was a problematic argument to be made against the Oriel Noetics. This made Jones's and Whewell's attack on speculative political economy not only a hard battle to fight but also a hard battle to win.[1]

At heart were questions of evidence on natural and revealed religion, and what these questions implied for the mechanism of society. These questions were answered very differently in Oxford and Cambridge. In what follows I discuss how Jones's and Whewell's own views on the structuring role of natural theology for questions of method and evidence in the sciences, including political economy, motivated their criticism of the method followed by the Ricardian political economists. From a comparison with Whately, we will see that natural theology was as structuring for him on these issues as it was for the Cambridge men. Whately's solution was, however, in conformity with the Ricardian predilection for theory over facts and carried the day in Victorian England.

Jones on Bentham's "Defence of Usury"

In its finished form, Jones's book consisted essentially of a detailed discussion of different rent-schemes that could be found in different parts

1. Apart from Jones's book, the most durable outcome of Whewell and Jones versus Ricardianism was the establishment of Section F of the British Association for the Advancement of Science in 1833 under the presidency of Adam Sedgwick, and of the London (now Royal) Statistical Society one year later.

of the world. In their long years of correspondence, Whewell and Jones had explicitly conceived of the book as a weapon and a showpiece—a weapon against the Ricardians and a showpiece to convince all those who were seriously troubled by the theories and learning of the political economists that in this department of knowledge something more "cheering" could be established on sound scientific principles. Whewell had pushed Jones to come forward with his book when John Ramsay McCulloch's restatement of Ricardo's *Principles of Political Economy* appeared in the early 1820s. When this moment was lost, Whewell just continued to question Jones about the state of his "Eurydice of political economy" and when it was to appear (Whewell 1827).

How this Eurydice would look could be gleaned from a somewhat lesser goddess Jones had published anonymously in 1825, in which he argued against the repeal of the usury laws.[2] In his preliminary remarks Jones argued that on "wide and sweeping general principles" the usury laws might be found to favor the landed interests while being disastrous to the interests of industry and trade. An investigation of the matter that rested on "acquaintance with its details" might, however, show that such principles were "delusions" that "can never throw any useful light upon the subject" (Jones 1825, 3).

Jones took particular issue with Bentham's *Defence of Usury*. This tract served as exemplar of the obtuse way in which "the maxims and speculations of theoretical writers" became completely mixed up with "the facts of the case in the public mind," so that he first had to clear the ground before any intelligible "practical inquiry" could be pursued. To this effect, Jones confronted his critical investigation of Bentham with the evidence brought before the committee of the House of Commons. The difficulty of Jones's investigation was aggravated by the high praise that greeted Bentham's tract. Jones quoted Sir Francis Baring, who hailed the book's "perfectly unanswerable" logic, and Dugald Stewart's equally high praise, which was then "echoed back by a thousand voices" (Jones 1825, 4–5). Quoting Father Buffier, Jones warned that there was a "species of madman," who made an "excellent logician," but was similar to the scholastic

2. *Reasons against the Repeal of the Usury Laws* is identified as Jones's in Whewell's own handwriting. It was collected in one of Whewell's own books, call mark S.14.66.1 in the Wren library at Trinity College. Strangely enough, I have found no reference to this book in all of the available correspondence between Whewell and Jones I know of, and this despite the fact that by 1825 Whewell and Jones corresponded intensively on the false method and false conclusions of political economists.

defenders of "metaphysical paradoxes" without being interested in the relation of fact and theory (20n).

Bentham was a fine example of such a madman. According to Jones (1825), Bentham's arguments made only a small part of *Defence of Usury*, which was mostly a "Parody on Blackstone, with whose bad political economy Mr. Bentham is much amused" (6). Bentham's arguments came to two: first, every man has the right to make the most of his property; second, freedom of trade is never interrupted without certain known bad consequences. This was also true for trade in money. Jones granted Bentham the liberty to flesh out the logical consequences of these propositions; what he disputed was the claim that these consequences had anything to do with facts. This split between theory and facts was clear from Bentham's "peculiar mode of discussion":

> "As the world," he [Bentham] says, "has no mouth of its own to plead by, no certain attorney by which it can come and defend its force and injury, I must even find arguments for it at a venture, and *ransack my own imagination for such phantoms as I can find to fight with*." And he afterwards states himself to have been combating with such arguments as fancy, rather than observation, has suggested to his view. (16)

The "marked inconvenience" of Bentham's speculative approach was that fancy might easily be mistaken for fact, so that the arguments "will be inapplicable and aimless, however ingenious" (16). This was exactly the conclusion Jones drew from a comparison of Bentham's fictions with the evidence given before the committee of the House of Commons. Bentham's first argument hardly needed refutation from this quarter, however, because it was a generally "recognised principle, that society has a right to interfere with the otherwise unrestrained dominion of the individuals which compose it," if the actions of individuals would be "inconsistent with the well-being of society at large" (7). For Jones, self-interest was no sure compass for the benefit of society. Bentham's one-sided emphasis on the alleged protection the usury laws provided to the landed interests overlooked that these laws served another and more important purpose, namely, the protection of the needy and poor. But Bentham and his followers simply substituted fictions for facts.

In evidence Jones quoted from Ricardo's statements for the committee. Asked to compare transactions at the legal and at market rate of interest, Ricardo answered that he "had no knowledge of any such transactions, but my opinion is very decided, that they have been more injured by having been prevented from borrowing money at the market-rate of interest" (quoted in Jones 1825, 53–54). For Jones (1825, 54), this was a good example of the "substitution of the conclusions of speculations for the results of experience. . . . it is the decision of a theory, not evidence to a fact." Ricardo's claim that market outcomes were always to be preferred was explicitly contradicted by the evidence given by no less than N. M. Rothschild, who in a separate letter to the committee pleaded to maintain the usury laws in the interests of the poor (quoted in Jones 1825, 97–98).

Going through the evidence, Jones concluded that Bentham and his allies had accused the landed interests without ground. The usury laws were designed to protect not the landed interests but, more important, the interests of the needy and poor. Of the evidence given, it could not be concluded that the interests of industry and trade were harmed. Therefore the usury laws should be preserved to continue their "wholesome influence on the constitution and manners of the country." Their "annihilation" might just be a "fearful and intricate experiment upon the moral habits of the great body of the people," with highly uncertain outcomes (Jones 1825, 1).

One may take this conclusion as a mere indicator of Jones's conservatism, which is true, but that does not do justice to Jones's fundamental point about the relation of theory and evidence in political economy. Bentham was happy to serve as spokesman for the facts if these refused to speak for themselves. Jones, by contrast, rejected policy conclusions drawn from a merely speculative investigation of society because of their seriously destabilizing consequences for the social order. To rely on self-interest was to draw a blind check on a supposed mechanism that would guide human conduct to the common good.

The "Dismal Systems" of Political Economists

In his *Essay on the Distribution of Wealth* of 1831, Jones basically followed the same strategy of discrediting the political economists by arguing that their speculative systems were based on arbitrary definitions and illegitimately generalized scant observations. From his introduction (which was written in close cooperation with Whewell) it became, however, more clear than we have seen so far that Jones's rejection of speculative political economy was motivated not only by his fears for a collapse of the social order but also by fundamental religious concerns. This held true in particular for Thomas Robert Malthus's law of population.

In their correspondence Whewell and Jones had already criticized the speculative nature of Malthus's law. In a letter of 28 June 1829, Whewell drew Jones's attention to a small-scale attempt of John Lubbock (a student of Whewell's) to give statistical precision to Malthus's law. Lubbock's suggestion was not based on found but on imagined statistical data, and so was not something Jones was eager to follow up himself (Whewell 1829). Apart from the problematic statistical status of Malthus's law, there was an even more pressing problem that was perceived not only at Cambridge but in Oxford as well, as we will see below. In his original essay Malthus made clear that the distressful position of the poor could not be attributed to the social arrangements of society but was the inevitable outcome of laws of nature, whatever the arrangement of society might be. Malthus considered even abstinence or postponement of marriages to provide only temporary relief to population pressure that would inevitably bring down the wealth of the masses to subsistence level. If this were so, there was no escape from poverty and pauperism for the greatest part of the population.[3]

Jones in particular took issue with this "dismal" message. It was a direct challenge to God's Providence. At the turn of the century it had become popular to prove the existence of God from the order of nature, a tradition referred to as natural theology. This loose reference is sufficient to see Jones's (and Whewell's) difficulties with Malthus. Jones ([1831] 1964, xiii) praised Malthus's theory of rent, which overcame many of his predecessors' "errors," but his theory of population pressure had distinctly thrown a "gloom over the whole subject" by enforcing "an apparent inconsistency between the permanence of human happiness, and the natural action of the laws established by Providence." If nature was so constituted that its laws kept large parts of humanity in a state of inescapable misery, this implied a direct challenge to God's wisdom and goodness.

Shielding Malthus, a Cambridge man himself, from too harsh criticism, Jones argued that it was the unfortunate fate of "really eminent men" like Malthus that not only their wisdom but also their errors should be "fertile in consequences" (ix). His "followers" misused him to develop those "dismal systems which teach that the whole human race is under the resistless dominion of an impulse, forcing ever its aggregate numbers forwards to the extreme limit they can procure; and that even wealth

3. Over the various editions of his essay, however, Malthus changed his views on this issue considerably. See, in particular, Waterman 1991. See also Winch 1996.

and plenty are only forces which impel communities gradually, but inevitably, towards want."[4] Jones blamed the Ricardians for extending the "gloomy fate, the constant tendency to decline" present in Malthus's law of population pressure to a conflict within the different layers of society itself. The Ricardian theory of rent showed "essential contradictions and differences" to exist between the "fortunes and varying relative position of the different orders of society." Hence it was for good reasons that a "feeling of dislike" crept over the public mind and that political economy, as a subject, became "distrusted" (xviii).

We see then that Jones's engagement with the political economists' "dismal system" was motivated by a wish to countenance its message that the providential order in nature was to push humankind permanently to a state of want, and the order of society was a permanent state of conflict. If, by contrast, political economists would proceed on the same inductive method followed in all of the sciences, it was readily seen that both conclusions lost their inevitability and even proved to be contradicted by the facts. "As soon as we draw our eyes from books to consult the statistical map of the world," Jones could show that the inevitable wedge between the increase of food and population did not exist or was even contradicted. An "unprejudiced observer" could see "populations, whose means are comparatively ample, increasing less rapidly than those who are confessedly most wretched." This at least suggested "causes which coming into action during progress of plenty and refinement" prevented men from falling into "misery" and "unmixed vice" (Jones [1831] 1964, xvii).

By comparing different social arrangements, Jones showed that rent did not universally result from Ricardo's principle of diminishing returns on marginal lands but was dependent on the specific social arrangements of different countries. Jones questioned the relevance of Ricardo's principle even for those nations that could be classified as having the (Ricardian) farmer's rent system (i.e., England and Holland). Hence Ricardo's conclusions were only valid under the artificial assumptions that farmers

4. This relatively mild treatment of Malthus was also motivated by Whewell's and Jones's conviction that Malthus was actually on their side against the Ricardians because of his opposite opinions on the repeal of the Corn Laws. They also considered him an adherent of an inductive approach to political economy and so asked him for support for establishing Section F of the British Association for the Advancement of Science. In a letter to Jones, Whewell wrote that he and Malthus were members of the "moral school" of political economy as opposed to the "speculative school" of the Ricardians. In correspondence with Whewell, Malthus made clear that his relation to Ricardo, in particular on questions of method, was more complex than Whewell considered. For a discussion of this correspondence, see De Marchi and Sturges 1973.

did not, or were not able to, improve the quality of the soil, or to improve yields by improving on farming techniques, an assumption contradicted by inspecting the available evidence.

Jones's conclusion was that no society, neither now nor in history, could be identified where the landed interests were opposed to those of the other classes in society. The more "cheering, because more comprehensive" conclusion was that "all systems were essentially false and delusive, which suppose that the permanent gain and advantage of the community, can be founded on the loss of another class" (Jones [1831] 1964, 328). On the negative side, then, Jones's classification of rent systems, and his comparative analysis of economic development in different nations, removed the dismal gloom from political economy. On the positive side it served to show that

> the same providence which has knit together the affections and sympathies of mankind . . . has, in perfect consistency with its own purposes, so arranged the economic laws which determine the social condition of the various classes of communities of men, as to make the permanent and progressive prosperity of each, essentially dependent on the common advance of all. (328–29)

Given David Levy's recent tracing of the origins of the phrase "dismal science" to Thomas Carlyle's controversy with John Stuart Mill over slavery in *Fraser's Review* in the 1850s, this last point may need some emphasis.[5] Levy very interestingly shows that Carlyle used "dismal science" as a label to refer to the political economists who opposed slavery. I don't dispute this. But before Carlyle coined this exact phrase, it was common usage, and I suspect not only in the Cambridge network that Jones and Whewell were a part of, to think of the systems of political economists as "dismal" because they put into question the goodness of the creation, the morality of humanity, and the reality of a society that gradually and harmoniously progressed toward a more happy state for all.

Whewell on Natural Theology and Induction

Whewell (1830) agreed with Jones that "modern economists . . . jump . . . from one or two trivial facts to the conclusion that every man will get as much money as he can, an axioma generallissimum." In contrast, Whewell

5. See Levy 2001.

praised Jones for following the proper method of scientific inquiry, induction. In the beginning of 1830 Whewell did not yet have his mature theory of induction of his *Philosophy of the Inductive Sciences* (1840).[6] From his notebooks of this period, Menachem Fisch (1991a) reconstructs Whewell's search for the philosophical foundation of the correct method of induction. We will not pursue Whewell's route here, but instead take a brief look at *Astronomy and General Physics, Considered with Reference to Natural Theology,* which he published in 1833. The book was commissioned as one of the Bridgewater Treatises, which were intended to show the conformity of science and religion.[7]

Analogies of the great clockwork of the heavens with God's intentional design had been commonly used to prove the existence of God in the eighteenth century. Such comparisons had lost some of their appeal by the time Whewell published his book, not so much because they were considered false but because they were considered too simple and so were not sufficient to prove the point (Brooke 1991b). The emphasis had shifted to proving God's existence from systems that were much more complex, like the human eye. This was one of Paley's examples, in his much-acclaimed *Natural Theology* of 1802.[8] Paley compared the complex mechanism of the eye with that of the telescope. He argued that the eye and the telescope should both be considered as instruments that showed "contrivance." That is, both the eye and the telescope were intentionally designed for a purpose. But Paley went on to argue that he did not just draw an analogy between the eye and the telescope. Rather, the eye and the telescope embodied essentially the same mechanism. And so, because the telescope was designed by an intelligence, man, so the eye, a much more refined but in its bare bones the same instrument, could not otherwise have come into existence than by an intelligent maker—God.

Paley considered the similarity of the mechanisms of the eye and telescope a sufficient refutation of the argument that such mechanisms could have come about by mere chance; they presupposed intelligence.[9] But

6. There is a wealth of literature on Whewell's philosophy of induction. In the space of just one essay, Menachem Fisch (1991a) provides a very complete account. See also Fisch 1991b, Yeo 1993, and Snyder 2006.

7. On the history and reception of the Bridgewater Treatises, see, for example, Brock 1966 and Topham 1998.

8. On the reception of Paley's *Natural Theology* at Cambridge, see Fyfe 1997. On the argumentative strategy of Paley in *Natural Theology*, see Nuovo 1992.

9. For a much more extensive reading of Whewell's views on natural theology, see Brooke 1977, 1991a, 1991b. See also Yeo 1993.

Whewell considered that if the argument for the existence of a deity hinged only on the similarity of human and divine design, it was easy for man to mistake himself for God. Whewell therefore became much more reserved to the kind of mathematics favored by the short-lived Analytical Society than he had been as a freshman in Cambridge.[10] The hubris to which the mathematician might fall victim was to "substitute for the Deity certain axioms and first principles, as the cause of all," with the consequence that he might be "thrusting some mechanic cause into the place of God" (Whewell [1833] 2001, 332).

Arguing against those "great [French] mathematicians who have laboured with such wonderful success in unfolding the mechanism of the heavens" (327), Whewell wrote that an appropriate conception of the "Divine purpose and agency" must "go beyond the analogy with human contrivances. We must conceive the Deity, not only as constructing the most refined and vast machinery . . . we must also imagine him as establishing those properties by which such machinery is possible" (360). Hence Whewell denied "mechanical philosophers and mathematicians of recent times any authority with regard to their views of the administration of the universe; we have no reason whatever to expect from their speculations any help, when we ascend to the first cause and supreme ruler of the universe" (334).

Arbitrary definitions and axioms were like a train in a tunnel; they might well help you find solutions quickly, but they did not show you how these definitions and axioms might have their grounds in nature itself—if indeed they had any such ground at all. For Whewell, symbolic algebra might be helpful as an organizational device, and as an instrument to find solutions, but it was not the appropriate tool to discover the true order in nature. Rather than disclose this order, it concealed it. In teaching, the moral drawback of such arbitrary notational systems was that students wrongly could get the idea that they gave order to nature, rather than that they were made aware that the order they were searching for was not arbitrary but already there.

For Whewell this meant that "deductive habits" of investigation had to give way to induction; one could not impose one type of laws as governing the universe. Rather, one should see God's hand from a gradual discovery of the various laws governing nature and society. Not incidentally, the

10. For a very good interpretation of Whewell's thoughts on mathematics, see Fisch 1991a, 1994. Whewell formulated his views, among others, in *Thoughts on the Study of Mathematics as a Part of a Liberal Education* (1835). See also Becher 1981.

chapter on inductive and deductive habits of thought was the one Whewell was most pleased with and anxious of to hear the opinions of his friends and colleagues.

From the foregoing, we can understand that Whewell's rejection of Ricardianism was motivated by methodological concerns. These were in their turn rooted in his theological convictions. When Whewell told Jones of his intentions to formalize the theory of rent of the Ricardians so that he could show that their conclusions were even false on their own "axioms," Jones warned him to make clear that he would proceed on their assumptions and not on his own; he should make it clear that he at no point subscribed to them. No mechanism, no laws could be imposed on society that did not emerge from a careful study of historical facts. It could not even be supposed that the laws governing society, if there were any, were of the same nature as those of mechanics.

The fundamental difference between Jones and Whewell, on the one hand, and the Ricardians, on the other, was that the latter imposed a theory on society and so ignored the order of society that had emerged over history. An investigation of this order could proceed only inductively, on the basis of the found facts of history. In response to McCulloch's claim that Ricardo did not use the term *rent* "in the ordinary and vulgar sense of the word," Whewell wrote in the preface to his edition of Jones's *Nachlass* that he left it to the reader "to decide for himself which subject of inquiry is better worth his notice,—the rents that are actually paid in *every* country, or the Ricardian rents, which are *not* those actually paid in *any* country" (Jones [1859] 1964, xii–xii).

A Mandevillian Budget of Paradoxes: Whately on Method

Whately had a very different way to reconcile contemporary political economy with Paley's *Natural Theology*. The Oxford men were as much concerned with the philippics of the political radicals against the established church and the old institutes of learning as the Cambridge network. As examples one may think of the Subscription controversy, of their proposals to extend the franchise, and of their notorious anticlericalism and atheism as expressed, for example, in Bentham's *Not Paul, but Jesus* that appeared anonymously in 1823. This book received the obvious reaction that its actual message was "Neither Paul nor Jesus" (quoted in Crimmins 1990, 231).

Just like Hume's essay *On Miracles*, Bentham's book was about the evidence of the scriptures, but it was written in a much more violent and uncompromising voice. T. S. Hughes, at the time the Christian Advocate of Cambridge University and officially assigned to respond to such literature, wrote that this book, in its attack on St. Paul, tried to "remove" one of the "main pillars, and principal ornaments" of the "Christian edifice" (quoted in Crimmins 1990, 230). Crimmins notes that if Bentham had published some of his manuscript materials, the public reactions would have been even more extreme. In them Bentham constructed from a literal reading of the New Testament a "Mandevillian interpretation" that made self-interest, rather than altruism, the prime motor of society. In Crimmins's words, "If all of us seek to do good to others whenever and wherever we can then we would destroy ourselves; by neglecting our labours to serve others . . . we would give up . . . our own preservation" (233–34).

Whately (1832, 4) of course never saw these manuscripts, and in his introductory lectures on political economy he used the word *Mandevillian* in opposition to the above, to denote those who argued for the "incompatibility or discordancy of national Wealth, and Virtue." Yet he made self-interest as central to his analysis as it had been for Mandeville and was for Bentham in arguing that self-interest and the common good were *not* incompatible. And here Whately centrally diverged from the Cambridge men. Whately first secured the propriety of political economy as a subject of study by distinguishing between its scientific and moral values.[11] From a study of the subject of wealth, and the principles that governed it, nothing followed as to its moral merits, nor could anything morally be derived from it. Just as a physician's advice to patients was to be taken to relate to their bodily health only, so did this hold for political economy; there was no "morally" prescriptive meaning to its conclusions. Nothing, then, prevented a systematic investigation of the principles governing the pursuit of wealth. There was nothing un-Christian in an open-minded investigation of the social mechanics of self-interest.

As Anthony Waterman observed, Whately, before being appointed Drummond professor in political economy, considered that his lectures might be used "as sort of continuation of Paley's 'Natural Theology'"

11. This point is much emphasized by Waterman, who considers Whately's distinction between the positive and the normative as a perfect example of the "Anglican genius" of finding a "*via media* through which to steer the ship of church and state." See Waterman 1991.

(Whately, quoted in Waterman 1991, 212). Just as Paley had shown "contrivance" to be central to natural theology, so Whately set out to show that there was not only "contrivance" in the "structure of organized bodies" of the natural world but that "an attentive study of the constitution of Society, would bring to light a no less admirable apparatus of divinely-wise contrivances, directed no less to beneficial ends" (quoted in Waterman 1991, 212). Almost explicitly referring to Mandeville, Whately (1832, 89) continued to draw a parallel, not between the eye and the telescope but between the bee and the beehive. Just as the "structure of the single bee" was "admirable," this was even more so for the "hive of bees, instinctively directing their efforts towards a common object." The very same instinctive, unconscious mode of operation could be found in human society.

> For instance, let any one propose to himself the problem of supplying with daily provisions of all kinds a city as our metropolis, containing above a million of inhabitants. Let him imagine himself a head-commissary, entrusted with the office of furnishing to this enormous host their daily rations. . . . this object is accomplished far better than it could be by any effort of human wisdom, through the agency of men, who think of nothing beyond his own immediate interest . . . and combine unconsciously to employ the wisest means for effecting an object, the vastness of which it would bewilder them even to contemplate. (93–96)

The presence of such a system showed that "Man, considered not merely as an organized Being, but as a rational agent, is perhaps the most wonderfully contrived . . . specimen of divine Wisdom" (100).

In more than one sense was Whately's famous example itself an example of a Mandevillian investigation.[12] First, because of its emphasis on self-interest as the unconscious motive power of human agency, which had been well put in place by "divine Wisdom." Second, because it was an example of what Whately called Mandeville's "hypothetical" approach. According to Whately, Mandeville argued that "*if* such and such" were the case, then these were the consequences. The great merit of Mandeville's notorious *Fable* was that it showed the general public that it was

12. Without referring to Whately, Paul Samuelson (1958, 37) adapted Whately's "famous economic example" in his economics textbook, arguing that it was "alone convincing proof that a competitive system of markets and prices . . . is not a system of chaos and anarchy. . . . It works." See also Waterman 1991, 212. I would like to thank Anthony Waterman for pointing me to this reference.

impossible to hold two contradictory hypotheses simultaneously. By showing these contradictions, Mandeville questioned the assumptions maintained by common sense. Referring to Francis Bacon, Whately (1832, 64) argued that "science" did not "dispense with common-sense" but used it "more profitably," just as "the adoption of Arabic numerals and of the Algebraic symbols, does not supersede calculation, but extends its sphere." According to Whately, there was no subject of study where "paradoxical theory" was more important than "in matters concerning Political-Economy." Examples such as that "a man is a benefactor to the community by building himself a splendid palace" was a "*paradoxical* truth" that might have "*sense*," even though no "*common*-sense" (72). The purpose of political economy was to clarify such paradoxes and so to gain insight into the true nature of society.

Whewell (1990, 80) had little more to say about Mandeville's *Fable* than that it was written "with little or no literary merit." It merely served him as an example of those "common and so licentious" attacks on "religion and morals" in the eighteenth century that played a role in contemporary "battles of speculators concerning Morals, Politics, and Religion" (81). In contrast, Whately turned Mandeville's approach to the study of society into the cornerstone of his reconciliation of the teachings of the political economists with natural theology. While Whewell and Jones refused to impose a theory or "mechanism" on society, Whately, much in Mandeville's footsteps, emphasized the unconscious working of self-interest to the benefit of the community as the principal "contrivance" that divine wisdom had incorporated into society to make it "work." Even though no *moral* meaning could be attached to this, its practical implication was that it was far better to rely on self-interest played out in the market than on state interventions for the benefit of all.[13]

There was, however, a high degree of "if-ness" about Whately's views; Whately based his opinion about the "paradoxical truths" of political economy on thought experiments like the food supply in London, rather than on a careful investigation of facts and institutions that historically were in place to provide this supply in the concrete. In Whewell's and Jones's views, Whately reveled therefore as much in hypothetical speculations and paradoxes as did Mandeville, Bentham, and the Ricardians.

13. It falls outside the scope of this article to investigate Whately's influence on the political economic discourse in Ireland. As shown by Tom Boylan and Tadhg Foley, the Irish famine "crucially challenged political economy" as advocated by the Oxford school. See Boylan and Foley 1996. See also Johnson 2005.

No History Please, We're Political Economists

It seems that Whewell and Jones became aware of their fundamental disagreement with the Oriel political economists on the method of political economy only when Jones's long-awaited "Miss Political Economy" was already in press.[14] Pietro Corsi (1987, 119–20) plausibly argues that the unnumbered page in Jones's book between the table of contents and page 1 was inserted only after Jones had read Whately's *Logic*. Immediately after reading this book Jones (1831a) sent an infuriated letter to Whewell in which he took high issue with Senior's claims in the appendix that "the foundations of political economy [were] a few general propositions—deduced from observation or from consciousness & generally admitted as soon as stated." This made Senior an exemplar of the "anticipators" whom Bacon had opposed and a "father of errors & destroyer of the sciences" (see also Maas 2005, chap. 3).

Whewell and Jones could have foreseen a clash between their view and that of the Oxford men from Copleston's two letters on issues of political economy to Peel. In the first letter, Copleston referred approvingly to Ricardo's *Principles* in which "the fact" appeared to be "well established, that a rise in wages is a diminution not of rent, but of profits." Copleston (1819, 36–37) commented that "whatever is theoretically true we may be sure is really acted upon by the interested party, however unconscious he may be of the abstract principle, and even unable to comprehend it," a conclusion that was of course unacceptable to Whewell and Jones.[15]

Also Whately's extremely witty and well-received *Historic Doubts Relative to Napoleon Bonaparte*, first published in 1819 and immediately very popular, should have warned Whewell and Jones for the strongly anti-inductivist bends of the Oxford Noetics. This small tract was published anonymously, however, but speculations about its authorship pointed in Whately's direction. It was a typical product of the lunch table conversations in the Oriel Common Room between Whately and Copleston. Discussing Hume on miracles, Whately and Copleston considered how easy it was to undermine historical evidence in ways similar to how Hume

14. The section heading is an allusion to Blaug 2001. The fraught relation of (political) economists to history seems to be remarkably persistent over time.

15. See Copleston 1819. These letters are part of Whewell's collections of political economy manuscripts, TCC S.17.6/2. To help Jones write his book, Whewell collected as many political economy tracts as he could lay his hands on. The first letter was on monetary issues, the second on the causes and consequences of the Poor Laws.

had questioned the evidence of the scriptures on their contradictory accounts of miracles.[16]

On the inserted page Jones defended his "omission" of a "regular definition of the word *Rent*" in his book.

> On a subject like this, to attempt to draw conclusions from definitions, is almost a sure step towards error. A dissertation, however, on the use and abuse of definitions would be out of place here. . . . If any reader . . . is really puzzled to know what we are observing together [in the book], I shall be sorry: but I am quite sure that I should do him no real service by presenting him in the outset with a definition to reason from.

Jones's provocation was not spilled on Whately, who answered with a blistering attack on the merits of the inductive method as propagated by the Cambridge men. Whately gave short shrift to Jones's efforts to ground political economy in history. To do so was to "rejoice in a fog" of ambiguity (Whately [1832] 1966, 242). In contrast, the "pure science" of political economy was better served by taking clear definitions as its starting point, just as Senior had proposed in his own introduction to the topic. The use of definitions was to clarify the resulting "confusion and inaccuracy" and was perhaps the "most essential step" to be made (Whately [1832] 1966, 228–29).

Whately made his attack in his ninth lecture on political economy, which he added to the second edition of his *Introductory Lectures*. Whately granted the Cambridge men that political economy started from facts, but immediately continued to ask what might be meant with this. It certainly could not be the "heap" of historical evidence that pointed only in different and contradictory directions. Those who (like Jones) started from collecting data "from all quarters—from History—Statistical Accounts—Travels, and all other sources" burdened "their memory with an immense, and . . . *confused* mass of materials" that was more likely to do harm than good. The first harm stemmed from the particular manner in which history and travel journals were written.

The facts of these tracts were more likely to be exceptional (and therefore worth noticing) than common. A naive collector of facts might thus be "heaping" his "materials together . . . into some, probably faulty, system, while he is not aware of the process going on in his own mind." By

16. The fourth edition of *Historic Doubts* of 1831 is listed in the catalog of Whewell's books, call mark 164.c.83.5/1. I have no evidence Whewell knew of the book and its author before this date.

focusing on the exceptional rather than the common, the political economist might easily overlook the obvious truths that he immediately would have touched on if he had started from the much greater set of common daily experiences. Hence a political economist relying on history might easily end up with an "erroneous theory" rather than with the true principles of the subject. "Yet such is History!" (Whately [1832] 1966, 235). Whately concluded that if political economy were to start with an inductive historical investigation, its conclusions most likely would be defective. By contrast, "the Logical, not the Physical investigation" should have priority in political economy (239).

Whately basically repeated Senior's claim that the position of political economy was somewhat "peculiar" because in contrast to sciences like geology, which did need to take account of historical facts or an extensive survey of facts, political economy was in need of just a limited number of facts that were, in principle, available to all who engaged in economic activity.[17] That is, "the facts on which the general principles of the science are *founded*, come within the range of every one's experience" and are no different from "those of Baring or Rothschild." Quoting from Senior's own introductory lecture on political economy of 1827, Whately ([1832] 1966, 229) subscribed to Senior's view that "it is in fact as impossible to avoid being a practical Economist, as to avoid being a practical Logician."

Whewell on the Use of Definitions

Jones and Whewell were clearly aware that it was much more difficult to "fight" the Oriel economists than to attack the Ricardians. In the various reviews he wrote of Jones's book, Whewell launched, as Corsi (1987, 121) notes, a "guarded attack" on the Oriel school. Jones warned him to not "unnecessarily provoke the Oriel men" (Jones 1831b).

In a letter of 1 June 1831 Jones complained that Whately had "*not sent*" his introductory lectures, confirming his suspicions of a rift between the Oxford and Cambridge men: "I hope not for if so it will come to a fight." If this were unavoidable, he suggested adding "a few pages" to his next

17. Whately most likely mentioned geology in reference to William Buckland, whose discovery of a long-extinct dinosaur in the fields of Oxford caused a stir and renewed investigations into natural theology. Buckland also wrote a Bridgewater Treatise. Even though Whately wrote a eulogy on Buckland, Buckland's attitude toward science was much closer to the men in the Cambridge circuit and the BAAS. See Brooke 1991b. See also Morrell and Thackray 1981.

book on labor "on the use & abuse of definitions," showing that "*we do* know something of their use." Examples of abuse should be taken from "Whatelys *own* books." Jones took particular offense at Whately's adoption of "man" as an "animal that makes exchanges" and that only in this regard was "contemplated by political economy." If this was all that political economy was concerned with, Jones challenged Whately, "do look around you . . . *the greater part* of wealth is never exchanged at all" and yet affected the wealth, habits, and social relations of all classes in society. But if this were excluded *by definition*, not much was to be expected from such an investigation.

At the end of January 1832, Whewell wrote to Jones that he had met Senior in the Athenaeum and had asked him his opinion about "his friend Whately's name of catallactician." On Senior's answer that he did not adopt the name, although he considered it an accurate description of the subject, Whewell "reminded him that more than half the wealth of the world is never exchanged." To this Senior "declared very frankly, that in that case he had no business with it" (Whewell 1832). This encounter may well have prompted Whewell to jot down his own thoughts on the use of definitions and to confront Whately directly.[18]

Whately's suggestion that all humankind, from practical experience, shared on a general level the same experiences as Baring and Rothschild simply passed over the fact that Jones had quoted in his tract against Bentham, that Rothschild was asked to give evidence for the committee of the House of Commons because he could draw on expert experiences that were *not* shared by everyone. Whereas Whately in his *Historic Doubts* and *Ninth Lecture* questioned how to weigh conflicting historical evidence, one might well turn this same question to Whately and ask him from what high grounds of experience he could claim there was a common experience that overruled specific experiences? According to Whewell and Jones, it was only by a dogmatic decision that the tedious inductive interplay between definitions, nomenclature, and empirical data could be "avoided."

Whewell published his small paper "On the Use of Definitions" in 1832 in the short-lived *Philological Museum*.[19] Drawing on Whately's distinction between geometry and the other sciences, Whewell argued that the

18. For an extensive investigation of the ensuing "fight" with the Oxford men, see Corsi 1987. See also Snyder 2006, esp. chap. 5.

19. I quote from a copy of Whewell's essay from his own library, TCC call mark 164.c.83.5[5].

case was different for geometry because there the definitions "*are* themselves the first principles of our reasonings," which were "independent of the external world." But this was not so for the empirical sciences. In all the other branches of knowledge, "exact definitions have been, not the causes, but the consequences of an advance in our knowledge" and "*followed* the settlement" of a scientific dispute (Whewell 1832, 2–3). To show the absurdity of starting with exact definitions, Whewell gave the example of a criticism of a paper read to the Geological Society titled "The Green Sand." On this occasion "a distinguished geologist" criticized the use of "The," "Green," and "Sand," because there were several green sands that were not green but "more commonly" red, and "more calcareous than siliceous." Even though the "subtlety" of this criticism was "applauded," it did not prevent geologists from referring to this class of sands in this way. If geologists should have waited for an "unimpeachable" definition of his subject of investigation, they should have "arrested [their] researches" on the spot (7–8).

The same was true for the study of political economy. "Voyages and travels, history and legislation, politics and statistics" would all be needed to "arrive at general classifications." It would only be "*then*" that "definitions enable us to express our laws." But the "most celebrated teachers" of political economy ignored this clear answer to how political economy should be studied, because they "scorn[ed] the prospect of collecting *their* principles by this slow and laborious process of observation and comparison. Their truths are to flow from the inexhaustible fountain of *definition without previous knowledge and classification of facts*" (9).

As we have seen, Whately had ridiculed Jones's disclaimer to give an exact definition of rent. The effect of Jones's warnings against exact definitions was in Whately's ([1832] 1966, 242) views only to put "a man of well-trained understanding . . . on his guard; well knowing what description of persons are usually foremost in a mob that is clamouring against Police and Gas-lights." Directly referring to Whately, Whewell rebutted that this allegation "touches not us." One might be "rash enough" to define rent "upon some conjectural hypothesis," but in doing so "our chance of any further success in our enquiry is gone. . . . The way is just as dark as ever, and the only consequence is that . . . we stumble over the lamps themselves" (Whewell 1932, 10).

Whately never responded to Whewell's short essay. As Corsi plausibly suggests, he may have never seen it, because the *Philological Museum* was a periodical that hardly circulated outside Cambridge. From De Marchi and Sturges 1973 we know Malthus read it because Whewell sent it to him. For a moment Malthus felt "a little alarmed" by it, because he thought himself to be Whewell's target. From their correspondence it also becomes clear how much closer Malthus was to the "deductive" political economists than Whewell and Jones could have tolerated. Their efforts to establish an inductive alternative was perhaps well received in the Cambridge network close to the British Association for the Advancement of Science (BAAS), but not in the community of political economists. It is illuminating that Whewell never visited the Political Economy Club, and Jones only twice or so.

As soon as Whewell considered that there was too much of this "rabble-rousing" in Section F of the BAAS and the Statistical Society of London, he lost his interest and even tried to abolish it. Science did not advance by polemics but by the inductive and joint efforts of scientists, that is, by the gradual discovery of truth on the basis of extensive and careful data collection. This was the purpose of the BAAS as it was seen by Whewell and the Cambridge network. A collective effort cultivated the moral character of the scientist and gradually revealed God's providential order in nature and society to them. Here, the explicit anti-utilitarian, anti-self-interested stance of Whewell and the Cambridge network finds its place. Though Whewell's pen was good enough for a row, his convictions about nature and science and the method of political economy made him effectively dodge an open fight with the Oxford Noetics by publishing his answer to Whately in the obscure *Philological Museum.*

Conclusion

In his 1991 book on Christian political economy, Anthony Waterman mentions Richard Jones only in his preliminary attempt to define what is and what is not to be understood under this label.[20] In contrast with Salim Rashid's use that includes "any English-speaking economist in Holy Orders from Joshua Tucker . . . to Richard Jones," Waterman (1991, 12) prefers a more restricted use that includes only those who combine "classical political economy . . . with Christian—specifically Anglican—theology in normative social theory."

Such a definition presupposes, however, that there was in the period a commonly accepted doctrine or body of knowledge, something that seems

20. See also Waterman, this volume.

to be Waterman's opinion. Yet we have seen that Oxford and Cambridge men drew very different consequences from Paley's *Natural Theology* in matters of political economy. While the Oxford Noetics were perfectly happy to embrace the idea of "contrivance" in society, in the form of self-interested behavior leading to the common good, this was not so within the Cambridge network. Rather than accept its utilitarian and selfish overtones, they dismissed all a priori imputations of an organizing mechanism on society. Just as nature could not be studied as one grand machine, so was a careful inductive study of society needed that gradually should reveal its various and diverse ordering principles.

It is only on the exclusion of the work of Jones and Whewell that Waterman can write that around 1820 political economy was studied in a united voice. According to Waterman, this unity was disrupted by controversies not so much over its appropriate method of study but over its "ideology." Apparently, "all good theory" followed the same abstract, analytic method. That is what made political economy scientific. On this reading, to question the abstract deductive method of theorizing of the Ricardians was not relevant for its relation to Christianity. Yet Jones and Whewell questioned this theory and this method, because it mistook fictions for facts. For Jones and Whewell, the deductive method of the Oxford Noetics and the political radicals was precisely at stake in their attacks; it was the a priori method of political economy that embodied its antireligious bent. Its political consequence was, of course, that no a priori trust could be set in self-interest and the market. In contrast, the Cambridge men put their trust in the received Anglican institutions and their controlling role in matters of morals, not in market "experiments" with highly uncertain and potentially dangerous outcomes.

It's a separate question, and beyond the scope of this article, to investigate why in the second half of the nineteenth century Cambridge and Oxford shifted sympathies with regard to the method of political economy. As far as Cambridge is concerned, Henry Sidgwick's Victorian virtuosity in finding a *via media* between utilitarianism and Whewell's intuitionist views on ethics surely was of importance.[21] The decline of natural theology after the publication of Charles Darwin's *Origin of Species* was important as well. After all, Darwin paid tribute to Malthus in sorting out the mechanism of natural selection. And what was this mechanism other than selfishness and competition played out in nature itself?

21. See Medema, this volume, and Backhouse, this volume.

However this may be, Darwin's *Origin of Species*, Sidgwick's *Method of Ethics*, and John Neville Keynes's *Scope and Method of Political Economy* all sealed the fate of pleas for the inductive method in political economy at Cambridge. Once faith was lost in Cambridge, a priorism reigned supreme.

On 14 July 1839 Whewell wrote Jones from Nuremberg and asked him, as he had done so often before, about the progress made on his planned books: "How do you and your books go on? But in truth I suppose they do not go on" (Todhunter [1876] 2001, 281). Indeed, although Jones still worked on the lectures he gave by then at Haileybury College, as successor in the chair of Malthus, most of his time was devoted to the Tithe-Conversion Committee. And as always, the subject appeared more complex, so that he was in need of more materials to come to conclusions. On 30 April 1848, Whewell asked Jones from Trinity Lodge if he had seen Mill's *Principles*, with which they did not have much to "disagree." It was clear that by this date Whewell had lost contact with the subject. He mused about the days gone by in which they had studied and discussed "Malthus and Ricardo" and wished those days might return. "I mean, I wish this, that I might have your help in getting hold of the subject now, as I had then. Besides, it was very pleasant—and would be so again. Adieu" (Todhunter [1876] 2001, 346).

References

Becher, H. W. 1981. William Whewell and Cambridge Mathematics. *HSPS* 11.1:1–48.

Blaug, M. 2001. No History of Ideas, Please, We're Economists. *Journal of Economic Perspectives* 15.1:145–64.

Boylan, T. A., and T. P. Foley. 1996. A Nation Perishing of Political Economy? In *"Fearful Realities": New Perspectives on the Famine*, edited by C. Morash and R. Hayes. Dublin: Irish Academic Press.

Brock, W. H. 1966. The Selection of the Authors of the Bridgewater Treatises. *Notes and Records of the Royal Society of London* 21.2:162–79.

Brooke, J. H. 1977. Natural Theology and the Plurality of Worlds: Observations on the Brewster-Whewell Debate. *Annals of Science* 34.3:221–86.

———. 1991a. Indications of a Creator: Whewell as Apologist and Priest. In *William Whewell: A Composite Portrait*, edited by M. Fisch and S. Schaffer. Oxford: Clarendon.

———. 1991b. *Science and Religion: Some Historical Perspectives.* Cambridge: Cambridge University Press.

Copleston, E. 1819. *On the Causes of the Increase of Pauperism, and on the Poor Laws.* Oxford: Murray.

Corsi, P. 1987. The Heritage of Dugald Stewart: Oxford Philosophy and the Method of Political Economy. *Nuncius* 11.2:89–144.

Crimmins, J. E. 1990. *Secular Utilitarianism: Social Science and the Critique of Religion in the Thought of Jeremy Bentham*. Oxford: Clarendon.

De Marchi, N. B., and R. P. Sturges. 1973. Malthus and Ricardo's Inductivist Critics: Four Letters to William Whewell. *Economica* 40.160:379–93.

Fisch, M. 1991a. A Philosopher's Coming of Age. In *William Whewell: A Composite Portrait*, edited by M. Fisch and S. Schaffer. Oxford: Clarendon.

———. 1991b. *William Whewell, Philosopher of Science*. Oxford: Clarendon.

———. 1994. "The Emergency Which Has Arrived": The Problematic History of Nineteenth-Century British Algebra—a Programmatic Outline. *British Journal for the History of Science* 27.94:247–76.

Fyfe, A. 1997. The Reception of William Paley's Natural Theology in the University of Cambridge. *British Journal for the History of Science* 30.106:321–35.

Johnson, P. 2005. Market Disciplines in Victorian Britain. Working Papers on the Nature of Evidence: How Well Do "Facts" Travel? No. 06/05.

Jones, R. 1825. *Reasons against the Repeal of the Usury Laws*. London: Murray.

———. 1831a. Letter to Whewell, 24 February. Add.Ms.c52/20, Whewell Papers, Trinity College, Cambridge.

———. 1831b. Letter to Whewell, 7 March. Add.Mss.c.52/26, Whewell Papers, Trinity College, Cambridge.

———. 1832a. Letter to William Whewell, 15 March. Add.Ms.c.52/49, Whewell Papers, Trinity College, Cambridge.

———. 1832b. Letter to William Whewell, 21 March. Add.Ms.c.52/51, Whewell Papers, Trinity College, Cambridge.

———. 1832c. Letter to William Whewell, 28 April. Add.Ms.c.52/53, Whewell Papers, Trinity College, Cambridge.

———. [1831] 1964. *An Essay on the Distribution of Wealth and on the Sources of Taxation*. New York: Kelley.

Levy, D. M. 2001. *How the Dismal Science Got Its Name: Classical Economics and the Ur-Text of Racial Politics*. Ann Arbor: University of Michigan Press.

Maas, H. 2005. *William Stanley Jevons and the Making of Modern Economics*. New York: Cambridge University Press.

Morrell, J., and A. Thackray. 1981. *Gentlemen of Science: Early Years of the British Association for the Advancement of Science*. Oxford: Clarendon.

Nuovo, V. 1992. Rethinking Paley. *Synthese* 91.1–2:29–51.

Paley, W. [1802] 2006. *Natural Theology: Or, Evidence of the Existence and Attributes of the Deity, Collected from the Appearances of Nature*. Edited by M. Eddy and D. M. Knight. Oxford: Oxford University Press.

Samuelson, P. A. 1958. *Economics: An Introductory Analysis*. New York: McGraw-Hill.

Snyder, L. J. 2006. *Reforming Philosophy: A Victorian Debate on Science and Society*. Chicago: University of Chicago Press.

Todhunter, I. [1876] 2001. *William Whewell: An Account of His Writings, with Selections from His Literary and Scientific Correspondence*. Bristol, U.K.: Thoemmes.

Topham, J. R. 1998. Beyond the "Common Context": The Production and Reading of the Bridgewater Treatises. *Isis* 89.2:233–62.

Waterman, A. M. C. 1991. *Revolution, Economics, and Religion: Christian Political Economy, 1798–1833*. Cambridge: Cambridge University Press.

Whately, R. [1832] 1966. *Introductory Lectures on Political Economy*. New York: Kelley.

———. 1985. *Historic Doubts Relative to Napoleon Bonaparte*. Berkeley: Scolar.

Whewell, W. 1827. Letter to Richard Jones, September. Add.Ms.c.51/41, Whewell Papers, Trinity College, Cambridge.

———. 1829. Letter to Jones, 28 June. Add.Ms.c.51/67, Whewell Papers, Trinity College, Cambridge.

———. 1830. Letter to Jones, 7 December. Add.Ms.c.51/93, Whewell Papers, Trinity College, Cambridge.

———. 1832. Letter to Jones, 25 January. Add.Ms.c.51/127, Whewell Papers, Trinity College, Cambridge.

———. 1835. *Thoughts on the Study of Mathematics as a Part of a Liberal Education*. Cambridge: Deighton.

———. 1990. *Lectures on the History of Moral Philosophy in England [and] Additional Lectures on the History of Moral Philosophy*. Bristol, U.K.: Thoemmes.

———. [1833] 2001. *Astronomy and General Physics, Considered with Reference to Natural Theology*. Bristol, U.K.: Thoemmes.

Winch, D. 1996. *Riches and Poverty: An Intellectual History of Political Economy in Britain, 1750–1834*. Cambridge: Cambridge University Press.

Yeo, R. 1993. *Defining Science: William Whewell, Natural Knowledge, and Public Debate in Early Victorian Britain*. Cambridge: Cambridge University Press.

An Inquiry into the Nature and Effects of Henry Thornton's Christian Faith on the Existence and Content of His Economic Writings

Neil T. Skaggs

> Evangelicalism explains Henry Thornton as much as ideas can explain any man. To an extraordinary degree, he and his friends, living amid the confusion of infant industrialism and the French Revolution, shaped their thoughts and lives to accord with their belief in God.
> —Standish Meacham, *Henry Thornton of Clapham*

Since Friedrich Hayek's "rediscovery" of *An Enquiry into the Nature and Effects of the Paper Credit of Great Britain* (1802) in the 1930s, Henry Thornton's name has occupied an honored place in the firmament of monetary economists. Although widely respected as a monetary economist in his own era,[1] Thornton was overshadowed throughout the nineteenth

I want to thank Harro Maas and the editors of this volume for valuable comments on earlier versions of this article. Worthy of especial thanks is Anthony Waterman, whose knowledge of eighteenth-century economics and theology prevented me from making many serious errors. Any remaining errors are solely mine.

1. Thornton was acquainted with David Ricardo and Malthus, not to mention Francis Horner and William Huskisson, with whom he served on the Bullion Committee of 1810. He was a good enough monetary theorist to draw the ire of James Mill (1966, 36–37, 163–65, 173–77), who could not countenance Thornton's rejection of certain of Adam Smith's monetary principles. J. R. McCulloch later included the *Paper Credit* in his catalog of notable works on political economy, *The Literature of Political Economy* (1845), though he disparaged Thornton's theory and was the source of the false belief that *Henry* Thornton had been a governor of the Bank of England.

History of Political Economy 40 (annual suppl.) DOI 10.1215/00182702-2007-065

century by his contemporary, David Ricardo. In the past several decades, however, Thornton has come to be recognized as a monetary theorist of the first order. In his own time, Thornton was even better known as an evangelical Christian, coleader with William Wilberforce of the "moderate evangelical" wing of the Church of England, financier of the anti–slave trade movement, and writer of Christian literature.

Thornton wrote in an era before economics was firmly separated from other disciplines, including theology. Given his lifelong devotion to God, contemporary readers might well have expected that Thornton's writings would blend economics and theology, much as the writings of his contemporaries William Paley and Thomas Robert Malthus did. But such readers would have been wrong; the *Paper Credit* is a purely technical exercise in monetary macroeconomics. Even when discussing a topic linked historically to theology—the usury law—Thornton eschewed theological analysis.

In this article I document both Thornton's wholehearted devotion to God and to doing God's work as Thornton perceived it, as well as Thornton's complete separation of theology and economics. I then speculate on the reasons that might have led him to partition his thinking in a manner uncommon until Richard Whately's demarcation of "scientific" and "religious" knowledge three decades later.

Thornton's Background

Thornton was the third and youngest son of John Thornton, who was from a family of merchants who traded in Russia and who were centered in Hull, Yorkshire. While retaining strong connections with relatives in Hull, John Thornton raised his family in Clapham, only five miles from the City, south of the Thames. Henry's older brothers were respected London merchants; Samuel, the oldest, served a term as governor of the Bank of England.

John Thornton, "the Great and the Good" (Hayek [1939] 1978, 13), was an exceedingly devout Christian. His willingness to give away thousands of pounds each year in acts of charity was legendary. The elder Thornton economized on both time and money in order to spread the Gospel at home and abroad. Henry noted that "ever since I knew him he appeared to me to be a man of commendable temperance & self denial" (Thornton 1802–8, 2).

John Thornton spent many thousands of pounds during his lifetime purchasing "livings" for evangelical clergymen in the Church of England.

His most famous client, the ex–slave trader John Newton, is still well known among English-speaking Christians as the author of the hymn "Amazing Grace." Not all of the ministers favored by his father found favor with Henry. John was more approving of "wild, half-antinomian" preachers than was his youngest son, for whom sound doctrine preached calmly, with ample applications to the Christian's life, was the measure of a good minister. Henry was an evangelical to the very core of his being, teaching his children the Bible and making use of any opportunity to speak of spiritual matters with anyone who would listen.

Although poorly educated in local schools, Henry was intelligent and serious. By his own account, he knew "little or nothing of English history, of mathematics, of natural philosophy, of logic, of belles letters, or of politics" (Thornton 1802–8, 16). However, Thornton possessed a sharp mind and was able to rapidly comprehend any topic he sought to understand. In practice, this meant he learned a great deal about banking, finance and economics, and politics, as well as about the Bible and the Christian ministries that occupied so much of his life.

When Thornton was "approaching the age of 19," he began working in the counting house of Geoffrey Thornton, his father's cousin, where he "chiefly was employed in carrying out bills to be accepted" (16). Two years later he entered his father's counting house, through which John Thornton conducted business under his own name, rather than under the auspices of Thornton Cornwall & Co., his major concern. In the time at his father's firm, Henry became disappointed by his father's "lax accounting habits" and rather haphazard approach to business decision making. Furthermore, young Henry was not earning much working for his father. So it was that he was inclined to listen to a proposition made by one Mr. Richard Poole of Woodford for joining him and his partner in the business of banking. Thornton accepted the offer, and the reconstituted firm of Down, Poole, and Thornton began business in 1784.

"Henry Thornton was undoubtedly a major 'catch' for an ailing banking house" (Acaster 1974, pt. 1, 50). Poole must have recognized that the young Mr. Thornton would soon inherit a sizable sum from his father. Furthermore, Henry was, since 1792, the MP for Southwark. Members of Parliament enjoyed franking privileges, and in the days before the Penny Post, bankers doing business with numerous country correspondents could save a pretty penny by having an MP as partner (51). The offer proved to be a good one for the bank. Thornton developed a sizable network of correspondents. In his words, "We owed much to the kindness of our friends and much also to the circumstances of many country banks rising up at the time, with which we were wise enough to become connected" (51). Much of the "wisdom" shown by the bankers apparently came from Thornton, for before long he was viewed as the master banker of the trio.

Assembling the Clapham Sect

While still single, Thornton purchased a house on Clapham Common and expanded it greatly by adding two wings. The library of Battersea Rise, as the house was known, became from 1792 the center of activity for the evangelicals who gradually gathered around the Common. Wilberforce, who had lived in Battersea Rise before Thornton's marriage to Marianne Sykes in February 1796, remained nearby. This suited Thornton well, as he viewed Wilberforce not only as a friend but as a mentor.

> I owed much to him in every sense soon after I came out in life, for my education had been narrow and his enlarged mind, his affectionate and condescending manners and his very superior piety were exactly calculated to supply what was wanting to my improvement and my establishment in a right course. (Meacham 1964, 38)

Many of the activities that occupied so much of Thornton's time were tied directly to his mentor's interests in social reform, which Wilberforce had expressed thus in 1787: "God Almighty has set before me two great objects—the abolition of the slave trade and the reformation of manners" (quoted in Armstrong 1973, 133).

In 1794 Charles Grant, a merchant in the East India Company who was determined to carry the Christian message to India, settled in a house Thornton had built nearby. John Shore, another East India Company man, later came to Clapham as well (Meacham 1964, 40–41). John Venn became the rector of Clapham in 1792, pastor to Thornton and Wilberforce and the rest of the Clapham Evangelicals. James Stephen, a lawyer who became an evangelical because of his hatred of slavery, later joined the group, as did Zachary Macaulay, who was furious at the treatment of slaves he had witnessed in the West Indies. Others became part of the sect without ever moving to Clapham: Thomas Gisborne, who preached at Yoxnall in Staffordshire, and Thomas Babington from Rothley Temple, Leicestershire, whose personality mirrored Thornton's. And, of course, there was Hannah More of Somerset, whose work with the poor in the Mendip Hills caught his attention. Thornton was, "of those at Clapham, her dearest friend" (Meacham 1964, 48). His financial support of her Sunday schools was crucial to their success. Common interests brought the sect together; Wilberforce and Thornton served as the magnets attracting other like-minded individuals.

Thornton's Faith: The Evangelicalism of Clapham

To really know Henry Thornton, one must begin with his Christian faith, for a large majority of his time as an adult—in and out of Parliament—was devoted to distinctively Christian social endeavors. The Clapham Evangelicals, brought together and given direction by Wilberforce and Thornton, altered British society in ways that would have been hard to imagine in 1790. They led the fight to end the British slave trade, organized and financed the Sierra Leone colony on the west coast of Africa as a home for repatriated Africans, and organized Christian mission outreaches to Africa and India. Thornton was heavily involved in all these affairs and more. Besides helping finance More's Sunday school program, he wrote a sizable portion of the materials used in it. He also wrote, under pseudonyms, numerous articles for and letters to the *Christian Observer*, the main journal of the "moderate evangelicals" in the Church of England.[2] The transformation of English society effected by the Clapham Evangelicals laid much of the foundation for the confrontations between Thomas Carlyle and the Romantic conservatives, on the one hand, and the alliance of utilitarian economists and Exeter Hall evangelicals, on the other, that were played out through the middle of the nineteenth century (Levy and Peart 2003).

What exactly did it mean to be an "evangelical" at the turn of the nineteenth century in Great Britain? Boyd Hilton (1986, 1) has argued, in *The Age of Atonement*, that the evangelical movement "began with an upper- and middle-class reaction against the French Revolution and English Jacobinism." According to G. M. Young, Wilberforce's *Practical*

2. Hilton (1986) differentiates between "moderate" evangelicals, such as the members of the Clapham sect, and "extreme" evangelicals (many of them Methodists) whose belief in the imminent return of Christ generated a "last days" mentality and immoderation in both doctrine and behavior. While moderate evangelicals worked to save the souls of individuals, the extreme evangelicals took an entirely different approach. In their eyes, "a successful ministry did not consist in 'this man or that man saved, much less is it nations saved by wholesale,' but in providing a faithful witness to the truth of an imminent millennium" (17).

View of Christianity (1797) and Malthus's *Essay on the Principle of Population* (1798) were the classic texts on which the movement was based (Hilton 1986, 1–2). But Hilton and Young are a generation off; the men of whom Hilton and Young speak were second-generation evangelicals. Thornton imbibed the rough evangelical Christianity of his father but practiced a more moderate, reasoned form of it. The French Revolution clearly did affect Thornton's thinking; initially, he favored the Revolution out of a general preference for freedom. However, the path taken by the Republicans horrified Thornton, and he soon changed his mind, voting with the government in its decision to go to war. On the other hand, Malthusian thought played no role in shaping his religious views, which were well formed before Malthus wrote his *Essay*.[3]

Hilton quotes a paragraph from a letter written by Wilberforce that indicates the nature of evangelical belief:

> Christianity appears to me to consider the world as in a state of alienation from God, as lost in depravity and guilt; pointing out at the same time "how we may escape from the wrath to come," from the natural consequences of that guilt and from the power of moral corruption. This must be effected by the power of the Holy Spirit. . . . It ought to be the grand object of every moral writer . . . to produce in us that true and just sense of the intensity of the malignity of sin . . . , and of the real magnitude of our danger which would be likely to dispose us to exert ourselves to the utmost to obtain deliverance from the condemnation and emancipation from the power of sin. (quoted in Hilton 1986, 4)

In short, the evangelicals believed in the literal truth of the ancient Christian doctrines of depravity—the separation of humanity from God by sin—and salvation through the atoning blood of Jesus Christ. Hence the death, burial, and resurrection of Jesus became the centerpiece of evangelical theology, both doctrinally and practically. This was hardly a revolutionary doctrine for the late eighteenth century, although the emphasis placed on sin and depravity and the consequent need for repentance and forgiveness drove a wedge between the evangelicals and many Church of England clergymen. Doctrine certainly mattered, but *attitude* was what really marked off the evangelicals from ordinary Anglicans.

3. Anthony Waterman, in conversation, has suggested that the writings of Wilberforce and Malthus were "tracts to re-convert the British upper classes," a thesis that fits well with the argument he makes in Waterman 2004, chap. 2.

Robin Furneaux's (1974, 41–42) understanding of the nature of evangelicalism, though deficient in important ways, captures one crucial fact: evangelicalism was "more an attitude towards religion than a faith with a particular doctrine" (44). Quite so: the Clapham Evangelicals cooperated regularly with Methodists, Quakers, and Dissenters with whose theological views or unruly worship services many disagreed. The majority of Clapham Evangelicals remained firmly within the Church of England.

The evangelical gospel also ran counter to the theological utilitarianism of Paley, who saw all events as part of a beneficent evolutionary pattern set in motion by the Creator (Hilton 1986, 3–4).[4] In a time of war, poor crops, rising birth rates, and social change, the evangelical message seemed closer to the truth to many educated people than did Paley's justification of beneficent evolution.

Thornton's own attitudes toward the Bible and how it should be handled are laid out in two letters to the editor of the *Christian Observer.* In January 1810, Thornton tackled the issue of truth. He began his essay with several quotations attesting the truth of mutually inconsistent positions. He then noted,

> A superficial observer of these numerous and contradictory claims to the possession of truth, might be tempted by them to become sceptical on the whole subject of religion; an effect which it will be one object of the present paper to obviate. But I shall first deduce a few important inferences which naturally occur.
>
> I begin with remarking, that a strong persuasion of our religious opinions is no proof that they are sound. Some of the men whose writings I have quoted have been good divines, but they cannot all have been in the right; for many of their doctrines stand opposed to each other, and yet all appear to have been confident. Let us not then mistake our own conviction that a thing is true for *evidence* of its truth. . . .
>
> . . . laymen should be a little cautious of believing doctrines on the mere authority of those who teach them. Our instructors may not intend to mislead us: they may feel sure of what they say, and yet they may be in error: and that error may possibly be gross and dangerous. . . .

4. Waterman (2004, chap. 7) indicates the extent to which Paley, following Bishop Joseph Butler and Rev. Josiah Tucker, harmonized Adam Smith's "increasing returns" economics with Christian theology, so that Christian doctrine and political economy were perceived as harmonious systems—until Malthus upset the applecart in 1798 with his "diminishing returns" economics. Thornton's writings, however, are completely devoid of any discussion of the issues that caused the rift between "economists and humans." Waterman (this volume) provides additional discussion of this shift in thinking.

> I observed that we ought to "prove all things." But is there no danger, it may be said, in doing this? May not we err in consequence of the presumption attending this very attempt? And, after all, how shall we know, amidst the endless diversity of judgments, whether we are of the happy number who are in possession of the truth? . . . Is not, in short, the search after truth rendered discouraging, and almost hopeless, by the multitude of delusions in the world? (Thornton 1810a, 17–18)

Thornton follows this skeptical rumination with a lead-in to his essay in the next volume: "Be assured that there is such a thing as religious truth. . . . the truth itself somewhere exists" (18). In the subsequent issue, Thornton lays out the proper ways to pursue truth. With the exception of enjoining his readers to make sure that the meaning of texts has not been altered by translation into a different language and culture, his approach is remarkably similar to that taken by present-day evangelicals.

> There are two principal modes, by no means incompatible with each other, in which religious truth is to be sought—the one, prayer to the Father of Lights; the other, the diligent and unprejudiced use of that reason and common sense with which God has endowed us. It is important not to disjoin these two; for God, as I apprehend, has no more promised to guide that man by his grace who allows every faculty to lie dormant, than he has engaged to introduce those to the truth who aim to arrive at it by the unassisted and unsanctified exercise of their natural understanding. . . .
>
> The Scriptures are the great depository of religious truth; and therefore both our prayer and diligence should be employed in endeavouring to deduce it from that source. . . . Doubtful texts are to be explained by the aid of those which are more clear; and the few passages in which obscurity remains are not to be rested upon as deciding points of great importance. Truths plainly, frequently, and variously inculcated are to be deemed of superior moment; and those doctrines which sustain each other ought to be considered as deriving confirmation from this circumstance. Care should be taken not to employ those texts, for the establishment even of important points, which were not intended for that purpose. (Thornton 1810b, 79)

Thornton followed these rules of sound interpretation with several exhortations and several warnings. He advised Christians to seek biblical truth with seriousness, perseverance, and impartiality (80). The last of these pertains to prejudices brought to the biblical text by the reader. Following "Lord Bacon," Thornton uses the "quaint term of idols" to characterize these prejudices or false appearances. First, said Bacon, there are "idols of the tribe" that spread among members of particular sects. Second, there are "idols of the cave or den, . . . prejudices belonging to our condition in life." Third, there are "idols of the theatre" that follow from an individual's disposition or outlook on life. Finally, there are "idols of the market," by which Bacon meant the changing meaning of words. Thornton notes that

> Mr. Locke conceives that more than half the differences among men may be referred to the diversity of the meaning of words; and Lord Bacon seemed to have been nearly of the same opinion. . . . we have not, perhaps, sufficiently considered that Scripture communicated religious truth at a time when language was far less precise than it is at present. On this account, the sacred writings fail to decide many questions, both of a nice theological and of a metaphysical kind, on which some theologians have dogmatized in succeeding days. (Thornton 1810b, 81–82)

Thornton closes his discussion of biblical interpretation by quoting two paragraphs penned by a "pious divine":

> Be sure to live on the great fundamentals of religion, and let not your attention to these be diverted by an intemperate zeal about lesser things. Place not your religion in disputable points and ineffectual opinions, but in those weightier matters of the law and Gospel which are of undoubted importance, and in which holy men, among all the different denominations of Christians, are better agreed than is commonly apprehended. Choose God for your portion and felicity; and live daily upon Christ Jesus as the only mediator by whom you can either have access to God or acceptance with him. Indulge no sin—plead for no infirmity—but make it the daily business of your lives "to mortify the deeds of the body."
>
> Rest not in a low degree of holiness, but love and long and strive for the highest. And for these purposes pray without ceasing for those promised influences of divine grace which can alone heal your diseased natures, and carry you forward from one degree of holiness to another, till, being ripened for glory, an entrance shall in due time be ministered unto you abundantly into the everlasting kingdom of our Lord and Saviour Jesus Christ. (82)

Thornton's serious attitude toward careful interpretation of scripture carried over to its application to life. In his *Family Prayers . . . with a*

Commentary on the Sermon on the Mount (1836), Thornton addresses the manner in which a Christian should live life, as indicated by the words of Jesus in the Sermon on the Mount. A couple of passages illustrate the nature of Thornton's practical faith.

In his commentary on Matthew 6:1–4,[5] Thornton addressed vanity or, as we might say today, a desire to create a particular perception of oneself in the public's eye. "God looks not so much at the act done, as at the motive for doing it." Vanity not only can lead one to craft an appearance of generosity or magnanimity but can even take the form of crafting a reputation for humility! The real issue is this: for whom are we really doing our good works? "Are we prompted to perform those good things which we do, chiefly by the desire of *appearing well before men?* Do we love, not so much *to do right*, as to be *thought* to do right?"

> Ask yourselves this question: "Supposing all my acquaintances to recommend something which I know to be wrong, should I dare to act against their judgment? And supposing them all to frown upon me for doing right, should I proceed to do it?" If your conscience cannot give a reply, which is in any degree satisfactory, then you, like the Pharisee, are under the domination of the love of praise. Men in general are enslaved by this principle. . . . There is an *extreme* of vice into which they rarely fall. But is not Christian virtue practiced almost as rarely? Is not true holiness almost as much avoided as gross sin? And for the same reason; both are discreditable. It is discreditable to be very profligate, to lie or to steal. It is also discreditable in this age to be accounted stricter than others in religion; and therefore, men choose to be neither in one extreme, as they call it, nor in the other. (Thornton [1837] 1849, 251–52)

A second passage worthy of mention is Matthew 6:24: "No man can serve two masters: for either he will hate the one, and love the other; or else he will hold to the one and despise the other. Ye cannot serve both God and Mammon." Thornton explicates the passage at length, but for our purposes his key point is this:

5. "Take heed that ye do not your alms before men, to be seen of them, otherwise you have no reward of your Father which is in heaven. Therefore, when thou doest thine alms, do not sound a trumpet before thee, as the hypocrites do in the synagogues and in the streets, that they may have glory of men. Verily I say unto you, they have their reward. But when thou doest alms, let not thy left hand know what thy right hand doeth: That thine alms may be in secret: and thy Father which seeth in secret himself shall reward thee openly."

> Most men, in entering their profession, especially if it be that of trade, propose to make their fortunes, as they call it. "What," say they, "is the use of following business, if we are not to gain money by it? We will labour to be rich, and even to be very rich; but we will use honest means, and take due care to fulfill, at the same time, all our religious and moral duties."
>
> Such persons mistake the nature of true religion. They understand not, that it consists in mortifying those earthly desires which naturally govern the heart, in order that by so mortifying them, God may reign without a rival there. (Thornton [1837] 1849, 293)

The picture of Henry Thornton that emerges from this brief recitation is of an intensely committed Christian willing to overlook reasonable differences of opinion on unclear biblical issues. However, he believed that the core doctrines of the faith were not in doubt, and he was unwilling to condone deviance from these settled doctrines. He maintained an attitude of charity in regard to differences in opinion on disputed doctrinal issues. But Furneaux's contention that evangelicalism is more an *attitude* than a *doctrine* appears correct. The real difference between evangelicals and nonevangelicals lay in the former's insistence that biblical faith must be lived out daily.[6]

Thornton's Life: A Doer of the Gospel

In February 1804, under the pseudonym "S.P.," Thornton published a letter to the editor of the *Christian Observer* attacking the "sect of the NON-DOERS." He thought it appropriate to draw attention to this sect because it was "a large and comprehensive body." Indeed, Thornton (1804, 77) doubted "whether it may not boast a superiority in point of numbers over every other religious party within this kingdom," a not-so-subtle dig at the perceived state of the Church of England. By the appellation, Thornton denoted "all that class of persons who maintain the profession of christianity [*sic*] without the practice, including some who are observant merely of its forms, and others who attend also to its doctrines; in short, all those *who say and do not do*" (77).

6. While simple biblical faith underpinned the lives of the first and second generation of evangelicals, the children of the second generation largely abandoned evangelicalism. Some returned to the high church, while others followed the same path away from the church as Henry Sidgwick (originally a high churchman) took, as described in Medema, this volume.

The sect of the nondoers was hardly new. Thornton finds Cain, the oldest son of Adam, guilty of membership in the sect, as was Saul, the first king of Israel, and the Jews in general for their failure to follow Moses through the wilderness during the exodus and for their later shortcomings as diagnosed by the Hebrew prophets. He argues that the errors of the scribes and Pharisees, pointed out by the Gospel writers, were not strictly doctrinal but comprehended their manner of living. "'Every tree,' said [Jesus], 'that bringeth not forth good fruit, is hewn down and cast into the fire. Wherefore by their fruits ye shall know them'" (quoted in Thornton 1804, 78). Thornton quotes the Apostle Paul at length, ending with the sentence from Romans 2:13, "For not the hearers of the law are just before God, but the *doers* of the law shall be justified" (79), before mustering a bevy of quotes from Jesus, Peter, and James and Jude (the brothers of Jesus) and ending with John's criticism of the church at Ephesus in Revelation 2:4–5: "I have somewhat against thee, because thou hast left thy first love. Remember, therefore, from whence thou art fallen, and repent, and do the first works; or else I will come unto thee quickly, and will remove thy candlestick out of its place" (80). Unfortunately, the sect of nondoers persisted past New Testament times. In later centuries, "popery . . . substituted a multitude of forms in the place of religious practice" (78). Though the sect diminished during and immediately after the Reformation, it unfortunately returned, affecting the Protestant churches as well as the Catholic. His diagnostic conclusion was gloomy: "This dangerous sect abounds, as I conceive, Sir, at this hour in our cities; it infests our towns; it pervades our villages; it enters our seats of learning and religion; and our very churches and meeting-houses are not free from it" (81). Thornton's standards were high:

> If we disbelieve the historic facts of the Gospel, then we are acknowledged infidels; if we deny the doctrines involved in the facts, then undoubtedly we are heretics; if admitting both the facts and the doctrines, and even if also observing the morality of believers,[7] we attain not to the evangelical practice enjoined by our Lord and his Apostles, we are then of that sect of the *Non-doers* of which I have been speaking. (81)

In the heated environment of the anti–slave trade era, Thornton did not lack for detractors. One thing they never accused him of was being a

7. The text says "unbelievers," which makes no logical sense and surely is a typographic error.

nondoer. His life was crammed so full of doing the work of the Lord that he barely had time to tend to his banking house (ultimately, with tragic consequences [Acaster 1974, pt. 2]). For every word he wrote about economic matters, he wrote many more about the matters that genuinely consumed him. Yet precisely because Thornton was a *doer*, he was moved to take a leading position on monetary issues. It was his duty to his constituents and to his fellow citizens to press the government to pursue the wisest course of monetary policy. That he himself, as a banker, stood to gain from sound monetary policies was not sufficient to move him to such a task as writing the *Paper Credit.* Simply by spending more time at the bank, watching more closely over his partners, he could have increased his income substantially. But income wasn't Thornton's primary motivation. As a financial expert and a servant of Christ, Thornton was compelled to be a doer.

Thornton the Economist: Parliamentary Evidence and the *Paper Credit*

In the *Paper Credit* Thornton argued that the Bank of England should not be blamed for the rising prices of grain and certain other basic articles in England over the preceding three years. Thornton works out his argument in terms strikingly similar to a "neoclassical synthesis" macroeconomic model that permits aggregate demand and aggregate supply to be affected by real, as well as monetary, factors. He argued in 1802 that real factors were to blame. Eight years later, as one of the three driving forces on the Bullion Committee, Thornton reversed course, arguing that the Bank of England had permitted its note issue to expand too rapidly, generating a significant increase of prices (Cannan [1919] 1969). Reluctantly,[8] Thornton the "moderate bullionist" joined his voice with those of the strict bullionists in calling for a return to the gold standard within two years, whether or not the hostilities with France were ended. To Thornton, the unwillingness of the directors of the Bank of England to admit that the Bank's issues had *any* effect on the market price of bullion indicated that the Bank could not be trusted to properly manage the paper currency. Thus he changed his policy prescription, going where the evidence led him.

8. Even while supporting a return to convertibility, Thornton ([1802] 1939, 329, 334) went to great lengths to make clear his aversion to any sudden, large reduction in the Bank's note issue, reminding his listeners that in the *Paper Credit* he had shown the harm that would result from an overly restrictive policy.

Compared with John Wheatley or Ricardo, Thornton appears flexible in his policy recommendations. He understood the complexity of the British economy and was unwilling to assume away adjustment mechanisms merely for the sake of strengthening his policy recommendations. Thornton's theory focuses on pursuing a policy that maintains reasonable price stability and international equilibrium, given the actual conditions prevailing. He attempted to explain how the central bank might pursue a first-best policy under various situations. As a polemical weapon, Thornton's complex analysis was inferior to Ricardo's stripped-down, easily understood, monetarist model, which largely explains Thornton's rapid—but far from complete—eclipse in the literature after his death.[9]

From 1793 until his death in 1815, Thornton was regarded as perhaps Britain's leading expert on monetary issues. He testified before parliamentary committees in 1793 (the only banker called to testify in the wake of the financial panic of that year) and again in 1797 (after the suspension of convertibility). In 1804 he was the moving force on the committee examining the state of the Irish currency, a committee whose very existence appears to have followed Thornton's call to investigate why the Irish pound had depreciated so dramatically relative to the English pound (Fetter 1955, 27). And, of course, Thornton joined with Francis Horner and William Huskisson in chairing the famous Bullion Committee of 1810 (Cannan [1919] 1969). Given the prominence of his parliamentary roles and the depth and breadth of the *Paper Credit*, as well as his stature as a London banker, it would be easy to believe that Thornton spent most of his time thinking about monetary matters. But, as I have shown, nothing could be farther from the truth. Despite his acknowledged expertise in banking and his thorough understanding of monetary theory, Thornton's primary interests lay in completely different areas, and he was more widely known during his lifetime for his religious writings than for the *Paper Credit*.

For the purposes at hand, the question that needs to be addressed is, to what extent, if any, did Thornton's religious views affect his economic model and his policy prescriptions? As I noted in the introduction, my answer is that neither Thornton's theology nor his rigorous application of it to daily life affected the content of his economics in perceptible ways. Unlike most economic writers of his age, Thornton was a *technical* economist; he paid little attention to political elements of economics

9. As I have argued elsewhere (Skaggs 1995, 2003), Thornton heavily influenced Thomas Tooke and other members of the Banking school, through whose writings Thornton's ideas remained alive during the nineteenth century.

and no attention to moral philosophy at all.[10] The *Paper Credit* is, from first to last, a technical work on monetary macroeconomics. In it, Thornton explains

- the nature of commercial credit and how the invention of paper credit expanded the use of commercial credit;
- how paper money circulates and how its velocity of circulation varies with interest rates and commercial confidence;
- why the Bank of England should never suddenly reduce the quantity of its notes to any great extent, elucidating the effects of illiquidity in his discussion;
- why the real bills doctrine is fallacious as a guide to monetary policy;
- the concept of the balance of payments and the theory of exchange rates and gold flows;
- the inability of the Bank of England to increase its gold reserves when the demand for gold by domestic citizens rises;
- the advantages and disadvantages of country banks;
- the tendency of an excessive issue of paper money to raise the market price of gold and trigger an outflow of gold;
- the flexibility of the connection between the quantity of paper money in circulation and its value;
- the lack of wisdom in demanding that the Bank of England follow a strict quantitative rule in issuing its notes.

All of this is technical stuff. Thornton was an expert on the British monetary system, and he wrote a technical book on how the system worked. There is no trace in his work of the sort of blending of economics and Christianity that one sees in the works of Malthus (Waterman 1991) or the Roman Catholic economists in Europe in the decades following Thornton's death (cf. Almodovar and Teixeira, this volume).

Thornton wrote the *Paper Credit* for the same reason that he provided testimony to House of Commons committees in 1793 and 1797, spearheaded the committee on the Irish currency in 1804, and helped chair the Bullion Committee in 1810: he was an acknowledged expert on these matters, and an expert's duty was to provide wise advice to his country in perilous times. A *doer* could do no less.

10. The *Paper Credit* does contain one instance of what we today would call a public choice analysis of the behavior of the directors of the Bank of England (on page 110), but beyond that its focus is strictly on how the economy works and how it is affected by monetary and fiscal policies.

David Levy's understanding of the alliance between evangelicals and utilitarians provides further evidence in favor of my reading of Thornton. In an attempt to compensate for his "inattention to Thornton elsewhere" in *How the Dismal Science Got Its Name*, Levy (2001, 53) followed J. S. Mill's dictum in summarizing Thornton's version of the "reciprocity norm": "First, markets work as the textbooks claim; second, slavery ends." Levy derives his evidence from Thornton's *Family Prayers* (1837).[11] Levy argues that at the time of the great debate over slavery, the evangelicals and the utilitarians agreed to regard the Golden Rule of Christianity and the Greatest Happiness Principle of the utilitarians as "formally identical" (53). If such was the case, we should be no more surprised that Thornton produced a technical, rather than a moral, guide to proper monetary policy than we would be that a utilitarian might produce such a technical work.

A second, unintentional, confirmation of the technical nature of Thornton's economics comes from Hilton's flawed argument about how the monetary writers of the restriction period entertained ambivalence about the nature of economic value. The British economy grew rapidly, sometimes chaotically, during the twenty-four years that the pound sterling was severed from gold. Industry and finance altered the economic landscape, much to the dismay of landowners, whose political power was threatened by the rising economic strength of the industrialists and financiers. But was this newfound wealth real? Or was it only chimerical, bound to disappear when the economy returned to normal? Hilton argues that those who thought the new economy was real tended to be antibullionists, wedded to paper currency and credit. Those opposing the new economy, who saw it as a temporary aberration bound to fail, tended to be bullionists.

Clearly, many people—including politicians and economic writers—believed that the gold standard was more than simply one among several alternative approaches to maintaining the value of the currency. And, according to Hilton, evangelicals typically sided with those who viewed the "ancient standard" in quasi-religious terms. "Moral bullionists," argues Hilton (1986, 129), "believed that with an absolute measure of value, like the Gold Standard, it would be possible to measure the *real* worth of economic enterprise." And it is true that the undoubted leader of the Currency school in the 1840s and 1850s—the successor to the strict bullionists—was Samuel Jones Loyd, Lord Overstone, a devout evangelical.

11. Levy (2001, 51) notes that Henry Thornton "is everyone's idea of a great economist. . . . He brings the same spare elegance in his *Family Commentary upon the Sermon on the Mount* that he did to *Paper Credit*."

According to Hilton (1986, 133–35), Overstone accepted the midcentury view of business cycles and the bankruptcies that accompanied them. The recurrent nature of business cycles had led Christian writers to give up the idea that depressions were specific acts of God intended to punish the nation for its sins. But the idea that individuals were still morally culpable when businesses failed was widely accepted within evangelical circles. Bankruptcies were not "mysterious visitations" but were the "logical outcome of sin," reflecting the "economic guilt" of the businessman. If the ultimate cause of the failures is human sin, then the government cannot, indeed *should* not, take action to ameliorate the situation.

Hilton then links Overstone to Thornton: "Overstone's analysis of the trade cycle, though technical and relatively unpolemical, rested characteristically on psychological factors. In this he followed Thornton, the first writer to emphasize how much such factors could affect public credit" (134).

It is all well and good to link Overstone to Thornton by focusing on their common discussions of psychological factors, but Hilton fails to complete the comparison. Overstone, following Ricardo, advocated a rigid approach to monetary policy. He and his Currency school allies successfully sponsored the passage of the Bank Charter Act of 1844, which quantitatively limited the supply of bank notes, whether issued by the Bank of England or by commercial banks. Under the act, the Issue Department of the Bank of England faced a 100 percent marginal reserve requirement on its note issue, above a £14 million "fiduciary issue" backed by Treasury debt. The note supplies of country banks were also limited to fixed maximum amounts. The rigid reserve requirement reflected the Currency school's belief that controlling the quantity of bank notes in circulation was the key to stopping the "speculation" that led to "over-trading" and an ultimate collapse of credit and widespread bankruptcies. *All of this flies in the face of Thornton's analysis.*

As I have argued multiple times (see especially Skaggs 1991, 1995, and 2003), Thornton's true heirs—the Banking school writers, including Thomas Tooke, John Fullarton, and John Stuart Mill—believed the Currency school's analysis of the problem was flawed and that the strict Ricardian approach would increase the probability of the very thing most feared by the Currency school writers: suspension of convertibility. And Tooke, Fullarton, and Mill were right. The Bank Act *did* worsen the periodical credit crises, forcing the Bank of England to seek authority to suspend the act on two occasions. Contrary to what Hilton argues, Thornton's intellectual heirs considered the legal framework—which restricted the elasticity of the money supply and generated liquidity crises—to be the root of the problem, not the supposedly sinful actions of individual traders and bankers. Thus, once again I conclude that Thornton's economics followed from his technical understanding of the economy rather than from his religious views.

A Technician with a Heart for God . . . and Man?

Can one be a devout Christian and not leave traces of one's faith in what one writes? If the question is applied to economists from our own era, I have no doubt that most people would respond in the affirmative. One example suggested to me even parallels Thornton in his interests: Brian Griffiths, a devout Christian whose reputation as a monetary economist in our secular age is outstanding. But Thornton lived in a very different time. Was it really possible for him to think in purely technical terms in an age when religious arguments were still routinely woven into economic, political, and even scientific treatises? Let's consider some possibilities.

First, Thornton treated the analysis of the monetary/credit system as an exercise in technical economics. Harro Maas, in a comment on an earlier draft of this article, pointed out that choosing to treat credit as a technical subject, rather than a moral or religious subject, is itself a *political* decision. Was Thornton "hiding behind" a technical approach to avoid discussing the moral dilemmas posed by the widespread use of credit? And if he was doing so, how would we recognize his ploy?

It is a fact that Thornton never addressed the morality of credit in the *Paper Credit* or in any of his parliamentary testimony. He was concerned with how the credit system worked, not with how it might be morally justified. What does appear obvious from his discussions of credit is that Thornton maintained a viewpoint that S. Herbert Frankel (1977) would call an "organic credit system."

> Rather than being constructed on some rational plan, such a system grew from individual relationships between and among many different lenders, borrowers, and guarantors. The success of such a system (Walter Bagehot argued), lay in the willingness of those possessing financial wealth to hold assets other than coin. That is, the system was successful because individuals possessing financial wealth were willing to entrust their money to those in need of liquid funds in exchange for

> promises to repay the loan principal plus interest in the future. For Bagehot (as for Frankel), trust lay at the center of England's financial system. (Skaggs 1998, 453)

In terms of his understanding of the monetary/credit system, Bagehot was approximately the second coming of Henry Thornton, who begins his treatise by analyzing the nature of commercial credit. Thornton recognized that the core of a credit relationship is the belief that a borrower will meet his or her commitment to repay, with interest, the sum borrowed. Honest people were able to carry on a large business with very little money, provided that they met their obligations on time, proving themselves worthy of the credit they received.

In the *Paper Credit* Thornton repeatedly cautions the Bank of England against restricting its note issue—that is, its willingness to discount bills of exchange—so sharply that honest borrowers are unable meet their commitments. Overly restrictive credit policy ruined honest traders who, but for the change in Bank policy, would have met their commitments.[12] It is *possible* that Thornton stressed this theme so strongly in his book because excessively stringent monetary policy not only shrank the fortunes of honest men but also tarnished their reputations. But one could equally argue that Thornton simply wished to avoid the unnecessary economic losses that accompany an excessively restrictive monetary policy.

It is also *possible* to see in Thornton's discussion of the effects of excessively tight monetary policy on industry, and hence on workers, a plea for charity toward those who had far lower incomes than did the commercial and financial magnates with whom Thornton associated. Thornton recognized, as Adam Smith had before him, that a downturn in business caused firms to release workers, since wages were no more downwardly flexible in the eighteenth and early nineteenth centuries than they are now.

A Marxist might see in Thornton an apologist for the bourgeois class, concerned only about maintaining the web of economic relationships that supported the bourgeoisie in wealth and power. But such a view hardly fits Henry Thornton the philanthropist and anti–slave trader. It seems more reasonable to believe that Thornton was what he appeared to be: a dedicated Christian who thought about the financial system in technical, rather than philosophical or political, terms. By his own admission, Thornton knew nothing about philosophy and little about history.

12. Thornton (1939, 188n) explicitly states that it is not the Bank's business to bail out those engaged in "rash" behavior.

Beyond the basics, what he knew he learned as an adult spent in the City, in the House of Commons, and in conversations with his Clapham associates. If he mixed his religion and his monetary economics, the mixture isn't readily apparent.

References

Acaster, E. J. T. 1974–75. Henry Thornton—the Banker. Pts. 1–2. *Three Banks Review* 104:46–57; 105:38–52.

Armstrong, Anthony. 1973. *The Church of England, the Methodists, and Society: 1700–1850*. Totawa, N.J.: Rowman and Littlefield.

Cannan, Edwin, ed. [1919] 1969. *The Paper Pound of 1797–1821: The Bullion Report*. Reprint, New York: Kelley.

Fetter, Frank W. 1955. *The Irish Pound, 1797–1826*. Evanston, Ill.: Northwestern University Press.

Frankel, S. Herbert. 1977. *Money: Two Philosophies*. Oxford: Blackwell.

Furneaux, Robin. 1974. *William Wilberforce*. London: Hamilton.

Halévy, Elie. 1949. *A History of the English People: England in 1815*. London: Benn.

Hayek, Friedrich A. [1939] 1978. Introduction to *An Enquiry into the Nature and Effects of the Paper Credit of Great Britain*. Reprint, Fairfield, N.J.: Kelley.

Hilton, Boyd. 1986. *The Age of Atonement*. Oxford: Clarendon.

Levy, David M. 2001. *How the Dismal Science Got Its Name: Classical Economics and the Ur-Text of Racial Politics*. Ann Arbor: University of Michigan Press.

Levy, David M., and Sandra J. Peart. 2003. "Who Are the Canters?" The Coalition of Evangelical-Economic Egalitarians. *HOPE* 35.4:731–57.

McCulloch, John R. [1845] 1964. *The Literature of Political Economy: A Classified Catalogue*. New York: Kelley.

Meacham, Standish. 1964. *Henry Thornton of Clapham*. Cambridge, Mass.: Harvard University Press.

Mill, James. 1966. *James Mill: Selected Economic Writings*. Edited by Donald Winch. Chicago: University of Chicago Press.

Skaggs, Neil T. 1991. John Fullarton's Law of Reflux and Central Bank Policy. *HOPE* 23.3:457–80.

———. 1995. Henry Thornton and the Development of Classical Monetary Economics. *Canadian Journal of Economics* 28 (November): 1212–27.

———. 1998. Debt as the Basis of Currency: The Monetary Economics of Trust. *American Journal of Economics and Sociology* 57.4:453–67.

———. 2003. Thomas Tooke, Henry Thornton, and the Development of British Monetary Orthodoxy. *Journal of the History of Economic Thought* 35 (June): 177–97.

Thornton, Henry. 1802–8. *Recollections*. Manuscript Department, Cambridge University, Cambridge.

———. [S.P., pseud.] 1804. Attack on the Sect of the Non-Doers. *Christian Observer* 3 (February): 77–82.

——. [S.P., pseud.] 1810a. Interpreting the Scriptures, Part 1. *Christian Observer* 9 (January): 17–19.
——. [S.P., pseud.] 1810b. Interpreting the Scriptures, Part 2. *Christian Observer* 9 (February): 79–82.
——. [1802] 1939. *An Enquiry into the Nature and Effects of the Paper Credit of Great Britain*. Edited by F. A. Hayek. Reprint, Fairfield, N.J.: Kelley.
——. [1837] 1849. *Family Prayers: To Which Is Added a Commentary on the Sermon on the Mount*. New York: Stanford and Swords.
Waterman, A. M. C. 1991. *Revolution, Economics, and Religion: Christian Political Economy, 1798–1833*. Cambridge: Cambridge University Press.
——. 2004. *Political Economy and Christian Theology since the Enlightenment*. New York: Palgrave Macmillan.

“Losing My Religion”: Sidgwick, Theism, and the Struggle for Utilitarian Ethics in Economic Analysis

Steven G. Medema

Sidgwick wanted it all: a rational, orderly universe that unfailingly maximized both collective and individual happiness. He wanted the philosopher to be armed with a cognitivist defense of the moral order of the universe that could substitute for the theologian’s and convert both the clerisy and the “sensual herd.” . . . For Sidgwick was, in a plain sense, searching for a new religion, a new synthesis combining the best of the classical and the Christian.
—Bart Schultz, *Henry Sidgwick: Eye of the Universe*

Henry Sidgwick’s loss of religious faith is central to understanding the origins of the Cambridge school of welfare economics. The most prominent “public” manifestation of this loss and its impact on Sidgwick’s thought was his *Methods of Ethics* (1874), which was at once the capstone work of classical utilitarianism, cementing Sidgwick’s place as one of the great philosophers of ethics during the Victorian period,[1] and the source of his deep-seated need for the very religion to which he himself could no longer subscribe. Sidgwick’s studies in political economy carried this ethical perspective into the economic realm, though the major

The author would like to thank Warren Samuels, Donald Winch, the editors, an anonymous referee, and the participants at the 2007 *HOPE* conference for instructive comments on an earlier draft of this article.

1. See, for example, Schneewind 1977 and Rawls 1981.

History of Political Economy 40 (annual suppl.) DOI 10.1215/00182702-2007-066

impact came via his influence on A. C. Pigou, whose welfare analysis was very much a restatement of the Sidgwickian view, but undertaken with Marshallian analytical underpinnings.[2]

The writing of *The Methods of Ethics* was motivated largely by Sidgwick's struggles with Anglican orthodoxy and the desire to free himself from it. The most public aspect of this struggle was the resignation of his Trinity College fellowship in 1869, because he found that he could not meet the fellowship's condition of subscription to the Thirty-nine Articles of the Church of England. Yet, in falling away from orthodox religion, Sidgwick did not reject the idea of a supreme force in the universe. Rather, his views evolved into a theism independent of doctrines—such as those of the Trinity, the virgin birth, and eternal damnation—reflected in the creeds of the church.

Sidgwick's theism included the idea that the universe has a moral ordering and that there exists a benevolent God. However, his move away from orthodox religion led him to search elsewhere for an ethical basis for evaluating individual and social action, and thus for what Sidgwick described as "a reconciliation between the moral sense and utilitarian theories" (letter to H. G. Dakyns, March 1862, in Sidgwick and Sidgwick 1906, 75). The results of this search, combined with his reformist inclinations, provided Sidgwick with a normative basis for analyzing economic, political, and legal issues.

This article discusses Sidgwick's crisis of faith and his subsequent attempt to devise an ethical basis for social life that was divorced from religious concerns yet consistent with his own more general theistic stance. It further shows how the results of this search affected Sidgwick's work in economics and, ultimately, the Cambridge welfare tradition.

The Crisis of Faith

Sidgwick's life (1838–1900) spanned the Victorian era, a period that saw a significant challenge to religious faith in England. While the Victorians covered England with parish churches and the absolute number of people attending religious services was on the rise, this was merely an artifact of increasing population rather than an increased religiosity. In fact, the percentage of the population attending church was falling. So, too, was subscription to orthodox religious beliefs: by the end of the Victorian era,

2. On Pigou and Sidgwick, see O'Donnell 1979, Backhouse 2006, and Medema 2007b.

it was harder to believe in hell, life after death, the Bible, and the church's traditional teachings.[3] The university was at once contributing cause and microcosm of this secularization. During the Victorian era, the ancient universities were opened to students of any religion, or no religion at all. The training grounds for the future clergy of the Church of England, who were to be educated in both virtue and knowledge, became increasingly focused on academic research (Chadwick 1972, 439–41). Some of this research, particularly in the natural sciences, contributed to the ferment, with the collision between religion, on the one hand, and science and reason, on the other, perhaps most famously (but by no means exclusively) illustrated in the controversy over Charles Darwin's writings. There was an increasing sense that religion and science were incompatible, with religion coming out on the losing end of the evidentiary test.

Despite the increased secularization, there was still widespread support for religion, as the data on the founding of new churches make clear. Owen Chadwick has suggested in his monumental study, *The Victorian Church*, that "the people felt a moral and social need of religion," even if they questioned its foundations and were reluctant to attend services. In the end, although the Victorian era witnessed a profound secularization, the Victorians also managed to "preserve a country which was powerfully influenced by Christian ideas and continued to accept the Christian ethic as the highest known to men" (Chadwick 1972, 472). This tension between Anglican orthodoxy and the evolving religious mood of the age preoccupied—one might even say tormented—Sidgwick for his entire adult life. Although he was "raised in the firm orthodox Christian certainties of his age and class," Sidgwick moved away from them to a view that J. B. Schneewind (1977, 21) has aptly characterized as "highly individual and deliberately tentative."

We know relatively little about Sidgwick's early life. His father graduated Trinity College, became a clergyman, and went on to head the grammar school in Skipton, Yorkshire. However, he died when Henry was only three years old and so had no influence on his son's religious outlook. The major familial influence on Sidgwick's early religious views came via E. W. Benson, an older second cousin and frequent visitor to the family home. Benson was a clergyman who eventually married Sidgwick's

3. See Chadwick 1972, 472, 423; see also 218–38. Backhouse (this volume) and Waterman (this volume) also touch on religion and economists' attitudes toward it in England during this period. Chadwick (1966, 1972) surveys the Victorian period in great depth.

sister, became the headmaster of Wellington College, and ultimately rose through the ecclesiastical ranks to become archbishop of Canterbury. It was Benson who persuaded Sidgwick's mother to send Henry to Rugby School, where Benson was an assistant master teaching classics, and he came to live with the family not long after Sidgwick entered Rugby.[4] Here, Sidgwick would likely have been exposed to a relatively conservative orthodox form of Christianity. But Benson's influence went well beyond schooling advice: his forceful personality and orthodox views deeply impressed the young Sidgwick, and Sidgwick speaks of Benson having an "unquestioned rule over" his mind in matters intellectual, moral, and practical (*Life of Archbishop Benson*, 1:150, quoted in Sidgwick and Sidgwick 1906, 10).

At Benson's urging, Sidgwick followed in his father's (and Benson's) footsteps, going on to Trinity College in 1855. Unlike his father, however, Henry never left. He became a fellow of Trinity in 1859, and his association with the college continued until his death. Sidgwick's studies focused on classics and mathematics, but he early on developed a great interest in philosophy as well. In his second year at Cambridge, he was invited to join the Apostles, the exclusive discussion group that had such a formidable influence on so many young men at Cambridge during the nineteenth century. This group made a profound impact on Sidgwick. Its Saturday evening debates were the highlight of his week, and the group's "pursuit of truth with absolute devotion and unreserve" was a characteristic that Sidgwick felt marked his own approach to intellectual inquiry (autobiographical fragment, in Sidgwick and Sidgwick 1906, 34).[5] The Apostles was only one of several discussion societies to which Sidgwick belonged over the years, and his interest in discussing religious questions was a significant motivation for him to join these groups. According to Sidgwick's biographer Bart Schultz (2004, 24), for Sidgwick, "the lure of discussion was always the same: free and open inquiry into issues of deep concern, usually involving religious or moral questions, and this as a search for unity in a conflictual world and an antidote to the dogma and dogmatism of school and church."

There can be little doubt that the questioning method of the Apostles struck a particular chord with Sidgwick. As he later described it, "No con-

4. The need for persuasion arose because Sidgwick's father had opposed public schools based on what he believed to be their poor moral state.

5. Sidgwick dictated some autobiographical material during his last illness, and this material was included in Sidgwick and Sidgwick 1906.

sistency was demanded with opinions previously held—truth as we saw it then and there was what we had to embrace and maintain, and there were no propositions so well established that an Apostle had not the right to deny or question, if he did so sincerely and not from mere love of paradox" (autobiographical fragment, in Sidgwick and Sidgwick 1906, 34–35). Looking back at his apostolic period shortly before his death, Sidgwick said that his attachment to it was "much the strongest corporate bond which I have known in life." At least as important, though, was the direction in which it pointed him: it revealed to him that "the deepest bent of [his] nature was towards the life of thought—thought exercised on the central problems of human life" (autobiographical fragment, in Sidgwick and Sidgwick 1906, 35).

By the time Sidgwick graduated Cambridge in 1859, he was "in a state of religious, moral, and philosophical turmoil" that lasted for a solid decade (Schultz 2004, 28). His association with the Apostles played no small role here, and the growth of the group's influence on Sidgwick was matched by a diminishing of Benson's influence. There was a significant demarcation between the two in Sidgwick's mind already in the early 1860s. He later wrote that he and others among the Apostles were working toward an ideal that had both philosophical and theological aspects:

> What we aimed at from a social point of view was a complete revision of human relations, political, moral, and economic, in the light of science directed by comprehensive and impartial sympathy; and an unsparing reform of whatever, in the judgment of science, was pronounced to be not conducive to the general happiness. This social science must of course have historical knowledge as a basis: but, being science, it must regard unscientific beliefs, moral, political, of past ages as altogether wrong,—at least in respect of the method of their attainment and the grounds on which they were accepted. History, in short, was conceived as supplying the material on which we had to work, but not the ideal which we aimed at realizing; except so far as history properly understood showed that the time had come for the scientific treatment of political and moral problems.
>
> As regards theology, those with whom I sympathized [i.e., the Apostles] had no close agreement in conclusions . . . and my own opinions were for many years unsettled and widely fluctuating. What was fixed and unalterable and accepted by us all was the necessity and duty of examining the evidence for historical Christianity with strict scientific impartiality; placing ourselves as far as possible outside traditional

> sentiments and opinions, and endeavoring to weigh the *pros* and *cons* on all theological questions as a duly instructed rational being from another planet . . . would naturally weigh them. (letter to A. C. Benson, 1897, in Sidgwick and Sidgwick 1906, 39–40)

Benson's outlook and his perspective on the day's pressing issues were very different from this. Christianity was the unquestioned starting point for thought rather than something to be subjected to the same critical and questioning processes of inquiry as everything else. As Sidgwick later described it,

> For him, the only hope of effective and complete social reform lay in the increased vitality and increased influence of the Christian Church: useful work might be done by those outside—his recognition of the value of such work was always ample and cordial—but it could only be of limited and partial utility. The healing of the nations could only come from one source; and any social science that failed to recognize this must be proceeding on a wrong track. (quoted in Schultz 2004, 37)

Benson considered attempts at unbiased (i.e., by Christianity's influence) inquiry dangerous and, unlike the Apostles, was not one for dispassionate argumentation.

Sidgwick's own ideas on religion and ethics developed simultaneously from the late 1850s through the late 1860s, a period that he referred to as his "years of 'storm and stress' as regards religious convictions and ecclesiastical relations" (Sidgwick and Sidgwick 1906, 33). The Apostles' increasing influence and Benson's diminishing influence are paralleled on the ethical and religious fronts: we see the major tenets of Sidgwick's ethical system worked out and solidified in his own mind as his religious beliefs progressively faded (Schneewind 1977, 51).

Evidence for the weakening of Sidgwick's religious commitment can be found in a letter written to his close friend and fellow Apostle Oscar Browning in 1860. Here, Sidgwick speaks of "a great gulf" between his views and those of the framers of the Thirty-nine Articles that set out the doctrinal perspective of the Church of England, to which Cambridge fellows (among others) had to subscribe. Given the breadth of meanings that could be said to fall within these very general Christian beliefs, Sidgwick allowed that "I think I could juggle myself into signing the Articles as well as any one else." At the same time, however, he was gripped by an internal ethical conflict, feeling that it was the duty of some, at least, not to sign off on a set of beliefs that did not accurately reflect their thinking—to avoid what he called "the best-motived perjury" (letter to O. Browning, Michaelmas term 1860, in Sidgwick and Sidgwick 1906, 62).

Looking back on this period some three decades later, Sidgwick said that, prior to 1862, he "had not in any way broken with the orthodox Christianity in which [he] had been brought up." He had, however, been seriously questioning, and through this had "become skeptical" about, many of the conclusions of orthodox Christianity "and generally with regard to its methods of proof" (autobiographical fragment, in Sidgwick and Sidgwick 1906, 36). In 1862, though, Sidgwick was clearly questioning whether, given his religious views, it was appropriate for him to continue to hold the fellowship. In June of that year he wrote to his good friend H. G. Dakyns that "at present . . . I am only a Theist." Yet he went on to express the hope that his continued studies would lead him to Christianity in the end, saying that, if he did not get there, it would not be for lack of trying (in Sidgwick and Sidgwick 1906, 82–83).

The problem here was in the "proof," or evidence: what passed for such within Christianity, and the conflict between this and his own scientific (as he saw it) approach. Sidgwick insisted that religious claims should satisfy the same evidentiary tests as scientific facts. Writing to fellow Apostle Roden Noel in early 1862, Sidgwick said, "I am sometimes startled to find to what a halt my old theological trains of thought and sentiment have come; I have never deliberately discarded them, but the scientific atmosphere seems to paralyse them" (in Sidgwick and Sidgwick 1906, 74–75). This tension between his felt religious needs and his scientific approach to inquiry, including theological inquiry, is perhaps best reflected in a letter to Dakyns in June 1862: "I want to be orthodox," he said, "and hunger after proofs." He did not see his desires here as at all unreasonable, particularly given what was at stake: "The distinctive tenets of Christianity are either *true* and final or not true and temporary," he said (quoted in Schneewind 1977, 24). Writing to Dakyns a few months later, he gave a clear indication of his position on beliefs that could not be empirically substantiated: "You see, I still hunger and thirst after orthodoxy: but I am, I trust, firm not to barter my intellectual birthright for a mess of mystical pottage" (in Sidgwick and Sidgwick 1906, 90).[6] Sidgwick felt that the

6. Speaking of an 1883 visit to Rome, Sidgwick said that "all that is connected with the form of Christianity centralised here is apathetic to me—partly, no doubt, because one almost never finds the Ages of Faith purely conveyed; the expression of them is almost always 'restored' and plastered over by the later ages of *make believe*" (letter to F. Myers, 28 January 1883, in Sidgwick and Sidgwick 1906, 367).

results of theologians' inquiries would be respected widely only if they adopted the methods of scientists (letter to Roden Noel, August 1866, in Sidgwick and Sidgwick 1906, 150; Schneewind 1977, 55) and that preachers of religion would be able to "retain their hold over educated men" only if they could "show in their utterances on sacred occasions the same sincerity, exactness, unreserved, that men of science show in expounding the laws of nature" (letter to his sister, 8 April 1870, in Sidgwick and Sidgwick 1906, 226).[7] Even so, Sidgwick was not ready to abandon Christianity, telling E. M. Young that he was "cling[ing] to the hope of a final reconcilement of spiritual needs with intellectual principles" (letter of 28 January 1862, in Sidgwick and Sidgwick 1906, 75).

His own attempts to accomplish such a reconciliation came via a lengthy historical study of Christianity, which, as he described it, was pointed toward solving "the great issues between Christianity and Scepticism or Agnosticism" (autobiographical fragment, in Sidgwick and Sidgwick 1906, 37). In 1862 Sidgwick read Ernest Renan's *Études d'histoire religieuse* (1857), which convinced him that a historical understanding of Christianity required encountering the original texts. This led him to an intensive study of the Arabic and Hebrew languages and then the relevant literature and history—a venture that occupied roughly three years of his life. By 1865, though, Sidgwick began to think that these historical studies would not help him answer "the great questions raised by the orthodox Christianity from which [his] view of the Universe had been derived" (autobiographical fragment, in Sidgwick and Sidgwick 1906, 37). What were these questions? They went to the truth of the foundational elements of orthodoxy: "Was Jesus incarnate God, miraculously brought into the world as a man? Were his utterances of divine authority? Did he actually rise from the grave with a human body glorified, and therewith ascend into heaven?" (38). And, he said, if one could not give a straightforward affirmative answer to these questions, "what element of truth, vital for mankind, could be disengaged from the husk of legend, or symbolised by the legend, supposing the truth itself capable of being established by human reasoning?" (38). Sidgwick's ultimate lack of confidence in the ability of historical studies to provide conclusive answers to these ques-

7. Nearly two decades later, Sidgwick would write in an address titled "Authority, Scientific and Theological" that "the deepest antagonism between Science and Theology lies in the difference in the authority derived from the *consensus* of experts in either case" (Sidgwick and Sidgwick 1906, 611). He considered the consensus of authority in theology as weaker than that in science, particularly given the divergence of opinions in the field on many questions.

tions, along with the influence of Auguste Comte's arguments about the necessity of religion, led him to turn his attention increasingly to the study of philosophy and theology.

The "storm and stress" of these years can be seen in the to and fro nature of his relationship with Christianity, and this comes out quite clearly in the *Memoir* (Sidgwick and Sidgwick 1906). Writing to Dakyns in 1866 about the struggles over continuing to hold his fellowship, Sidgwick said, "I sometimes think again of resigning. . . . My dear boy, this remaining in the Church of England is just—humbug" (in Sidgwick and Sidgwick 1906, 142). But then a month or two later he writes again to Dakyns about approaching "complete practical reconciliation with the Church" (145). Sidgwick's simultaneous desire to hold on and move away can be seen in his decision to participate as a founding member of the Free Christian Union in 1868. The union's objective was "to invite 'to common action all who deem men responsible, not for the attainment of Divine truth, but only for the serious search for it; and who rely, for the religious improvement of human life, on filial Piety and brotherly Charity, with or without more particular agreement in matters of doctrinal theology'" (189–90).

Despite the waning of religious belief in England at the time, Sidgwick felt very alone on the theological front and told Dakyns in 1863 that, as a religious skeptic, "There is no man in England who reflects my notions in print, no, not one" (letter of 22 March 1863, in Sidgwick and Sidgwick 1906, 94). He sensed a decided lack of interest in grappling with the questions that he considered so central. Yet it is not as if Sidgwick was the only fellow who did not agree with Church of England orthodoxy. Leslie Stephen, who had earlier resigned his fellowship on religious grounds, described the situation thusly:

> The average Cambridge don of my day was (as I thought and think) a sensible and honest man who wished to be both rational and Christian. He was rational enough to see that the old orthodox position was untenable. He did not believe in Hell, or in "verbal inspiration" or the "real presence." He thought that the controversies upon such matters were silly and antiquated, and spoke of them with indifference, if not with contempt. But he also thought that religious belief of some kind was necessary or valuable, and considered himself to be a genuine believer. He assumed that somehow or other the old dogmas could be explained away or "rationalised" or "spiritualised." He could accept them in some sense or other, but did not ask too closely in what sense.

> Still less did he go into ultimate questions of philosophy. He shut his eyes to the great difficulties or took the answer for granted. (quoted in Schultz 2004, 122)

The problem for Sidgwick was that he could not continue to maintain what he considered a religious charade.

In June 1869 Sidgwick finally took the step of resigning his fellowship. He did so, as he described it to Benson on 13 June, "in order to free myself from dogmatic obligations" (in Sidgwick and Sidgwick 1906, 198)—specifically, the particulars of the Apostle's Creed. He also informed Benson that he did *not* wish to secede from the Church of England, of which he felt he could remain a member even though not subscribing to the creed. His confidence in taking this step comes through very clearly in a 4 June letter to his mother, where he said that "whatever happens I am happy and know that I have done what was right. In fact, though I had some struggle before doing it, it now appears not the least bit of a sacrifice, but simply the natural and inevitable thing to do" (197). In the end, Trinity appointed him lecturer in moral sciences, which meant that he continued to perform essentially the same duties as under his fellowship, but at reduced compensation.[8]

Forsaking his fellowship did not, however, mean forsaking God. Sidgwick said in 1870, "I find . . . in me an inherited predisposition to this faith" (in immortality) (quoted in Schultz 2004, 442). As Schultz has put it, "Reverence, a prayerful attitude, these were things Sidgwick would not give up, elements of what he took to be the religiously oriented psychology of human beings" (679). Sidgwick considered himself at this time to be a theist and said that he could not see how unbelievers could be "content with, happy in, a universe in which there is no God" (letter to F. Myers, 26 June 1870, in Sidgwick and Sidgwick 1906, 227–28). Sidgwick had little tolerance for those who looked down on the religious attitudes of others, and he regarded "insouciant atheism or agnosticism as shallow, insensitive to the religious experience and the demands of the human heart" (quoted in Schultz 2004, 43).

Given his views on "proof," one might surmise that Sidgwick had some empirical grounding for his theism. But this was not the case:

8. One can read more of Sidgwick's own thoughts on this whole episode in the various letters that he wrote during this period, which have been published in Sidgwick and Sidgwick 1906, 198–202, and in Schultz 2004, chap. 3. Religious tests were abolished by an act of Parliament in June 1871, and Sidgwick was reappointed to his fellowship not long thereafter (Sidgwick and Sidgwick 1906, 219).

> I myself regard Theism as a belief which, though borne in upon the living mind through life, and essential to normal life, is not self-evident or capable of being cogently demonstrated. It belongs, therefore, to a class of beliefs which I do not dispute the general reasonableness of accepting, but which I think have to be considered carefully and apart in estimating the grounds of their acceptance—assumptions for which we cannot but *demand* further proof, though we may see no means of obtaining it. (Sidgwick 1902, 242; quoted in Schultz 2004, 684–85)[9]

There was, for Sidgwick, an "indestructible and inalienable minimum of faith which humanity cannot give up because it is necessary for life; and which I know that I, at least so far as the man in me is deeper than the methodical thinker, cannot give up" (letter to Lord Tennyson, mid-1890s, in Sidgwick and Sidgwick 1906, 541).[10]

Ethics and the Dualism of Practical Reason

Sidgwick's interest in philosophy dates to his undergraduate days, and his entry point into the subject was the study of the works of J. S. Mill. However, the classics and the historical case for Christianity occupied most of his attention until the mid-1860s, when he was led back to philosophy by his struggles over whether he had the right to retain his fellowship. It was in dealing with this question that he went through the thought processes that eventually were systematized in *The Methods of Ethics*, a book in which he wanted to show that religious "doubt did not necessitate a falling off of moral standards" (Schultz 2004, 138).[11]

Sidgwick has indicated that his "first adhesion to a definite Ethical system was to the Utilitarianism of Mill," and this interest in utilitarianism goes back at least to 1860. The attraction was related in part to his religious struggles: he found in utilitarianism a "relief from the apparently external and arbitrary pressure of moral rules which [he] had been educated to obey, and which presented themselves to [him] as to some extent doubtful and confused; and sometimes, even when clear, as merely dogmatic, unreasoned, incoherent" (Sidgwick [1907] 1981, xvii). Early

9. See also Sidgwick [1898] 1906.

10. One can find more by Sidgwick on his religious views in the 1880s and 1890s in Sidgwick and Sidgwick 1906, especially 346–48, 508.

11. See also the autobiographical fragment in Sidgwick and Sidgwick 1906, 36–38. "A method is a rational procedure 'for determining right conduct in any particular case'" (Schultz 2004, 150).

on, Sidgwick seems to have found a degree of consistency between utilitarianism and his religious beliefs (Schneewind 1977, 41–42).[12] And indeed, one can find in some writers a sense that utilitarianism, with its golden rule–type implications, reflected Christ's teachings.[13] Yet Sidgwick ultimately came to reject the view of an essential continuity here, seeing the state of the heart rather than the nature of the act as determining goodness in the eyes of Christ (Sidgwick [1866] 1904, 23; Schneewind 1977, 45–47).

The tangle between Sidgwick's religious and utilitarian views extended to his decision to resign his fellowship. We noted earlier his increasing conviction that he could not in good conscience maintain his fellowship when he did not subscribe to Church of England theology. His resignation, and the moral stance behind it, was clearly grounded in his utilitarianism, as we see from his letter to Blanche Clough written shortly after his resignation:

> It is my painful conviction that the prevailing lax subscription is not perfectly conscientious in the case of many subscribers: and that those who subscribe laxly from the highest motives are responsible for the degradation of moral and religious feeling that others suffer. It would require a very clear and evident gain of some other kind to induce me to undergo this responsibility. And such gain I do not see. (letter, 31 July 1869, in Sidgwick and Sidgwick 1906, 200–201)

In fact, Sidgwick's pamphlet *The Ethics of Conformity and Subscription* (1870) was a utilitarian attempt to settle the subscription issue. His approach to religious questions, reflected in the pamphlet, among other places, was very much like the approach he ascribed to utilitarian analysis: "Answering questions about actual practice in terms of realistic appraisals of the facts and the probabilities." And in situations of conflicts between duties (such as truth and church), the conflict should be resolved by an appeal "to what is expedient or useful or least harmful—by an appeal, in short, to some form of the utilitarian principle" (Schneewind 1977, 51).[14]

12. As David Levy (2001, 53) has noted, the golden rule and utilitarianism were considered "formally identical" by a number of prominent thinkers in England during this period. Others, though, saw utilitarianism and religion as fundamentally opposed. See, for example, the discussions in Almodovar and Teixeira, this volume, and Waterman, this volume.

13. See, for example, Mill and the Cambridge historian J. R. Seeley's *Ecce Homo: A Survey of the Life and Work of Jesus Christ* (1866).

14. See also Schultz 2004, 133.

The ethical hedonism of Mill's system—the idea that people ought to seek the general happiness—was very attractive to Sidgwick (1907, xvii), who found it "morally inspiring." But he was also attracted by Mill's psychological hedonism—the idea that each person seeks his or her own happiness—owing to what he considered "its frank naturalness" (xvii), and because common sense suggested to him that egoism, or the pursuit of self-interest, is reasonable (bk. 2, chap. 1). Sidgwick did not initially perceive a conflict between self-interest and duty, but an increasing sense that there was an incoherence here led him to make a more systematic study of how the two could be reconciled.[15]

The basic problem with the conflict between self-interest and duty has been excellently described by Schneewind (1977) in his study of Sidgwick's ethics. Schneewind restates Sidgwick's two ethical axioms as follows:

> P6: Maximizing the agent's own good is an ultimate right-making characteristic.
>
> B6: Maximizing the universal good is an ultimate right-making characteristic. (373)

If both of these principles are true, as Sidgwick asserts, an act is "right" only if they hold simultaneously. This means that there must be a perfect coincidence between the acts dictated by P6 and by B6, or at least that acts dictated by one are neutral with respect to the other. In fact, though, said Sidgwick, this will not be the case, as an empirical matter: "The inseparable connexion between Utilitarian Duty and the greatest happiness of the individual who conforms to it cannot be satisfactorily demonstrated on empirical grounds" (503). Elsewhere, Sidgwick spoke of the "inevitable divergence, in this imperfect world, between the individual's Duty and his Happiness" (journal entry, 16 March 1887, in Sidgwick and Sidgwick 1906, 472).[16] Having set out to discover what practical reason demands of human action, he was forced to conclude that it "inevitably makes contradictory demands" (Schneewind 1977, 374). Because of this, he could not help but conclude that his work here was a failure.[17]

15. The issue of this conflict between egoism and utilitarianism seems to have preoccupied him already in the early 1860s.

16. Sidgwick began to keep a journal in the summer of 1884 and continued it for several years. Much of this material is reprinted in Sidgwick and Sidgwick 1906.

17. Contrast this with Bastiat, who considered self-interest a God-given positive motive force (Faccarello and Steiner, this volume).

Sidgwick felt self-interest and duty would be aligned only if some external force worked to bring about such a harmonization, and he was convinced that the sanctions of this world alone could not do it. This brought him back to the issue—indeed, the necessity—of religious belief: there would have to be an afterlife that made acts in this world, such as benevolence, which satisfy the dictates of duty, also consistent with individual happiness, even though that would not seem to be the case by the dictates of this world. What was needed, in effect, was an invisible hand that would direct the pursuit of self-interest to the greater good, simply because it is God's will that people do—and thus in people's self-interest to work toward—the greater good. The threat of divine sanction meant that benevolence was in the individual's self-interest if the effect on eternal life is taken into account. As Schultz (2004, 15) put it, "Without a theistic postulate that the universe has a friendly moral order, there was ever the potential for a basic conflict between acting for one's own greatest happiness and acting for the greatest happiness of all, each option presenting itself as what one has most reason to do."[18]

The problem, of course, is that Sidgwick (1874, 470) could not find evidence for the existence of a deity who had imposed such an order:

> I find that I undoubtedly seem to perceive, as clearly and certainly as I see any axiom in Arithmetic or Geometry, that it is "right" and "reasonable," and the "dictate of reason" and "my duty" to treat every man as I should think that I myself ought to be treated in precisely similar circumstances and to do what I believe to be ultimately conducive to universal Good or Happiness. But I cannot find inseparably connected with this conviction and similarly attainable by mere reflective intuition, any cognition that there actually is a Supreme Being who will adequately reward me for obeying this rule of duty, or punish me for violating it.

This left Sidgwick with a problem or, rather, another conflict—this time between his concern about the implications for his system of ethics and his empirical nature: "The whole system of our beliefs as to the intrinsic reasonableness of conduct must fall, without a hypothesis unverifiable by experience reconciling the Individual with Universal Reason, without a belief, in some form or other, that the moral order which we see imper-

18. Interestingly, Richard T. Ely did not believe that, in practice, religion was necessarily the answer, either. As Frey (this volume) points out, Ely was concerned that selfishness led people to (incorrectly, in his view) see religion as being about the attainment of a personal afterlife rather than about the redeeming of the society in which they live.

fectly realized in this actual world is yet actually perfect" (473). Because he considered the existence of the afterlife necessary "in order to effect that harmony of Duty with Happiness which seemed to me indispensable to rational moral life," he followed Immanuel Kant in provisionally postulating "the continued existence of the soul" and set out in search of empirical evidence to support this hypothesis (journal entry, 28 January 1887, in Sidgwick and Sidgwick 1906, 467).[19]

Sidgwick's search for empirical support for the afterlife focused largely on exploring psychic phenomena. This interest, which began during his undergraduate days and continued throughout his life, explicitly linked the religious and the ethical: it was motivated largely by a desire to find scientific evidence, or proof, of another world and thus to provide a measure of scientific support for religious belief—some form of theism at least, if not Christianity itself—but had the added effect that it would provide the underpinnings for belief in an underlying moral order within the universe that harmonized self-interest and duty (466–67).[20]

Of course, Sidgwick's psychical studies did not bear any fruit. Even with this lack of empirical success, though, Sidgwick could not allow himself to jettison his belief in duty, writing in 1880 that, if he did so, he would "feel that the last barrier between [himself] and complete philosophical scepticism, or disbelief in truth altogether, was broken down." Therefore, he said, "I sometimes say to myself 'I believe in God'; while sometimes again I say no more than 'I *hope* this belief is true and I must and will act as if it was'" (letter to Major Carey, 8 August 1880, in Sidgwick and Sidgwick 1906, 347–48).[21] But as he was led increasingly toward the conclusion that he was unlikely to find proof of life after death, or of the soul's immortality, he was forced to confront the question of whether he could continue to postulate the existence of a deity who would accomplish the necessary harmonization of self-interest and duty. The import of this had deep personal implications for Sidgwick, who then asked himself, "Have I any ethical system at all?" This, in turn, led him to question whether he could consistently continue to be a professor of ethics (journal entry, 28 January 1887, in Sidgwick and Sidgwick 1906, 467).

19. Schultz (2004, 213): "As C. A. J. Coady has neatly put it, Sidgwick seems to be envisioning a God that has so effectively harmonized the world of practical reason that both the principles are 'true, and possibly self-evident, and it is the appearance of a contradiction between them that is wrong.'"

20. See also Schultz 2004, 276–77.

21. Major Carey was an old Rugby schoolfellow of Sidgwick's.

The import of the dualism of practical reason, for Sidgwick, went far beyond the personal to the social implications of the larger controversy over religion in England at the time. Religion was widely thought to provide the foundation for morality and, as Schneewind (1977, 20) has put it, "was needed to control the passions and desires of human beings, and to assure social order." If the only issue was one's happiness in this world, people would act far differently than they did under the threat of divine sanction. The promise of eternal salvation—or the sanction of eternal damnation—was the force that would motivate people to act benevolently in this life. Yet the status of religion in society was increasingly in question, and Sidgwick was afraid of destroying the existing moral order if Christianity was dismantled. As he said in 1881,

> In fact, the reason why I keep strict silence now for many years with regard to theology is that while I cannot myself discover adequate rational basis for the Christian hope of a happy immortality, it seems to me that the general loss of such a hope, from the minds of average human beings as now constituted, would be an evil of which I cannot pretend to measure the extent. I am not prepared to say that the dissolution of the existing social order would follow, but I think the danger of such dissolution would be seriously increased, and that the evil would certainly be very great." (letter to J. R. Mozley, 30 July 1881, in Sidgwick and Sidgwick 1906, 357)[22]

In light of this, Sidgwick was eager to "take part unhesitatingly in any social action to adapt and sustain" religion (letter to F. Myers, 26 June 1870, in Sidgwick and Sidgwick 1906, 227–28). He believed that churches met "a social need of fundamental importance" and had great social utility because of their "systematic teaching of morality" (Sidgwick 1897, 584). His support for religion, then, was utilitarian—to save society from moral collapse—not based on empirical evidence for the existence of God.

While Sidgwick regarded Christianity as "indispensable and irreplaceable . . . from a sociological point of view," his doubts about its truth were as solid as his conviction of its utility. Writing in his journal on 27 August 1886, he said that he found it "more and more incomprehensible how any one whom I feel to be really akin to myself in intellectual habits and culture can possibly find his religion in [it]." He described his alienation as

22. This gives weight to Keynes's characterization of Sidgwick, quoted in the concluding section of this article.

completely grounded in intellectual objections and wondered how—though pleased for the result, in light of his concerns about the demise of religion—so many possessed of intellectually able minds can be drawn to the clergy (in Sidgwick and Sidgwick 1906, 455).

Political Economy and the Dualism

Mill's influence on Sidgwick was not limited to philosophy; Sidgwick's time spent studying Mill's writings also led him to the study of politics and political economy (autobiographical fragment, in Sidgwick and Sidgwick 1906, 36; Sidgwick 1897, vi).[23] Sidgwick's interest in economics, theology, and utilitarianism were closely linked:

> I desire only studies that however abstract in . . . reasonings have for their end human happiness. Thus Political Economy to make men happier and better en masse: Theology, to know, not what conduces to *my* eternal weal, but to *our* &c. The strongest conviction I have is a belief in what Comte calls "altruisme": the cardinal doctrine, it seems to me, of Jesus of Nazareth. (quoted in Schultz 2004, 42)

That is, as with theology, Sidgwick was attracted to the study of political economy for utilitarian reasons—its potential to improve societal well-being.[24] More important, though, utilitarian considerations were, for Sidgwick (1897, 42), the "ultimate standard of right and wrong" in adjudicating the rightness of economic and political outcomes.

Yet Sidgwick (1901, 402) considered self-interest a centerpiece of human motivation, noting in his *Principles of Political Economy* that "the motive of self-interest does work powerfully and continually." He allowed that individuals at times were motivated by moral considerations, even in the economic realm (Sidgwick 1901, 581; [1885] 1904, 184). But such was his sense for the import of self-interest as a motivating force that he even went so far as to wonder whether his own ostensibly altruistic acts might actually be motivated by "enlightened selfishness" (Schultz 2004, 42). In fact,

23. Sidgwick was reading political economy already in the 1860s and said that he did so "as a ballast to my necessarily busy selfishness which would otherwise be intolerable to my real self" (letter to Dakyns [Lent term 1861], in Sidgwick and Sidgwick 1906, 66). He seems to have developed a particular interest in political economy in the 1870s, when he began to both write and deliver lectures on the subject (Schultz 2004, 534).

24. This perspective even extended to sport: Sidgwick found curling to be a "fine game" and loved the spirit of it because "the individual has to be subordinated to the common interest" (journal entry, 1 January 1887, in Sidgwick and Sidgwick 1906, 465).

Sidgwick was very much aware of the utility of self-interest in the economic sphere, to the point where "the difficulty of finding any adequate substitute for it, either as an impulsive or as a regulating force, is an almost invincible obstacle in the way of reconstructing society on any but its present individualistic basis" (Sidgwick 1901, 402).[25] He was not, however, a cheerleader for self-interest but, instead, as Schultz (2004, 42) has put it, "was apt to regard the prevalence of self-interest as akin to the prevalence of sin, something that had to be recognized and dealt with realistically, though certainly not applauded."

If the good of society is the ultimate criterion and individuals are motivated by self-interest, we are back to the question of the extent to which we can assume that self-interested action redounds to the best interest of society—the question that, in an ethical context, gave rise to the dualism of practical reason. In his *Elements of Politics*, Sidgwick (1897, 45) argued that the case for laissez-faire requires both "the psychological proposition that every one can best take care of his own interest" and "the sociological proposition that the common welfare is best attained by each pursuing exclusively his own welfare and that of his family in a thoroughly alert and intelligent manner." The latter is nothing more than the economic application of the ethical axioms P6 and B6, set out above. If self-interest and promoting the general welfare are the two ultimate moral goods, they will be simultaneously realized in the economic arena when the pursuit of self-interest redounds to the general welfare. As Sidgwick pointed out, ideal competitive markets translate self-interested action into the "morally *right* price"; here, "the self-interest of the seller seems to be working as a necessary factor in the realisation of the economic harmony of society" (Sidgwick 1901, 586). As with the God who resolves the dualism of practical reason issue, we have an invisible hand that directs the pursuit of self-interest to the greater good.

But just as Sidgwick (1897, 43) could not find empirical support for the equivalence of self-interest and duty in the ethical context, so, in the economic realm, he saw self-interest as "inadequate to produce the attainable maximum of social happiness" in many instances.[26] His *Principles of Political Economy* reveals an extensive list of divergences between private and social interests, both where laissez-faire's wealth-maximizing results

25. Sidgwick's *Principles* was originally published in 1883. References given here are to the third edition, which was published in 1901.

26. He also did not believe that each individual could always best see to his or her own interest. See, for example, Sidgwick [1886] 1904, 202–5; 1901, 425.

are not in society's best interest because there are "extra-economic considerations" that are more important than wealth and where laissez-faire does not even generate the wealth-maximizing result (Sidgwick [1886] 1904, 203; 1901, 399–418).[27] He was concerned that orthodox political economy had "often produced a blind confidence in the economic harmony resulting from natural liberty," to the point where it even seemed to neglect to note the opposition between the monopolists' interests and those of the community (Sidgwick 1901, 588).

This lack of confidence in the ability of natural liberty to harmonize self-interest and social interest led Sidgwick to suggest that improvements could come via government intervention. Sidgwick's qualms about the market were matched, though, by a concern that government interference could make matters worse, owing to the various incentive problems that worked against an efficiently operating governmental machine. As such, he insisted that intervention be implemented on a utilitarian basis—that is, the gains had to outweigh the costs. The same empirical perspective evidenced on the religion side comes through in his political economy. His sense that policy choices involve imperfect alternatives made him critical of the supporters of both laissez-faire and socialism, and of the idea of finding a golden mean between the two.[28] Such a mean implies "that both extremes are right, if each would only see the other's side, and that truth can be arrived at by harmoniously compounding the two." Sidgwick, in contrast, believed that "both are proceeding from unwarranted premises to uncertified conclusions, and that scientific truth on the subject of dispute is only to be reached, if at all, by a road that neither has found" (journal entry, 25 September 1886, in Sidgwick and Sidgwick 1906, 457).

Hands, Visible and Invisible

Sidgwick's ethics and his political economy were both characterized by the search for a harmonizing element. He wanted harmonization via invisible

27. See also Medema 2007a. The English school of welfare economics, discussed by Backhouse (this volume) broadened this even further.

28. Sidgwick used the French term *juste milieu*. One might legitimately ask how the extremes of laissez-faire and socialism referred to by Sidgwick can be reconciled with the notions of excess and deficiency, which are central to Aristotle's notion of the golden mean. Sidgwick does not speak to this directly, but in his *Principles of Political Economy* and his *Elements of Politics*, it is clear that Sidgwick sees self-interest as a useful but imperfect coordinating force. Laissez-faire, then, gives rise to an excess of self-interested action, and socialism a deficiency of it.

hands—God, perhaps, and whatever it was that equated private and social interests in the economic realm. But while the champions of Christianity and laissez-faire each touted the virtues of their particular religion, Sidgwick could not find empirical evidence for either. He could not rely on morality absent a divine sanction to get the job done on the ethical front, and he had little confidence in the ability of the economic system to channel self-interest toward the larger social interest.

Absent a harmonizing set of invisible hands, Sidgwick was forced to rely on hands more visible—the church in the moral realm and the state in the economic—to get the outcomes mandated by utilitarianism. In the former case, he hoped for the continued beneficial influence of Christianity on morality; in the latter case, he held out hope that government action could nudge the economic system in directions that redounded to the general interest. He did not have a great deal of confidence in either, although he hoped that what he saw as a theistic mood within society at large would be sufficient on the moral end and that improvements in governance would help on the economic front.[29]

Sidgwick (1901, 590) would almost certainly have numbered himself among the many (and not just socialists) who he said see the incentives for action under self-interest as very useful economically "yet feel the moral need" to make people conscious that their work is "a social function only rightly performed when done with a cordial regard to the welfare of the whole society." This, of course, would be thoroughly consistent with his interest in socialism, itself a natural outgrowth of the centrality of benevolence in his ethical system. The problem, of course, was that Sidgwick felt self-interest often failed to promote the general interest, yet the general-interest promoting socialism would fail because of the effects of self-interest.[30]

Even so, Sidgwick remained incredibly optimistic about what Christianity and government had to offer, and saw the possibilities of the latter in some sense tied to those of the former. In early 1891 he described his "attitude towards Christianity" as follows:

> (1) I think Optimism in some form is an indispensable creed—not for every one, but for progressive humanity as a whole. (2) I think Optimism in a Theistic form—I mean the belief that there is a sympathetic

29. See Backhouse and Medema 2008 and Medema 2007a.

30. On the role of self-interest in state action, see Backhouse and Medema 2008 and Medema 2007a.

> soul of the Universe that intends the welfare of each particular human being and is guiding all events of his life for his good—is, for the great majority of human beings, not only the most attractive form of optimism, but the most easily acceptable, being no more unproven than any other form of optimism, and certainly more than satisfying to the deepest human needs. (3) I think that no form of Optimism has an adequate rational basis; therefore, if Theism is to be maintained—and I am inclined to predict the needs of the human heart will maintain it—it must be, for Europeans, by virtue of the support that still obtains from the traditional belief in historical Christianity. (letter to Mozley, 11 January 1891, in Sidgwick and Sidgwick 1906, 508)

On the economic front, Sidgwick (1901, 416) suggested that, over time, "moral and political progress [in society] may be expected to diminish" the extent and severity of the shortcomings associated with government intervention. This, in turn, would increase the range of activities that government can carry out in a manner superior to market forces. This optimism is most strikingly expressed in his assessment of socialism. While concerned that any attempt to institute a collectivist system in the late nineteenth century would "arrest industrial progress" and bring about "equality in poverty," he saw something potentially quite different for the future:

> It is, I think, quite conceivable that, through improvements in the organization and working of governmental departments, aided by watchful and intelligent public criticism—together with a rise in the general level of public spirit throughout society—the results of the comparison [between individualism and collectivism] will at some future time be more favourable to governmental management than they hitherto have been. (Sidgwick 1897, 159)

This optimism about the improvability of the state, and thus for the ability of state action to enhance economic welfare, was to become a hallmark of the Cambridge welfare tradition, as elaborated by Alfred Marshall ([1907] 1925, 336; 1926, 395) and Pigou (1912, 250; 1932, 333–35).

Sidgwick was, at heart, a skeptic who at once demanded empirical proof yet allowed his desires on this score to be partially overridden by his own hopes and optimism. When preparing his address to the British Association for the Advancement of Science in 1885, Sidgwick wrote of economics in a way that consciously paralleled his view of religion:

> My problem . . . is to put as optimistic a colour as possible on the rather low view that I take of the present state of our economic knowledge. Really, in this as in other departments, my tendency is to skepticism, but skepticism of a humble, empirical, and more or less hopeful kind. I do not argue, or even think, that nothing is known, still less that nothing can be known by the received methods, but that of what is most important to know we, as yet, know much less than most people suppose. (journal entry, 15 July 1885, in Sidgwick and Sidgwick 1906, 417)

Keynes said of Sidgwick that "he never did anything but wonder whether Christianity was true and prove that it wasn't and hope that it was" (quoted in Schultz 2004, 4). Both religious and economic dogmas suffered at the hands of Sidgwick's empiricism. Yet, in losing his religion, Sidgwick was forced to confront the inability of invisible hands to harmonize self and social interests, and thereby to search for institutional structures that could bring about results that comported with utilitarian dicta.

References

Backhouse, Roger E. 2006. Sidgwick, Marshall, and the Cambridge School of Economics. *HOPE* 38:15–44.

Backhouse, Roger E., and Steven G. Medema. 2008. Public Choice and the Cambridge School: A New View. Working paper, University of Colorado Denver.

Chadwick, Owen. 1966. *The Victorian Church, Part 1.* New York: Oxford University Press.

———. 1972. *The Victorian Church, Part 2.* 2nd ed. London: Black.

Kloppenberg, James T. 1992. Rethinking Tradition: Sidgwick and the Philosophy of the Via Media. In *Essays on Henry Sidgwick*, edited by Bart Schultz. Cambridge: Cambridge University Press.

Levy, David M. 2001. *How the Dismal Science Got Its Name: Classical Economics and the Ur-Text of Racial Politics.* Ann Arbor: University of Michigan Press.

Marshall, Alfred. [1907] 1925. Social Possibilities of Economic Chivalry. In *Memorials of Alfred Marshall*, edited by A. C. Pigou. London: Macmillan.

———. 1926. Memorandum on Fiscal Policy of International Trade. In *Official Papers by Alfred Marshall*, edited by J. M. Keynes. London: Macmillan.

Medema, Steven G. 2003. The Economic Role of Government in the History of Economic Thought. In *The Blackwell Companion to the History of Economic Thought*, edited by Jeff Biddle, John B. Davis, and Warren J. Samuels. Oxford: Blackwell.

———. 2007a. The Hesitant Hand: Mill, Sidgwick, and the Evolution of the Theory of Market Failure. *HOPE* 39:331–58.

——. 2007b. Pigou's *Prima Facie* Case: Market Failure in Theory and Practice. Working paper, University of Colorado Denver.

O'Donnell, Margaret G. 1979. Pigou: An Extension of Sidgwickian Thought. *HOPE* 11:588–605.

Pigou, A. C. 1912. *Wealth and Welfare*. London: Macmillan.

——. 1932. *The Economics of Welfare*. 4th ed. London: Macmillan.

Rawls, John. 1981. Foreword to *The Methods of Ethics*, by Henry Sidgwick. 7th ed. Indianapolis: Hackett.

Renan, Ernest. 1857. *Études d'histoire religieuse*. Paris: M. Lévy.

Schneewind, J. B. 1977. *Sidgwick's Ethics and Victorian Moral Philosophy*. Oxford: Oxford University Press.

Schultz, Bart. 2004. *Henry Sidgwick: Eye of the Universe*. Cambridge: Cambridge University Press.

Seeley, J. R. 1866. *Ecce Homo: A Survey of the Life and Work of Jesus Christ*. London: Macmillan.

[Sidgwick, Arthur, and Eleanor Mildred Sidgwick]. 1906. *Henry Sidgwick: A Memoir*. London: Macmillan.

Sidgwick, Henry. 1870. *The Ethics of Conformity and Subscription*. London: Williams & Norgate.

——. 1874. *The Methods of Ethics*. London: Macmillan.

——. 1897. *The Elements of Politics*. 2nd ed. London: Macmillan.

——. 1901. *The Principles of Political Economy*. 3rd ed. London: Macmillan.

——. 1902. *Philosophy: Its Scope and Relations*. London: Macmillan.

——. [1866] 1904. Ecce Homo. *Westminster Review*. In *Miscellaneous Essays and Addresses*. London: Macmillan.

——. [1885] 1904. The Scope and Method of Economic Science. In *Miscellaneous Essays and Addresses*. London: Macmillan.

——. [1886] 1904. Economic Socialism. In *Miscellaneous Essays and Addresses*. London: Macmillan.

——. [1898] 1906. On the Nature of the Evidence for Theism. In *Henry Sidgwick: A Memoir*. London: Macmillan.

——. [1907] 1981. *The Methods of Ethics*. 7th ed. Reprint, Indianapolis: Hackett.

Faith, Morality, and Welfare: The English School of Welfare Economics, 1901–29

Roger E. Backhouse

In the first three decades of the twentieth century, a group of economists sought to bring religious convictions explicitly into economics as the foundation for judgments about welfare. These economists, described by Walton Hamilton (1919) as an "English welfare school," created a welfare economics that was distinct from the more "scientific" welfare economics associated with the Cambridge school of Henry Sidgwick, Alfred Marshall, and A. C. Pigou.[1] This article focuses on three of the former group—J. A. Hobson, R. H. Tawney, and Henry Clay. Their political views and their religious beliefs differed substantially (Tawney was a socialist and a committed Anglican, whereas Hobson was a Liberal and an agnostic humanist), but all three sought explicitly to maintain a space for religious beliefs within economics. This focus immediately makes this a story about Oxford.[2] That is no accident, for their beliefs owed much to the Oxford environment and the influence of teachers such as Benjamin Jowett and T. H. Green.

I am indebted to Donald Winch, the editors, and two anonymous referees for comments on an earlier draft of this article, although they bear no responsibility for such inadequacies as remain.

1. Quotation marks are placed around *scientific* to denote that the meaning of the term was highly contested in this period (see Maas, this volume).

2. It should of course be remembered that Marshall passed through Oxford and that although he developed welfare economics differently, he and his Cambridge colleagues shared many of the ethical commitments discussed here.

History of Political Economy 40 (annual suppl.) DOI 10.1215/00182702-2007-067

In creating that space they were addressing challenges faced by the Victorian church, which ran much deeper than simply Darwinism and evolution. Society was believed to rest on a morality that in turn rested on traditional Christian beliefs, and when these were challenged this was seen as a threat to the social order. The Victorians responded in many ways, some abandoning Christianity, others reinterpreting traditional beliefs, yet others reaffirming them, and discussions of these questions came to be tied up with questions of "socialism," which at this time was an extremely loose and more ambiguous term.

The present article begins by summarizing the Victorian doubts over religion and morality that provide the context for the work of these three economists. The discussion then turns to Tawney. His work came directly out of the nineteenth-century Christian socialist tradition, and he lay squarely at the center of the church establishment. His close friend Charles Gore was both a leading Christian socialist and a prominent bishop. Hobson illustrates what might be thought of as the other extreme of the religious spectrum: the humanism found in the ethical societies or the "Ethical Church." The Victorian church needs to be understood as comprising a confused spectrum of beliefs that cannot be reduced to a simple dichotomy between belief and unbelief. Clay, on the other hand, shows how similar ideas on welfare could be incorporated into a more conventional economics, without following Tawney or (to a lesser extent Hobson) toward socialism. The article concludes by placing this episode in the context of Waterman's (2004) discussion of "establishment" views, represented both by churchmen (William Smart, Josiah Stamp, and William Temple) and atheists (John Maynard Keynes).

Doubt and the Moral Foundations of Society

Morality was central to the doubts that plagued the Victorians, arguably ranking above science and biblical criticism in the list of problems confronting religion.[3]

> English thinkers found it easy to be Christian because the grounds of reason looked probable enough. As they searched the realms of nature they traced the beauties of pattern and of purpose. In 1830 science sustained the head truths of religion. Englishmen were sure that God existed

3. The following paragraphs draw extensively on Chadwick 1970, chapter 8, and 1976, chapter 3.

> and revealed himself. They believed the contrary doctrine untrue *less because they could prove it false than because they could see it as immoral.* The atheist or agnostic was not welcome in polite society. A man who said that he was irreligious lost public face. (Chadwick 1970, 527; emphasis added)

The immorality of unbelief, whether deism or unbelieving rationalism, had been demonstrated by the excesses of the French Revolution.[4] The result was that "the bases of Christianity—creator God, Christ divine, inspired Bible, future life—were as entrenched among the axioms of ordinary Englishmen in 1837 as fifty years before" (527).

However, the position of the English church in society had changed dramatically, the most significant break with the past being Catholic emancipation in 1828. This measure was passed not because of popular support (it was widely opposed as threatening the social order) but because the incorporation of Ireland, with its overwhelmingly Catholic population, into the United Kingdom made it a political necessity. The right of Catholics to participate in the political process called into question the identification of the state with the established church—the perceived foundations of the social order. It inaugurated an era of vigorous competition between Christian denominations and within them and there developed the greater earnestness in religion that forms the background against which Cardinal Newman sought an infallible assurance of faith, a process ending with his move to Rome.

By the 1850s the threats had grown. Darwinism is the most well-known challenge, but it was neither the first nor the most profound. More important were the related challenges from biblical criticism and from morality. Modern biblical criticism dates from D. F. Strauss's *Life of Jesus*, published in German in 1835. Although his book was largely unread in Britain because of the language barrier, and untranslated because of the blasphemy laws, it became notorious after his election to a chair in Zurich created a political storm that caused the government of the canton to fall. Strauss's name (and with it German thought more generally) became "a ghostly whip, a bogey, a talisman" (Chadwick 1970, 527). It was not until it was ruled that serious work did not constitute blasphemy that the book could be translated, in 1846, by Mary Ann (later, Marian) Evans, the nov-

4. For an account of British responses to the French Revolution, see Stedman Jones 2004.

elist George Eliot (Strauss 1846). The moral challenge to faith came from the Old Testament and from certain Christian doctrines. The doctrines of a substitutionary atonement and of eternal hellfire for unbelievers were thought offensive and inconsistent with a God of love. The Old Testament portrayed a God who commanded the Israelites to murder innocent people. This came when readers were beginning to think more historically about the Bible, seeing it as a series of books written over a long period.

German biblical scholarship played a twofold role in this process. It posed a challenge to the idea that the Bible was infallible yet provided a weapon for defenders of Christianity to show that it was not necessary to either believe that the Bible was completely true or reject it as a fabrication. The biblical writers could be seen as honest men, writing the truth as they saw it. This was particularly important when questions were asked about the New Testament: it was, for example, far more acceptable to claim that the Gospel writers relied on sources who thought they had seen Jesus walking on water (when he was actually walking around a lake), or who attributed healing arising from natural cures to supernatural intervention, than to suggest that they sought to deceive. Thus while conservatives might be frightened of German scholarship, responding by reiterating the doctrine of divine inspiration and the Bible's literal truth or by denying reason, there were others for whom Strauss "free[d] Christian truth from the shackles of history and so the mind from the torment of doubt" (Chadwick 1970, 532).

The broad church school that emerged in the 1850s comprised individuals who turned to German critical methods to reformulate Christian doctrine in a way that took seriously the problems with traditional beliefs. For the present argument, the two most important of them were F. D. Maurice, at Cambridge, and Benjamin Jowett, at Oxford. Their significance lies in the way they sought to redefine Christian doctrine not through science but through religious experience or through seeing religion as an ethical parable. Maurice represented the former; Jowett the latter. The broad churchmen faced problems—Maurice was dismissed from his chair at King's College, London; Jowett was required by Oxford to reaffirm his assent to the Thirty-nine Articles after publishing a series of critical essays—but by the 1860s their position was secure.

From the 1860s to the end of the century, the significant religious question became that of unbelief. Again, although science provided a key ingredient, the key issue was morality:

> For the serious non-Christians—George Eliot, John Morley, Leslie Stephen and the like—the problem was morality. The morals of their society were based upon religion. . . . If the religion declined, as they hoped, the decline brought danger that the public morality would decline, which they did not hope. They needed to find for themselves, and to make plain to the public, why the fall of religion would not lead to the fall of moral standards. (Chadwick 1976, 120)

There were people who felt that religion could be removed from society without loss, but they were few. More common were those who believed that although ethics need not be based on religion, religion was in fact the basis for morality and would remain so for a considerable time. This was the background to the late-nineteenth-century search for principles of ethics that would stand apart from Christian doctrines, which included philosophical treatments by Green, Stephen, Sidgwick (and, at the end of the century, G. E. Moore), and Eliot's novels.

As with their broad church antecedents, such as Maurice, this generation included men who were an inspiration to their contemporaries. At Oxford, Green sought to reformulate Christian doctrine as a system of morality; although expounding a system of ethics that drew heavily on Hegelian idealistic philosophy, and giving ample ground for critics to wonder whether he was propounding a message that was at its heart secular, it was Christian in language and form. Some of his most influential lectures took the form of lay sermons (included in Green 1885–88; see also Richter 1964). Idealism, which in Hegel's hands had been a conservative doctrine, was reinterpreted as an ideology of social reform. Much of what he said may have gone over the heads of his listeners, but it still inspired them. When Marshall was in Oxford, he noted the hundreds of students flocking to hear Green, and later contrasted this with the very small number that Sidgwick was attracting in Cambridge (see Harvie 1976, 200). His was a practical, socially oriented Gospel, expressing itself as much through activities such as the settlement movement as through doctrine.

At Cambridge Sidgwick was the central figure. He did not attract students in the same way as Green, but he was nonetheless an inspiration to many of his contemporaries: he was even spoken of as saint.[5] Unlike Green, who sought to reinterpret Christian doctrine, Sidgwick's philosophy was explicitly secular (subject to the qualifications implied by the

5. See Schultz 2004 for an invaluable account of Sidgwick's life.

attitudes discussed by Medema, this volume). His philosophical perspective was determined not by idealism but by utilitarianism, with which he engaged in a continuing debate, seeking, but failing, to find grounds on which he could prove that selfishness was inferior to concern for the welfare of the community. Keynes, somewhat unkindly, said of Sidgwick, "He never did anything but wonder whether Christianity was true and prove it wasn't" (quoted in Moggridge 1992, 101). Although Keynes, following Moore, was impatient with Sidgwick's agonizing over religion and ethics, this was something with which many of his contemporaries could identify.

This was the context out of which welfare economics emerged in Britain in the hands of Sidgwick, Marshall, Pigou, and their contemporaries. Cambridge welfare economics, well known because it engaged with the concerns of economists in the 1930s and beyond, was an attempt to provide a scientific analysis of welfare, using what were, broadly, utilitarian arguments about markets and welfare.[6] This narrowed the scope of their work to what could be analyzed scientifically, as they understood that term. It was this narrowing to which Hobson, Tawney, and Clay took exception, developing an alternative analysis that, although seen as "welfare economics" by Hamilton and Wesley Mitchell, was not even recognized as such by most Cambridge economists, Lionel Robbins, or subsequent generations. Perceived canons of what it meant to be "scientific," which had been important in the time of William Whewell and Richard Jones (see Maas, this volume), proved important in a later period.

Christian Socialist Ethics: R. H. Tawney

Christian socialism dates back to around 1850, as a solution to the difficulties the Church of England had in reaching out to the working classes. It combined high church doctrines with a critique of political economy and laissez-faire, although not of the basic institutions of society, making it less radical than many critics of political economy and laissez-faire. However, although Maurice was often seen as the origin of Christian socialism, it is appropriate here to focus on the later development of this movement that started in the 1870s and 1880s and was represented by the Guild of St Matthew, established in 1877, and the Christian Social Union

6. The qualifier "broadly" is inserted because, in different ways, Marshall and Pigou both sought to distance themselves from utilitarianism.

(CSU), established in 1889. Both were established to increase the Church of England's engagement with social questions, thereby showing the relevance of the Incarnation especially in slum parishes in the East End of London. Although Stewart Headlam, the founder of the guild, was forced to quit his parish because of his views, the CSU achieved a wide following among the bishops, Gore being a prominent example. Christian socialism was largely about replacing principles of competition and laissez-faire with ones of fellowship and social concern. The extent to which it should be considered socialism at all is debatable, one historian arguing strongly that

> the Christian "Socialists" of the C.S.U. School were, like Maurice in the 1850s, not really socialists at all. They represented the synthesis of Victorian intellectual liberalism with Chamberlain's "constructionism" or collectivism. They differed only in the scale of their moralizing from those of their class and profession whose criticisms of Political Economy, and partial acceptance of collectivist functions of the State, were marked features of the last three decades of the century. So far were they from being the daring social theorists of their own imagining, and so respectable did their attitudes become, that between 1889 and 1913, sixteen of the fifty-three episcopal appointments went to members of the Christian Social Union. (Norman 1976, 176)

Others, however, have emphasized the combination of conservatism in religious doctrine with views about Christian social responsibility that were sufficiently radical to offend conservatives and that, in the terminology of the day, could be considered socialist. The CSU was at its peak in late Victorian and Edwardian England, but by the First World War it was clearly in decline, Gore having resigned from it a few years earlier. In 1919 it merged with the Navvy Mission Society (established in 1877) to form the Industrial Christian Fellowship (ICF).[7]

The CSU provides the context for Tawney's writings on welfare. He was at Balliol from 1899 to 1903, a contemporary of William Beveridge, soon to become his brother-in-law. Green's influence, with its focus on social concern, was still strong, although for Tawney a key figure was Gore, who became a close friend. Gore, who became the first bishop of Birmingham in 1905 and bishop of Oxford in 1911, was among those who sought to combine broad church liberalism (with its strong social concern and

7. See Studdert-Kennedy 1982, 4–5, 15.

willingness to accept that parts of the Bible should be understood metaphorically) with high church Anglicanism, as expressed in *Lux Mundi* (1889), of which Gore was editor. Although focusing on the Incarnation, this needed to be made a reality through actions in the world. They might be "the holy party," but their devotion found expression in social concern. Christian ethics needed to be worked out in society in concrete terms. Gore did not share Green's idealist philosophy, and, unlike Green, he adopted a strict view of the historical accuracy of the New Testament (although his willingness to concede that the theological value of the Old Testament did not require its historicity but might rest on treating it as allegory or myth caused a rupture with traditionalists in the Tractarian tradition). His founding of the Community of the Resurrection reflected a belief in the centrality of fellowship, a theme associated with Tawney (see the subtitle and chapter 9 of Terrill 1973).

Tawney left Oxford with Beveridge, moving to Toynbee Hall, a settlement established by a Church of England curate, Samuel Barnett, in one of the poorest parishes in London's East End, to encourage members of the privileged classes to live and work among the poor, thereby educating the future rulers about conditions there. Tawney was inspired by the Master of Balliol's challenge "to discover why with so much wealth, there was also so much poverty in London" (Wright 1987, 2). He then moved, via Glasgow University, to the Workers Educational Association (WEA, founded in 1903 to meet the educational needs of working men), an organization he remained close to for many years. He later described the experience of teaching there as the best part of his education (Wright 1987, 6). After six years of working at the WEA, he moved to LSE in 1912 as director of a foundation established to investigate the causes of poverty. He remained a friend of Gore, in whose house he recovered after being wounded on the first day of the battle of the Somme, and also a friend of William Temple, later archbishop of Canterbury, whom he involved in the WEA and to whom he dedicated his first book.

His socialist views were established while at Oxford. There, from Balliol and from Gore, he became attuned to the importance of ethics, a view confirmed by his experience at Toynbee Hall, where he concluded that poverty went along with a poor ethical atmosphere (Wright 1987, 4). In his years at the WEA before 1912 he established himself as an economic historian of the sixteenth century, the upshot of which was that he considered morality to lie at the heart of efforts of social reform. On 18 September 1912, he wrote in his diary,

> What is needed for the improvement of society is not so much that men should have profound information as to the possible result of their actions, but that they should have a keen sense of right and wrong, that they should realize that the conceptions of "right and wrong" apply to *all* relations of life, including those where their application is most inconvenient, such as those of business, and that they should act on their knowledge. (Tawney 2006, 30)

This moral knowledge, he continued, was "the common property of Christian nations" (31). Christianity thus lay at the heart of his social thought.

Tawney's most important work is generally believed to be three books published between 1921 and 1931: *The Acquisitive Society* (1921), *Religion and the Rise of Capitalism* (1926),[8] and *Equality* (1931). In a sense, *Religion and the Rise of Capitalism* was fundamental, because it provided a historical explanation of where capitalism, and the values on which it was based, originated. *Equality* later proved highly influential in the Labour Party and on the left. However, Tawney's attitude to morality and economics can be seen in *The Acquisitive Society* and the earlier pamphlets on which it was based.

For Tawney (1920, 17) an acquisitive society was one where a priority was given to protecting economic rights, in particular property rights, while leaving economic functions to fulfill themselves (except under exceptional circumstances).

> By fixing men's minds, not upon the discharge of social obligations, which restricts their energy, because it defines the goal to which it should be directed, but upon the exercise of the right to pursue their own self-interest, it offers unlimited scope for the acquisition of riches, and thereby gives free play to one of the most powerful of human interests. (18)

Such a society, Tawney argued, had come into existence, in Britain, in the seventeenth and eighteenth centuries, with the rise of individualism.[9] This historical thesis is a side issue for the present argument, but it is worth noting that Tawney believed that it was only after the Industrial Revolution that private property became a problem. Before the Industrial Revolution, the right to private property had provided a defense for

8. Gore wrote a prefatory note to this book.

9. Similar to the development that MacPherson (1962) would later describe as the rise of possessive individualism.

the small producer against the state; it was only after the development of modern industry that absolute property rights (absolute in that they were associated with no economic function) resulted in the separation of ownership of capital from work and became a cause of great inequality of opportunity.

Tawney argued that goods and activities had to be judged according to the contribution made to the public purpose. People were not isolated individuals but parts of societies that had common goals and purposes, or moral principles. After saying that increased production was important, he claimed that "plenty depends upon co-operative effort, and co-operation upon moral principles" (Tawney 1920, 5). However, individualism had destroyed these moral principles and the purpose, without which society could not exist.

> The will to economic power, if it is sufficiently single-minded, brings riches. But if it is single-minded it destroys the moral restraints which ought to condition the pursuit of riches, and therefore also makes the pursuit of riches meaningless. For what gives meaning to any economic activity, as to any other activity is . . . the purpose to which it is directed. (18)

There were, until they were eroded by individualism, moral principles that found general acceptance (Tawney 1921, 225). In the above quotation the crucial phrase is "single-minded": the problem was not with economic criteria themselves but that economic criteria had pushed aside all else. The vehemence with which he argued this is worth quoting at greater length:

> The burden of our civilization . . . is that industry itself has come to hold a position of exclusive predominance among the human interests, to which no single interest, and least of all the provision of the material means of existence, is fit to occupy. . . . That obsession [with] economic issues is as local and transitory as it is repulsive and disturbing. And it is a poison which inflames every wound and turns each trivial scratch into a malignant ulcer. (Tawney 1920, 86)

He explicitly rejected the utilitarian criterion, the greatest happiness of the greatest number, as it denied any role and meaning for society.

> But to say that the end of social institutions is happiness, is to say that they have no common end at all. For happiness is individual, and to

> make happiness the object of society is to resolve society itself into the ambitions of numberless individuals, each directed towards the attainment of some personal purpose. (17)

Society was not an economic mechanism but a community of wills (Tawney 1921, 227). Given this view that societies had, or should have, common purposes, he was able to argue that some goods and activities were better than others, and that part of wealth was waste, which should never have been produced when there was still useful work to be done (Tawney 1920, 21).

Tawney's welfare economics was permeated with values that he took from Christianity. The basis for equality was that all were equal before God. Christianity was the source of his judgment that economic activity should be a means, not an end, and of the idea that society should be structured so as to meet collective rather than purely individual needs. Thus rather than a society based on rights (rights derived from ownership), there should be a society centered on functions performed. If people performed useful social functions, whether making goods or performing services, they should be rewarded. But there was no justification for incomes that corresponded to no function (monopoly profits, ground rents, mineral royalties, or even interest): "The man who lives by owning without working is necessarily supported by the industry of someone else, and is, therefore, too expensive a luxury to be encouraged" (Tawney 1921, 84).

The Acquisitive Society ended with an appeal for an explicitly Christian standard of social conduct (228). Tawney often gives the impression that Christian conduct is too obvious to need spelling out in detail, although some things become clear. It did not mean maximizing one's income.

> No one has any business to expect to be paid "what he is worth," for what he is worth is a matter between his own soul and God. What he has a right to demand, and what it concerns his fellow-men to see that he gets, is enough to enable him to perform his work. *When industry is organised on a basis of function, that, and no more than that, is what he will be paid.* . . . If a man has important work, and enough leisure and income to enable him to do it properly, he is in possession of as much happiness as is good for any of the children of Adam. (175; emphasis added)

Christian social conduct, therefore, involves regarding consumption not as an objective but merely as the means that enables one to serve others.

Humanist Ethics: J. A. Hobson

Hobson (1938, 15), born in 1858, came, as he put it, "from the middle stratum of the middle class of a middle-sized industrial town of the Midlands," predisposing him toward "a complacent acceptance of the social order."[10] In describing himself as what might be thought of as a typical Victorian, he focused on social class. However, religion was an integral part of this background, helping mold his social thinking.

> Derby was a religious community in which the Established Church and leading Nonconformist sects were strongly supported. Church and chapel going was universal and, for the young, compulsory; family prayers were pretty general, and piety played a considerable part in ordinary life. (19)

The divide between church and chapel was less doctrinal than socioeconomic, those aspiring to move upward often joining the Church of England. He was brought up in what he called "a moderate puritanism which eschewed all taint of Romanism," one of his earliest memories being "walked out" of the church when the vicar wore a white surplice instead of a black gown. His father protested by letter, and the family moved to the church of the well-known evangelical preacher the Reverend Sholto Douglas Campbell Douglas, who "oversatisfied our religious ardour by sermons of an hour and a quarter." Hobson recounted this as a time when active piety took his "childish mind" away from social problems. At the age of sixteen he attended a Cambridge University Extension Board course in political economy, taken by a clergyman, the Reverend Ede, on the moral underpinnings of the subject.

His disillusion arose from applying reason to Christian doctrines, his earliest two publications dealing with religious doctrine.

> The failure to satisfy my elementary sense of reason and of justice in the doctrines of the atonement and of everlasting punishment for unrepentant sinners were, I think, the earliest evidence of a humanism which in early manhood led me to the abandonment of orthodox Christianity. (20)

As was noted above, such reasoning was typical of the period. It led to his going up to Oxford a "religious heretic," excused the duty of attending

10. See also Backhouse 2007.

chapel.[11] However, despite his skepticism, he was susceptible to the influence of many "broad church" figures.[12]

> I think that my mind received from these years of study a disposition and a valuation that were of immense service in liberating me from the easy acceptance of the current ideas and feelings of an age rightly designated as materialistic and narrowly utilitarian. Something more than that I received from the atmosphere of an Oxford in which Jowett, T. H. Green, and Mark Pattison were leading figures, though my only personal contact, not a close one, was with Pattison, in his declining years. (26)

The precise nature of the "something more" is not elucidated, but he makes clear that unbelief in orthodox doctrine did not imply a materialistic outlook.

On leaving Oxford, Hobson, after some years working as a schoolteacher, during which he met his American wife, moved to London in 1887. There he joined the rationalist circles, becoming close to J. M. Robertson, a close associate of the notorious atheist Charles Bradlaugh. However, of more significance was his involvement with ethical societies (Hobson 1838, 49–58; Clarke 1978, 51–54). He initially joined the London Ethical Society and, through that, the Charity Organisation Society, eventually reacting against its individualism and its application of double standards to rich and poor. In 1897 he moved to the South Place Ethical Society, with which he remained associated for the rest of his life, becoming one of its regular lecturers.

The South Place Chapel had been built in 1822 to house a congregation that had, since 1802, been Unitarian, under the guidance of its pastor William Johnstone Fox, who "preached a humanized theism" (Sylvester-Smith 1967, 105). His successor, a charismatic American, Mercure Conway, moved the congregation away from Unitarianism toward what they hoped could be a "pure and universal religion" that would emancipate humankind from superstition and create "fellowship among liberal thinkers of all classes," and promote the "moral welfare of mankind" (115).[13]

11. Note the different meaning of "chapel," innocent of any connection with nonconformity, in this context.

12. Pattison was rector of Lincoln College, Oxford, and one of the reformers, along with Jowett, seeking to encourage scholarship by rewarding academic success.

13. These phrases are taken from the deliberations of a Congress of Liberal Thinkers that Conway helped organize at South Place in 1878.

The ambiguities of this movement came to a head under Conway's successor, another American, Stanton Coit, who took over South Place in 1887. Coming from Columbus, Ohio,

> he brought with him influences of a Freethinking mother, a background of spiritualism (which he abandoned when he was nineteen) and a head full of Ralph Waldo Emerson. In addition, [he] was heavily influenced by Sir John Seeley, Professor of Modern History at Cambridge. Seeley rejected Christianity, but insisted that religion had always been the basis of societies. (124)

He helped with founding a series of ethical societies, the first from Toynbee Hall in 1886, with further ones in 1890 (East London), 1891 (West London), 1892 (South London), and 1895 (St. Pancras). Out of the West London society emerged the Ethical Church in Bayswater in 1909. He preached what has been described as a socialized religion, the basis of which lay in the social order (126). The ambiguous relationship with the established church is shown by the fact that he thought of the Ethical Church as a model for reform, not a sect but an "unacknowledged party within the Anglican Church, striving . . . to bring to it a new conception of its national task" (126).

In 1911 the Union of Ethical Societies published an extensive summary of its principles and aims (Bridges et al. 1911). This spoke of the supremacy of ethics, that authority in ethics was essential:

> The doctrine of self-assertion is pushed to the most extravagant lengths. Men who would not venture to trust their own unaided judgment on any detail of physics or chemistry are yet ready to preach revolution against the ancient sanctities of humanity, even when the whole weight of expert opinion is opposed to their innovations. The most quixotic utterances of Nietzsche are accepted as oracles, and the notion of good and evil as a fundamental distinction in human actions and dispositions is dismissed as obsolete by people who have never read a treatise on ethics or given an hour's consideration to its problems. (67–68)

This was not a mere matter of moral instruction for the young: "The unnatural and pernicious association of ethics with supernaturalistic theology must be ended" (70). There were major moral problems to be solved. Drawing on arguments based on the psychological basis for religious experience, Coit and his colleagues asserted, using almost mystical language, that "it is the duty of an ethical fellowship to be a powerhouse, generating currents of energy which stimulate the intelligence, the idealism, and the will-to-service of all who belong to it" (137).[14]

This is the organization with which Hobson was associated for over forty years. Shortly after he joined the South Place Ethical Society, Hobson wrote *John Ruskin: Social Reformer* (1898) and began to see the logic of Ruskin's position. Concepts such as wealth, value, and profit had to be seen in their proper relation to life, and not interpreted so as to serve a business mentality. These ideas were developed in lectures to the CSU and published in Coit's *Ethical World*, a Saturday penny paper started in 1898, to which Ramsey MacDonald, the future Labour prime minister, was also a significant contributor.[15] Hobson and MacDonald were also contributors to Coit's *Ethical Democracy* (1900), in which Hobson wrote on the ethics of industrialism. These ideas were more fully written up as *The Social Problem* (1901), perhaps the first full statement of Hobson's position. Hobson's organicism—his view that individuals cannot be understood apart from the society of which they form a part—and his emphasis on the social basis of ethics, which permeates all his thinking, are but a short step from the principles and aims of the Ethical Movement, as outlined by Coit. Also, although Hobson may have given these ideas much greater intellectual substance, he remained in many ways a preacher.

That Hobson's outlook remained essentially religious, despite his rejection of Christianity and belief in God (cf. the parallel cases discussed by Emmett, this volume, and Faccarello and Steiner, this volume), is shown by remarks made at the end of *God and Mammon* (1931). He wrote of the need for "a religion, stripped of all theology and magic" that could supply principles and ideals on which economic institutions could be based (56). He rejected moral individualism: not only was it inherently repugnant, it failed to take account of the co-operative nature of much social activity. What was needed was a rationalist religion that, avoiding the errors of Auguste Comte's positivism, would "conceive man, individual and collective, as the most finely composed part of nature, directed in his behaviour by a more definitely conscious urge than is discernible in the rest of the animate world" (58). The function of this urge was "to establish . . . some standard of values, some ideal of a good life," a process that he described as "an enlightened utilitarianism in which

14. The ambiguities involved in the Ethical Movement meant that this period was its heyday, for it could not survive the strains of the First World War.

15. On the *Ethical World*, see MacKillop 1986, 147–61.

bodily satisfactions would have their proper place along with the spiritual, under a system of thought in which the division of body and spirit is not regarded as an ultimate division of labour."

This call for an "enlightened utilitarianism" echoed Hobson's call, thirty years earlier, in *The Social Problem*, for a "new utilitarianism" based on a Ruskinian calculus that took account of the human costs of production and consumption.[16] He provided a much fuller account a few years later, in *Work and Wealth* (1914), the aim of which he described as being to complete the task identified by Ruskin, "to determine what are in reality useful or life-giving things, and by what degrees and kind of labor they are attainable and distributable" (*Munera Pulveris*, quoted in Hobson [1914] 1992:10). He sought to develop a human standard of value by which the welfare of society could be established. Society was, he claimed, an organic whole and had to be analyzed as such. "Organic welfare" was a measure of welfare that took account of society as an organic structure, the value of whose parts depended on their role in the whole. This might be little more than "a synonym for good life" (12), but it acquired content as Hobson applied it to the process of production and consumption of wealth.

The most-neglected aspect of the problem, Hobson claimed, was the study of consumption. To work out the human value of national income it was necessary not only to look backward to the processes in which goods were produced but also to look forward to the processes in which they were consumed. Echoing Thorstein Veblen, whose *Theory of the Leisure Class* (1899) he cited with approval, he argued that organizing business for profit led to consumption that was harmful, to the degradation of many consumption goods, and to the stimulation or suppression of wants according to the interests of business rather than the interests of consumers (Hobson 1914, 112). Many wants were "artificial" (118).[17] Interestingly, however, given Hobson's largely middle-class perspective and his evangelical, puritan upbringing, he argued that there could be value in certain activities that economists frequently dismissed as wasteful working-class spending, such as high spending on public holidays, on drink, and on funerals (127).

In *Wealth and Life* (1929), Hobson moved toward what he called a more social view of welfare, based on the assumption that people might be

16. Discussed in detail in Backhouse 2007.

17. Of course, this was one of Marshall's themes, although he did not press it to the same extent.

mistaken in judging their own needs. He argued that a broad, human assessment of goods was required, that this required evaluations that were qualitative as well as quantitative. Quantitative analysis, based on the assumption of a selfish, gain-seeking "economic man," could never capture this broader, humanist view (Hobson 1929, 454–55).

> The economic treatment will remain essentially quantitative, the humanist treatment qualitative. The former will seek to answer the question, "How many men can live with the highest average standard of economic life upon this area?" The latter will ask, "What population will yield the best results in terms of human personality as expressed in due satisfaction of all physical and spiritual needs?" (456)

Hobson clearly believed that welfare cannot be reduced to a single dimension that will permit quantitative comparisons to be made: because there are many "physical and spiritual needs" that cannot be reduced to a common denominator, comparisons of welfare can only be qualitative.

Christian Ethics and Economic Liberalism: Henry Clay

Henry Clay was another economist trained at Oxford, not Balliol but University College, from 1903 to 1906. His career started in charitable work followed by a settlement in Sheffield, from which he went on to the WEA, where he worked from 1909 to 1917. During the war he became a civil servant in the Ministry of Labour, and after it he embarked on an academic career, at Oxford and then Manchester. In 1930 he moved to the Bank of England. Although he later returned to Oxford as warden of Nuffield College, his career was from then on solely in the policymaking sphere, where he acquired a high reputation as a monetary economist "unrecognised by the academic world" (Sayers 1976, 2:462, 489).

Clay's (1918, ix) writing on welfare dates from the first phase of his career, at the WEA, where he became a friend of Tawney, whose assistance he acknowledges. Tawney's (2006, 33, 56) diary mentions occasions where he picked up stories about working-class life from Clay. It was out of his lecturing in WEA classes that he wrote *Economics: An Introduction for the General Reader* (1916). This was, as its title implies, an elementary textbook. As economic theory, it was in no sense a match for the work of Marshall or Pigou. It was, however, taken very seriously by contemporaries. The British edition (1916) and the American (1918) were widely reviewed, including a ten-page review article in the *Journal of Political Economy* (Hamilton 1919). The significance of the book here is that its final three chapters (chapters 23–26) contain an extensive, substantially original, analysis of welfare.

Clay points out that wealth can mean either "economic wealth" or welfare. The former comprises all goods that satisfy wants and are in limited supply. Economic wealth is thus the output of the economic system and comprises both good and bad wants (Clay 1918, 415–17). It is measurable, at least in principle. In contrast, welfare depends on ethical views, counting only certain kinds of want. This means that there is disagreement over what welfare means, and it may not even be measurable. This is why economists have avoided the concept.

> Because there are these divergent conceptions of welfare, varying with every variation in ethical, aesthetic and political views, economists have chosen to leave on one side the study of wealth in this second sense [as welfare], and have confined themselves to wealth in the commoner, agreed sense [economic wealth]; they have studied the organisation for satisfying wants, without considering distinctions in the kind of wants. (422)

Given that welfare depends on ethical views and is hard to define, Clay confines himself to asking what he describes as "the important practical question; how far, and under what circumstances, an increase of wealth is an increase of welfare" (422). He found many reasons why one could not assume a close relationship.

The first reason was that welfare depends on what Clay called "internal" and "external" causes. The external causes of an individual's welfare are the goods and services he or she consumes, but causes internal to the individual (which determine wants) are also important. There are widely diverging views about the relative importance of internal and external causes:

> Materialism is the subordination of the internal sources of satisfaction to the external; most religions exalt the internal over the external, and teach that welfare lies in the former, to which the latter must be sacrificed: "The Kingdom of Heaven is within you." (447–48)

Thus in some systems of morality, welfare is independent of wealth. Another system of morality was the utilitarian, according to which different kinds of satisfaction could be added up and maximized (434).

Clay did not agree with this, seeing different satisfactions as incommensurable, some being "higher" than others. Such arguments do not establish what the relation is between wealth and welfare, but they are enough to establish that to assume they are closely linked (as did Pigou) is to make a strong ethical judgment.

This was a purely negative argument against seeing wealth as the measure of welfare. His offered positive arguments were much more conventional, many of them familiar to Sidgwick and his Cambridge successors. Some free goods contributed to welfare, causing wealth to diverge from welfare. There were externalities and wants that were endogenous, depending on social standards. The latter could mean that "the rich *as a class* are no happier and no better than the poor *as a class*" (449). The same was true over time: "If we compare ages and countries, we are struck by the apparent unimportance of wealth" (449). Ages might be measured by art or by religion, according to which the modern age fares less well in relation to its predecessors.

Welfare depends on ethical beliefs, and these vary greatly. Divergent conceptions of welfare were, Clay believed, a major obstacle to bringing economic organization in line with "society's general conception of welfare" (475). However, to draw the conclusion that welfare could not be analyzed, because of these disagreements, would be to abandon the application of economics altogether. The aim of policy is to increase welfare, which means that economics simply cannot be applied without some notion of welfare and some moral system.

An argument to which Clay paid much attention was the argument that the business system was neutral, on the grounds that under a system of free enterprise activity will conform to the wants and tastes of the time, and hence the ethical values of the time. He offered many arguments why this was not the case. The first was that a system of free enterprise took account of demands and not needs; inequality in the distribution of income caused these to diverge, and those "who subordinate everything else to money-getting will exercise the greatest influence," whereas those who "devote themselves to altruistic objects and neglect the pursuit of private wealth" will have little influence (452). Saint Francis, devoted to a life of poverty, would have no influence at all. Clay also maintained that people did not know what was good for them. It was also common for people to know what was good for them (perhaps not drinking too much) but not to do it. They needed, sometimes, to be forced to do what was good for them.

However, Clay's most interesting argument is perhaps the argument that the economic organization is not independent of moral standards but reacts to them (455–60). Wealth is definite and measurable, and hence people attach greater weight to it than they should. Insecurity means that people struggle to get above the minimum that they need, which generates inequality; this raises wants, for those with less will want more, and as a result welfare will not rise proportionately to income. Free enterprise also means that some will profit from actions that lower welfare, such as the publican who earns more by getting someone drunk than from keeping him sober. Furthermore, under free markets many receive incomes for which no service has been provided (e.g., the unearned increment of land values), which "obliterates" the distinction between "social and anti-social effort": "Wealth is respectable however won, and great wealth is honoured, because it is powerful, whatever its source" (460). Dishonesty was admired as much as honesty. The result, Clay contended, was that the economic organization of his day strengthened materialistic tendencies at the expense of idealistic ones. Wealth had come to be unconsciously equated with welfare, and the pursuit of wealth had become a habit. Quoting William Morris, he concluded:

> It was this materialism, or "utilitarianism" as Morris called it, "which, being interpreted, means the reckless waste of life in the pursuit of the means of life," that the idealists of the nineteenth century, Carlyle, Ruskin, and Morris, attacked; all attributed it to the same cause, the influence of the economic system established by the Industrial Revolution; and all extended their attacks to the economists who explained the system, *for ignoring the effects of the system on standards of taste and conduct.* (463–64; emphasis added)

Although the terminology is different, there is a clear link here with Tawney. Clay does not go so far as Tawney in his view of society as involving a shared purpose, or in arguing for a functional view of society, in which rewards are clearly linked to the functions performed, where these are valued in relation to society's goals. However, they share the views that social welfare has to be judged against shared moral values and that the dominance of commercial activities can undermine those moral values.

Unlike those of his friend Tawney, Clay's religious convictions are implicit only in his published work. While he clearly rejected utilitarianism, he presented religious ideals in a way that, although clearly highly sympathetic, was ostensibly neutral. His biographer in the *Dictionary of National Biography* fails to mention his religious convictions. What is significant, however, is that here we have an economist developing a welfare economics very similar indeed to that put forward by Tawney, and having much in common with Hobson's, but who remained, unlike either of them, a nineteenth-century liberal.

The Boundaries of Faith and Economic Science

Waterman (2005, chap. 13) writes of a change in establishment social thinking toward the end of the nineteenth century. Midcentury, at the time of Richard Whately, there was still an Anglican social doctrine that amounted to a synthesis of classical political economy with Christian theology. By the end of the century the situation changed, the religious establishment having come largely to identify itself with the opponents of economics—with those who have been called, emphasizing their links with the Romantics, "the self-appointed spokesmen for human beings" (Winch 1996, 418). This split reflected the gradual secularization of British intellectual life after 1860 (Waterman 2005, 216). The CSU, with its enormous support in Oxford and among the episcopacy, is a central part of that story. Waterman (2004, 216–17) exemplifies this by citing the divide between Marshall and Tawney, although he could equally have pointed to the different emphases of the *Economic Journal* and the CSU's *Economic Review*.

Waterman's 2004 discussion fills out some of the detail in this larger picture but also shifts the emphasis. Rather than simply echo the established view (Waterman 2005, 214 n. 26) that English Christian socialists were "naive and confused about economic matters," the claim is that a small group of economists challenged the division of labor between economics and religion, arguing that moral judgments rooted in religion had to form a part of welfare economics. The Christian socialist, Tawney, worked alongside the humanist, Hobson, and the Liberal, Clay. Their attempts to keep a space within economics for ethics, arguably the obsession of secular as much as Christian intellectuals in late Victorian England, arose directly from the Victorian crisis of faith.

This is not to deny that many Christian socialists may have been naive in their attitude toward economics.[18] Tawney's dismissal of Marshallian ideas, cited by Waterman, may represent naïveté about the need to understand "positive economics," and Hobson certainly failed to understand *some* components of the orthodox economics he was attacking (see Backhouse 1988). Their belief that ethical values were so widely shared that identifying them posed no significant intellectual problem, was no doubt

18. Neither do I wish to affirm this.

naive but common for their generation. However, their ideas should not be too readily dismissed. Hobson, for example, developed the implications of ideas that Marshall and Pigou recognized but then brushed aside (see Backhouse 2007). Marshallian influences are pervasive in Hobson's writing.[19] The welfare economics of Tawney and Hobson made little headway in British academic economics, but it was taken seriously in the United States (see Rutherford 2007), and all three were highly significant figures in the worlds of politics and policymaking. There was a divide between professional economist and religious moralizer—this adds another dimension to Hobson's rejection by the economics establishment—but in this period it was far from sharp.

What Waterman calls the establishment view of the relation between economics and religion may have taken slightly longer to become entrenched than he suggests. Tawney, Hobson, and Clay all came through Oxford, home of the Oxford movement, Jowett, Green, and the CSU.[20] All three were involved in adult education in the period before the First World War, when the activity of the CSU was at its height, and it was then that their ideas on welfare were formed (before Tawney and Clay had moved into established academic positions). During this period, Gore and his contemporaries in the CSU preached a message that, although one can question whether it was sufficiently radical to be described as socialist, nonetheless posed a serious challenge, much as did the Social Gospel movement in the United States (see Davenport, this volume, and Bateman and Banzhaf, this volume) or contemporary Catholic thinking (see Almodovar and Teixeira, this volume). By the end of the First World War, the situation had changed. The *Economic Review*, the CSU's main organ, ceased publication in 1914. The CSU's successor, the ICF—exemplified in its "Messenger," the ex–First World War army padre, Woodbine Willie—preached an intellectually shallow evangelical piety that was a world apart from prewar Christian socialism (see Studdert-Kennedy 1982). The profound divisions of the late Victorian and Edwardian eras gave way to the softer conservatism of Stanley Baldwin, facilitating the rapprochement between economics and establishment religion in the 1930s that Waterman correctly identifies with figures such as Stamp and Temple.

19. I wish to thank Donald Winch for making me see the extent of Hobson's debt to Marshall.

20. Edwin Cannan, another member of Hamilton's "English welfare school" also came through Oxford.

Conclusions

The dominant challenge for many Victorian intellectuals was not reconciling faith with evolution but maintaining the morality on which social order was believed to rest. At Cambridge, Sidgwick sought, and failed, to find a secular, philosophical argument for nonegoistic, utilitarian behavior. Marshall and Pigou developed what they considered a scientific welfare economics, following the approach of most nineteenth-century economists of excluding values, as far as possible, from economics (see Waterman, this volume). In doing so, they came up against the "extrascientific" issues raised by Hobson, Tawney, and Clay, but after token gestures, ignored them. For other Cambridge economists, Moore's ethics provided an alternative basis for welfare judgments, but the notion that moral judgments were things that could be intuited directly was hardly persuasive as a basis for welfare. Ralph Hawtrey (1926) made moves in that direction, but Keynes, although his work was suffused with moral judgments (see Backhouse and Bateman 2007) and although he sensibly never sought to construct any systematic principles of welfare economics, never published his highly original ideas about ethics (see Baldwin 2006).

In contrast, Tawney, Hobson, and Clay refused to exclude ethics from economics, being much less concerned about whether the subject was "scientific." Their personal histories, involving in various measures Oxford, Green, the CSU, and the extension movement, help explain why Tawney, Hobson, and Clay sought to develop the ideas about welfare that they did. However, the fact that, in this period, a group of economists was embarking on such a project has to be set against the challenges posed, many decades earlier, to the beliefs of the Victorian church. Whether this should be considered "keeping faith" depends crucially on how this term is defined.

References

Backhouse, R. E. 1988. J. A. Hobson as a Macroeconomic Theorist. In *Re-appraising J. A. Hobson*, edited by M. Freeden. London: Allen and Unwin.

———. 2007. J. A. Hobson as a Welfare Economist. Unpublished paper.

Backhouse, R. E., and B. W. Bateman. 2007. Keynes and Capitalism. Unpublished paper.

Baldwin, T. 2006. Keynes and Ethics. In *The Cambridge Companion to Keynes*, edited by R. E. Backhouse and B. W. Bateman. Cambridge: Cambridge University Press.

Bridges, H., S. Coit, G. O'Dell, and H. Snell. 1911. *The Ethical Movement*. London: Union of Ethical Societies.

Chadwick, O. 1970. *The Victorian Church*. Part 1. London: Black.

———. 1976. *The Victorian Church*. Part 2. London: Black.

Clarke, P. 1978. *Liberals and Social Democrats*. Cambridge: Cambridge University Press.

Clay, H. 1916. *Economics: An Introduction for the General Reader*. London: Macmillan.

———. 1918. *Economics: An Introduction for the General Reader*. London: Macmillan.

Coit, S., ed. 1900. *Ethical Democracy*. London: Grant Richards.

Gore, C., ed. 1889. *Lux Mundi*. London: Murray.

Green, T. H. 1885–88. *Works of Thomas Hill Green*. Edited by R. L. Nettleship. 3 vols. London: Longmans Green.

Hamilton, W. H. 1919. An Appraisal of Clay's Economics. *Journal of Political Economy* 27.4:300–309.

Harvie, C. 1976. *The Lights of Liberalism*. London: Lane.

Hawtrey, R. G. 1926. *The Economic Problem*. London: Longmans, Green.

Hobson, J. A. 1898. *John Ruskin: Social Reformer*. London: Nisbet.

———. 1901. *The Social Problem*. London: Nisbet.

———. 1929. *Wealth and Life*. London: Macmillan.

———. 1931. *God and Mammon: The Relations of Religion and Economics*. London: Watts.

———. 1938. *Confessions of an Economic Heretic*. London: Allen and Unwin.

———. [1914] 1992. *Work and Wealth*. Reprint, Bristol, U.K.: Thoemmes.

MacKillop, I. D. 1986. *British Ethical Societies*. Cambridge: Cambridge University Press.

MacPherson, C. B. 1962. *The Political Theory of Possessive Individualism*. Oxford: Clarendon.

Moggridge, D. E. 1992. *Maynard Keynes: An Economist's Biography*. London: Routledge.

Norman, E. 1976. *Church and Society in England, 1770–1970*. Oxford: Clarendon.

Richter, M. 1964. *The Politics of Conscience: T. H. Green and His Age*. London: Weidenfeld and Nicolson.

Rutherford, M. 2007. American Institutionalism and Its British Connections. *European Journal of the History of Economic Thought* 14.2:291–323.

Sayers, R. S. 1976. *The Bank of England, 1891–1944*. 2 vols. Cambridge: Cambridge University Press.

Schultz, B. 2004. *Henry Sidgwick: Eye of the Universe*. Cambridge: Cambridge University Press.

Stedman Jones, G. 2004. *An End to Poverty*. London: Profile Books.

Strauss, D. F. 1846. *The Life of Jesus: Critically Examined*. Translated by George Eliot. 3 vols. London: Chapman Brothers.

Studdert-Kennedy, G. 1982. *Dog-Collar Democracy: The Industrial Christian Fellowship, 1919–1929.* London: Macmillan.
Sylvester-Smith, W. 1967. *The London Heretics.* London: Constable.
Tawney, R. H. 1920. *The Sickness of an Acquisitive Society.* London: Fabian Society/Allen and Unwin.
———. 1921. *The Acquisitive Society.* London: G. Bell and Sons.
———. 1926. *Religion and the Rise of Capitalism.* London: Murray.
———. 1931. *Equality.* London: Allen and Unwin.
———. 2006. *R. H. Tawney's Commonplace Book.* Edited by J. M. Winter and D. M. Joslin. Cambridge: Cambridge University Press.
Terrill, R. 1973. *R. H. Tawney and His Times: Socialism as Fellowship.* Cambridge, Mass.: Harvard University Press.
Veblen, T. 1899. *The Theory of the Leisure Class.* New York: Macmillan.
Waterman, A. 2004. *Political Economy and Christian Theology since the Enlightenment.* London: Palgrave Macmillan.
Winch, D. 1996. *Riches and Poverty: An Intellectual History of Political Economy in Britain, 1750–1834.* Cambridge: Cambridge University Press.
Wright, A. 1987. *R. H. Tawney.* Manchester: Manchester University Press.

Part 3
The United States

The United States: Introduction

The three sections of this book follow a natural progression. Just as the Church of England inherited the traditions of the Catholic Church, so, too, did American Christianity inherit much of its initial impetus from British Protestantism. Likewise, just as French political economy had an important impact on the development of British political economy, the latter played an important role in the development of American economics.

The chapters in this section demonstrate these historical connections. We begin with Stewart Davenport's study of the reception in antebellum America of Adam Smith's two chief works, *The Theory of Moral Sentiments* and the *Wealth of Nations*. A particular problem was how to resolve *das Adam Smith Problem* within the framework of "faculty psychology," in which prudence occupied an uncomfortable middling ground between the higher virtues and the more base passions. Davenport describes two schools of American thought on the matter. The first was "the clerical school" of political economy, comprising Francis Wayland, John McVickar, Alonzo Potter, Henry Vethake, Francis Bowen, and others, all of whom held prominent academic posts, and a number of whom were church leaders as well. These clerical economists emphasized that God had so constituted the world that acting prudently would bring prosperity and harmony to a nation. As prudence is a virtue, albeit a lesser one, the corollary was that virtuous living had this happy consequence. A second school, which Davenport refers to by the shorthand "pastoral moralists," was primarily

History of Political Economy 40 (annual suppl.) DOI 10.1215/00182702-2007-068

composed of pastors who wrote and preached on economic matters, but were not necessarily academic scholars. While they agreed that prudence and the pursuit of self-interest may bring prosperity, they also feared that prudence could become the ally of the passions as well as of the virtues. Moreover, they were not content with the hedonistic outcomes but insisted that economic relationships build moral character as well.

In the next chapter, Stephen Meardon considers a set of individuals and overlapping political movements that might be grouped with Davenport's pastoral moralists. Meardon provides a complex story of the way religion, politics, and political economy were intricately entangled during the years of the Second Great Awakening, provoking religiously grounded debates over free trade—and over the boundary between the private and public role for religion. He focuses especially on two individuals, the Reverend Joshua Leavitt and the Reverend Calvin Colton, both evangelical ministers and social proselytizers, born within five years of one another, both from western Massachusetts and both educated at Yale. Yet their similarities end there. A dedicated abolitionist, Leavitt found an intellectual basis for freeing slaves in the principle that individuals have a property right to their own labor. From there, it was a short step to the idea that they also have a right to sell the fruits of their labor at a market price. By this reasoning, a consistent abolitionist would also support free trade. Pragmatically, Leavitt also developed a political coalition for his Liberal Party by recruiting western farmers, whose interest was in freer markets for their exports. Colton, on the other hand, reacted strongly against the abolitionist movement, which he viewed as an extension of the excessive moralizing emanating from religious revivals and moral societies. In his view, such meddling was injurious to religion and thrust religion into the political sphere, where it did not belong. Although personally opposed to slavery, he felt the movement threatened national harmony. To him, the chief national political goal was to build America's greatness. Taking the same road as Leavitt but in the opposite direction, Colton found this position consistent with supporting the tariff and found both those positions politically expedient for bringing southern and some western votes to the Whig Party.

In the third essay in this section, Donald Frey shows how new ideas imported from Continental Europe could shake up these debates. Frey takes up the case of Richard Ely, an economist who, motivated by his dedication to the Social Gospel, wanted to use the tools of economics to make the world more hospitable to the poor and oppressed, that is, to make it more just. However, inheriting an American tradition of political economy shaped by Davenport's clerical economists, Ely had first to disarm the laissez-faire critique that any state intervention in the economy would be unable to achieve its objectives, or do so only at high ancillary costs. Studying in Germany under Karl Knies, Ely returned to America convinced that such doctrines reflected a fallacious, ahistorical absolutism. Denying the existence of any absolute laws such as those of laissez-faire, Ely argued that economic truths were contingent on the cultural context from which they emerged and in which they operated. This, in turn, led Ely to a much more inductive methodological posture, not unlike that advocated by Richard Jones and William Whewell (as described in Maas's earlier essay in this volume). Notably, this posture toward social science was also fully consistent with Ely's liberal Protestantism, which had digested historical criticism of the Bible and Friedrich Schleiermacher's emphasis on subjective religious experience.

The final chapter, by Ross Emmett, is about an individual who may seem out of place in a volume on religion: Frank Knight. Knight's open hostility toward organized religion is well documented in his own published writings and in numerous personal anecdotes. Based on their experience in his courses, Chicago graduate students used to joke, "There is no God, and Frank Knight is his prophet." Yet Knight, for all his hostility, was no less thoughtful about the connection between religion and economics, and the role of religion in an economy. Emmett shows that Knight worked according to a set of principles held together in precarious tension. First, he held that economics is the scientific study of the allocation of resources in a market economy; essentially, it is price theory. Second, Knight believed economics, as a science, could not bow to religious principles either in its methods or in its policy recommendations. Third, he believed that Christian and other religious principles were guides for *personal* relationships, and that as such they had little role to play in *impersonal* market transactions and had little to say about problems at the level of economic organization. In this respect, Knight is as far removed in his commitments as he was in time and space from Germaine de Staël, Benjamin Constant, Claude-Henri Saint-Simon, and others in the opening chapter to this volume, who felt that religion was needed to maintain social harmony in such settings. Fourth and finally, however, Knight also carefully circumscribed the role of economics. Economics may be the scientific study of market relationships, but this did not prove that the market economy was the best institutional arrangement for production and distribution. This is an ethical question that has a higher status than economics itself. Similarly, at the micro level, price theory could describe the choices people made according to utility maximization, but value theory could not be reduced to the utilitarian calculus. Price theory takes wants as given, but "the chief things which the common-sense individual actually wants is not satisfactions for the wants which he has, but more, and better wants." That is, we desire to be better people. Thus, in the end, Emmett portrays a Frank Knight who ironically played an influential role in safeguarding a space for ethical and spiritual considerations, a space in which other economists might "keep the faith."

Das Adam Smith Problem and Faculty Psychology in the Antebellum North

Stewart Davenport

Where are ethical concerns in Adam Smith's *Inquiry into the Nature and Causes of the Wealth of Nations*? In one of his most famous passages Smith wrote, "It is not from the benevolence of the butcher, the brewer, or the baker, that we expect our dinner, but from their regard to their own self-interest. We address ourselves not to their humanity but to their self-love" (Smith [1776] 1981, 26–27). Thankfully, in the wonderful world of *The Wealth of Nations*, these same individuals, driven by "self-interest" but fortunately guided by the "invisible hand," ended up working for the good of the whole. Thus in its daily operations, the mechanism of market capitalism appeared to have no place for benevolence—or "sympathy" as Smith had called it in his earlier tome, *The Theory of Moral Sentiments*—but it ultimately did more good than harm. Smith's vision of a self-interested commercial society was not as problematic as the "Private Vices, Public Benefits" described by Bernard Mandeville in *The Fable of the Bees*, but it was still unclear exactly where Christian ethics and a Christian God fit into Smith's capitalist economics. This essay investigates how some of the first inhabitants of the world that Smith had wrought—Christians in the developing market-capitalist antebellum North—sought to resolve the modern tensions between the ethical and the economical.

This essay comes out of my 2008 book *"Friends of the Unrighteous Mammon": Northern Christians and Market Capitalism, 1815–1860* and is published here with the permission of the University of Chicago Press.

History of Political Economy 40 (annual suppl.) DOI 10.1215/00182702-2007-069

When one opens up this can of worms called "Christian ethics and capitalist economics," however, one quickly discovers that the range of issues involved is simply enormous, covering everything from the cosmic to the quotidian. Thus while aware of the discursive nature of the subject, this essay nevertheless attempts to bring some order to the chaos. The first section introduces *das Adam Smith Problem* as a major intellectual challenge from 1776 to the present and summarizes the best recent scholarly attempts to resolve it. In the second section I argue that the antebellum paradigm of faculty psychology provides a useful vocabulary for addressing the problem, although it might complicate matters because it takes an issue that was originally binary and makes it tripartite. The next two sections investigate how two groups of antebellum Protestants, the "clerical economists" and "pastoral moralists," used faculty psychology to solve *das Adam Smith Problem* to the best of their abilities and according to their own set of ethical priorities.

Originally Sinful: *Das Adam Smith Problem*

When it came to the questionable ethics of Smith's economic system, the fundamental problem—which later German scholars simply called "*das Adam Smith Problem*"—was that Smith had written two influential books and not one. The difficulty was in harmonizing *The Theory of Moral Sentiments*, which emphasized people's sympathy for other people, with *The Wealth of Nations*, which presumed the individual's overriding tendency to act according to self-interest. Another way to state the problem is simply to ask where was morality in *The Wealth of Nations*, or what kind of morality did it presuppose and possibly sanction?

Broadly considered, the answers to the questions posed by *das Adam Smith Problem* are various and all too often depend on whether or not the answerer was (or is) an advocate of market capitalism.[1] Those who admire Smith and the world that he helped create insist that there never was any Adam Smith problem. Political economy, they argue, simply is moral philosophy and reflects, even if "invisibly," the values and assump-

1. For the views expressed here about *das Adam Smith Problem*, I am deeply indebted to three excellent articles: Leonidas Montes (2003), "*Das Adam Smith Problem*: Its Origins, the Stages of the Current Debate, and One Implication for Our Understanding of Sympathy"; Spencer J. Pack (1997), "Adam Smith on the Virtues: A Partial Resolution of the Adam Smith Problem"; and Amos Witztum (1998), "A Study into Smith's Conception of the Human Character: Das Adam Smith Problem Revisited."

tions of this earlier discipline from which it emerged.[2] Smith's ideological opponents, however, insist that Smith did separate political economy from moral philosophy as a discrete field of study, divorcing ethics from economics and implicitly sanctioning an amoral commercial realm where almost anything goes.

But ideological commitments aside, the general scholarly consensus is that there is an Adam Smith problem and that its solutions are rather elusive. For example, Spencer Pack (1997, 127, 137–38), who insists that the two books were parts of "a grand system," nevertheless confesses that they "are not tightly linked" and, after much labor to harmonize their competing principles, concludes that "the Adam Smith problem will always remain, or rather it can be only partially resolved." Another scholar who worked even harder to harmonize the two books into one ethical synthesis likewise confessed that while "it is unlikely that one will find an inherent contradiction, it is not inconceivable that Smith had not fully considered the implications of his observations in the [*Wealth of Nations*]" (Witztum 1998, 490). Whether this "problem" was by design on Smith's part or simply an oversight is open to debate. But what is clear is that "there is a problem worth addressing" (Otteson 2000, 70) that has been a burden to all those seeking integrity between the ethical and the economical from the eighteenth century to the twenty-first.[3]

For many Protestants in the nineteenth century, however, this "problem" was both an academic exercise and much more than that. Among the first American professors of political economy, the clerical economists wrote some of the most influential texts on the subject, fought to include it in the core curricula of their colleges, and even delivered public lectures on the new science to dispel any misconceptions and prejudices that people might have about it. Apparently, not all Americans—and especially those who were Christian—were so enamored with the new science, and the clerical economists felt the need to allay their fears. The main objection was that political economy never paid attention to moral factors. In all of its counting and calculating, political economy seemed to care only

2. See, in particular, Himmelfarb 1985, especially the second chapter, "Adam Smith: Political Economy as Moral Philosophy" (47–49); Sowell 1979, 3–18; and Cropsey 1979, 165–76. See also Raphael and Macfie 1976, 20; Winch 1978, 10; and Haakonssen 1981, 197 n. 19, quoted in Montes 2003, 78–79.

3. For even more on *das Adam Smith Problem*, see Brown 1994, Dickey 1986, Griswold 1999, Khalil 1990, Lamb 1974, Levy 2001, Morrow [1923] 1969, Nieli 1986, Pack 1991, Sen 1987, Teichgraeber 1981, and Young 1997.

about how profitable a commercial exchange might be, not how much harm or good it might do. “It has been often questioned whether Political Economy be a moral science,” John McVickar admitted in 1825, and then confessed: “The decision of Adam Smith and his followers is against it; the production of material wealth is the only question they admit” (160). What place did a Christian ethic of altruism have in commercial transactions? And if political economy was the so-called science of such transactions, how could it be consistent with this Christian ethic?

For their part, the clerical economists recognized that the religious community’s skepticism about their discipline was no minor issue. If the principles of political economy led to conclusions inconsistent with Christian theology or morality, how could they subscribe to it and encourage others to do the same? These were the obstacles that the clerical economists had to overcome if they were going to convince Protestants of the trustworthiness of their discipline and the overall goodness of economic modernization.

The Paradox of Commercial Civilization and Faculty Psychology as an Interpretive Tool

In the antebellum era many social observers were convinced that Smith’s commercial civilization was yielding its bitter fruit in the hearts of men. All good republicans recognized that there was a paradox inherent in the workings of an advanced economy. “Among the elements of the nation’s greatness,” William Arnot (1853, 57–58) warned, “lie the seeds of its sure decay. The very abundance of our material resources, and the very excess of our mercantile enterprise, seem to be forcing into earlier maturity the vices that will lay our glory in the dust.” Accompanying the development of a commercial civilization were some obvious vices such as competitiveness, along with pride, and the traditional republican bugbears of luxury and greed. Many Northerners, however, and especially the American clerical economists, esteemed the goal of a commercial civilization. In their opinion, a nation in the civilized state was unequivocally better off than a nation in the savage state. But civilization—and here is where the paradox emerged most clearly—brought with its blessings a whole host of new threats. As Francis Wayland (1842, 18–19) described it: “Civilization by presenting new object of desires [*sic*], has only whetted to a keener edge the appetite of cupidity.” Or, as Orville Dewey (1848, 248), one of the pastoral moralists, lamented: "We are, if I may say so, in an unfortunate dilemma. . . . Our political civilization has opened the way for multitudes to wealth, and created an insatiable desire for it."

Here both the clerical economists and the pastoral moralists made an important, and perhaps unconscious, distinction that was central to their understanding of ethics and economics. In the early nineteenth century, the word *passion* was almost always a pejorative term meant to describe an impulse in human beings that had to be held in check. As many antebellum Protestants understood them, people's passions were usually for less-than-virtuous ends such as excessive wealth or the lustful, gluttonous, or drunken gratification of the senses. Dewey (1848, 197), for example, complained of an "insane and insatiable passion for accumulation" in American culture. The term *desire*, on the other hand, especially when used by the clerical economists, did not have a negative connotation but was thought to describe a range of tastes that were natural and good in and of themselves. As Wayland ([1837] 1854, 15) wrote on the very first page of his *Elements of Political Economy*: "The universe around us is composed of objects suited to gratify our desire, and thus minister to our happiness." Desires were good, in other words, because they led to a personal happiness that was not self-destructive. Problems arose, however, when natural and God-given desires morphed into uncontrollable passions, as many observers thought was happening on a widespread basis in the first half of the nineteenth century.

This emphasis on the passions brings up the intellectual paradigm of faculty psychology, an understanding of the human person that was pervasive in antebellum culture. As Daniel Walker Howe describes it, the ideal of faculty psychology was to develop a "balanced character"—one that had rightly ordered the three internal faculties of the moral sense (or conscience), self-interest (or prudence), and the passions. According to this paradigm, human beings possessed all three faculties, but the virtuous person had them hierarchically arranged within himself or herself in precisely this order: conscience at the top, the passions consigned to the bottom, and self-interest in the middle. But, as Howe (1997, 12–13) points out, the problem was that "the strength of the faculties of the will varied inversely to their rank in the sequence of rightful precedence." In other words, the passions were naturally (or sinfully) the strongest and always threatened to dominate the other two. The virtuous person was the one who had developed a robust enough conscience through moral education and earnest training to win the majority of those inner struggles and keep the passions in their place.[4]

There is a key ambiguity, however, in that prudence, or self-interest, occupies the middle space between conscience and the passions. Some views of human nature were simpler and more binary. There were always the passions, which were considered base or animal, and which always needed to be constrained by faculties that were more divine: either reason, which was more strictly intellectual, or conscience, which was more moral. The faculty psychology of the antebellum era, however, was tripartite, adding prudence to the mix—an important variation that highlights key differences in the thought of these two groups of Protestants about ethical economic activity. As Howe explains, including prudence in the previously more dualistic understanding of human nature was a product of the Enlightenment. "At the beginning of the period," he writes of the eighteenth century, "self-interest had generally been considered one of the passions, but by the end, moral philosophers had definitely promoted it to the rank of a rational faculty" (Howe 1997, 28). In the antebellum era, self-interest was still considered morally inferior to conscience, but it had risen in the hierarchy to occupy this middling and thoroughly ambiguous position.

In *das Adam Smith Problem*, there is an apparent inconsistency between Smith's emphasis on sympathy in *The Theory of Moral Sentiments* and his emphasis on self-interest in *The Wealth of Nations*. The obvious connection to this discussion of faculty psychology is that Smith's first book prioritized the higher faculty of conscience, and his second the inferior faculty of prudence.

Some scholars seeking to reconcile the two works have come to what they have called only "a partial resolution" (Pack 1997, 127) to the problem. They claim that the two texts can be harmonized by going back to *The Theory of Moral Sentiments*, recognizing that in that text Smith declared prudence itself a virtue, and then seeing how that definition "implicitly defended the acquisitive, commercial society analyzed so thoroughly in [*The Wealth of Nations*]." The connection between the two books, in other words, was this emphasis on prudence, which Smith proclaimed a virtue, although an inferior one. Consistent with faculty psychology, Smith believed in "a hierarchy of virtues" (Pack 1997, 127, 133),

4. For more on faculty psychology, see Hirschman [1977] 1997 and Sklansky 2001.

with sympathy at the top and prudence in the middle. According to this "partial resolution," therefore, *The Wealth of Nations* was not devoid of ethical considerations. It was not, in other words, an entirely amoral text, but it did promote what amounted to a secondary or inferior morality.

This "partial resolution" leaves two unresolved dilemmas for Smith's disciples, though—dilemmas that return to the paradox of commercial civilization. The first is that the now sacrosanct but secondarily virtuous prudence can actually inflame the passions—a problem that critics of commercial civilization throughout history have been quick to point out. Basing a society on self-interest might provide "a virtuous underpinning to the logic of acquisitive, self-interested commercial society," but it can also end up working in alliance with the basest of the faculties. "For Aristotle," as Pack writes, "the use of money to make more money knows no limit; this mode of acquisition tends to become an all-consuming passion." But Smith never addressed this question, and, as Pack (1997, 134–35) concludes, his "silence is significant." For their part, the clerical economists followed in this tradition. They were aware of the problem, but like Smith they always ignored it. Being the defenders of commercial civilization that they were, they were always happy instead to point out the good utilitarian fruit that a society based on self-interest would yield. The pastoral moralists, as I explain below, did not ignore commercial society's threat to the individual's virtue but instead addressed the subject head-on while still upholding the ideal and the reality of a liberal-capitalist society.

The second unresolved issue is that although prudence might unify the two texts, it is still an inferior virtue. This is why Pack calls it a "partial resolution"—prudence might be a part of both texts, but the virtue of sympathy, which is central to *The Theory of Moral Sentiments*, is nowhere to be found in *The Wealth of Nations*. This is why there was an Adam Smith problem to begin with. And for those seeking a seamless fusion of the two books, there is still a gaping hole. There might be a "virtuous underpinning" (Pack 1997, 134) of prudence in the commercial society that Smith described in *The Wealth of Nations*, but there is still no sympathy in it. In other words, there is a consonance between the two texts, but literally a devalued one—one that comes only when one lops off the concern for sympathy entirely and focuses instead on the inferior virtue of prudence. And this, again, was the world that the clerical economists were happy to live with, but the pastoral moralists were not.

There is an alternative solution to *das Adam Smith Problem*, however, one that the pastoral moralists subscribed to and one that does not reduce all the virtues to prudence and prudence alone. One can synthesize Smith's two texts such that sympathy still matters and is in relation to the prudence of *The Wealth of Nations* but, unsurprisingly, is in tension with it. Drawing on faculty psychology, this other resolution to *das Adam Smith Problem* recognizes that the individual is not uniform (operating on either sympathy, self-interest, or the passions alone) but is internally divided and constantly in pursuit of the balanced character that comes from the interaction of these three faculties. The difficulty with this solution, as Amos Witztum describes it, "is that the different components of human character can be considered in *complete segregation*," with Smith principally concerned with sympathy in *The Theory of Moral Sentiments* and prudence in *The Wealth of Nations*. This is a "complete segregation" of the human person, however, that is consistent with the faculty psychology of the antebellum era. The way through this difficulty, as Witztum (1998, 495) goes on to explain, "requires the tying together of sympathy, as a capacity, and self-interest, as a motive"—a balancing act that is also consistent with faculty psychology. Or as another Smith scholar describes it, self-interest is "a motivating force" and sympathy, "a regulating force" (Montes 2003, 74). One supplies the drive while the other the necessary governance and occasional restraint of that drive. The sympathy of *The Theory of Moral Sentiments* and the self-interest of *The Wealth of Nations* can and do coexist within individuals, but they do so only with tension. As Witztum puts it: the fact that all "human beings are naturally *motivated* to pursue their own affairs . . . does not mean that they cannot be endowed with the *capacity* to feel for others." The existence of self-interest, in other words, does not make such a person "incapable of sympathy" (Witztum 1998, 489, 507), but they are different impulses acted on in different circumstances.

Just as there was a tension between the passions and self-interest, there also existed a tension between self-interest and conscience. In both cases the inferior one was the driving force and the superior the regulator of it. The clerical economists were primarily concerned with the first relationship, and they, like Smith, wanted to hallow self-interest as an effective, even if morally inferior, social stabilizer and check to the passions. The pastoral moralists wanted to explore the more challenging ethical territory that existed between prudence and conscience. In other words, they were concerned with the point at which the motive of self-interest, which they did not consider to be itself base or evil, crossed the line and led to actions that were clearly vicious.[5] The conclusion that the pastoral moralists reached—and one that squares with the faculty psychology solution to *das Adam Smith Problem*—was that it was acceptable for self-interest to drive an individual, but sympathy-driven conscience ultimately had to keep that self-interested activity within its proper limits.

According to the pastoral moralists, this type of self-interest within the bounds of conscience alone is what made a Christianized liberal society possible. It is also what made it acceptable. Recognizing that there would always be a tension between prudence and conscience, the pastoral moralists decided to live with it and sought to better understand the nature of the relationship and where the nebulous boundary was between the two. A religiously inspired sympathetic disposition did not make self-interested commercial behavior impossible, they concluded, but provided an important check to it. The pastoral moralists therefore accepted commercial activity as somewhat inevitable, but they also issued a stern warning to those Christians engaged in it that not all activity was permissible. In their vision of society, Christianity needed to adapt to meet the new challenges of changing times, but the market also had to conform to the inviolable principles of the Christian faith, and in particular to the dictates of the golden rule. What they sought in their inquiries were ways to apply the timeless moral truths of Christianity to the shifting economic landscape of modernizing America. Christianity, after all, was "a religion for universal man" and thus "must be capable of meeting him in these new, ever-varying, and complex relations, and of prescribing adequate rules for his guidance therein" (Atwater 1853, 390). For their part they wanted to identify those rules as best they could and pass them along to their listeners and readers. According to the clerical economists, on the other hand, both self-interested commercial activity and the market capitalist mechanism that it powered were not only inevitable but good—visible manifestations of the benevolence of the Creator who had made humankind to flourish by obeying the natural laws of the economy.

5. Almodovar and Teixeira (this volume) includes an excellent discussion of some European Catholics who similarly approved of economic modernization but critiqued the excessive, and sinful, behavior that it could foster. See, in particular, their treatment of Charles Périn and Pope Pius XI.

The Clerical Economists: People, Project, and the "Partially Resolved" Problem

From 1815 to 1860 the clerical economists insisted that their fellow citizens and churchgoers should not only accept political economy as something useful but wholeheartedly embrace it as a positive good, entirely compatible with their faith and intrinsically supportive of its central theology and morality. "I cannot but reverence the claims of free commerce as something holy," wrote John McVickar (1830, 34), "something allied to the policy of a higher power than man." Henry Vethake (1838, 406) similarly called "the spirit of political economy, like that of Christianity itself, . . . a spirit of peace and good-will to all mankind." Alonzo Potter (1840, 26) encouraged his readers "to behold that perfect harmony which the Creator has established between his moral, intellectual and economic laws"; Francis Wayland ([1837] 1854, 15) added that the science itself was "a systematic arrangement of the laws which God has established"—in this case the laws of producing, exchanging, distributing, and consuming wealth. Finally, Francis Bowen (1856, 27) argued that political economy had discovered an economic order in the world that, to his mind, made "manifest the contrivance, wisdom and beneficence of the Deity."

These five men—McVickar, Vethake, Potter, Wayland, and Bowen—make up what some historians have called "the clerical school" of political economy. Their common project, although not the central purpose of their lives, was to introduce Americans to a Christianized version of political economy, "clerical laissez faire," as Henry F. May called it. In the antebellum North, what they wrote and taught about the subject, despite the differences among them, constituted an almost singular voice on the economic issues of their day, one that "dominated American economic teaching" for "at least a generation and in many institutions for far longer" (May 1949, 14).

All five were able to spread their ideas in large part because of the influential positions they held during their careers as educators. Wayland (1796–1865), a Baptist minister, was president of Brown University from 1827 to 1855, during which time he wrote some of the most widely used textbooks on moral philosophy and political economy in the antebellum era. Potter (1800–1865) taught these same subjects at Union College in New York from 1826 to 1841 and was named vice president of the college in 1838. He was also a trustee of the University of Pennsylvania as well as a powerful figure in the Episcopal Church, eventually becoming the bishop of Pennsylvania from 1845 until his death in 1865. Vethake (1792–1866), a Presbyterian layman, taught mathematics and natural philosophy at several antebellum colleges before landing at the University of Pennsylvania, where he taught from 1836 to 1855. McVickar (1787–1868), an Episcopal priest, taught political economy at Columbia College for forty years from 1817 to 1857, and Bowen (1811–1890) taught political economy at Harvard during a long tenure there from 1833 until after the Civil War.

Although a Unitarian, it is interesting that Bowen was perhaps the most conservative of the clerical economists. This is largely because he had an absolutely unshakable faith in Scottish commonsense philosophy and natural theology—the intellectual glue that most united these men. Called the "old Roman" by some, he unabashedly attacked everything that appeared the slightest bit radical, and he took special aim at the intellectual predecessors and heirs of the French Revolution: Jean-Jacques Rousseau, Claude-Henri Saint-Simon, Auguste Comte, and others whom he considered naive utopians and dangerous philosophical speculators (Dorfman 1946, 835–36). Theological heterodoxy aside, therefore, Bowen was a valued member of this academic club that sought to uphold social and economic stability.

When it came to discussing the morality of Smith's commercial civilization, the clerical economists had two main responses. The first was to deal as much as possible with—for lack of a better phrase—macroeconomic issues. The clerical economists felt confident that they could address the nagging ethical questions about economic development on that scale. Obeying the doctrines of political economy, they argued, especially the doctrines of free trade and the division of labor, would invariably lead a nation to wealth, civilization, and peace with its national trading partners—three results that they argued were thoroughly consistent with the principles and morals of Christianity. In fact, inasmuch as the doctrines of political economy helped usher in world peace, it was very much an active agent of Christian progress, in partnership with the Gospel, rather than in opposition to it. "If Political Economy is listened to, this it would effect," McVickar (1830, 273) wrote about world peace: "It [political economy] would make nations and states a brotherhood of love." Thus the commercial mechanism that political economy described apparently passed the morality test, at least on the international scale.

The clerical economists' second response was to highlight the natural and God-given harmony that existed between individual virtue and the creation of wealth. As Wayland ([1837] 1854, 131) put it succinctly: "Where virtue, frugality, and respect for right exist, riches will, by natural consequence, accumulate." And as Potter (1838, 19) elaborated, Christians should perceive "the hand of God in the dispensations of nature—giving to virtue the 'world that now is, as well as that which is to come.'" In other words, God rewarded virtuous actions both on earth—that is, in business—and in heaven. Such a system of rewards was the obvious and, in their words, "natural" state of affairs. The cherished principles of natural theology simply forbade any other conclusion, and the new discipline of political economy merely explained in greater detail how the specifics of these natural, just, and God-given laws worked. For the individual, virtuous behavior led to wealth. But the clerical economists also believed that the prospect of wealth naturally encouraged virtue in an individual. As McVickar expressed the idea: "The honest pursuit of wealth is still the greatest safeguard of virtue." And with the skeptic in mind, he added: "Let the speculative moralist declaim against it [the pursuit of wealth] as he will, let him with Plato teach us that gold and virtue are balanced against each other in opposite scales" (McVickar 1830, 273). In the clerical economists' vision of society, by contrast, the self-interested pursuit of wealth and the development of character always worked in tandem. The pursuit of wealth inspired certain virtues in an individual (industry, sobriety, frugality, integrity, etc.), while the failure to pursue it actually developed certain vices (sloth, drunkenness, prodigality, untrustworthiness, etc.).

This was the place where virtuous behavior and the self-interested pursuit of wealth overlapped—an alliance that the clerical economists celebrated because they saw it as part of God's good plan for the ordering of human society. The new science of political economy thus "shews that to be their interest," McVickar wrote, "which religion has shewn to be their duty." And, as he continued, it was ultimately "the will of that wise and good Providence which has made our duty and interest the same." "Truth, genuine truth," he reminded his listeners, returning once more to the sine qua non of natural theology, "under all its forms, must be one and the same thing." Again, political economy had revealed the Creator's wise intention of making religious duty and economic self-interest reinforce one another and have the same good effects on the nation. And convincing their countrymen of this fortunate partnership of Christianity and political economy was one of the clerical economists' main objectives. They had merely wanted to show that the pursuit of wealth was not inconsistent with a virtuous life and that a nation composed of such pursuers would actually be stable and moral rather than unstable and immoral. The commercial society that Adam Smith described in *The Wealth of Nations* might be founded on an inferior set of virtues, but they were virtues nonetheless. And inasmuch as that society inspired at least these minimal virtues and produced wealth at the same time, the clerical economists would defend it against all other competing social visions. The self-interested pursuit of wealth, McVickar (1830, 273) wrote, "in a national point of view is decidedly favorable to the formation of moral character. In the mass of men it is the only security." This was the clerical economists' conclusion of the matter.[6]

Relating this back to faculty psychology, the clerical economists therefore thought of prudence as an inferior but supremely useful virtue when it came to shoring up social stability. When it came to the higher faculty of conscience, they simply rejoiced that it and prudence were so similar that they could be combined and together overpower the passions—a joint operation that was obviously the design of a good God. The clerical economists continued to recognize the distinctiveness of these two faculties and that one was superior to the other, but they never spoke openly or clearly about conscience and what restrictions it might put on the commercial activity of the prudent man. In other words, they never addressed—and outright refused to address—how conscience might be at odds with prudence and might actually have to restrict the behavior of the self-interested economic actor. A prudential person, for example, might successfully subdue passion or patiently delay gratification, but also regularly cheat competitors or customers. People acting according to self-interest, in other words, ran the risk of acting selfishly, even if they were in

6. Two essays in this volume provide an especially instructive point of comparison with the subject treated here. The first is Steven Medema's treatment of "ethical hedonism" and "the conflict between self-interest and duty" in "Losing My Religion": Sidgwick, Theism, and the Struggle for Utilitarian Ethics in Economic Analysis." The other is A. M. C. Waterman's helpful metaphor of the alliance that was briefly but fatefully forged between theology and the natural sciences in the early nineteenth century. Considering political economy an ally rather than a subject of theology acknowledged its epistemological separation from religious inquiry (and its constraints) but also allowed for the co-optation of the science for pragmatic ends. In Waterman's essay this end is principally intellectual—to hold together a cosmos defined by natural theology. Because of space considerations I am not able to elaborate on these important themes in intellectual history. I do cover this subject in some detail, however, in "*Friends of the Unrighteous Mammon*." In the present essay, I treat the subject of how the alliance between religion and political economy was meant to serve the pragmatic end of making the American republic both moral and wealthy.

control of their passions. This is where Christian faith and commercial activity—conscience and prudence—could still be dramatically at odds with one another. The clerical economists, however, always emphasized the harmony of conscience and prudence, as well as the fortunate alliance between them, and never the potential tension. The pastoral moralists, on the other hand, dwelt on the tension that could exist between conscience and self-interest and devoted their studies to exploring how an individual could engage in commercial affairs prudently while being guided and restricted by the higher faculty of a Christian conscience.

The Pastoral Moralists: Project and Promises, Liberalism and Limits

The goal of identifying the ethical boundaries of economic activity was not a full-time occupation for any of the pastoral moralists. Unlike the clerical economists, who thought a great deal about economic matters over many years, the pastoral moralists were mostly pastors who wrote or preached only occasionally on this subject, and usually only once in their lives. In other words, they did not develop anything like a repertoire, or show a development of thought over time, because there was no discernible development. As a result—although some biographical information is included when necessary, relevant, and possible—this section is more focused on the sources themselves than on the men who wrote them. Among the most important of these texts are sermons such as Joseph Emerson's *Christian Economy* (1813), David McConaughy's *Duties and Dangers of Prosperity* (1817), Joshua Bates's *Discourse on Honesty in Dealing* (1818), and three book-length treatments of the subject: Orville Dewey's *Moral Views of Commerce, Society, and Politics* (1838), Henry Augustus Boardman's *Bible in the Counting House* (1853), and the American version of William Arnot's *Race for Riches, and some of the pits into which the runners fall* (1853). In addition to these sources, there are many sermons on the "hard times" of 1837. The financial panic of that year apparently inspired a great deal of introspection about the developing market economy and people's virtuous or vicious participation in it.

Calling these men "pastoral moralists" is therefore merely a shorthand way to identify this disparate group of antebellum ministers who addressed a common set of questions. They had no real corporate identity as such. Still, despite the fact that they wrote only once on these issues and often decades apart from one another, the literature does form a remarkably coherent whole. They shared a similar approach to the subject, identifying key issues and making tentative recommendations that can in many ways be considered an antebellum "party line" on the Christian morality of everyday business affairs. There apparently were rules out there to be found that would apply "the Word of God to the Traffic of Men" (Arnot 1853, 1), and the pastoral moralists wanted people to know what they were.

In many ways competition was the crux of the matter. The commercial world was built on it, but the principles of Christianity seemed to be set against it. This is the place where self-interest could bump up against the interests of others and potentially do violence to others, according to the golden rule. "While we are endeavoring to secure our own property," Emerson (1813, 7) explained simply, "we may be tempted to injure our neighbor. His interest and ours may clash." What was the good Christian to do in this situation—renounce competition entirely? Did putting one's neighbor before one's self always mean losing? And what about winning? Did success in one's own endeavors have to mean the failure and ruin of your competitors? One group of earnest and justice-minded Congregationalists in Rhode Island was so suspicious of "both the reality and the appearance of . . . competition" that they resolved to avoid it "as far as possible." But as they went on to say: "Of course, this cannot be avoided entirely" (First Congregational Church 1837, 6).

This type of realistic assessment of competition was the pastoral moralists' starting point. Like trade itself, they reasoned, competition was simply a reality—a fact of life in a liberal society that needed to be navigated properly, not condemned categorically. To them the unavoidable truth of the matter was that self-interested competition was a necessary component of a commercial society. In the language of faculty psychology, competition was the motivating engine that drove the economy but that also had to be restrained. "We are indeed to do to others as we would have them do to us," Orville Dewey wrote, referencing directly the golden rule as his ethical guideline for commercial activity. But, as he went on to argue, there was nothing "in Scripture, or in the laws of human brotherhood, that forbids this honest, not fraudulent, but honest competition between men's exertions, faculties and wits" (Dewey 1848, 154, 161). Scripture might not overtly sanction competition, but neither did it overtly forbid such activity.

In general, the pastoral moralists were resigned to the fact that America was going in a certain direction—away from republican notions of "community" and toward a more liberal notion of "society"—and that life within that society had to be lived in a certain way. As Boardman, the esteemed pastor of the Tenth Presbyterian Church in Philadelphia wrote, an economic "revolution" had "come over the world within the last half-century." "Whether this revolution could have been prevented, or whether it is not on the whole beneficial," he continued, "is not a question now before us" (Boardman 1853, 14–15). In other words, it was simply useless to criticize the system itself or long for a different or now-past social order. As the pastoral moralists acknowledged, there were some costs associated with modernization, to be sure, but the current structure of American civilization was generally good and not going away. "Trade," as Dewey (1848, 153) put it, "being a part of the inevitable lot of cultivated humanity, the question is, not about abolishing, but about the moral principles that are to regulate it." Or as Boardman (1853, 77) concluded, commerce, far from being an evil, was in fact "founded on the organic structure of the globe and mercifully designed by the Author of our being, to subserve the most salutary ends in our physical and moral training."

Boardman's statement illustrates perfectly both the similarities and differences that existed between the pastoral moralists and the clerical economists. Both groups agreed that, in general, commerce and commercial activity were God-ordained and good for meeting humankind's physical needs. But for the clerical economists, this hedonic lowest common denominator was as far as they went, largely because that was as far as Adam Smith went. As Lisa Hill (2001, 11) describes it, Smith believed that the global commercial order was "designed with a hedonistic goal in view: our happiness, prosperity, perpetuation and material comfort. . . . The *telos* of human [economic] activity is not, as might be expected, the attainment of moral perfection." For the clerical economists, such a view of the commercial mechanism was consistent with an understanding of a good and caring God, and thus evidence against the Malthusian pessimists and skeptics.

But, as Hill makes clear, Smith's economic mechanism, which provided exceptionally well for people's material needs, seemed to be entirely unconcerned with their ethical development. For their part, the clerical economists merely followed Smith's lead and likewise emphasized the human "happiness" and "prosperity" that commercial development would effect while ignoring entirely the goal of "moral perfection." The pastoral moralists, on the other hand, thought of the grand mechanism of commerce as meeting, in Boardman's (1853, 77) words, "the most salutary ends in our physical and moral training." As Orville Dewey (1848, 187) expressed the idea: "Business, in its ultimate, its providential design is a school. . . . Man is placed in this school, as the learner of lessons for eternity." Boardman (1853, 83) put it another way: business was "an essential part of that great scheme of Providence by which men are to be trained to the practice of virtue." This was the pastoral moralists' point of departure from the clerical economists. To them, instead of being an example of God's benevolence, the commercial mechanism was instead the training ground for virtuous souls.

The problem was that people could fail in this school of character and go just as far away from true virtue as they could go toward it, and this was exactly what the pastoral moralists feared was happening. In their perhaps naive opinion, too many people had forgotten "the moral end of business"—the development of virtue—and had begun to think of commercial activity as simply a way to amass a personal fortune. Wealth had replaced virtue as the good end of trade, and impatient self-will had replaced God's grace as the means to that end. As William Arnot (1853, 64) complained: "The love of money has now taken the place of a God-fearing, man-loving sense of duty as the motive power in this man's soul." And as Dewey (1848, 225) summed it up: "That very [economic] structure, built for the gain of earth, may be the gate of hell!" God's commercial mechanism ("that very structure") was generally good. But fallen individuals, as always, were abusing the new opportunities that the structure afforded them and were placing themselves, their families, their neighbors, and their nation in grave danger as a result.

In the simplest terms, when thinking about a remedy for these potential social ills, the pastoral moralists' interests lay not with the structure of the new economy but with the culture that had grown up alongside it. The developing structure of economic modernization, in their opinion, was generally good and here to stay. What the moralists wanted to investigate, and felt they could change, was the spirit that animated the structure. For Lyman Atwater, a Congregationalist minister, the new economy needed "a baptism by the Spirit that will sweeten and hallow the relations of life, whatever the external form may be." The pastoral moralists recognized that "the external form" of commercial life had changed dramatically over the past half century. The only way to baptize that form was if, as Atwater (1853, 396) prescribed, the "Christian principle should permeate every sphere, and regulate all the practices of commercial life." In other words, the pastoral moralists sought to change the spirit of modern commerce by targeting individuals, who once personally transformed and in great enough numbers would transform the marketplace in which they worked.

There turned out to be quite a dilemma, however, over exactly how to apply the "Christian principle" to "the practices of commercial life" (Atwater 1853, 396). As the pastoral moralists confessed, it was difficult to come to moral clarity about even the most basic commercial transaction. Take, for example, the following scenario:

> You offer to sell to your neighbor an article of merchandise. . . . Conscience will hardly mark down the just price in your account book. Conscience, indeed, commands us to do right; but the question is, what *is* right? (Dewey 1848, 154)

This question—"What *is* right?"—applied to "the thousand-fold processes of daily business" (154), such as setting a profitable but fair price, dogged the pastoral moralists on every page of their work. The modernizing economy had created a new set of human relationships and a complex set of moral questions about those relationships. How was one supposed to love one's neighbor in this new economy? Who, after all, was one's neighbor? Or more specifically, who was one's more important neighbor: immediate family members or business partners, customers, and employees?

Because of the expansive and near infinite nature of these ethical dilemmas—with one question leading to another, which led to another, and so on—the pastoral moralists adopted a common strategy in their discourses. They attempted to articulate as clearly as possible what the line or boundary between ethical and unethical commerce looked like while leaving "to the honest judgment of the trader" (Dewey 1848, 157–58) what was the appropriate moral decision for any particular situation. At the beginning of his sermon "Christian Economy," for example, Joseph Emerson (1813, 7), a Congregationalist minister, quickly explained that "it is not my design to lay down particular rules and methods of operation; but to offer some general directions as to the temper of heart." Joshua Bates, another Congregationalist minister and president of Middlebury College, did exactly the same thing. "In discoursing on this subject," he wrote, "I have only *to illustrate the duty of honest dealing between man and man*; or, in other words, *to point out the boundaries between honesty and fraud, and apply the subject to every enlightened conscience*" (Bates 1818, 4). Henry Boardman (1853, 385) likewise concluded his four-hundred-page discourse, *The Bible in the Counting House*, with a similar evasion: "The great lesson I have wished to enforce in these discursive remarks is, that we should live *to do good. . . . How* you are to do this, must be left to your own enlightened discretion." This was about as specific as the pastoral moralists dared to get.

Occasionally they would try to reduce commercial morality to a simple formula. As Bates (1818, 4) put it: "The religion of the Bible . . . commands us in *general terms, to do unto others, as we would that they should do unto us.*" This is the golden rule, the timeless and universal bedrock of Christian social ethics. But the devil, so to speak, was always in the details. As Orville Dewey (1848, 154) confessed, the "Scriptures, like conscience, are a general directory. They do not lay down any specific moral laws of trade." Even Francis Wayland (1837, 13) admitted that "the confines of justice and oppression are separated by a very shadowy limit." Nevertheless, he and the rest sought that limit, having faith that it was out there and sometimes defining it along the lines of the golden rule. But ultimately the original question remained: "What *is* right?" Thus the best that the pastoral moralists could do was try to identify the boundary between ethical and unethical commercial transactions, and leave the really difficult decisions about application up to "the honest judgment," "temper of heart," or the "*enlightened conscience*" of the individual merchant or trader—a strategy thoroughly consistent with the inner checks and balances of faculty psychology.

This was also how the pastoral moralists resolved *das Adam Smith Problem* to their own liking. They were content to let self-interest be the motivating engine of their liberal-capitalist society, but they also thought that that engine needed to be regulated by a robust conscience. In "the language of this science [of political economy]" the clerical economist John McVickar wrote, subtly criticizing his own discipline in a way, "man is but a machine for the creation of value." Destitute "of personal virtues," he continued, "man is a machine out of order" (McVickar 1832, 342). But because he was speaking as a political economist and had willingly capitulated to the amoral language of his discipline, he dared to make only this observation. He did not propose any solutions. It was up to the pastoral moralists to elaborate, to explain how to find this "order" or "balance" that faculty psychology so cherished, a balance that involved dividing self-interest right down the middle. Starting out, as William Arnot wrote, were "emotions and energies that are in themselves innocent." But if unchecked and unregulated, those same energies could become "possessed by an unclean spirit, . . . animated by a sordid lust, and prostituted to objects hateful to God, and hurtful to his creatures" (Arnot 1853, 64–65). This was the difference between the self-interested but still good "desire" to provide for oneself and one's loved ones, and the selfish "passion" for riches that could ruin an individual and a whole society.

References

Arnot, William. 1853. *The Race for Riches and some of the pits into which the runners fall: six lectures applying the word of God to the traffic of men*. Philadelphia.

Atwater, Lyman. 1853. Review of H. A. Boardman's *The Bible in the Counting House*. *Biblical Repertory and Princeton Review* 25:390–409.

Bates, Joshua. 1818. *A Discourse on Honesty in Dealing: Delivered at Middlebury, on the Annual Fast: April 15, 1818*. Middlebury, Vt.

Boardman, Henry A. 1853. *The Bible in the Counting House: A Course of Lectures to Merchants*. Philadelphia.

Bowen, Francis. 1856. *The Principles of Political Economy Applied to the Conditions, the Resources, and the Institutions of the American People*. 4th ed. Boston.

Brown, Vivienne. 1994. *Adam Smith's Discourse: Canonicity, Commerce, and Conscience*. London: Routledge.

Cropsey, Joseph. 1979. The Invisible Hand: Moral and Political Considerations. In *Adam Smith and Modern Political Economy: Bicentennial Essays on the Wealth of Nations*, edited by Gerald P. O'Driscoll. Ames: Iowa State University Press.

Dewey, Orville. 1848. *Discourses on the Nature of Religion: and on Commerce and Business; with some Occasional Discourses*. Vol. 2 of *The Works of Orville Dewey D. D.* New York.

Dickey, Laurence. 1986. Historicizing the "Adam Smith Problem": Conceptual, Historiographical, and Textual Issues. *Journal of Modern History* 58:579–609.

Dorfman, Joseph. 1946. *The Economic Mind in American Civilization, 1606–1865*. Vol. 2. New York: Viking.

Emerson, Joseph. 1813. *Christian Economy: A Sermon, Delivered before the Massachusetts Missionary Society at their Fourteenth Annual Meeting, in Boston, May 25, 1813*. Boston.

First Congregational Church. 1837. *Report and Proposal to the Public on the Subject of Female Wages: By a Committee of the Female Benevolent Society*. Providence, R.I.

Griswold, Charles. 1999. *Adam Smith and the Virtues of Enlightenment*. Cambridge: Cambridge University Press.

Haakonssen, Knud. 1981. *The Science of a Legislator: The Natural Jurisprudence of David Hume and Adam Smith*. Cambridge: Cambridge University Press.

Hill, Lisa. 2001. The Hidden Theology of Adam Smith. *European Journal of the History of Economic Thought* 8.1:1–30.

Himmelfarb, Gertrude. 1985. *The Idea of Poverty: England in the Early Industrial Age*. New York: Vintage Books.

Hirschman, Albert O. [1977] 1997. *The Passions and the Interests: Political Arguments for Capitalism before Its Triumph.* Twentieth anniversary edition. Princeton, N.J.: Princeton University Press.

Howe, Daniel Walker. 1997. *Making the American Self: Jonathan Edwards to Abraham Lincoln.* Cambridge, Mass.: Harvard University Press.

Khalil, Elias L. 1990. Beyond Self-Interest and Altruism: A Reconstruction of Adam Smith's Theory of Human Conduct. *Economics and Philosophy* 6:255–73.

Lamb, Robert B. 1974. Adam Smith's System: Sympathy Not Self-Interest. *Journal of the History of Ideas* 35:671–82.

Levy, David M. 2001. *How the Dismal Science Got Its Name: Classical Economics and the Ur-Text of Racial Politics.* Ann Arbor: University of Michigan Press.

May, Henry F. 1949. *Protestant Churches and Industrial America.* New York: Harper and Row.

McVickar, John. 1825. *Outlines of Political Economy, Being a Republication of the Article Upon that Subject Contained in the Edinburgh Supplement to the Encyclopedia Britannica: Together with Notes Explanatory and Critical, and a Summary of the Science.* New York.

———. 1830. *Introductory Lecture to a Course of Political Economy: Recently Delivered at Columbia College, New York.* London.

———. 1832. Review of Thomas Chalmers' *On Political Economy. Churchman,* 10 November, 342–43.

Montes, Leonidas. 2003. *Das Adam Smith Problem*: Its Origins, the Stages of the Current Debate, and One Implication for Our Understanding of Sympathy. *Journal of the History of Economic Thought* 25.1:63–90.

Morrow, Glenn R. [1923] 1969. *The Ethical and Economic Theories of Adam Smith.* New York: Kelley.

Nieli, Russel. 1986. Spheres of Intimacy and the Adam Smith Problem. *Journal of the History of Ideas* 47:611–24.

Noll, Mark A. 2002. Introduction to *God and Mammon: Protestants, Money, and the Market, 1790–1860*, edited by Mark A. Noll. New York: Oxford University Press.

Otteson, James R. 2000. The Recurring "Adam Smith Problem." *History of Philosophy Quarterly* 17.1:51–74.

Pack, Spencer J. 1991. *Capitalism as a Moral System: Adam Smith's Critique of the Free Market Economy.* Aldershot, U.K.: Elgar.

———. 1997. Adam Smith on the Virtues: A Partial Resolution of the Adam Smith Problem. *Journal of the History of Economic Thought* 19.1:127–40.

Potter, Alonzo. 1838. Review of Henry Carey's *Principles of Political Economy. New York Review* 3.7:1–19.

———. 1840. *Political Economy, Its Objects, Uses and Principles Considered with Reference to the Condition of the American People.* New York.

Raphael, David D., and Alec A. Macfie. 1976. Introduction to *Adam Smith: The Theory of Moral Sentiments*, edited by David D. Raphael and Alec A. Macfie. Oxford: Oxford University Press.

Sen, Amartya K. 1987. *On Ethics and Economics*. Oxford: Blackwell.

Sklansky, Jeffrey. 2001. *The Soul's Economy: Market Society and Selfhood in American Thought, 1820–1920*. Chapel Hill: University of North Carolina Press.

Smith, Adam. [1776] 1981. *An Inquiry into the Nature and Causes of the Wealth of Nations*. Indianapolis: Liberty Fund.

———. [1759] 2000. *The Theory of Moral Sentiments*. Amherst, N.Y.: Prometheus Books.

Sowell, Thomas. 1979. Adam Smith in Theory and Practice. In *Adam Smith and Modern Political Economy: Bicentennial Essays on the Wealth of Nations*, edited by Gerald P. O'Driscoll. Ames: Iowa State University Press.

Teichgraeber III, Richard F. 1981. Rethinking Das Adam Smith Problem. *Journal of British Studies* 20:106–23.

Vethake, Henry. 1838. *The Principles of Political Economy*. Philadelphia.

Viner, Jacob. 1972. *The Role of Providence in the Social Order*. Philadelphia: American Philosophical Society.

Wayland, Francis. 1837. *The Moral Law of Accumulation, the substance of two discourses delivered in the First Baptist Meeting House, Providence, May 14, 1837*. Boston.

———. 1842. *A Discourse delivered in the First Baptist Church, Providence, R.I. on the Day of Public Thanksgiving, July 21, 1842*. Providence, R.I.

———. [1837] 1854. *The Elements of Political Economy*. 4th ed. New York: Leavitt, Lord.

Winch, Donald. 1978. *Adam Smith's Politics: An Essay in Historiographic Revision*. Cambridge: Cambridge University Press.

Witztum, Amos. 1998. A Study into Smith's Conception of the Human Character: Das Adam Smith Problem Revisited. *HOPE* 30.3:489–513.

Young, Jeffrey T. 1997. *Economics as a Moral Science: The Political Economy of Adam Smith*. Cheltenham, U.K.: Elgar.

From Religious Revivals to Tariff Rancor: Preaching Free Trade and Protection during the Second American Party System

Stephen Meardon

The religious awakening of the early-nineteenth-century United States, culminating in the mid-1820s through the mid-1830s, opened deep rifts in the generation that overlapped and followed it. The rifts emerged from questions of religious doctrine and evangelical method, then widened to encompass worldly politics and ideologies. The generation, specifically the period 1828–54, was the era of the second American party system.

Both of the major parties of the period, the Democratic and Whig parties, had evangelical Christians in their ranks. Democrats, however, tended to separate religious convictions from party purposes; for Whigs they were closely related. As the parties wrestled with each other for dominance, they did so also within their ranks: coherence of platform was balanced precariously against the attempt to prevent supporters' defection to other parties, including the Anti-Masonic, Liberty, and (later) Free Soil parties. For the Whigs, religious convictions, traceable in one way or another to the waves of religious revivals of preceding years, fomented these struggles. The momentous clash over the existence and extension of slavery comes first to the present-day mind. But to the mind of the late 1820s to the early 1850s, the question of slavery was neither unrivaled in its gravity nor unique in the relevance of religious revivalism to one's political and ideological allegiances. The tariff question, in particular, was more than a controversy of political economy during the second party system. It was also, indirectly but importantly, a religious controversy.

History of Political Economy 40 (annual suppl.) DOI 10.1215/00182702-2007-070

The story of religion's influence on the U.S. tariff controversy is absent from the outstanding U.S. trade policy histories (Taussig 1892; Stanwood 1903). Parts of the story have been written, piecemeal, by authors whose interests lay elsewhere. Charles C. Cole Jr. (1954) and Richard Carwardine (1997) have shown in detail the political consequences of the "Second Great Awakening." Several authors have explained the evangelical roots of certain moral and political causes—above all, the political abolition of slavery—that were related to the tariff in ways they left unexplained. In addition to Cole and Carwardine, they include Gilbert Hobbes Barnes (1933), Alice Felt Tyler (1944), David Brion Davis (1962), Aileen S. Kraditor (1967), Daniel Walker Howe (1991), and Mark A. Noll (2006), to name only those who have influenced the present essay. Others have studied the evangelical orientation of political parties and so have treated the subject of religion and the tariff at least obliquely. The evangelical impression on the Whig Party has been documented by Howe (1979) and, by way of his broader history of the party, Michael Holt (1999). Eric Foner (1970) has shown the like impression on the radical wing of the Republican Party, which grew out of the ruins of the Whigs and other fragments of the second party system.

The foregoing works contribute to a common narrative about the role of religion in the rise and fall of the second party system. The narrative includes a role for the tariff that is minor and deceptively simple. The evangelical imperative of "national redemption," the narrative holds, was central to Whig political culture (Howe 1979, 167). Even the party line on such matters as the public debt and the tariff was drawn in religious hues: the public debt was sacrosanct; tariff protection was required "as much by the theory of benevolent action for one's fellow man . . . as by current economic theory" (Carwardine 1997, 108).

There ends the part of the narrative relating religion to the tariff. In the sequel, evangelicals in growing numbers construed national redemption to call not only for the staples of the Whig economic program but also for the abolition of slavery. Conservatives and Southerners resisted. Partisanship between the two major parties intensified; at the same time, so did factionalism within the Whig Party, which began to splinter. The more adamant antislavery Whigs became so wary of compromises permitting expansion of the slave system that they were willing to abandon their national party for a regional one representing more faithfully their priorities. Conservative Whigs were more wary of disunion. After the Kansas-Nebraska Act of 1854—which Northerners of all political convictions, even conservatives, believed to have conceded too much to slavery—the party's splintering accelerated. By 1856, in the North, the splinters were larger than the party. When the majority of them united in the emergent Republican Party, they outpolled the remaining Whigs.

Sophisticated versions of the narrative acknowledge that although evangelicalism inspired the Whig Party's fervent antislavery types, it inspired as well conservative Whigs who (until the party's disintegration) opposed them. The latter group's disdain for "ultraism" and inclination toward prudent compromise, writes Carwardine (1997, 182), was "derived not so much from [their] political pragmatism as from their conservatism in temperament, in social philosophy—and in theology." Howe (1979, 33) goes a step farther and attributes the evangelical-conservative temperament to Whigs in general, not just a subset of them. Their "aggressive didacticism," he writes, was due to "the rise of the missionary spirit in religion that accompanied the Second Great Awakening"; yet most of them channeled that spirit toward seeking the imposition of moral standards of "self-control and restraint." In sum, just as some evangelicals were impelled by the missionary spirit to brook no compromise with slavery, others who originated in the same political party were impelled by the morality of self-control and restraint to accommodate it. Both groups, of course, found justification in the Bible, but neither one could manage to do so definitively (Noll 2006).

The sophisticated treatment of religion's influence on the slavery controversy has not been extended to the tariff controversy. The common narrative holds the tariff to have been a matter of interparty, not intraparty, rivalry. Inasmuch as religion touched the matter, it contributed to the Whig Party's protectionism. American Whigs, writes Howe (1979, 33–34), were "evangelical reformers" who "typically assumed moral responsibility for others." Having assumed it, they exercised it actively with "reliance on government planning rather than the invisible forces of the marketplace" (34). The protective tariff, land policy, internal improvements, and federal revenue sharing—all of these economic policies were of a piece, all of them tinted with evangelicalism.

This explanation is persuasive as far as it goes. Compared with the explanation of religion's influence on the slavery controversy, however, it does not go very far. If religion was capable of inspiring such different views of slavery in the United States from the late 1820s to the early 1850s, why did it inspire such uniform views of the tariff?

The British experience sows doubt that it did. Simon Morgan (2007) recounts how leaders of the anti–Corn Law agitation in Great Britain, during and after the birth of their mass movement in 1836–39, appealed directly to the religious sensibilities of supporters of the antislavery movement. Although slavery had been abolished nominally in British territories in 1833, former slaves remained bound to their masters afterward by a system of "apprenticeship." British evangelicals led opposition to the system. Having vanquished it in 1838, they turned their attention to abolishing slavery worldwide. The evangelical Quaker Joseph Sturge organized the British and Foreign Anti-Slavery Society in 1839, the same year that Richard Cobden formed the Anti–Corn Law League. Cobden and Sturge perceived their causes to be allied by evangelical impulse, ideological orientation, and, in most cases, tactics. Sturge was a member of both groups at their beginnings; Cobden relied from the outset on Sturge's advice and appropriated, for the cause of free trade, the rhetoric of "abolition" and emancipation from "bondage." Thus, at the very time when a growing faction of American evangelical Whigs was gravitating toward political abolitionism, British evangelicals had formed an ideological and practical alliance between abolition and free trade. Yet in America, the common narrative holds, as evangelicals continued to hew to protectionism.

Either American intellectual and political currents were uncharacteristically insulated from the British, or the narrative requires amendment. Morgan rules out the first possibility: Sturge and Cobden both made trips and kept correspondents in the United States; evangelical abolitionists from the United States traveled overseas to form alliances with their British brethren; and the idea of arguing against the Corn Laws on the particular grounds that their repeal would promote the abolition of slavery in the United States, thereby "proving that free trade itself was part of a divine Providential order," was recommended to Cobden by an American (Morgan 2007, 13). Religion was indeed capable of inspiring different views in the United States about the tariff, just as it did about slavery. The purpose of the present essay is to show how.

The influence of religion can be seen in the political and economic ideas of two men in particular. The Reverend Joshua Leavitt (1794–1873) and the Reverend Calvin Colton (1789–1857) were evangelical ministers and social proselytizers of the same generation, from the same Connecticut River region of Massachusetts, with the same college pedigree. The religious denominations in which they were ordained, Congregationalist and Presbyterian, were not identical, but were aligned in evangelical purpose by the "Plan of Union" of 1801 and in political purpose, in the northeast at least, by their members' steady support for the Whig Party (Carwardine 1997, 122–24). Both men were swept up in the religious revivals of the 1820s and became, over the following two decades, leading contributors to the second party system's controversies over slavery and the tariff. Yet they were on opposite sides: Leavitt plumped for free trade in the 1840s while Colton grew more committed to protection.

Leavitt and Colton represent the different positions on free trade and protection that evangelicalism could inspire even in those who originated in the same political party. But that is not the limit of their significance. They were among the most important agents of that inspiration. They allow us to see the moral, intellectual, and tactical paths by which evangelicals, following their lead, arrived at their positions on the tariff. Finally, they allow us to see how the tariff controversy partook of the rancor within the Whig Party as much as it did between the parties during the second party system.

The Theological Impetus for Worldly Policies

The paths from evangelicalism to free trade and protection both traveled through opposition to slavery. Before evangelical Whigs parted ways on slavery—not on the question of whether the institution should end but on when and how—their political thinking was congruent. They agreed that religion should exert its influence in the politics of worldly affairs.

The Whig Party inherited the imperative of "national redemption" from the Federalist Party that preceded it during the first party system. New England, the stronghold of Federalism, was also the wellspring of Puritan piety. Among the galvanizing ideas of the Puritans were those of election and covenant. The account in Exodus of God's election of the people of Israel to be his own, and their acceptance of a covenant with him in which they did the same, had special significance to the Puritan emigrants. The covenant offered the Israelites God's guidance, through the wilderness, to a new land free of enemies and full of bounty. It required of them fidelity to God in continual choices between right and wrong. The possibility of their failing to choose well and honor the covenant was terrifying; the prospect of their succeeding was blissful. In the New Israel, righteousness would prevail, and the world would be redeemed (Stephanson 1995, 7–8).

Associated with the covenant's ultimate promise was the Book of Revelation's prophecy of the millennium. After an age of unabated struggle between good and evil, the Messiah would reappear to imprison Satan and reign together with the faithful for a thousand harmonious years. At the end of the thousand years, Satan would break free and heaven would descend to defeat him and all evil. A final judgment would be made on all souls, living and dead, and the unredeemed would burn eternally in hell (9).

A tension is evident between the idea of the covenant, which implies personal choice, and the ideas of election and prophecy, which would seem to preclude it. The Puritan mind favored prophecy over choice. One was predestined either to burn or to be saved; one's choice lay in understanding and cooperating with God's will or closing one's eyes and defying it (7–9). The tension was heightened in the ferment of the Great Awakening of the 1730s and 1740s, when dramatic group revivals were employed by evangelists like the Congregationalist Reverend Jonathan Edwards in the Connecticut Valley to "harvest" converted souls for Christ. Edwards was a strict predestinarian (Smith 1984, 7); to inspire voluntary conversion by people whose destinies were predetermined required not only the power of persuasion but also some finesse. When the Second Great Awakening gathered force in the 1820s, it was served well by a softening of Edwards's Calvinist doctrine. Arminianism, which taught that salvation was available to all, had long been known as the softer doctrine; but those who embraced it explicitly and in swelling numbers, principally Methodists, bore to many minds the stigma of low breeding and disrepute (Carwardine 1972, 330, 338–40). The project of bowing toward Arminianism, whether consciously or not, without venturing so far toward rationalism and free agency as to promote distaste for revivals and divorce from Congregationalism (as did the Unitarians of eastern Massachusetts), beckoned early-nineteenth-century theologians. The one who responded most effectively was Nathaniel William Taylor of the Yale Theological Seminary.

Taylor's innovation was to put Scottish "commonsense" philosophy to work for American Protestant evangelism. The philosophy held that the existence of things and the validity of moral principles were understandable intuitively to people. Moral behavior was a matter of common sense because its dictates were integrated in "the very nature and structure of the mind" (Taylor 1859, 200; Smith 1984, 6–7). If one had thus the mind to choose between damnation and salvation, Taylor determined, one also had the will. The Calvinist belief that this choice was terribly consequential was correct—and its correctness, he reasoned, is precisely why God must have made people free to choose their destinies. If they were not, then they were not responsible for wrong choices, and if they were not responsible, then to suppose that some were destined for heaven and others for hell would be to imply that God acted arbitrarily toward all and meanly toward many. But God was not arbitrary and mean. So people must be free moral agents.

Taylor's teachings at Yale, beginning in 1822, constituted the highbrow theology of the "New School" of evangelism. Taylor was not himself one of the popular evangelists, although he trained some of them and lent the rest greater respectability. The most effective popular evangelist of the Second Great Awakening was Charles G. Finney, whose revivals in the Mohawk Valley of New York from Troy to Rome, on the Erie Canal, attracted national attention in 1826 and sparked imitation. Finney's methods included the use of colloquial speech, extravagant gestures, admission of women to his services, appeals to emotion, and employment of the "anxious seat" and assistants to aid him in the harvest (Cole 1954, 61, 64). As for his ideas, his insistence that "there are means of regeneration" available to the sinner, who could embrace them of his or her own volition, was as important to the revivals as were his methods. It also put him decidedly within the New School (Finney 1876, 154; Cole 1954, 64–65).

The works of Taylor and Finney, and others of similar minds and methods, made the New School's doctrine remarkably broad in scope. Its breadth was observable in at least two dimensions. First, the New School was interdenominational: its teachings appealed at once to Congregationalists and Presbyterians, who were identical theologically and differed (into the 1830s, at least) mainly in their organization and geographic reach. Congregationalists predominated in New England, Presbyterians in New Jersey and Pennsylvania (Carroll 2000, 34–39). The two denominations' Plan of Union of 1801 enabled them to cooperate on establishing churches and schools in western New York, Ohio, and other parts of the western frontier (62). The New School ideas generated enthusiasm for the effort. Baptists and Methodists, too, were caught up in the enthusiasm: their numbers had already swelled in the eighteenth century precisely because they embraced free will and emotional fellowship during a time when such notions and practices were not accepted by the Calvinists of the Congregational and Presbyterian churches (42–45).

Second, as New School evangelism brought the Second Great Awakening to culmination in the early to mid-1830s, revivals entailed much more than individual commitments to reform individual behavior. In the 1740s and even as late as the early 1800s, revivals had as their purpose the salvation of the unconverted. By the 1830s, the purpose of revivals lay increasingly in the salvation of the world; the revival itself was but the first step toward fulfilling it. Finney's preaching expressed, as Cole (1954, 75) put it, "an aggressive activism; the mission of the church was ideological conquest—to spread the gospel to the farthest reaches of the globe." Missionary organizations like the American Board of Commissioners for Foreign Missions (established in 1810) and the American Home Mission Society (1826) swelled with new members and support. At the same time, new organizations sprang up with objectives that were as much political as religious.

Religious enthusiasm weighed more directly on more questions of worldly, temporal, and public importance than it had in the past. Finney and other revivalists, including even the equally renowned but more conservative Lyman Beecher, enjoined their listeners to participate in societies promoting particular social reforms: temperance was chief among them in the early 1830s. In time, so too were antislavery and commercial policies (Cole 1954, 77).

Evangelicalism and Abolitionism

The Whig Party, which would be the political vehicle for evangelicals' social reform from the 1830s to the early 1850s, began to coalesce (without its eventual name) in 1828 (McCormick 1966, 335). The leaders of the incipient Whigs in that year were "National Republicans" who supported President John Quincy Adams's reelection campaign. Their stalwarts and guiding lights were, in the North, Daniel Webster of Massachusetts, and in the West, Henry Clay of Kentucky. Their unifying issue was nationalism; their platform, made explicit in 1831, embraced Clay's "American system" of tariff protection and internal improvements (McKee 1901, 28–30). Recharter of the Second Bank of the United States, too, was a formative cause (Marshall 1967, 445–46). Their supporters, therefore, especially in the North, were erstwhile or continuing Federalists—for the Federalist creed, as inscribed in part by Alexander Hamilton ([1787] 1961, 151), had envisioned a sufficiently "energetic government" to accomplish their designs. Erstwhile Federalists from rural areas and small towns were particularly reliable supporters: theirs were the areas ablaze with revivals during the Second Great Awakening.

Joshua Leavitt was born in northwestern Massachusetts in the small town of Heath, whose founders included both of his grandfathers. His paternal grandfather was a Congregationalist minister, and his father was at various times a representative to both houses of the Massachusetts legislature. Like most others in the town—and in like towns of the region at the turn of the century—his father's politics were Federalist. Such political views implied a conservative attitude toward the existing social order: property rights were to be respected and the potential for violent uprisings feared. The Federalist view of slavery, for instance, perceived threateningly if not urgently on the Southern horizon, held the institution to be morally contemptible but not publicly actionable. Closer to home, the social order demanded pious observation of one's duties to family and church. This was the intellectual and cultural setting of Leavitt's youth, toward the end of which, by 1810, a respected Congregational minister from another town together with the local pastor had prepared him for the entrance examination for college (Davis 1990, 1–8).

Harvard, by then under Unitarian influence, would have been an unlikely choice. Yale, which had remained unshakably Congregationalist and also happened to have graduated the ministers who were Leavitt's grandfather and his exam tutor, was more suitable. Leavitt's training under President Timothy Dwight emphasized the value of public morals and works in addition to private piety, and of public organization to promote them. Dwight was a cofounder in 1812 of the Connecticut Society for the Reformation of Morals and the Suppression of Vice; Leavitt, following his example, was cofounder in 1813 of a Yale College Benevolent Society that raised money for the liberal education of indigent youth. Thus were the seeds of activism for the reform of public morals, inspired by religion and fostered by political organization, planted in Leavitt during his college education. They sprouted after he graduated, worked as a teacher and lawyer for several years, and returned to Yale in 1823 to enter the recently established Theological Seminary. There Leavitt came under the influence of Nathaniel Taylor (Davis 1990, 8–17, 26–27).

Under Taylor, Leavitt's commitment to seeking the "means of regeneration" of humanity and society deepened. To be a pastor was no longer the obvious vocation for one with such a commitment. The benevolent and missionary societies that were proliferating when Leavitt finished his training in late 1824 required educated men to be their organizers, secretaries, and propagandists. After three and a half years as pastor of the First Congregational Church in Stratford, Connecticut, during which time he also spoke and wrote actively for educational reform and Sunday schools, against lotteries and slavery, and served as traveling agent for the American Temperance Society, Leavitt found an opportunity to cease ministering to individual congregants and devote himself wholly to his larger causes. He moved to New York to become secretary and periodical editor for the American Seamen's Friend Society (Davis 1990, 35, 38).

The society's periodical, *Sailor's Magazine*, proposed to save the souls of its readers by steering them away from rough manners, gambling, tobacco, drink, theater, and solicitation of prostitutes (Davis 1990, 54). Its unpopularity among those it purported to help merits hardly a mention and no explanation (53). But the society and magazine were only the first of several of Leavitt's evangelizing efforts in New York City. He would find, arguably, greater success—and certainly greater recognition—as editor of the *Evangelist*, an evangelical newspaper of more general interest. The paper was established in 1830 in the wake of Finney's arrival in New York City; Leavitt took up its editorial duties soon after (68). He would use the *Evangelist* to intensify his attacks on slavery and would eventually concentrate most of his efforts toward its abolition. But to do so required a reordering of his priorities, and he took two years to come around to it.

Like most antislavery advocates of the 1820s, Leavitt supported the American Colonization Society's program of Negro resettlement in Liberia. The program had broad appeal: it was consistent at once with the purposes of evangelical foreign missionaries, conservative antislavery types who sought eventual and "natural" rather than political abolition, white workers anxious about Negro competition, and whites of all classes anxious about the prospect of a slave uprising. In the early 1830s, however, the appeal of resettlement narrowed. William Lloyd Garrison (1885, 224–26) disavowed resettlement and called for immediate emancipation in the first issue of his newspaper, the *Liberator*, in 1831. By 1833 the ranks of converts to "immediatism," while still small in number, had grown. On the one hand, South Carolina's nullification of the Tariff of 1832 was answered with Clay's Compromise Tariff of 1833. Whatever an ardent antislavery advocate thought of the tariff law that sparked the crisis, the subsequent concession by Clay's Whig Party to the slave power was dismaying. On the other hand, the British Parliament's decision to abolish slavery in the West Indies, also in 1833, demonstrated what could be accomplished with sufficient determination. Late in the year Leavitt helped organize the New York City Anti-Slavery Society, modeled explicitly after the British abolitionist movement and dedicated to the doctrine of immediatism. When the American Anti-Slavery Society was organized in Philadelphia shortly thereafter on the same principles, Leavitt became prominent in the national movement (Davis 1990, 98–103).

The religious influence on abolitionism in the United States has been mentioned in this volume by Donald Frey; Leavitt's prominence as an agent of that influence is acknowledged by most of the lengthier studies of the subject, including those by Barnes (1933), Tyler (1944), Kraditor (1967), and Carwardine (1997). Even those who acknowledge his prominence, though, have no more than a passing interest in Leavitt and other evangelicals as agents of religion's influence on political-economic thought concerning matters other than slavery. Yet there, too, his and their importance was profound. The peregrination of leading evangelicals from advocacy of general moral reform to abolitionism is only the beginning of the story to be told here. The terms and tenor of debates over U.S. commercial policy in the 1840s and for the rest of the nineteenth century were established amid, and in consequence of, the religiously fueled controversy over slavery in the 1830s.

Evangelicalism and Anti-Abolitionism

The example of Joshua Leavitt shows that the intellectual and political path from evangelicalism to abolitionism was not a short one: Leavitt spent at least a decade traversing it. But one can say more. Evangelicalism did not necessarily lead to abolitionism at all, even at length. Many evangelicals of the 1820s followed another path entirely—a path that led them to a contrary position in the slavery controversy.

Decades earlier, in 1803, Lyman Beecher had already anticipated a reaction to some of the new currents in evangelical Christianity. His sermon of that year, titled "The Practicability of Suppressing Vice, by Means of Societies Instituted for that Purpose," promoted the establishment of "moral societies" like the one at his Congregational church in East Hampton, Long Island. The societies would be devoted to communal vigilance against individual misdeeds such as profane swearing, profanation of the Sabbath, intemperance, "and other immoralities." If virtuous citizens were united and organized, Beecher decided, they could reform public opinion and stigmatize the behavior they abhorred. Giving voice to the obvious objection, the quicker to dismiss it, he asked, "Will it be suggested that such institutions may create dissentions in society?" Perhaps they may, Beecher (1803, 15) answered, but "dissentions" presented much less cause for worry than did the "unrestrained progress of vice."

But Beecher did not only anticipate a reaction to the new currents; in some ways he fomented it. Apprehensive of excessive application of the "new measures"—women praying alongside men, the minister's calling on repentant sinners by name from the pulpit, itinerant and lay evangelists operating heedless of the authority of settled pastors—he set out to restrain the evangelists who practiced them, above all Charles Finney. In 1827, and largely at Beecher's behest, prominent Presbyterian and Congregational ministers from New York and New England gathered at New Lebanon, New York, a couple of miles from the Massachusetts border, to try to reach a consensus about the appropriate methods of religious revivals. Beecher, who now ministered to a well-to-do Boston congregation and was at the apex of his renown, expected that the Finneyites, whose strongholds were generally more western and therefore more rural and less urbane, would be bowled over by resolutions opposing the rumored excesses.

In the event, the rumors appeared to be somewhat overblown, the convention was divided, and the Finneyites held their own against the more strident resolutions. Beecher was put on the defensive. To Finney he burst out, "I know your plan, and you know I do; you mean to come to Connecticut, and carry a streak of fire to Boston. But if you attempt it, as the Lord liveth, I'll meet you at the state line, and call out all the artillery-men, and fight every inch of the way to Boston, and then I'll fight you there" (Cole 1950, 395).

The apprehensions of Beecher and other revivalists of a more conservative bent turned out to be not merely, and arguably not mainly, about the "new measures." The conservatives approved, after all, of religious revivals. What they disapproved of were the increasingly "mechanical" methods of conducting them—methods that seemed less reliant on the Holy Spirit than contrived by men, particularly by itinerant men who did not respect the prerogatives of stationary and established ministers. They disapproved, too, of exhortations to conversion that crossed the line between passion and theatrics and thus were characteristic of low breeding or Methodism (Carwardine 1972). Beecher's outburst in New Lebanon, coming *after* the Finneyites had been exonerated of the most severe allegations of such methods, betrayed that there was rather more at stake in the matter than the souls that might be saved or lost. At stake also were which ministers would hold the balance of esteem and power, and which section and class of people would decide the norms of religious practice.

After 1828 and the election of Andrew Jackson, sectional and class antagonisms, expressed often in religious terms, loomed larger than ever. Arthur Schlesinger Jr. (1945, 2–3) illustrated vividly the gloom felt by upstanding and pious Northeasterners after President Adams's defeat. Jackson was, from their perspective, a frontiersman of notorious character with a platform that was egalitarian in the worst sense—specifically, in that it elevated his lowly ilk to power. So great was the perceived threat to the social order that, despite their sharpening theological contrasts, Presbyterians of the Old and New Schools, Congregationalists, Unitarians, and Universalists were largely united in presidential politics. Where their denominations dominated, Adams won. The popular votes of all the New England states went for Adams; so would have New York's if it were not for New York City's four congressional districts and its environs; and so too did those of New Jersey, Delaware, and Maryland.[1] To state the result differently, Jackson won wherever the preeminent religious dominations were those that appealed vigorously to the common man—namely, the Methodist and Baptist churches, which, despite their large differences and mutual antagonism, had at least that much in common (Carwardine 2002, 87–89). The popular vote was Jackson's in all states from Pennsylvania to the west, where expansion was proceeding rapidly, and also, with the exception of coastal Maryland and Delaware, in all states to the south. That "the ungodly were in the ascendancy" may have been, as Schlesinger wrote, the common Northeastern view of the election result, but it was belied by the large support garnered for the democracy among evangelicals of certain denominations. An equally partisan but more apt characterization of the result replaced "the ungodly" with "King 'Mob'" (Schlesinger 1945, 6).

The united political front of Northeastern evangelicals belonging to the long-established and socially preeminent denominations dissolved as Jackson's presidency wore on. Disunity did not result from the mitigation of sectional and class antagonisms: they remained severe. It resulted instead from the growing perception, to the minds of Old School Presbyterians and others with roots sunk deep in Calvinism, that Congregationalism, New School Presbyterianism, and Unitarianism and Universalism fostered a kind of political radicalism not unlike that of Jackson's "mob." The wedge was exactly the moral reformism embodied by the likes

1. See Petersen 1963 and Martis 1982, 69.

of Rev. Joshua Leavitt. So long as moral reform implied what Lyman Beecher had in mind in 1803—suppression of Sabbath breaking and intemperance and similar vices—those of a conservative bent in religion and politics could view its effects as benign, even if its motive and methods were theologically suspect. But when moral reform implied at last the abolition of slavery, they could not abide it, and everything associated with it that they once tolerated was now tainted.

The mirror image of Joshua Leavitt, embodying the reaction to his religious premises and political advocacy, was the Reverend Calvin Colton. Colton, like Leavitt, was born in western Massachusetts, although five years earlier, in 1789, and near the southern border with Connecticut rather than the northern one with Vermont. What is more, Colton attended Yale College during the presidency of Timothy Dwight—graduating in 1812 after having overlapped for two years with Leavitt, who matriculated in 1810 (Cave 1969, 1; Davis 1990, 8). But there end the similarities between the two men. Whereas Leavitt graduated to practice law and returned to Yale to study theology only in the 1820s, by which time the college's theological school had been established and made a vehicle for disseminating the innovative thought of Nathaniel Taylor, Colton went immediately after graduating to the Andover seminary, which was established in reaction to the threat of Unitarianism at Harvard. He was ordained as a Presbyterian in 1815, then served for eleven years as a pastor in the "Burned Over District" of western New York. At last he resigned in a state of illness and depression, due in part to personal loss but also to disgust with low pay, overwork, and Finneyite religious innovations, in 1826 (Cave 1969, 1–2). Thus, just as the intense wave of religious revivalism of the mid-1820s was propelling Leavitt into the ministry, its backwash was repelling Colton.

Thereafter Colton traveled and wrote. He lived in England from 1831 to 1835, writing foreign correspondence for the *New York Observer* and publishing books on the side. It is notable that his writings from this period were not opposed to revivalism, and one of them, *The History and Character of American Revivals of Religion* (1832), presented a defense to a skeptical English audience. Among his other books, *The Americans* (1832) was a rebuttal of characterizations in popular travel narratives by Captain Hall and Francis Trollope of Americans' coarseness of manners and excesses in religion. More audaciously, in *A Manual for Emigrants to America* (1832), Colton averred that those who would seek their fortunes in the United States should either be confident of the worthiness of their own character or stay at home. In an aside that takes on greater significance in light of his later contributions to the slavery controversy, he also suggested that if one did choose to migrate, then the choice of region required special attention. New England offered a suitable home for those of good name and education, the West for most others, and the South for hardly anyone, for "the existence of slavery—an entailed, grievous, and lamented evil—generally constitutes a sufficient objection against voluntary emigration there" (quoted in Cave 1969, 10–11). On the other hand, because slavery was so abhorrent, it would surely "be abolished in the United States, utterly and forever" (29).

On his return to the United States, Colton treated differently the subjects of revivalism and slavery. He did not profess to have changed his views; rather, he witnessed a change of circumstances, both religious and political. Although the changes might already have been detectable when he departed his Presbyterian pastorate in 1826, in the intervening decade (and particularly during his sojourn abroad) they had become so disturbing that he chose to switch his religious affiliation—and to state his reasons in another book, *Thoughts on the Religious State of the Country: With Reasons for Preferring Episcopacy* (1836). "When I returned to this country in the spring of 1835," he explained, "I had not been here long before I discovered that America was another world than that, which I had left behind me in 1831. Of course I mean principally in a religious point of view; I might add in some others" (Colton 1836, 23).

From the religious point of view, Colton was troubled to observe, first, that "the great majority of religious excitements in this country, called revivals, have entirely changed their character" (15). Twenty years before, Presbyterians and Congregationalists had regarded the Methodists' modes of operation "in the light of extravagance, not to say fanaticism"; since then, "ruthless hands" working in those once-sober denominations had surpassed even the Methodists in "rash experiment" (41). The minister's pretense of determining particular parishioners' salvation or damnation on the spot of the sermon and in public, for instance, was a practice unseen in respectable churches in the previous generation, according to Colton, but common in the 1830s. In general, "to frighten, shock, and paralyze the mind with alternations and scenes of horror, carefully concealing the ground of encouragement and hope, till reason is shaken and hurled from its throne, for the sake of gaining a convert," he argued, was unseemly—and worse. Such practices would "do injury to the cause of religion" because their likely effect was, "in making a convert, to make a maniac" (44–45). Nor did Colton mean "maniac" to be read as hyperbole. Insanity had become epidemic: "It is but a little while since I visited an insane hospital, and wandered through its cells and more public rooms. I was struck with the predominance of religious mania" (41).

A second troubling observation was that parishioners were not the only ones being driven to insanity—and beyond—by religious excess. The overwork that Colton had suffered in the clergy until 1826 had worsened for those who remained. The cause was rooted in the organization of the Presbyterian and Congregational churches, where the prerogatives of pastoral government were divided between pastors and groups of "elders" or "deacons," who were laymen in either case. Such diffusion of power, and the mutual oversight that it implied of laymen and clergy, was an outgrowth of the supposed "covenant of mutual watch and care." The covenant held that members of a congregation, including the minister, were "bound to watch over each other, implying the right and duty of each member to have an eye on the conduct of every other" (47). Colton thought it preposterous. Laymen were rarely competent to supervise and judge their minister, and in submitting to their supervision and judgment, the minister debased himself: "To have elders and deacons to rule over him, is to be a slave—is not to be a man" (35). Like a slave, too, the minister risked wearing himself out and even dying by servicing the whims of his illegitimate masters. A bit of histrionics made the point colorfully: "I see my brethren fallen and falling around me, like the slain in battle, the plains of our land literally covered with these unfortunate victims" (41).

A third and supremely important observation was as much from the political as the religious point of view. To Colton, the covenant of mutual watch and care promoted "meddling and impertinent interference" (73)—not only by laymen in the business of their ministers but also by laymen in each others' business. The problem, however, was not the violation of everyone's privacy; it was the violation of time-honored inequalities of status. In other words, Colton objected not to "meddling" per se but to its being done irrespective of the relative stations in life of the meddler and the meddled. An evocative passage hints at the implications of this line of thinking to larger political questions:

> If the principle recognized in the covenant of "mutual watch and care" were attempted to be carried out, it would set society on fire, or rend it asunder. A man in the lowest condition of life is thereby authorized to look into the private concerns of the highest, and determine upon his conduct, and rebuke him, if he sees fit. The servant may rise to judge his master, and the maid her mistress. . . . None of the common

> and sacred relations of society could be maintained on this principle, if it be supposed, that persons in all these relations are members of the same church, associated under a solemn covenant to rebuke a fault wherever they see it, and consequently to treat every one according to his personal merits, themselves being judges, each for himself. Could any theory of society be more false—more unscriptural? The reason why it does little hurt, is because it is seldom put in practice. Society could not tolerate it for a moment. (50–51)

From his *Thoughts on the Religious State of the Country*, no large leap of reasoning was required of Colton to arrive at his subsequent condemnation of the abolitionist movement. He almost certainly had it already in mind.

Abolitionism was yet another example, albeit an especially pernicious one, of "impertinent meddling." That its inspiration was religious was the first step of his argument: "We trust it will be obvious to all, that it was impossible to treat Abolitionism according to its merits, or to exhibit its true character, without regarding it as a RELIGIOUS MOVEMENT" (Colton 1839, v). In particular, the movement was organized by "moral societies" whose origins could be traced to designs like Beecher's. The point was important because, having made it, Colton set out to demonstrate that the movement was a grotesque variant of those designs.

Like much of what issued from the religious enthusiasm of the 1830s, Colton argued, the new societies dishonored the institutions that they shaped themselves after and then perverted. The exemplar and chief offender was the American Anti-Slavery Society (AASS); Leavitt, who edited the society's official organ, *The Emancipator*, beginning in 1837, was thus implicated in Colton's indictment. The society's offense was deviating from the legitimate course of moral advocacy and entering, contrary to its originally stated intention, into politics. As Colton put it, the society had "betrayed and violated the principles of the Religious and Benevolent Society system, by first assuming its model, and then passing over into the field of political action" (vii).

Indeed, Colton contended that an organization devoted to abolishing slavery had necessarily to be a political organization, because the institution to be abolished was expressly permitted by the nation's defining political contract. The U.S. Constitution would have to be changed or set aside—a political act. And if the AASS did not propose to change the Constitution by constitutional means, which would be unlikely to surpass the several legislative barriers, then on what authority did it propose to act, Colton asked, and what action did it propose? His answers: the society presumed "that slavery is wrong by a higher and more imperative law than that of the country" (17), and it aimed "to face the Government of the country in open conflict, and to erect its batteries against that Constitutional fabric, which has hitherto been so dear to American citizens" (14). Abolitionism, therefore, was seditious. It followed that the movement should be "checked and suppressed" (12), not only by persuasion but also by force of law. And where that failed, in some instances Colton would even countenance mob violence (Cave 1969, 36–37).

The contrast of Colton's manner of speaking about slavery in 1832 with his manner of speaking about abolitionism in 1839 did not, to his mind, present any contradiction. In fact, it was common among conservative or "cotton" Whigs, who deplored slavery but believed, even into the 1850s, that the institution would wither away if only slaveholders were not antagonized by belligerence and affronts to their moral character. "What conservatives found particularly offensive," wrote Eric Foner (1970, 188), "was the constant moralizing of abolitionists and radicals about the peculiar institution." If one sought the extinction of slavery, thought conservatives like Colton (or, among political leaders, Henry Clay and Daniel Webster), one should begin by treating it "as a problem in political economy, not as a moral abstraction" (189). Stephen Colwell (1851, 257), an elder on the Old School side of the Presbyterian Church and a prominent author on subjects of political economy, wrote in 1851 that "when the object is to abolish slavery, the Christian process will be to incite masters to love and cherish their slaves as immortal beings under their charge, and to teach the slaves to love and obey their masters, under whom, in the order of Providence, they are placed. Under this teaching, a patriarchal relation will arise between the master and his slave; the fetters will drop off." One could inquire with propriety into establishing economic conditions that would allow the fetters to drop off more quickly, but one could not use the threat of compulsion, which would "stem the whole current of the Divine administration, and stop the course of Providence" (248).

Henry C. Carey, an even more prominent political economist than Colwell, as well as his friend and intellectual patron, inquired into the subject keenly and formulated an elaborate theory. Economic progress requires technological progress that originates in manufacturing industry, Carey argued; the vitality of manufacturing depends on the physical proximity of its customers, many of whom are employed in cultivating the land, to the seats of industry. Where industry is diversified—where "the natural tendency of the loom and the anvil to seek to take their place by the side of the plough and the harrow" is unhindered—agriculturalists are able to witness and adapt for their own uses the innovations of industry, thereby to cultivate land more intensively (Carey 1853, 50). Intensive cultivation of land with machinery obviates the need for large parcels of territory and the slaves indispensable to farming them. To extinguish slavery, Carey concluded, one should foster industry. That the conclusion was opportune to producers of iron, steel, and machinery in his native Pennsylvania is immaterial to the argument's ingenuity.

The reverberations of anti-abolitionism to other outstanding political questions, however, did not begin with Carey's argument of the 1850s. In *Abolition a Sedition*, Colton had already referred to abolitionism as but one example of a generic class of ill-advised reforms based ultimately in unsound theology and religious mania. He "had averred the philosophical connexion of antecedent and consequence between *Abolitionism and violent reforms*" (Colton 1839, v). In so doing, he pointed up the salience of other political causes, similarly troubling, that were also consequences of the thirst for violent reforms and were to be opposed for the same reasons.

Abolitionism and Free Trade

It has been observed elsewhere that, to their more doctrinaire mid-nineteenth-century exponents, abolitionism and free trade were kindred causes (e.g., Meardon 2006; Morgan 2007). The "free labor" doctrine embraced them both. If it is presumed that workers have a right to appropriate their own labor, then it is a short leap to the presumption that they have a right to sell the fruits of their labor at market price. Indeed it can be (and was) argued that either presumption is meaningless without the other. To those who accepted the presumptions, tariff protection took on the appearance of theft and redistribution. The logic is clear enough, but what is easily lost in it is the reason why the presumptions were made in the first place.

It was not their obviousness. To evangelical abolitionists, the idea of slaves' property rights to their own labor was useful to buttress an antislavery argument that was grounded originally in Christian benevolence. Likewise, the idea of a right to sell dear and buy cheap, without hindrance of "class legislation" and without which right one is effectively enslaved, was hardly manifest to most abolitionists, especially in the early years of the movement toward immediatism.

There were exceptions. As early as 1831, in a lecture mainly on the abolition of slavery (and thereby the fulfillment of the "predictions of Revelation"), Henry Dwight Sedgwick (1831, 23, 25–26) of Massachusetts veered significantly toward the tariff: it was "a partial, qualified, disguised slavery," he insisted, for it embodied the presumption that "one set of men have a right to prescribe to another set of men what they shall purchase, and from whom the purchase shall be made." Even so, Sedgwick did not neglect to consider the expedient as well as the moral connection of the two subjects. "It would be a beautiful spectacle, interesting alike to the philanthropist and economist," he reflected, "to observe how emancipation from the minor restriction—that imposed on commerce—would aid in the emancipation of the slaves from bodily thralldom" (47). But few evangelical abolitionists would find the right of free trade manifest, as Sedgwick did, until its expediency was clearer.

Given the abolitionists' Federalist lineage, the manifest right in commercial policy might instead have been tariff protection (Cole 1954, 180). The unexpected but congenial marriage of abolitionism and free trade arose from circumstances around the end of the 1830s: the calamitous panic of 1837, the presidential election of 1840, and inspiration from Great Britain's Anti–Corn Law League. Thomas P. Martin (1928, 206) observed that by the late 1830s, the disposition among New England and New York abolitionists—"particularly among those of commercial New York," including Leavitt—was to confront slavery aggressively with political action and economic pressure; their disposition "needed only an opportunity for positive expression."

The opportunity was elusive: effective pressure would require political organization on a large scale, and that would imply either changing substantially the Whig Party platform or peeling away support from the Whig and Democratic parties alike in several states. Neither strategy could have succeeded through most of the 1830s. Whigs were inclined generally toward gradualism, not immediatism, and outside the New England states and certain pockets of New York, abolitionism had little appeal. Even within New England, abolitionists were viewed with more disfavor than regard. Although motivated originally by evangelical Christianity, they had moved subsequently ahead of the movement's mainstream and ventured, to most minds, into the ominous realm of "ultraism." Leavitt witnessed the extent of public antipathy toward abolitionism firsthand during the New York City anti-abolitionist riots in the summer of 1834, when, as he recounted in a letter of 12 July to his parents, he was pursued by the mob and narrowly escaped injury (Leavitt n.d.). The incident foreshadowed dramatically the difficulty of establishing an abolitionist political program with mass appeal.

A matter of curiosity for the historian (if not the mob at Leavitt's heels), and a crucial matter for the linking of abolitionism and free trade, is that the real "ultraists" were those abolitionists who were most disinclined to direct involvement in politics. Colton's 1839 missive against the AASS for advocating political abolitionism was applicable, in truth, only to a sizable faction within the organization. That faction, which Kraditor (1967, 100–101) labels confusingly the "conservatives" and synonymously and more aptly the "evangelical abolitionists," was engaged at the moment in a bitter dispute with the "radicals" over the tactics that the organization would employ toward its great objective. The radicals, who eschewed direct political action, were led by Garrison; their embrace of the principle of nonresistance implied their unwillingness to participate in the political system so long as government was premised on the use of force. Besides, participation in the system would result inevitably, they believed, in pandering to nonabolitionists to win votes and thereby diluting the abolitionist program. Better to reform public opinion first and let politics follow (159–60).

One did not have to be a nonresistant to believe that an abolitionist political party was inexpedient. Leavitt, for instance, was hardly inclined to nonresistance, yet he wrote in 1838 that the creation of an abolition party would be "suicidal" (Davis 1990, 142, 147). But between 1838 and 1840, the evangelicals, who had no principled objection to coordinated political action, began to change their views of its expediency. Notwithstanding the political efforts of individual abolitionists, their abstention as a group was arguably abetting slavery where the federal government had the constitutional power to extinguish it (as in the District of Columbia and federal territories) or prevent its absorption into the union (as in the Republic of Texas, the annexation of which was a particularly menacing prospect to abolitionists in the late 1830s). At the same time, evangelical abolitionists hardened their objection to the principle of nonresistance, which set back the cause of abolitionism in other ways than by impeding coordinated political action. Like women's suffrage—another reform that Garrison advocated—the notion was far-fetched, brought the whole abolitionist movement into disrepute, and threatened to undermine the efficacy of any political action that might be entertained.

Leavitt allowed the objection to nonresistance to be aired in *The Emancipator* by James G. Birney, who by the end of the year had migrated from Southern slaveholder to Cincinnati abolitionist editor of national repute to corresponding secretary of the AASS (Davis 1990, 134; Dumond 1938, 1:xii–xiv). Birney had also become a steadfast opponent of Garrison (Kraditor 1967, 33). "The 'no-Government' doctrines," he charged, "seem to strike at the root of the social structure; and tend . . . to throw society into entire confusion, and to renew, under the sanction of religion, scenes of anarchy and license that have generally heretofore been the offspring of the rankest infidelity and irreligion" (*The Emancipator*, 2 May 1839; quoted in Kraditor 1967, 101). To Birney, it was not sufficient that the AASS remained officially neutral, as Garrison wished, toward nonresistance and women's rights. It should repudiate them. Only then would the abolitionist political program be at once sound and salable.

When a steamboat load of New England Garrisonians packed the May 1840 convention of the AASS, frustrating the evangelical abolitionists' efforts to refashion the organization to their design, the evangelicals formed the American and Foreign Anti-Slavery Society (A & F), with Birney and Leavitt among several notable others (Arthur and Lewis Tappan, Henry Stanton, John Greenleaf Whittier, Gerrit Smith, and thirty more) on the executive committee (Barnes 1933, 169–70). The constitution of the A & F, which Leavitt inserted in a letter of 1 July to his brother, "urge[d] on all the duty of exercising their political power in behalf of the slave" (Leavitt n.d.).

Leavitt, in fact, had already proceeded to do so. In April, he acceded to the transfer of *The Emancipator* from the AASS to the New York City Young Men's Anti-Slavery Society (Davis 1990, 158). After the transfer, Leavitt no longer faced resistance to his using the newspaper to urge "independent nominations" for political offices—as he had begun to do, despite the opposition of much of the AASS as well as his own earlier reservations, in October 1839 (150–56). Now he took up the task with abandon. A new political party, independent of Democrats and Whigs, directed toward the aims of evangelical abolitionists, and soon to be designated "Liberty," had by mid-1840 both a prominent organ to promote its candidates and (at least in theory) a national antislavery society to supply it with workers and spread its ideas (Carwardine 1997, 136, 370; Kraditor 1967, 142).

Yet the aims of evangelical abolitionists were not inscribed easily in a political party platform. Among the several difficulties was determining what their core principles implied with respect to other issues besides slavery. Another was determining whether it was expedient for the Liberty Party to take official stands on those issues. These matters were clearly on the minds of Leavitt and the other members of the nascent party who convened at City Hall in Albany on 1 April 1840 to nominate their national election candidates (who were, in the event, James Birney for president and Thomas Earle of Pennsylvania for vice president) and state their intentions in a series of resolutions. Their tenth resolution was a clear statement that although the party's principal objective would be abolition, they would "by no means lose sight of numerous other questions" in which they were deeply interested. All such questions should be decided by the same "fundamental principle"—namely, that all men are, "as men, entitled to an equal participation in the benefits of our government." They should be decided, therefore, "in favor of the widest and largest liberty that can flourish under just laws" (*The Emancipator*, 9 April 1840).

The mention of liberty, and more specifically of equal participation in the benefits of government, gives an inkling of the conventioneers' thinking about the other objectives of their party. Leavitt's letter of 19 May to Birney, reporting that Earle accepted his vice presidential nomination only on condition of "the passage [at the recent A & F meeting] of a resolution declaring our opposition to all exclusive privileges and monopolies," offers another clue (Dumond 1938, 1:574). The alliance of American and British abolitionists, which Leavitt himself helped to cement (Thistlethwaite 1971, 113, 195), considered together with the large overlap between the British abolitionist and anti–Corn Law movements (Morgan 2007), offers yet another. Still, the Albany conventioneers did not state the other objectives precisely, nor did they decide whether to advance them actively and simultaneously with abolition or passively and in consequence of it.

The reason for their reticence was surely the belief, evident also in Birney's letter of 11 May accepting his nomination, that the new party expected to draw its support from erstwhile Whigs more than Democrats. A large proportion of Whig abolitionists would vote for General Harrison, Birney foresaw, notwithstanding their disgust at his "'bowing the knee to the dark spirit of Slavery,'" because they thought that protection of certain pecuniary interests neglected by President Van Buren were of "primer importance" than the immediate abolition of slavery (Dumond 1938, 1:566). Not least among those interests were the ones propped up by a protective tariff. If the Liberty Party came out unambiguously against protection, it would alienate many sympathetic voters. If it remained ambiguous about its free trade inclinations, it could win them over. This was the "strong motive," according to Kraditor (1967, 147–48), if not the principled justification voiced more often, of the party's dalliance after the Albany convention with "one-ideaism": *acknowledgment* that other matters were relevant, but *advocacy* only of abolition. The imprecision of the Albany conventioneers' language prevented their being bound by one-ideaism while allowing their resolutions to be construed as consistent with it.

In the summer and fall of 1840, Leavitt was inclined to go well beyond the one idea. "I had hoped to send you some statistics on the Corn Laws," he wrote to Birney on 19 May; "I think much on the subject" (Dumond 1938, 1:574). His thoughts had percolated through seemingly disparate events over the preceding three years: the Anti–Corn Law League's activities in Great Britain and the ensuing parliamentary debate, which was reported in the United States beginning in March 1839 (Martin 1928, 209); the distress of Northwestern farmers as agricultural prices fell and credit disappeared after the panic of 1837; and the reluctance of Northwestern abolitionists, let alone more moderate antislavery Whigs and Democrats, to support independent nominations (Rayback 1948). In all this Leavitt apprehended an opportunity for the Liberty Party: one could argue that the structure of British tariffs, which discriminated against Western wheat flour in favor of Southern cotton, was a corrupt bargain with the slave power. Strike down the laws, facilitate transatlantic trade in Western grain, and in one blow slavery would be weakened and the West would prosper. Simply by making the argument, the Liberty Party could improve its electoral prospects at once among two constituencies, Northwesterners and Democrats, the latter of which could be enticed by generalizing the anti–Corn Law position to embrace free trade. "I can see it all clearly now," wrote Leavitt to Birney on 1 October. "We must go for free trade; the voting abolitionists can all be brought to that, and it will secure us the Democracy, and the corn movement will give us the West." Perhaps sensing that his reasoning was an awkward fit for a party of principle, he added, "Providence guides our minds, and designs some great and good results to our cause, our nation, and universal humanity" (Dumond 1938, 2:604).

And yet, despite his private will to campaign for free trade as well as the endorsement of providence, Leavitt refrained from making the case directly and publicly. To select audiences, like a Liberty convention in Ohio in late 1841, he called for free trade (Martin 1932, 473). To most others, his responsibilities as a prominent spokesman for the party compelled him to use his voice and its amplifier, *The Emancipator*, with caution, taking care not to express views far in advance of his compatriots. So he stayed in line with the resolutions of the Albany convention, pitching free trade obliquely—or, more often, making other arguments that appealed to many of the same voters and were compatible with free trade but stopped short of it. The Corn Laws argument, which pressed for a more liberal trade policy mainly on Great Britain's part, was such a one (e.g., *The Emancipator*, 1 May, 10 September, 24 December 1840; Leavitt 1841, 1842). Another suggested that the gravest problem with the tariff was not that it was high or low but that it gyrated from one Congress to the next; the gyrations were a deliberate tactic of the slave power to prostrate the North. The question of whether the nation should settle at last upon free trade or protection, therefore, was a matter that should be decided only after slavery was vanquished, for until then "any attempt at adjustment can only be temporary" (*The Emancipator*, 15 October 1840).

Yet another argument that was especially well received, according to Gamaliel Bailey, successor to Birney as editor of the *Cincinnati Philanthropist*, was one that Leavitt presented to Ohio abolitionists in September of 1840 (Bretz 1929, 256). "We are all aware that it is 'hard times' at present," Leavitt acknowledged—and what else could that mean but that "money is scarce"? (Leavitt 1840). Money was scarce, he explained, because credit from free states flowed inexorably to slave states, facilitated by the late Bank of the United States' practice of equalizing across all regions the cost of transferring money from one region to another. If not for that practice, credit would be expanded in the North and curtailed in the South because of the higher risk of entering into transactions with slave owners: "The free expect to pay their debts, if it takes years of toil and self-denial; the slaveholder likes to pay debts if it is convenient, but to work and save to pay an old debt enters not into his thoughts" (Leavitt 1840). Credit was scarce in the North, in other words, because of the lingering effects of bad legislation—specifically, the Bank's charter. The scarcity was exacerbated by the general distress that ensued when cotton prices fell, profligate Southerners could not or would not pay their debts, and Northern creditors were bankrupted.

Irrespective of its factual merits, the argument was politically astute. It blamed slavery for the economic crisis, thereby appealing to antislavery Whigs who were equally concerned with other matters, even as it reached out with its anti-Bank hook to wavering Democrats. It was similar in effect if not content to Leavitt's free trade argument, which prudence caused him to muffle.

After the election of 1844, in which Birney received less than 2.5 percent of the popular vote even on his second try, a growing number of

Libertymen failed to see how prudence recommended against drawing distinctly the connection between abolition and free trade. They had also become convinced that principle demanded it. William Goodell addressed the New York State Liberty Party convention at Port Bryon in July 1845, citing at length the numerous resolutions of past conventions that had proclaimed the party's devotion to equality and impartial government and its antagonism to monopolies of all kinds. "Can it be difficult to foresee the course," asked Goodell (1845, 9), "that such a party, if remaining true to its principles, must ultimately take, in respect to the question of protective tariff or free trade?" He continued:

> Abolitionists, including Liberty party men, have always stigmatized the slave system as being the most odious and grinding "MONOPOLY" in the land—as unjust *because* legislating for the benefit of one particular caste or CLASS at the expense of another—as anti-republican because it creates and sustains castes and classes. . . . How then can the Liberty party, with any show of impartiality and consistency, do otherwise than to repudiate *all* monopolies, and castes, and class legislations, whether bearing upon white men at the North, or colored at the South? If the slave has a right to dispose of his own labor, has not every other man the same right, including, of course, the right to dispose of the avails of his labor in whatever market he chooses?" (9)

True free trade had the added virtue of attacking slavery by compelling its taxation. If Federal revenues came not from customs, then direct taxes would have to be levied on incomes and property. Taxable incomes and property would include, Goodell presumed, slaveholder incomes and property in slaves. "Such a process the slave system could with difficulty survive, for a single year" (10).

As Goodell was articulating the foregoing views for his fellow Libertymen, he was also doing so in modified form to the congregants in his church in Honeoye, New York. In a sermon of 14 November 1847, titled "The Relief of the Poor," Reverend Goodell (n.d.) attributed much of the poverty witnessed in the country to laws that discriminated in favor of the wealthy. "By the Tariff, the burthens of the National Government . . . are taken off from *Capital* & thrown on to *consumption*, or *persons*! Thus the poor pay the greater part of the whole, the rich are comparatively exempt." Other causes of poverty were slavery and intemperance. Goodell inveighed against all of them for the same reason, which he expressed in his opening words by quoting from Deuteronomy 15: "Thou shalt open thy hand wide unto thy brother, to thy poor, to thy needy in thy land" (Goodell n.d.). His reasoning echoed Leavitt's, from a decade and a half earlier, as he ventured from evangelicalism to temperance to abolitionism. Only a new cause was added.

Goodell's challenge to one-ideaism put Leavitt in the uncomfortable position of defending the existing Liberty Party platform against views with which he heartily agreed except in the narrowest of tactical respects. Leavitt treated Goodell gently, praising his "logic, honesty, and good old fame" before observing that even those who agreed with his views were unwilling to see the Liberty Party adopt them officially (*The Emancipator*, 9 July 1845). When Goodell repeated his argument two years later to a nominating convention at Macedon Lock, New York (Goodell 1847)—engineering a split in the party and bringing forward Gerrit Smith as candidate of the "Liberty League," an abolitionist, free trade, and general reform party—Leavitt was more dismissive. He expressed respect for the offshoot's leaders and its candidate, with whom, "looking to the ends they have in view," he could find no fault. But he determined their party was impracticable and would make no great impression. In any event, he was sure that his readers would remain aloof from it, for "as Liberty party men, aiming in our organization only at one object, we have nothing to do with it" (*The Emancipator*, 3 July 1847).

A strange irony of the year that followed is that Leavitt was eventually willing to compromise one-ideaism—albeit by helping to fold the Liberty Party into the Free Soil coalition, whose platform was committed merely to nonextension of slavery, not abolition, and who therefore pursued the "one idea" with considerably less vigor than the Liberty Leaguers showed in pursuing that idea together with several others. The steady pressure of Western abolitionists, who were more interested in compromise and coalition building than the Easterners, was the driving force behind the coalition that Leavitt finally endorsed (Rayback 1948).

The irony and its cause, however, should not obscure a more relevant fact. The Free Soil coalition, while not committed to free trade, did stand for a "revenue tariff" as opposed to a protective one. Thus, when one-ideaism met its political demise in 1847 and 1848, the options at the ballot box for political abolitionists consisted of one party that stood for free trade and another that stood for freer trade. As one of the earliest proponents of hitching abolitionism to free trade, Leavitt must have been pleased by the similar trade-policy orientations of both alternatives.

Anti-abolitionism and Protection

The 1840s was a period of development of the protective doctrine, no less than free trade doctrine, amid intensification of the tariff controversy. The controversy had, of course, existed before, and particular incidents in it (like the nullification dispute of a decade earlier) had sparked thought on both sides. The difference in the 1840s was that protection was challenged by traditional Whig constituencies, among whom there had previously been only muted disagreement on trade policy. Now the dispute was familial and rancorous. It was associated with acrimonious debates about not only the integrity of the federal government and preservation of the union, as happened during the nullification period, but also religion and slavery. The stakes were considerably greater than in the past.

This was the context in which Colton, under the pen name "Junius," wrote a series of pamphlets from May 1843 to June 1844 on questions of political economy. The pamphlets supported the presidential candidacy of Henry Clay, with whose political program Colton identified closely; one of them offered a justification of Clay's "American system" of tariff protection. The arguments were generally restatements of Clay's own, most notably those contending that protecting manufacturers created a "home market" for producers of agriculture, thus benefiting them, too (Colton [1843] 1874, 10–11)—and that, over time, protection made manufactured goods cheaper because domestic competition and innovation would drive down costs (11). A more original argument was legal rather than economic. There can be no right to free international trade, Colton stated, because in trading with people of other countries, U.S. citizens are acting as "public agents" who "hold in their hands political powers of vital importance of the nation they represent" (2); therefore, they are rightly subject to regulation. The argument that Colton stressed more than any other, however, was patriotism: "Every true American will duly appreciate such an unblushing proposal [as free trade] to revive the old system of *Colonial* dependence. . . . Such always *has* been and *still is* the plan of British commercial policy, and such will be its end, if unopposed by an American system" (5). Anti-British sentiment had not been a fixture of Colton's youth, which was spent in territory friendly to Federalism and hostile to Jefferson's embargo. The fact that it surfaced now was due likely to the threat posed in Great Britain by the Anti–Corn Law League, whose moral crusade for free trade in grain could be expected to spawn imitation in the United States.

The culminating efforts of the movement to repeal the Corn Laws in 1846 did, in fact, contribute toward a substantial tariff cut in the United States in the same year. Clay had lost the election of 1844, and President Polk was more congenial to liberal trade. Colton reacted to the distressing reversal of the American system in a short book, *The Rights of Labor* (1846), which would be the core of his magnum opus, *Public Economy for the United States* (1848).

The Rights of Labor, notwithstanding its title, was entirely about free trade versus protection. The reason for the title becomes clearer, given the Whig Party's long-standing attempt to position itself as the party of labor and the necessity of responding to the repeal of the Corn Laws with opposing arguments that would appeal to that constituency. "This republican empire was founded on labor," wrote Colton (1846, 9); its political system had succeeded in securing to labor its fair reward. Yet another country, namely Great Britain, was working to undo all of the gains. "That old political system, which depresses labor, and holds it in bondage, has maintained and fortified its position," explained Colton. Specifically,

> what it could neither arrest, nor subdue, by force of arms, it has undertaken to conquer by policy; and the great political contest of the age is, whether THE RIGHTS OF LABOR, as established on American soil, and nourished by American blood, shall be maintained, and extend their empire; or whether they shall be crushed by political devices. (9)

The "political devices" of the Old World that threatened to enervate the rights of labor included, above all, the Corn Laws' abolition. The real purpose of ending the Corn Laws, Colton claimed, was protection for British manufacturers: with less-expensive food available, they could pay their workers less and undersell manufacturers from the United States. The main sufferers would be American workers (13). Tariff protection for Americans, if it were permitted, could sustain their standard of living.

By the mid-1840s, however, if a Whig who was ostensibly antislavery was to make an explicitly prolabor argument, then he also had to spell out the effects of his proposal on slave labor. Carey's proposal of encouragement for domestic manufacturers, for instance, which he claimed would benefit laborers as much or more than capitalists, would arguably help the slave to be emancipated gradually. It is telling that by 1846 Colton made no such argument. Instead he insisted on the compatibility of slavery with the protective tariff. Free and slave labor had "worked under the same system, for the same [agricultural] markets, during the whole history of the country . . . without jealousy or complaint" (7). Tariff protection posed no threat to the relationship. Indeed, he averred, the only threat came from the antiprotective tariff of 1846, which created the possibility that slave labor would be used outside its traditional place in agriculture as producers scrambled to cut labor costs. In iron, for instance, the dismantling of protective duties would cause the domestic industry to disappear from Pennsylvania, while that which remained would be located in Virginia, where iron would be produced with cheaper slave labor (6–7).

Colton's aim was decidedly not to persuade antislavery voters in his own Whig Party that his favored trade policy was the best way to emancipate slaves. Rather, he sought to convince Southern, Western, and border-state voters who were antagonistic toward emancipation and might cast votes for Democrats that protection would *not* free the slaves—and to convince workers in both parties who were indifferent toward emancipation that free trade threatened white workers' jobs. While Leavitt's religiously grounded abolitionism led him to an unexpected position on the tariff, Colton's religiously grounded censure of abolitionism led him to an unexpected rationale for the opposite position, which he had long held, and to defend it with growing vehemence.

Conclusion

The connections between evangelical and national party purposes were indistinct in the 1820s. It was the imperative of moral reform arising in consequence of the Second Great Awakening that established those connections. Moral reform introduced party cleavages, particularly within the Whig Party, that impelled partisans of emerging factions to discover or accentuate political differences that were previously absent or small. Chief among the differences were those concerning slavery and the tariff. Two men who represent the paths from religious awakening to tariff partisanship from the 1820s to the 1840s, and also contributed to clearing the paths, are the Reverend Joshua Leavitt and the Reverend Calvin Colton. Leavitt turned to free trade in consequence of his becoming an abolitionist, which he did to cleanse the nation of the sin of slavery. Colton's arch protectionism can be attributed in part to his being an antislavery advocate who nevertheless repudiated abolition, which he did in reaction to the religious excesses of his opponents.

Like Stewart Davenport (this volume), I am concerned with the starkly different ways in which evangelical Christianity filtered into the attitudes and ideas of a group of antebellum American thinkers whose intellectual contributions were both religious and economic. Unlike Davenport, I view politics as the filter. As differences emerged between Leavitt and Colton with regard to the tariff, they did so because of the conflict over slavery within the Whig party, and between the Whigs and other parties, to which each man adjusted his ideas. In this respect the story told here is similar to that of Roger Backhouse (this volume), who studies the interactions of Christian ethics, welfare economics, and the welfare state through the ideas of several different economists at a much different place and time.

That is not to say that evangelicalism, by provoking the conflict over slavery within the Whig Party, sparked the tariff controversy in the United States. The controversy had roots in sectional and ideological interests apart from religion. Among them were the interests of regions that were home to export industries versus those of regions with import-competing industries, and the interests of political leaders and constituents who envisioned the United States as comprising predominantly an agrarian economy versus those of others who preferred a balance between agriculture and manufacturing. Thomas Jefferson ([1785] 1788) and Alexander Hamilton ([1791] 2003) contributed to the controversy along those lines when the influence of religion on political and economic thought in the United States was at low ebb.

The religious awakening of the early nineteenth century neither allowed the controversy to continue in the same manner nor erased and replaced it with a new one of a religious character. Religion inspired political-economic and religious thinkers to amend old arguments and inscribe new ones onto the controversy, as on a palimpsest. It introduced new purpose, content, and tone to the controversy while the contours of the old remained apparent.

References

Barnes, Gilbert Hobbs. 1933. *The Antislavery Impulse, 1830–1844*. New York: Appleton-Century.

Beecher, Lyman. 1803. *The Practicability of Suppressing Vice, by Means of Societies Instituted for that Purpose: A Sermon Delivered before the Moral Society, in East-Hampton, (Long-Island)*. New London, Conn.: Green.

Bretz, Julian P. 1929. Economic Background of the Liberty Party. *American Historical Review* 34.2:250–64.

Carey, Henry C. 1853. *The Slave Trade, Domestic and Foreign: Why It Exists, and How It May be Extinguished*. Philadelphia: Hart.

Carroll, Bret E. 2000. *The Routledge Historical Atlas of Religion in America*. New York: Routledge.
Carwardine, Richard. 1972. The Second Great Awakening in the Urban Centers: An Examination of Methodism and the "New Measures." *Journal of American History* 59.2:327–40.
——. 1997. *Evangelicals and Politics in Antebellum America*. Knoxville: University of Tennessee Press.
——. 2002. Charles Sellers's "Antinomians" and "Arminians": Methodists and the Market Revolution. In *God and Mammon: Protestants, Money, and the Market, 1790–1860*, edited by Mark A. Noll. New York: Oxford University Press.
Cave, Alfred A. 1969. *An American Conservative in the Age of Jackson: The Political and Economic Thought of Calvin Colton*. Fort Worth: Texas Christian University.
Cole Jr., Charles C. 1950. The New Lebanon Convention. *New York History* 30 (October): 385–97.
——. 1954. *The Social Ideas of the Northern Evangelists, 1826–1860*. New York: Columbia University Press.
Colton, Calvin. 1836. *Thoughts on the Religious State of the Country: With Reasons for Preferring Episcopacy*. New York: Harper and Brothers.
——. 1839. *Abolition a Sedition [by a Northern Man]*. Philadelphia: Donohue.
——. 1848. *Public Economy for the United States*. New York: Barnes.
——. [1843] 1974. The Tariff [The Junius Tracts, No. III]. In *The Junius Tracts and the Rights of Labor*, edited by Michael Hudson. New York: Garland.
——. [1846] 1974. *The Rights of Labor*. 3rd ed. In *The Junius Tracts and the Rights of Labor*, edited by Michael Hudson. New York: Garland.
Colwell, Stephen. 1851. *New Themes for the Protestant Clergy*. Philadelphia: Lippincott, Grambo.
Davis, David Brion. 1962. The Emergence of Immediatism in British and American Antislavery Thought. *Mississippi Valley Historical Review* 49.2:209–30.
Davis, Hugh. 1990. *Joshua Leavitt: Evangelical Abolitionist*. Baton Rouge: Louisiana State University Press.
Dumond, Dwight L., ed. 1938. *Letters of James Gillespie Birney, 1831–1857*. 2 vols. New York: Appleton-Century.
Finney, Charles G. 1876. *Memoirs of Rev. Charles G. Finney*. New York: Barnes.
Foner, Eric. 1970. *Free Soil, Free Labor, Free Men: The Ideology of the Republican Party before the Civil War*. New York: Oxford University Press.
Garrison, Wendell Phillips. 1885. *William Lloyd Garrison, 1805–1879: The Story of His Life, Told by His Children*. Vol. 1. New York: Century.
Goodell, William. 1845. Address Read at the New-York State Liberty Convention, Held at Port Byron, on Wednesday and Thursday, July 25 and 26, 1845. Goodell Anti-Slavery Collection, pamphlet no. 15, Oberlin College Special Collections, Oberlin, Ohio.
——. 1847. Address of the Macedon Convention, by William Goodell, and Letters of Gerrit Smith. Goodell Anti-Slavery Collection, pamphlet no. 4, Oberlin College Special Collections, Oberlin, Ohio.

———. n.d. Papers. Series 2 of Goodell family papers, Oberlin College archives, Oberlin, Ohio.

Hamilton, Alexander. [1787] 1961. The Necessity of a Government as Energetic as the One Proposed to the Preservation of the Union. No. 23 of *The Federalist*, edited by Jacob E. Cooke. Middletown, Conn.: Wesleyan University Press.

———. [1791] 2003. *Report on Manufactures*. Vol. 2 of *Encyclopedia of Tariffs and Trade in U.S. History*, edited by C. C. Northrup and E. C. Turney. Westport, Conn.: Greenwood.

Holt, Michael F. 1999. *The Rise and Fall of the Whig Party: Jacksonian Politics and the Onset of the Civil War*. New York: Oxford University Press.

Howe, Daniel Walker. 1979. *The Political Culture of the American Whigs*. Chicago: University of Chicago Press.

———. 1991. The Evangelical Movement and Political Culture in the North during the Second Party System. *Journal of American History* 77.4:1216–39.

Jefferson, Thomas. [1785] 1788. *Notes on the State of Virginia*. Philadelphia: Pritchett and Hall.

Kraditor, Aileen S. 1967. *Means and Ends in American Abolitionism: Garrison and His Critics on Strategy and Tactics, 1834–1850*. New York: Pantheon Books.

Leavitt, Joshua. 1840. The Financial Power of Slavery; The Substance of an Address Delivered in Ohio, in September, 1840. Printed document, Pitts Theology Library, Emory University, Atlanta.

———. 1841. Memorial of Joshua Leavitt, praying the adoption of measures to secure an equitable and adequate market for American wheat. 26th Cong., 2nd sess., Feb. 25, S. Doc. 222.

———. 1842. Memorial of Joshua Leavitt, praying that, in the revision of the tariff laws, the principle of discrimination may be inserted in favor of those countries in which American grain, flour, and salted meat, are admitted duty free. 27th Cong., 2nd sess., S. Doc. 339.

———. n.d. Family papers. Library of Congress, Washington, D.C.

Marshall, Lynn L. 1967. The Strange Stillbirth of the Whig Party. *American Historical Review* 72.2:445–68.

Martin, Thomas P. 1928. The Upper Mississippi Valley in Anglo-American Anti-Slavery and Free Trade Relations: 1837–1842. *Mississippi Valley Historical Review* 15.2:204–20.

———. 1932. Free Trade and the Oregon Question, 1842–1846. In *Facts and Factors in Economic History: Articles by Former Students of Edwin Francis Gay*, edited by the Graduate School of Business Administration, Harvard University. New York: Russell and Russell.

Martis, Kenneth C. 1982. *The Historical Atlas of United States Congressional Districts, 1789–1983*. New York: Free Press.

McCormick, Richard P. 1966. *The Second American Party System: Party Formation in the Jacksonian Era*. Chapel Hill: University of North Carolina Press.

McKee, Thomas Hudson. 1901. *The National Conventions and Platforms of All Political Parties, 1789–1901*. 4th ed. Baltimore: Friedenwald.

Meardon, Stephen. 2006. Richard Cobden's American Quandary: Negotiating Peace, Free Trade, and Anti-Slavery. In *Rethinking Nineteenth-Century Liberalism: Richard Cobden Bicentenary Essays*, edited by Anthony Howe and Simon Morgan. Aldershot: Ashgate.

Morgan, Simon. 2004. Richard Cobden's Critique of British Imperialism. *Journal of Liberal History* 45 (Winter): 16–21.

———. 2007. Moral Reform in a Material World: Transatlantic Perspectives on British Anti-Slavery and the Anti-Corn Law League. Working paper, University of Leicester.

Noll, Mark A. 2002. *America's God: From Jonathan Edwards to Abraham Lincoln*. New York: Oxford University Press.

———. 2006. *The Civil War as a Theological Crisis*. Chapel Hill: University of North Carolina Press.

Petersen, Svend. 1963. *Statistical History of American Presidential Elections*. New York: Ungar.

Rayback, Joseph G. 1948. The Liberty Party Leaders of Ohio: Exponents of Antislavery Coalition. *Ohio State Archaeological and Historical Quarterly* 57.2:165–78.

Schlesinger Jr., Arthur M. 1945. *The Age of Jackson*. New York: Little, Brown.

Sedgwick, Henry Dwight. 1831. *The Practicability of the Abolition of Slavery: A Lecture, Delivered at the Lyceum in Stockbridge, Massachusetts*. New York: Seymour.

Smith, David L., ed. 1984. *Horace Bushnell: Selected Writings on Language, Religion, and American Culture*. Chico, Calif.: Scholars.

Stanwood, Edward. 1903. *American Tariff Controversies in the Nineteenth Century*. 2 vols. Boston: Houghton, Mifflin.

Stephanson, Anders. 1995. *Manifest Destiny: American Expansionism and the Empire of Right*. New York: Hill and Wang.

Taussig, Frank W. 1892. *The Tariff History of the United States*. New York: G. P. Putnam's Sons.

Taylor, Nathaniel W. 1859. *Lectures on the Moral Government of God*. New York: Clark, Austin & Smith.

Thistlethwaite, Frank. 1971. *The Anglo-American Connection in the Early Nineteenth Century*. New York: Russell and Russell.

Tyler, Alice Felt. 1944. *Freedom's Ferment: Phases of American Social History to 1860*. Minneapolis: University of Minnesota Press.

The Impact of Liberal Religion on Richard Ely's Economic Methodology

Donald E. Frey

Richard T. Ely intertwined social-scientific and religious-ethical statements in the major writings of his early career (the decade of the 1880s). To label his writings as part of the Social Gospel, while accurate, may obscure the most important part of what Ely was doing. Besides his overt discussion of ethics, often in religious terms, Ely was simultaneously employing an economic methodology that served rather naturally as a critique of laissez-faire economics. This was important, and integral to Ely's ethical agenda, because laissez-faire economics held that the very conditions Ely wanted reformed were unchangeable outcomes of economic laws. For ethics to have meaning, the changes mandated by morality must be possible; there is little obligation to change what cannot be changed. Specifically, Ely employed a methodology whose premise was that economics was fundamentally a human activity, or even invention, and so subject to human choices. This perspective was consistent with moral choice being a relevant possibility in economics; laissez-faire essentially neutralized ethics because its perspective was that change either was not possible or would only make things worse.

This essay explores the roots of Ely's methodology, which he learned from German mentors who were greatly influenced by German liberal religion. Economists have rarely noticed Ely's connection with liberal religion, through what might seem the unlikely channel of economics. Ely himself made little of it. Even in his later career, when he kept explicitly

History of Political Economy 40 (annual suppl.) DOI 10.1215/00182702-2007-071

ethical statements separate from his more purely economic writings, Ely continued to emphasize a methodology that placed economics within the realm of human choice (and so of ethics), and outside a realm of inexorable laws that put economics beyond the reach of human choice.

1. Connecting an Economic Methodology with Liberal Religion

The immediate intellectual influences on Ely, of course, were his studies in Germany. In his autobiography, Ely (1938, 41–47) credited his German mentors in economics for their influence on him; however, his autobiography did not bother to delve into the possible sources that lay behind his German mentors' ideas. Perhaps guided by Ely's silence on the subject, subsequent interpreters of Ely did little to clarify a larger story of the development that led to the historical and empirical approach to economics that Ely learned in Germany.[1]

Ely gives much credit to the influence of his professors. John Everett (1946, 78) summarizes the essential points made by Ely's favorite professor, which in various ways reappeared subsequently in Ely's own work:

> [Ely's teachers] felt that their primary task was to trace the historical development in terms of preceding cultural patterns. It was [Karl] Knies who challenged the absolutism of theory and substituted the doctrine of relativism. Absolutism of theory took two forms—perpetualism, or the teaching that a certain policy is good for all time; and cosmopolitanism, the teaching that a policy is good for all countries.

Already, in this short capsule of Knies's teaching, we see kernels of Ely's later critique of the "absolutism" of laissez-faire theory. In place of universal economic laws, Ely would portray economic practices and institutions as being *contingent* on the culture in which they emerged, and their history in that culture. However, the teachings of Ely's mentors are significant not only for their influence on Ely but also as a development

1. For example, John Everett (1946, 1–25), in his introduction, covers a variety of intellectual influences of Ely's time but does not mention the historical emphasis in German liberal religion. Nor does he mention it when summarizing the essential elements of Ely's mentors. Benjamin Rader (1966, 47) only vaguely alludes to an alliance between Ely's German teachers and "reformers in politics, jurisprudence, and theology." Robert Nelson (1991, 171–76) attempts to link Ely to a longer intellectual tradition, but not to the historical thought of German liberal religion, and not through Ely's teachers.

of methods rooted in German religious liberalism. The German historical school, of which Knies was a prominent member, reflected emphases of liberal religion in Germany, and its analytic methods (adapted to social science) resembled those used by liberal biblical scholars (the so-called higher critics) and historians of church doctrine.

Modern liberal Protestantism is traced to Friedrich Schleiermacher (1768–1834), whose starting point in theology was subjective religious experience. For Schleiermacher's school, "the emotional experience on which religion was based was an empirically verifiable fact. Schleiermacher himself saw religious experience as the antidote to speculative philosophy and theology" (Herbst 1965, 78). In short, Schleiermacher turned what became liberal Protestantism away from abstract doctrines understood to be fixed for all time; instead, he rooted religion, and even the understanding of church dogmas, in human experience. If the starting point of religion was experience (albeit subjective experience), then empirical methodology in the study of religion became appropriate. Given the long history of Christianity, Schleiermacher stressed that religious experience was "historical fact, shared by many and institutionalized in the church." It also could be "studied as a phenomenon of the human consciousness" (78–79). The historical nature of experience led to church history becoming a "scholarly discipline" and to the "emergence of historical scholarship" more generally (96–97).

A nineteenth-century German historian of church doctrines provides a good example of the working assumptions of this approach:

> Dogma is an exceedingly complicated historical structure. It has in its various constituent parts, constructed as they have been in the face of multifarious forms of opposition, and under the inspiration of many . . . impulses and external (political and canonical) occasions, received the impress of different theological tendencies. Thus dogmas have been "deepened," or "disintegrated" and superficialized—logically developed, or, under the influence of advancing views, transformed, restored, and again newly interpreted. (Seeberg [1895] 1964, 19–20)

Behind the complex, Germanic structure of this quotation is the point that even religious doctrine is a *human* product and so can change dynamically. The historian adds the obvious, that the historical approach "excludes, first of all . . . the view that the Dogma of the church is as such infallible" (20). He continues with logical extrapolation from his method: that because doctrines were expressed in the "intellectual apparatus of the times in which they were originated," that very apparatus might subsequently bias the perceived meaning. Finally, in case the point was missed, the historian Reinhold Seeberg adds, "Dogma is perpetually subject to . . . interpretation" (21). Similar developments occurred in the historical (or "higher") criticism of scripture. The questions asked included the following: what was the meaning of this concept in the society in which it arose and what were the purposes of those who articulated this concept when they did?

The assumptions made by the historian of church doctrines point very naturally to the kinds of assumptions made, and questions asked, by Ely's mentors in economics. There was a clear parallel between this approach to church dogma and Knies's approach to economic dogmas. That is, economics is a human activity, an assertion that rules out viewing its doctrines as eternal verities, free of place and time; the meaning and application of economic ideas depends on their cultural setting and their long history. Following his mentors, Ely critiqued major premises of laissez-faire economics by posing the same kinds of questions originated by liberal scholars of church doctrine and of scripture. For example, what was the source of an economic concept (such as property rights) within human history, and how has its meaning developed? Ely assumed of economic doctrines (as the liberal religious scholars did of religious doctrines) that they were human expressions and highly contingent in meaning on the cultural situation, rather than unchanging laws. In sum, the German historical school of economics extrapolated significant trends in liberal Protestant scholarship into the realm of economic life. Elsewhere in Europe, some economic thinkers would move beyond liberal scholarship to propose a practical application of liberal religion: basing economic morality on "religious feeling," a statement obviously influenced by Schleiermacher (see Faccarello and Steiner, this volume, on Germaine de Staël and Benjamin Constant).

In America, the main thoughtful opposition to German historicism came from adherents of the old Scottish Common Sense philosophy (see Marsden 1994, 90–93, 211; or Herbst 1965, 59–64). This philosophy dated to postcolonial times in America and posited a single, unchanging truth attested by (1) revelation (scripture), (2) the natural (or social) order, and (3) the very way the human mind worked. This philosophy clearly served an apologetic purpose for traditional Christianity, and it was popular in the denominational colleges of the nineteenth century. It was conservative in that the natural order and the working of the human mind were believed to correlate with fixed revelation, traditionally understood. This philosophy reinforced a Protestant interest in empirical natural science by its assurance that the study of nature would confirm the truths of the faith. For Protestants, this conveniently distinguished the reformed position from that of Catholicism, which was perceived to depend too heavily on authority and speculative concepts.

In American economics, Common Sense was used by clerical promoters of laissez-faire, such as Francis Wayland. For example, Wayland demonstrated the absolute validity of property rights by invoking scripture (the commandment "Thou shalt not steal" implied that property must exist), a discussion of the human mind (the possessive pronoun is universal in all languages, he said), and casual empiricism of the outside world (the Native Americans, with their common property, were economically inefficient, Wayland asserted) (Frey 2002, 226). In practice, of course, Wayland's argument was more a defense of John Locke's essentially secular ideas of absolute property rights than a defense of scripture, and his casual appeal to supposed observations on Native Americans was not equivalent to what empirical evidence would have meant in natural science.

The clash between German historical method and the old Common Sense in the nineteenth century is documented by George Marsden (1994, 211–12). Marsden describes the issue among Presbyterians, whose faith was defined by the Westminster Confession, "which they treated as a doctrinal statement that should stand for all time." In short, they held to "fixed truths." Compared with this, wrote Marsden, "modern historicism was entirely alien." Its premise was "that the human mind plays a creative role in defining what is reality and then added that various cultures, subcultures, and *individuals each created their own definitions of truth*, adapted to a particular time and place" (212; emphasis added). Marsden's final point—that the historical method could lead to pure relativism—may or may not be correct, depending on the person using historical assumptions. A conservative user of the historical method might believe he or she was peeling away historical and cultural accretions to arrive at the core of meaning found in scripture and then, perhaps, reinterpreting that meaning in contemporary idiom. (For a discussion of Ely's possible views, see section 5.)

The German historical economists were not the sole influence on Ely's outlook. There is some evidence that Ely's studies merely confirmed tendencies that Ely had exhibited well before traveling to Germany. As a young man, Ely rebelled against the deterministic elements of his father's Presbyterian Calvinism. Although in many ways Ely seems to have revered his father, and so sought to "become a good Presbyterian," he ultimately could not accept doctrines (e.g., election of only some, predestination) that made God so absolute and left so little to human will. Indeed, in reaction, he reports that to "the great distress" of his father he seriously considered studying for the Universalist ministry (Ely 1938, 16). While the young Ely surely did not reject Calvinism because of exposure to German historical methods (which he had not yet encountered), it is clear that his perspective toward received doctrines that minimized human agency must have been similar to that of the religious liberals. It is also unlikely that Ely would reject theological determinism as a youth and be accepting of a rather materialistic determinism in economics (which is what laissez-faire offered). In short, Ely's German studies probably reinforced, and certainly provided an intellectual component to, a perspective he had already developed.[2]

2. A Longer Protestant Scientific Tradition: Empiricism

Historical research to liberal religion was seen as a form of empirical research, as applied to social, human activity. Protestant affinity to empiricism was not new with the liberals. Protestantism and empirical natural science had a long relationship. As noted, even the Common Sense philosophy was allied with empiricism in the study of the natural order (and a casual empiricism, to judge from Wayland, in his study of the social order). Only with nontheistic natural science, after Charles Darwin, did this alliance break down. Although Great Britain and the United States were home to a relatively nonempirical, laissez-faire tradition in economics, these countries otherwise welcomed the empirical approach in the natural sciences. There is a large literature connecting the rise of science with the rise of Protestantism, in general, and the kinds of Protestantism found in England and America, in particular (see, e.g., Harrison 1998, 5–8).

Robert K. Merton, an American sociologist, argued that seventeenth-century English Puritan culture in fact nurtured empirical science. Merton ([1938] 1970, 69) notes that "physics, understood always as the study of

2. Ely eventually became an Episcopalian, without giving much explanation of that choice in his autobiography. However, the history of the Anglican Church in England and the American Episcopal Church essentially guaranteed that these churches contained many strands of theological opinion; the Episcopal Church had the latitude for a religious liberal to find a compatible religious home.

God in his works, is the favorite Puritan scientific discipline." Puritans valued science, too, for its leverage in dealing with the utilitarian problems (72). Among Protestants, "Reason takes on a new connotation: the rational consideration of empirical data. Logic is reduced to a subsidiary role. . . . the test of reality comes not from scholastic logic . . . but from the observation of facts" (Merton 1970, 71). Another historian, after remarking on the "unobstructed advance of the new physics among orthodox Puritans," adds that the "experimental method was presented as not only an assistance to piety but practical benefit to mankind" (Miller 1953, 441).

Given the clerical laissez-faire school in American Protestant colleges, it is clear that these empirical tendencies in Protestantism did not necessarily deeply influence disciplines outside the natural sciences. As noted in the example of Wayland's defense of property rights, a casual reference to social patterns among Native Americans was the closest Wayland came to empiricism. And, of course, laissez-faire itself, which Ely criticized for its lack of empirical content, was largely the product of thinkers in predominantly Protestant England and America. This is underscored by the fact that the empiricists Richard Jones and William Whewell were unsuccessful in attacking a priori political economy in English universities (see Maas, this volume). It is clear that the Protestant affinity for empiricism did not easily carry over from the natural to social sciences in England and America. It is equally clear, however, that when Ely attempted to move the economics profession in a more empirical direction, he was not moving in a direction foreign to Protestant thought.

As with his rejection of determinism, Ely's attraction to empiricism may have been influenced by his family. Ely (1938, 22) describes his Calvinistic father—whose influence on him is emphasized in his autobiography—as being a careful observer of nature and something of a lay scientist.

3. The Protestant Reform Tradition

Just as methods of scholarship learned in Germany fit well with Ely's youthful inclinations, so his discovery in Germany of the potential for economic reform probably only confirmed his reforming inclinations. Ely's autobiography makes much of his family lineage, suggesting strongly that Puritan New England habits migrated with his branch of the family when it moved to New York State. Indeed, the very first page of his autobiography affirms that the "heritage and traditions built up since 1660 have been a strong and inescapable influence in my life" (Ely 1938, 1). Part of that New England, Calvinist, family tradition was social reform. He states that "looking back on my father and the Elys who preceded him, I seem to have come honestly by this tendency to be a rebel" (23). As Ely admiringly describes him, his father was "a humanitarian and a believer in social progress. Whatever might be our Fate in the Hereafter, it was our job to make the present world better—this was his philosophy" (23). Although Ely could never accept the *theological* determinism of his father's conservative Calvinism, he revered his Calvinist drive for social reform. All that his German studies needed to do was open his eyes to the possibilities.

Anglo-American Puritanism was indeed a reform movement. The tendency toward social reform emerged in American revivalist Protestantism of the early nineteenth century, addressing a host of social ills—from physical and mental disabilities to prison reform, literacy, and abolition (Ahlstrom 1972, 427). The Social Gospel, although its intellectual basis was liberal religion, was nevertheless continuous with this reform tradition. The Protestant churches that Ely confronted in the late nineteenth century appear to have lost any sense of a social component of the reform tradition. Ely blamed this passivity on the doctrines of laissez-faire, which presented the status quo as an inevitability.

4. Ely's Use of These Methods

Although Ely's reputation was as a reformer, the reader of his proposed reforms will find them unremarkable. In fact, he was a rather cautious reformer. At the midpoint of the 1880s, he was sympathetic to workers, yet his recommendations always sought to conciliate the other social classes, particularly employers. He wrote that "measures initiated by the masses should be examined and discussed by the more learned, prudent, and cautious . . . , who should at times exercise a controlling and restraining power" (Ely 1886, 53). He was explicitly critical of the class antagonism of Marxism (as well as its materialistic outlook), and he rejected violent labor protest. Generally, he accepted existing institutions and simply called for reform within the context of those institutions. Although he wrote favorably of socialism in the 1880s, Ely never explicitly endorsed the doctrine; and in the 1890s, when he was attacked on the issue, he distanced himself farther from socialism.

Although a cautious reformer, Ely was more aggressive and persistent in attacking laissez-faire. As noted, laissez-faire made reform difficult by portraying the existing order as inevitable. Popular versions, perhaps including mixtures of Social Darwinism, were convenient in providing employers, and others holding economic power, with reasons for ignoring costly reform proposals. In attacking the tenets of laissez-faire, Ely used arguments reflecting the intellectual assumptions of German historicism. His systematic effort in this direction was his 1889 *Introduction to Political Economy.* In the text he attacked the idea that the economic status quo was the inevitable outcome of economic laws akin to natural laws, and that such bulwarks of the status quo as property rights were unchangeable. To the contrary, he stated emphatically in his textbook that "the will of man is the main factor in all politico-economic phenomena" (Ely 1889a, 126). Concepts such as property, or the proper relationship between labor and employer, he said, are continually in flux (36). History reveals "the folly of those who would prescribe the same laws for all people and for all times" (37). Although there may be some limits, "we can have just such a kind of economic life as we wish" (38). Because human will shapes the economy, there is a moral responsibility for the type of economy that exists (65). Further, history is important, for reform efforts expand with time to include problems that once would have been ignored: "Things trouble us now which one hundred years ago we would have taken as a matter of course" (65). In short, Ely consistently presented the view that economic life is contingent on human history and is not a manifestation of fixed laws.

Occasionally, the reader detects assertions from Ely that might reflect the approach to scripture pioneered by the German liberals. Arguments "drawn from Adam Smith, and *intended for entirely different circumstances*," are used inappropriately to oppose factory reform legislation (Ely 1886, 317; emphasis added). Of interest, Ely did not proclaim Smith to be in error; rather, his words are valid in a certain context, but are not timeless truth. That is, the error of universalizing, or making absolute, what is conditional is a scientific error. The similarity to Knies's dictum and to the methods of the higher critics of scripture is obvious.

In his textbook, Ely juxtaposed what he considered a priori laissez-faire with historical economics. The old economics rests on a few axioms (i.e., self-interest as motive, Malthusian population growth, capital as the source of productivity, and diminishing returns), which proponents claimed "explained all facts of the socio-economic organism" (Ely 1889a, 118). In short, Ely stated that laissez-faire claimed to embody unchanging truths, which explained enough of economic life that no room was left for other influences, such as ethics. The deductive method misleads because "men will choose premises even unconsciously which will lead to the conclusions desired by them" (120). The idea that people choose the axioms, which are subsequently portrayed as self-evident or otherwise immune to question, seems to parallel the kind of considerations that Reinhold Seeberg expressed about the formulation of church doctrines (see above). To Ely (1889a, 322), Ricardo was a prime illustration of "the dangers of the deductive method."

Ely also discussed the particular axioms of laissez-faire. A major axiom was that of the self-interested economic actor. Ely's critique of self-interest did not deny its existence, but noted that personal character and circumstances are as important in determining behavior as self-interest itself (125–26). In his earlier *Social Aspects of Christianity*, Ely (1889b, 94) had directly denied the central premise of Malthusian scarcity: "Sufficient goods to satisfy all rational wants of men can be produced." That is, scarcity is inevitable only when human reason is eliminated from the distribution process.

As is often reported, Ely boldly recommended that churches devote half of ministers' education to social science. Yet, in his essays addressed to the churches, he was very unclear as to just what he expected the clergy to gain from knowing economics. His answer to what the clergy should study was implied in his textbook, which in fact came to be required by some denominations. The study of economics (as understood by Ely) would clear away the errors of laissez-faire, which the (possibly naive) clergy had too easily accepted. What Ely offered was to free the clergy from a thought system that marginalized biblical morality by rationalizing the economic status quo to be inevitable—and therefore immune to reform. For Ely (1889b, 86), freeing the churches to be ethical was crucial for their own sake, for without what he called "philanthropy," religion amounts to "superstition, persecution and cruelty." Perhaps it is not too much an extrapolation to say this means that, without ethics keeping churches grounded in real human needs, religion is subject to the evils created by "absolutism" of ideas.

Ely surely sought to ground economics in the real world. During his early career Ely was active in forming professional associations for economists. The founding statements suggested the need for an alternative to laissez-faire. As quoted by Ely (1938, 140), the statement of principles of the proposed American Economic Association included the statement that "we look, not so much to speculation as to the historical and statistical study of actual conditions of economic life."

Ely remained an intellectual reformer. Later in his career, editions of his textbook had grown in length and represented the work of several coauthors. The text continued to advocate whatever reforms were current, but sidestepped explicit ethics to justify reform. Instead, it simply invoked democracy as the decisive factor in reforming society. Explicitly religious statements were not found in the textbook (contrary to what one had found in the early, large work *The Labor Movement in America*). Nevertheless, the continued influence of liberal religion through economic method was still very evident. Ely continued to warn against absolutism in economic doctrine and to make room for human choice even in writing directed to an economics audience. That alone represented continuity with his earlier writings and served to make room for ethics as an influence in economic policy. In a revision of his economics textbook, years after it had first appeared in 1889, economics remained an "approximate and partially descriptive science" (Ely et al. [1916] 1918, 11). Economic truths, as in Ely's earlier work, remained conditional because a change of the conditions or the actors "invalidates theories, laws, general principles, institutions and enterprises" (6–7). The text continued to critique premises of laissez-faire: the Malthusian theory, he wrote, was the product of its day, whereas present conditions were different (437–38). Ely stated clearly in 1916 what he held earlier: economic rights exist by sufferance of human society (22). They are not part of natural law but are subject to the state's "continually placing limitations and restrictions on the right" (23). In short, rights are not absolute but contingent on the human condition.

Between the 1880s and 1916, the marginal-product theory had replaced the wages-fund. Although this was a major theoretical advance against laissez-faire (for it replaced the wages-fund), the main American exponent of the theory, John Bates Clark, had at least tentatively suggested that marginal-product wages were *just* wages because they linked reward with what the representative (marginal) worker produced. Alongside a clear technical exposition of marginal product, Ely's text made sure readers recognized that "the principle of marginal productivity is an illuminating way of stating the problem of the distribution of wealth, rather than a solution of it" (400). Any results that the theory yields, the text said, are conditional on context, and that context, by implication, could be influenced by moral actions. Ely was willing to tell his readers to accept that factors receive their (marginal) products in competitive markets, but then warned that "there are definite limitations to the meaning and significance of this claim" (403). He argued that the wages may equal marginal product in *many* contexts and at very different values for the wage and product:

> We can imagine an *economic order very different from the present one* in which it would still be true that incomes would tend to equal products. . . . To attempt to avoid this difficulty by assuming that the present order, or a purely competitive order, is the "natural" order of things, is to beg the whole question in favor of the existing status. (404; emphasis added)

In this statement, the lifelong vigilance against the status quo being made "absolute" as the "natural order of things" remains. In a world where wages were greatly increased by legislation, the text argued, marginal product would still equal the wage after market adjustments had occurred. Thus such theory may hold in some limited sense, yet it operates within conditions subject to human choice.

In sum, Ely took on the role of intellectual reformer, whose recommendations for particular reforms seem secondary. For the most part, the reforms he supported were advocated by others. Ely was more ambitious in seeking to overthrow the doctrines that had been used to make reform seem impossible. The deterministic framework of laissez-faire minimized the role of human will, and so of ethics, which guides the will.

5. The Religious Liberals' Perspective

It would be easy to conclude that the religious liberals' reliance on historical context to clarify things might ultimately lead to pure relativism or agnosticism about the meaning of received beliefs. As noted by Marsden, Common Sense critics of the German historical approach claimed this was a fatal problem. Yet there was a more conservative use of the historical methods in the religious arena. If the approach were viewed narrowly as clearing away historical accretions and misinterpretations, it could be seen as being in the service of finding the pure meaning of Christianity. As Sydney Ahlstrom (1972, 79) put it when describing the ethical liberals, "Ethical imperatives became central to the Christian witness, and the Sermon on the Mount was often regarded as the heart and core of the Bible." Thus at least some of the liberals did not become entirely relativistic.

All this is illustrated by the words of Walter Rauschenbusch, the major theological expositor of the Social Gospel. According to Rauschenbusch (1912, 66), Jesus' contemporaries

> expected the Kingdom [of God] to be set up by force . . . ; [but] Jesus repudiated the use of force. . . . They connected it with the hope of self-aggrandizement . . . ; [but] he democratized the idea of the Kingdom and put all who sought it under the law of service. They connected it with ceremonial and ecclesiastical religion; he set it within the domain of secular and ethical relations. To many of them the material benefits were the main thing . . . ; to Jesus fullness of ethical and religious life for all was the real end and substance of the hope. They expected it by catastrophe; he worked toward the law of gradual growth.

Rather than arrive at agnosticism or relativism, the ethical liberal Rauschenbusch effectively claimed to have captured the essence of Jesus' message. The selection shows at least superficial marks of the liberal approach: Rauschenbusch claimed to disentangle Jesus' message from ideas that he imputed to Jesus' contemporaries. Significantly, Rauschenbusch's portrayal of Jesus' contemporaries makes them look much like proxies for Rauschenbusch's fellow American Protestants.

While, according to Rauschenbusch (1912, 194), many of his fellow Christians were ignoring the ethic of Jesus, as he saw it, its modern expression was being acted out by the labor movement, which was less about material benefits than "a spiritual demand for a fuller and freer manhood." Rauschenbusch was critical of the materialism in socialist doctrine, but thought it was not integral to socialism. In fact, socialism's "fundamental aims are righteous," he wrote (405).

Ely's earlier writing anticipated Rauschenbusch on this score. The lead essay in *Social Aspects of Christianity* accused the churches of having substituted "all sorts of beliefs and observances" for ethics (Ely 1889b, 6). People will be pious on Sunday, "if on week days they may devour widows' houses" and "skin their fellows and sell their hides" (7). As was the case with Rauschenbusch, Ely did not follow liberal methods all the way to relativism (although religious conservatives might have seen it that way). He seemed to have viewed Jesus' teachings as the core Christian teachings, stripped of religious accretions and diversions ("all sorts of beliefs and observances"). Having discovered the core teachings, he apparently felt they embodied what could be detected in society and history.[3] Like Rauschenbusch, he did not limit Christ's ethic to Christians, and wrote that "the labor movement . . . is the strongest force outside the Christian church making for the practical recognition of human brotherhood" (Ely 1886, 138). The significance of Ely imputing such an ethical role to the labor movement is all the greater when one considers that some economists, who were losing their own faith, were convinced that traditional religion, of the sort promising rewards and punishments, was needed to keep the mass of people moral (see, e.g., Medema, this volume, on Sidgwick).

Rauschenbusch and Ely were remarkably similar in their reading of the core ethical message of Jesus, their little respect for the formalities of religion, and their willingness to see movements outside the churches in possession of Jesus' message, thus translating that core message into contemporary terms. This essentially reversed the old Common Sense approach, in which worldly experience would confirm static revelation; in the liberal rendition, the contemporary situation dictated how the core would appear in society. The contemporary meaning of ethics could be rather humanistic for the liberals. Ely (1889b, 123), again sounding much like Rauschenbusch, defined the end point of ethics as "the most perfect development of all human faculties in each individual."

6. Conclusion

Ely's methodology was representative of the historical methods developed by German liberal Protestantism to study church doctrines and

3. Everett (1946, 97) suggests that Ely retained elements of the Common Sense philosophy that he had encountered as an undergraduate. In rare places Ely implies a three-way harmony of knowledge through the mind, experience, and revelation that is reminiscent of that approach. He wrote at one point that ethics has "grown up as a result of intuition combined with historical experiences, and which has been clarified by religion" (Ely 1889a, 68). It would be difficult to ascertain the reason Ely used this particular formulation. However, he did not regularly make use of this kind of assertion. Rauschenbusch and Ely indeed suggested that labor groups outside the churches were in harmony with the Christian ethic. However, this may have served functionally to rebuke the churches, which they thought had lost the ethic. The claim did not seem to serve, as in Common Sense, as a separate confirmation of traditional, and specific, revelations. For Common Sense, experience helped confirm revelation. For Ely, religion merely "clarified" what seems to have been built into history. It is perhaps not surprising that a man who was, first, a social scientist would place heavy emphasis on what could be inferred from the observation of social movements. Ultimately, both Ely and Rauschenbusch articulated a very humanistic end point for ethics that Common Sense did not.

scripture. Ely also drew, to some extent, on a longer and more general Protestant inclination in favor of empirical science. His motivation in all this was the reform tradition of New England Calvinism, into which he was born, and exemplified by his father. To attribute Ely's methodological outlook to a "German historical school," limited exclusively to political economy, is to ignore the broader connections of this school, and its methods, to a movement of liberal Protestantism in the Germany of the nineteenth century.

Ely's Social Gospel was not notable for innovative or radical reform proposals. Rather, much of his emphasis was to undermine the methodological assumptions of laissez-faire, which played a significant role in justifying the status quo and so preventing social and economic reform. His critique embodied the same critical arguments found in biblical criticism and studies of the church dogma. His motive and his goal were essentially moral, for laissez-faire was deterministic, which ruled ethics out of the realm of economics entirely; meaningful ethical norms require the human will to make meaningful choices. Ely's sharp criticism of other church members, and of clergy, seemed largely directed at what he perceived to be their uncritical acceptance of the laissez-faire argument that the economic status quo was an inevitable consequence of unchanging economic laws. This had reduced them to moral passivity, and Ely pointed to how little the words of Jesus were followed. His call for the education of clergy to include economics appears to have been intended to immunize clergy against the rationalizations for the status quo in economics provided by laissez-faire and Social Darwinism.

Ely's writing in the 1880s was explicitly religious, even that which was not directed to church audiences (e.g., in *The Labor Movement in America*, he addressed the working movement with the assurance Christ was on their side). Years later, except when he was addressing church audiences, explicit religion and ethics were not easy to find in his writings. Indeed, his 1916 *Outlines of Economics* attempted to reach a broad audience and did not appeal to religious ethics. However, it retained the method that he had taken from liberal religion. The message was that economic life is a human activity, subject to the human will, and he continued to disabuse readers of the notion that economics has inevitability about it. He said this explicitly in many ways. Implicitly, the large portion of the text devoted to describing the details of economic institutions made it clear to readers that economic institutions are the creations of humans and could be arranged differently.

References

Ahlstrom, Sydney E. 1972. *A Religious History of the American People*. New Haven, Conn.: Yale University Press.

Ely, Richard T. 1886. *The Labor Movement in America*. New York: Thomas Y. Crowell.

———. 1889a. *Introduction to Political Economy*. Microfiche. New York: Chautauqua Press.

———. 1889b. *Social Aspects of Christianity and Other Essays*. Microfiche. New York: Thomas Y. Crowell.

———. 1938. *Ground under Our Feet: An Autobiography*. New York: Macmillan.

Ely, Richard T., Thomas S. Adams, Max O. Lorenz, and Allyn A. Young. [1916] 1918. *Outlines of Economics*. 3rd rev. ed. New York: Macmillan.

Everett, John Rutherford. 1946. *Religion in Economics*. New York: King's Crown Press.

Frey, Donald E. 2002. Francis Wayland's 1830s Textbooks: Evangelical Ethics and Political Economy. *Journal of the History of Economic Thought* 24.2:215–31.

Harrison, Peter. 1998. *The Bible, Protestantism, and the Rise of Natural Science*. Cambridge: Cambridge University Press.

Herbst, Jurgen. 1965. *The German Historical School in American Scholarship: A Study in the Transfer of Culture*. Ithaca, N.Y.: Cornell University Press.

Marsden, George M. 1994. *The Soul of the American University: From Protestant Establishment to Established Nonbelief*. New York: Oxford University Press.

Merton, Robert K. [1938] 1970. *Science, Technology, and Society in Seventeenth Century England*. New York: Howard Fertig.

Miller, Perry. 1953. *The New England Mind: From Colony to Province*. Vol. 2. Boston: Beacon Press.

Nelson, Robert H. 1991. *Reaching for Heaven on Earth: The Theological Meaning of Economics*. Savage, Md.: Rowman and Littlefield.

Rader, Benjamin G. 1966. *The Academic Mind and Reform: The Influence of Richard T. Ely in American Life*. Lexington: University Press of Kentucky.

Rauschenbusch, Walter. 1912. *Christianizing the Social Order*. New York: Macmillan.

Seeberg, Reinhold. [1895] 1964. *Text-Book of the History of Doctrines*. Vol. 1. Translated by Charles E. Hay. Grand Rapids, Mich.: Baker Book House.

The Religion of a Skeptic: Frank H. Knight on Ethics, Spirituality, and Religion during His Iowa Years

Ross B. Emmett

> We cannot go naked, spiritually; we have to be somebody, . . . or else cease to exist altogether.
> —Frank Knight, *Play, Art, and Work: A Little Book on the Value Problem for Students of the Social Science*

The Usual Account

Tales of Frank H. Knight's antagonism to religion abounded at the University of Chicago. One story often reported suggests that the university once refunded the tuition of a Jesuit seminarian who had enrolled in one of Knight's courses because he said the course was simply a ceaseless

The title of the present essay is the same as the title of a presentation that Frank Knight gave to the philosophical club at the University of Iowa on 10 May 1921. No notes for that presentation remain. The author wishes to thank Jerry Nordquist for his research on Knight's Iowa years, a "Frank Knight tour" of Iowa City in July 2006, which included a visit to the Unitarian Universalist Church, and comments on an earlier draft of this essay. Bette Sikes provided information about Knight's relationship to the First Unitarian Church of Chicago. Useful comments on an earlier draft were provided by Don Frey, Dan Hammond, Steven Medema, and the editors of this volume. The University of Chicago Library's Special Collections Research Center is gratefully thanked for permission to use material from the Frank H. Knight Papers and the University of Chicago Department of Economics Records. I am also grateful to the Christian Theological Seminary in Indianapolis for permission to use material from the Frederick D. Kershner Papers. A less complete version of the essay was presented at the session "The Role of Religion in Twentieth Century Political Economy: Insights from Hayek, Knight, Smith, and Viner," sponsored by the Association of Christian Economists at the ASSA meeting, Chicago, January 2007.

History of Political Economy 40 (annual suppl.) DOI 10.1215/00182702-2007-072

tirade against his religion. Based on their experiences in the same courses, economics students used to say, "There is no God, and Frank Knight is his prophet" (Buchanan 1982, xi). George Stigler (1987, 55) told a tale relayed to him by Frank's brother Bruce: after a particularly emotionally charged altar call at their church one Sunday, Frank marched the younger children out behind the barn, lit a small fire, and told the kids to burn the cards they had signed because "pledges made under duress are not binding." And Edward Shils (1981, 183) recounted meeting Knight on campus after his retirement and being told that Knight's sleepless nights were the fault of "that damned religion."

Such stories are supported by a litany of attacks on religions, particularly Roman Catholicism, by Knight in his published record. Within eight lines of his presidential address to the American Economic Association, for example, Knight manages to identify the pope with Hitler and Stalin as heads of authoritarian hierarchies; label the medieval church as dogmatic, intolerant, and obscurantist; and suggest that our modern moral confusion stems from the historical imposition of the liberal ethic of extreme freedom based on personal liberty on top of the Christian ethic of obedience based on social status (Knight [1951] 1999, 378). His commentary on Mortimer Adler's "God and the Professors" speech closes with the comment: "And now abide Positivism, Pragmatism, and Scholasticism, these three: but the worst of these is Scholasticism. It is on a level with the other positions or methods in philosophical naivety, and surpasses them in its vicious implications for action" (Knight [1940] 1999). And his series of attacks on the social ethics of the Roman Catholic theologian Jacques Maritain are capped by an article bearing the inauspicious title "Natural Law: Last Refuge of the Bigot" (Knight 1949).

Once we get past the vituperative rhetoric of Knight's responses to Catholicism, his central message about applying Christian ethics to the modern world emerges from two concerns. The first is the use of a personal ethic to place value on individuals' actions in a world of impersonal association. The second is the substitution of a moral authority structure for personal decision making. The two issues are related but initially can be treated separately.

When discussing religious ethics and economics, Knight often returns to the personal-impersonal division. The argument was simple: most religions, especially Christianity, have a personal ethic appropriate for face-to-face relations, but modern society requires a social ethic that accounts for the impersonal organization of market interaction. Evaluating the market system requires a different ethical standard than evaluating one's actions in face-to-face encounters. An ethical focus on only the personal aspects of decision making creates problems at the level of social and economic organization. Jesus's Gospel message is a good example of the problem of a personal ethic: the command to "love your neighbor as yourself" clearly focuses on personal interaction; what could it mean for judgments about the consequences of an impersonal economic organization? Would it serve as good advice for policymakers concerned with a change in the political and economic organization of trillions of interactions across billions of people? The clearest statement comes from Knight's 1939 essay "Ethics and Economic Reform":

> there is . . . little to be found in Christianity in the way of moral principles or ideals which can serve for the ethical guidance of deliberate political action. The question whether any proposed measure is in harmony with the "spirit" of Christianity commonly admits of no clear answer or at least none of a sort which will be accepted by Christians as a solution for practical political issues. Indeed, evil rather than good seems likely to result from any appeal to Christian religious or moral teaching in connection with problems of social action. Stated in positive form, our contention is that social problems require intellectual analysis in impersonal terms but that Christianity is exclusively an emotional and personal morality; and this, while unquestionably essential, does not go beyond providing or helping to provide the moral interest, motive or "drive" toward finding solutions for problems. This is not only a very different thing from furnishing the solutions or even indicating the direction in which they are to be sought, but the teaching that it does furnish solutions has results which are positively evil and decidedly serious. (Knight [1939] 1999, 46–47)

Knight's insistence of the inapplicability of a personal ethic to evaluating the consequences of impersonal association emerged from his understanding of the nature of liberal society. Liberal societies depend on two institutions for their organization: markets and democracy. Economic theory revealed for Knight (1933) how the price system coordinated the actions of individuals in socially beneficial ways without personal association. In a like manner, liberal democracy for Knight was coordinated by intelligent discussion among free individuals. While such discussion would often have to assume a moral position about what was good for society as given, placing that moral position itself beyond discussion was to deny liberalism's primary value—freedom. Individuals must remain free to pursue their own interests, including their interest in figuring out what they really value. In the short term, we accept some values as "final" for the purposes of decision making here and now, but Knight argued that these could be accepted only as "relatively absolute absolutes," always left open to change in the future. The acceptance of a moral authority was, for Knight, incongruent with liberalism. Systemic acceptance of any authority—ethical or scientific—was, for him, a denial of the freedom and openness to change required in a liberal society (Knight and Merriam 1945; Knight 1960).

All of this is familiar ground and part of the lore surrounding Knight's skepticism and cynicism about religion, morality, knowledge, and society.[1] *But could that most skeptical of religious skeptics have had religion?* We know that Knight did have religion at one point: he grew up and received his early college education amid the Disciples of Christ.[2] But Knight's religious past is often treated as just that: a past he left *before* he entered economics. The Knight that Chicago economists encountered seemed to have shed religion: in their view, it certainly did not continue to influence his thinking, except as a foil for intelligent social action.

But what if the Chicago story about Knight's religion is wrong? What if Knight's approach to economics and social science after his return to Chicago were a continuation of at least part, if not the whole, of a perspective informed by the development of his views while he still identified himself with a religious tradition? To reorient ourselves to examine that question, we need to stop reading Knight's religious views *backward*—starting with what Knight said at Chicago in the 1940s and assuming he thought that all

1. For critical treatments of Knight's views on religion, ethics, and economics, see Boyd 1997; Emmett 1992, 1994; Greer 2001; Hammond 1991; Kern 1988; Nelson 2001; and Raines and Jung 1986.

2. Both Frank and Minerva (his wife) Knight grew up in a moderate Disciples of Christ tradition that rejected denominationalism, emphasized what Protestants believed in common, and focused on a biblically informed practice. One element that distinguishes Knight's religious background from evangelicalism is the inclusivity of the Disciples tradition. But although he was sympathetic to the Progressive movement, Knight did not follow Ely and others into the Social Gospel movement (see Frey, this volume). See Dewey 1990 for information on Knight's early religious background.

along—and instead read them *forward*—find out where he started and follow his path to the 1940s.[3]

Rather than go all the way back, however, I focus in this article on the period immediately preceding Knight's return to the University of Chicago in 1928. Long skeptical of the truth claims of traditional Christianity, and inactive in any church congregation since his graduation from Milligan College in 1911, he nevertheless became an active participant in the Iowa City Unitarian congregation during the nine years he spent as a professor at the University of Iowa (1919–28). How did he maintain the tension between his skepticism and his religious participation?

Iowa City

In January 1919, a couple of months after his thirty-third birthday, Knight began a tenured position as associate professor of economics at the University of Iowa. He had completed his doctorate three years before at Cornell and had taught for a year and a half as an instructor at the University of Chicago. At Iowa, he replaced the retiring Isaac A. Loos and assumed primary responsibility for teaching economic theory (Nordquist 1997). Over the next nine years he rose to the top of the American economics profession following the publication of *Risk, Uncertainty, and Profit* (Knight 1921) and a string of famous articles on cost, value, and ethics in economics (see appendix 2 for a list of those on value theory, economics, and ethics). Meanwhile, Frank and his wife, Minerva, settled into their home on South Clinton Street, a short distance from campus and just a block or so from Iowa City's Unitarian association.

The fact that Knight had an active religious life in Iowa City is surprising not only because of what we know from the standard story recounted above but also because he had largely withdrawn from active church participation, if not attendance, over the previous decade. In a letter to

3. The argument here puts Knight in company with Henry Sidgwick (see Medema, this volume), Henry Clay, and J. A. Hobson (see Backhouse, this volume), but with his own twist on the issues. With Sidgwick, Knight appreciated what is lost when one loses one's religion. With Clay and Hobson, Knight sought to find a quasi-religious basis for an ethical idealism appropriate to the modern world. But unlike all of them, Knight remained a defender of market organization.

Frederick D. Kershner,[4] a Disciples of Christ leader and scholar, written in 1916 just after Knight had completed his dissertation at Cornell, he admitted that he had "had nothing at all to do with the Church since leaving Milligan, and must say that in addition to complete skepticism of religion historically and metaphysically (which I have always felt), I no longer believe in it as a social institution" (Kershner 1916). In Chicago, prior to the move to Iowa City, the Knights were loosely associated with the Disciples' University Church, where the liberal theologian Edward Scribner Ames was pastor, but they were not active participants.[5] What affiliation with the Disciples remained was largely social, perhaps held together by the general drift among liberal members of the Disciples toward religious humanism. In Iowa City, however, he attended services, taught Sunday school, led discussions for the young adults, attended the men's group, participated in the Unitarian Laymen's League, and served as a delegate for the local congregation at the regional association.

Why the Unitarians?

Iowa City's First Christian Church, the local Disciples congregation, was moderate enough, although it undoubtedly did not have as progressive a pastor as Ames in Chicago. In fact, we have almost no record of

4. Kershner was Knight's professor at both American College, Harriman, Tennessee (1905–7), and Milligan College (Tenn.) (1908–11). He served as president of Milligan while Knight attended, and also departed in 1911, to become president of Texas Christian University. Kershner taught about half of Knight's courses at the two colleges, and they became lifelong friends. Both American (now defunct) and Milligan were associated with the Disciples of Christ. American was part of the more conservative branch (which, in 1906, became the Churches of Christ), while Milligan has always sought a more moderate position. Kershner also straddled both sides of the divide in the Disciples: he is the only person who could publish in the *Christian Standard* (the Churches of Christ magazine) while editing the *Christian Evangelist* (the Disciples' magazine). After editing the *Christian Evangelist*, Kershner spent most of the 1920s at Drake University in Des Moines, Iowa (near the Knights), then moved to Indianapolis to be dean of the School of Religion at Butler University.

5. Ames was well known as a religious humanist and part of the Chicago school of pragmatism. Any affection Knight might have felt for Ames (who was a good friend of Kershner's) did not prevent him from criticizing Ames's *Psychology of Religious Experience* (1910) as a "shining example" of the "perversion" of attempting to "rationalize mysticism and bring it under the form of 'adaptive activity'" (Knight 1923b, 7 October). For Knight, the contrast between religious experience and rational activity was more essential than their similarities. When he returned to Chicago (the same year Ames assumed the deanship of the Disciplines' Divinity House), he did not return to University Church.

the Knights' church attendance during the first couple years of their time in Iowa, although his extensive correspondence with Kershner during this period indicates that he did keep in touch with other friends in the Disciples tradition.[6] But in November 1922, Knight signed the Unitarian congregation's membership book; it is likely that he had been affiliated with the Unitarian men's group before that and probably had attended the church for some time, as well.

Jerry Nordquist (1997) argues that two things prompted the move to the Unitarians. The first was the men's club. The club, which met monthly for dinner and conversation in the church hall, was a meeting place for progressive-minded academics and community leaders. While we do not know exactly when he began attending, we do know that Knight eventually became the club's president and gave at least two talks to the group (see appendix 1). Some of the men's group members were also involved in three other groups that provided important sounding boards for Knight's ideas during his Iowa years and probably formed the bridge between the academy and the church. At the university, Knight's involvement in both the philosophical club and the political science club brought him into contact with academics involved in the Unitarian association. Knight also regularly met with a group of students to discuss social philosophy and policy. We do not know if this student group was an informal continuation of conversations at the two clubs already mentioned or a separate organization. But the group included students with whom Knight was to have a lifelong association: Henry Simons, Homer Jones, and Ethel Verry. From the material available, we cannot determine the extent to which this group overlapped with a similar group that Knight eventually led at the Unitarian Church. Some interconnection between the two groups, however, seems inevitable.

The second thing that Nordquist suggests may have prompted Knight's affiliation with the Unitarians was the arrival in 1920 of Frank C. Doan, the dynamic Unitarian minister whom Knight quickly became acquainted with through the university's philosophical club. Doan had studied at Harvard with William James and also at Heidelberg and the Sorbonne, had taught at Meadville Theological Seminary in Chicago, and had authored *Religion and the Modern Mind* (1909). From a letter to his mentor Kershner,

6. Knight did attend a Disciples' church at least once in Iowa City. In a letter to Kershner dated 8 March 1919, he indicates that he learned about the Kershners' impeding move to Des Moines when he took his mother to church while she was visiting.

we know Knight thought highly of Doan.[7] But Doan left Iowa City before Knight joined the Unitarians, so even if Knight had been attending the men's group and occasional services, he did not affiliate himself with the Unitarians because of Doan's leadership. Knight's own explanation of his affiliation is quite simple: "I am about committed to casting my fortunes with the local Unitarian association," he told Kershner in November 1922. "I want some sort of religious connection, and while these people are really about as dogmatic and opinionated as any of the rest of them, at least they stand theoretically for a truth-seeking attitude" (Kershner 1922f).

Over the next five years, Knight was an active participant in the Unitarian association, and even gave one of his men's club talks in February 1928, in the midst of his move back to Chicago. Appendix 1 provides a list of the various talks and notes related to Knight's religious activity in Iowa City that we have either copies of in his papers or information about from church records.

And Behind the Scenes: Knight and Kershner

Mention has already been made of Frederick Kershner, Knight's mentor. The two men corresponded frequently during the early 1920s. Their letters are full of personal news: family events, visits back and forth (Kershner spent most of the 1920s at Drake University in Des Moines, and the two families saw each other frequently), and news of friends and extended family (Knight's brothers Melvin and Bruce had also been Kershner's students). But the letters also frequently deal with religion. Kershner's response to Knight's decision to affiliate with the Unitarians reveals both his own views and his tolerance for the associations his friend took:

> Churches are so purely matters of local grouping that I cannot pass judgment upon your attitude toward the Unitarian fellowship. As a general proposition, I should say that Unitarianism has proved a failure in the religious world. Even my good friend Professor Ames admits this fact and hence vigorously resents any accusation of being a Unitarian

7. In 1922 Doan departed Iowa City for a church in Rochester, New York. Knight wrote to Kershner: "He was too big a man for this place, but I hoped he would stay." Interestingly, the same letter includes Knight's news of his own offer from the University of Michigan, but he decided to "stay here for the present" (Kershner 1922d).

himself. After all, however, names count for very little in comparison with realities. (Kershner 1922c)

Many of the letters include news of theological discussions the two men had with others; Knight mentions books he is reading on Christian history, ethics, and the interpretation of Jesus' message and asks Kershner for other book recommendations. Knight's presentation of "The 'Concept' of Spirituality" to the regional association of Unitarians in October 1923 is confirmed in a letter of 12 October; Kershner had hopes that Knight would attend Disciples' conventions with him, although none of the letters confirm Knight's attendance. Two letters in November 1922 indicate that Knight and Kershner met (separately) with Bishop Paul Jones of the Fellowship of Reconciliation.[8] Knight described him as "an idealist without being under many illusions"—a quality Knight obviously admired, despite his own skepticism (Kershner 1922f).

The relation of Christian ethics to value theory is a recurring theme. A letter from Knight in 1921 kicks it off: "Our philosophy club . . . discussed the meaning of philosophy, . . . [and] soon came around to what seems to me the problem of problems and essentially the problem of religion, whether any sort of value has any 'objectivity' or any reality other than the brute fact that somebody at the moment cares about it" (Kershner 1921). Over the next two years, they discuss Knight's ([1922] 1999, [1923] 1999) Harvard lectures on ethics and economics. Kershner remarks that Knight's interpretation of value theory in those lectures seems to allow only two options: maximization as economists see it and "the idea of want-evolution continued infinitely," with its embedded Nietzschean assumption of a fundamental disquietude in human nature. Kershner suggests that a Christian viewpoint would emphasize "the ordered harmony of ethical and spiritual values which permits one . . . to achieve a type of happiness which contains essentially spiritual elements" and brings a "calmness of soul" that is not "nirvana for it carries with it the idea of infinite aspiration, but . . . is certainly something quite different from the idea of 'divine dissatisfaction' in which you appear to rest as an ultimate" (Kershner 1922a). In a later letter, Kershner says that for Jesus the supreme purpose of life is

8. Jones was a bishop of the Episcopal Church until 1918, when his pacifism during the First World War led to calls for his resignation. Jones complied with the request and never served as bishop again. He was a key leader in the early years of the American branch of the Fellowship of Reconciliation. Knight's brother Bruce wrote a book in 1936 advocating pacifism by pointing out the cost of war (Knight 1936).

the unselfish devotion to the good of all and points Knight to the work of Tolstoy, who, although exaggerated, "has gotten at the heart of Christian ethics" (Kershner 1922b). Knight continues to worry about these issues after the Harvard lectures, asking Kershner if pragmatism isn't merely a "dogmatic development" of paganism—which he identifies with the idea that "life is the end of all"—hence, eliminating religion. He insists that "life has to look toward and be a means to something beyond sense perception or intellectual cognition if it is to be satisfying" or at least tolerable (Kershner 1922e).

The fundamental problem of ethics and religion that Knight struggles with throughout the 1920s is identified clearly in the same letter in which he casts his lot with the Unitarians:

> I can't get away from the fact that the spirit of western civilization is the antithesis of Christianity, nor see how it could be western civilization if it weren't. The problem to me is how far one can go toward Christianity without giving up material and scientific progress, which I am not willing to do. I wish the world were so mature and organized that one could live on Christian principles and at the same time live fairly decently and approximately pay his way, but I cannot see that it is so. (Kershner 1922f)

Their correspondence from the Iowa years concludes in an exchange of letters in March 1925. Knight writes after an interlude of several months to ask Kershner for help in identifying books that could shed light on arguments made by Werner Sombart and Max Weber about the relation between religion and economics. He is particularly interested in the differences between "the attitudes of Catholicism and early Protestantism toward economic life" (Kershner 1925a, 1925b). Both men disagree with Weber, suggesting that Catholicism tended toward utilitarianism and capitalism, while the early Protestants (Kershner says the English and early Lutherans) adopted a form of asceticism. Given their earlier correspondence, it is clear that Catholicism's tendency toward economic rationality reduces its value as a religion—a surprising result, perhaps, but a reflection of the combination of Knight's desire to protect the spiritual from the economic and the Disciples' tradition of anti-Catholicism.[9]

9. Knight's attacks on Roman Catholicism have already been identified. Kershner (1938) wrote a book for the Disciples that detailed the foibles of medieval Catholicism.

Is There a Connection to His Economics in the 1920s?

The easy transitions in the Knight-Kershner correspondence between religious or philosophical themes and economic issues is indicative of the interconnections Knight himself saw between his economics work and his interest in religion and philosophy. His published essays from the Iowa years provide ample evidence of those connections, as do his unpublished writings (see appendix 2).

The most obvious connection is in the theme mentioned frequently in both the Kershner correspondence and Knight's religious presentations: value theory. When they heard that term, neoclassical economists thought of price theory; institutionalists, on the other hand, decried its nonscientific status and wished to replace it with modern psychology and the study of institutional processes. Knight heard the term and thought of the study of the price system as an institutional process *and* of the need for an ethical evaluation of different institutional processes. Knight's value theory, then, combines price theory, institutional analysis, and an ethics that transcends instrumental rationality entirely.[10] In "Social Economic Organization," a handout prepared for his classes at Iowa in 1924 and subsequently published as the first chapter of *The Economic Organization*, Knight said that the first function of an economic system was to establish a standard of value for society:

> In a world where organizations were absent, where each individual carried on his life activities in isolation and independence of all others, the matter of standards would be simply a matter of individual choice. But when the production of wealth is socialized, there has to be a *social*

10. Knight generally avoided language that suggested that a transcendent realm existed, because of the notion's association with an absolutist ethics. But in "The Concept of Spirituality," a speech to a Unitarian regional association meeting, he did say:

> "*Is* there, perhaps a realm of reality, where those who seek shall find, or might we even say do find, where to seek is to find, where the whole means-and-end relation is transcended completely as it is partially in the field of art? May it be *true* that the poor in spirit are blessed immediately, that there *is* the kingdom of heaven, where all 'taking thought' for the future or for the present is entirely out of place? The essence of value realization in such a sphere would be the very antithesis of the scientific-utilitarian methodology. Instead of relying upon procedure demonstrated in the face of skeptical attitude (necessary for science) the essence of it would be the deliberate engendering of an attitude of creative faith. Instead of 'intentions' being nothing they would be everything" (Knight 1923a, 7–8).

> decision as to the relative importance of different uses of productive power, as to which wants are to be satisfied and which left unsatisfied or to what extent any one is to be satisfied at the expense of any other. (Knight 1951, 8)

Robinson Crusoe's decisions would be solely a matter of individual choice in the presence of scarcity. Civil society required a choice about the institutions used to coordinate individual choices, and that was as much an *ethical* choice as it was an economic one. The choice of organizational form could not be solved by price theory, which was simply the analysis of how resources were allocated in the competitive enterprise form of social organization, given a particular set of individuals whose wants and needs had already been determined. To the extent, then, that economics was defined by price theory—and Knight thought that economic theory was price theory—economics was limited in its application to the context of competitive enterprise economies.

> Economics deals with the *social organization* of economic activity. In practice its scope is much narrower still; there are many ways in which economic activity may be socially organized, but the predominant method in modern nations is the price system, or free enterprise. Consequently it is the structure and working of the system of free enterprise which constitutes the principal topic of discussion in a treatise on economics. (Knight 1951, 6)

The link between value theory, ethics, and the social choice of organization began increasingly to occupy Knight's attention while he was at Iowa. His disagreements with the American institutionalists—largely on the basis of their interest in substituting psychology for value theory (Knight [1925] 1935, [1925] 1999)—led him to engage the German historical school, especially the work of Sombart and Weber (Knight [1928] 1999; Weber 1927). In fact, Knight's translation of Weber's *General Economic History* introduced the German writer to the English-speaking world.

But even within the confines of economics proper, Knight's concern about the linkage between value theory and ethics found expression. Three of his most famous essays from the Iowa years (Knight [1922] 1999, [1923] 1999, [1924] 1999) are concerned with the twin arguments that economics cannot explain all of human conduct and that value theory cannot be reduced to a utilitarian calculus. "The chief thing which the common-sense individual actually wants is not satisfactions for the wants which he has, but more, and better wants" (Knight [1922] 1999, 42).

> Life is at bottom an exploration in the field of values, an attempt to discover values, rather than on the basis of knowledge of them to produce and enjoy them to the greatest possible extent. We strive to "know ourselves," to find out our real wants, more than to get what we want. This fact sets a first and most sweeping limitation to the conception of economics as a science. (Knight [1924] 1999, 1)

In consequence, Knight reaches the string of conclusions that has confused interpreters of his methodological work ever since because they place him between the neoclassicists and institutionalists: (1) price theory is scientific; (2) economics is the scientific study of the allocation of resources in market economies; (3) yet the problems of social organization in a market economy transcend price theory because they require decisions about the quality of our choices and the question of what kind of people we want to become. The latter requires an ethics that does not reduce to constrained utility maximization. Consideration of his writings on religion during the 1920s helps us understand the rationality he ascribes to that string of conclusions.

How Should We Then Live?

How, then, does one live in a world that is not reducible to economics, if one believes, as Knight (1923a, 2) did, that intellectual honesty required us to "admit once for all that science has made it *impossible* to be religious in any theistic sense, orthodox or liberal." To put it the other way around, how does one cultivate a rational approach to life in a society bent on limiting rationality to what science can comprehend of human existence? Knight's address to the Unitarian regional association in October 1923 takes up this challenge right at the start:

> The controversy over "Fundamentalism," so-called, has helped to bring to a focus the essential problem of liberal religion, the problem of finding some middle ground between the type of religion represented by the orthodox Christian creeds on the one hand and a completely irreligious view of the world and of life on the other. In the writer's opinion any satisfactory and tenable solution of this problem is much more difficult than it is commonly pictured to be by members of the liberal churches, and liberal members of other denominations. Their danger, we suggest, is in putting all the emphasis on liberalism, to the point of getting away from religion altogether. This paper is a

> plea for liberal religion, and a protest against the tendency referred to above. It is a plea for "fundamentalism," in a sense, for the view that there are things which cannot be given up without ceasing to be religious; it is a plea for Spirituality. (Knight 1923a)

A life that searches for truth that does not reduce to either scientific rationality or moral authoritarianism may be disquieting to some, but it was, for Knight, the only option in a society committed to freedom and liberal democracy. Everything Knight wrote in the 1920s stressed the *limits* of scientific knowledge and the dynamic, multifaceted, and explorative nature of human experience. Aesthetic expression, for example, remained outside the boundaries of rational, scientific explanation, as did morality. We could reason about art and morality, Knight believed, but the act of aesthetic expression itself, or "good" conduct, remained a mystery. It was easier, he repeatedly said in his notes for public presentations on religion, to say what art, morality, and religion are *not*, than to say (i.e., to speak rationally about) what they are. Religion, especially. For what art or morality is to science is what spirituality is to art and morality. Poetry uses rational discourse (words) to create an aesthetic expression; religion in turn uses poetry to express the spiritual (Knight 1923a).

Despite its irrationality, religion was important to Knight during these years. Although he rejected both traditional Christianity's historical and theological claims, and opposed its moral authoritarianism, he nevertheless desired a religious context for life. His association with the Unitarians, therefore, was not so much about belief, even a liberal faith in rationality and freedom, but about community—the willingness to engage with questions within a common commitment to open inquiry and an exploration of the multiplicity of dimensions of human experience.

What Happened Next?

In early March 1927, Knight received a letter from Leon C. Marshall, chair of economics at the University of Chicago. The letter indicated that the department was interested in getting Knight back to Chicago to take charge of the new offerings in economic theory and to provide critical analysis of the developing use of quantitative methods in economics, and because "other things that never occur to one . . . keep arising from time to time" (Marshall 1927). On 14 April Knight gave a seminar in Chicago, using a paper titled "Some Observations on the Why of Economic Behavior" that he previously delivered at the University of Iowa's political science club in early January. Arrangements were made by May, and Knight began teaching at the University of Chicago in the summer quarter. His contract with the university provided a leave of absence without pay for the winter quarter of 1928, when he returned to Iowa City to teach and wrap up his domestic affairs. On 20 February 1928, he spoke for the last time at the Unitarian men's club—the topic is unknown. That spring, his final gift to the church was a special donation to help build the sanctuary's new roof.

Perhaps of greater importance for his religious activity, however, was the end of his first marriage that same summer. Whether the move to Chicago precipitated the divorce or merely facilitated it, in July 1927 Frank and Minerva "dissolved partnership"—as he described it to Kershner more than a year later (Kershner 1929). The marriage had obviously been deteriorating for some time—Knight spoke to Kershner of "the situation for years"—but their parting caused a large stir in the community. The *Daily Iowan* reported that Knight wanted "congenial and more intellectual companionship" and freedom from family responsibilities in order to have more time for his studies. His notes for a February 1927 presentation to the Fireside Club at the Unitarian Church on types of personal association, which begin as an exploration of the connection between the themes of personal and impersonal association that form the basis for his criticism of the application of Christian ethics to social questions, end with the following remark about love and marriage:

> Face the facts as to the uncertainties of the love feeling, make friendships between men free and get rid of the idea that love is a crime outside of marriage and family life. Let the coincidence be the ideal, to be attained where practicable, even by re-arrangement when mistakes have been made and discovered. (Knight 1927, 5)

Whatever the reason, Frank left for Hyde Park, and Minerva and the children stayed in Iowa City (Emmett 1997).[11]

11. Minerva Knight took a job at the University of Iowa in 1927 and eventually completed her PhD in philosophy, writing a dissertation on considerations of free will in Dostoyevsky's work. She remained active in the Unitarian association until she followed her daughter to California in 1946.

Shortly after his move to Chicago, Knight became reacquainted with Ethel Verry, a former member of his young adults group at the Iowa City Unitarian Church. They were married in September 1929. She had left Iowa City for graduate education in the mid-1920s and was finishing her degree in the College of Social Service Administration when they met. "Miss Verry" ran the Chicago Child Care Society and was an active member of the First Unitarian Church of Chicago near the university campus until her death in 1991. Knight himself occasionally attended the Chicago Unitarian Church, and even preached a few times, but was not a member (Knight 1963 is one of his sermons). His ashes are interred along with Ethel's in the church's cinerary urn crypt.

Appendix 1: Religion in Frank H. Knight's Work during the Iowa Years

The list below includes published essays and unpublished manuscripts or notes that have been identified with Knight's years at the University of Iowa. Presentations that have no surviving materials are also included, marked by an initial asterisk. The list is culled from Emmett 1999a and Nordquist 1997; more details are available there and in Emmett 1999b. Although Knight began his tenure in Iowa City in 1919, no dated documents on these topics exist prior to 1922. Box and folder identifications are from the Frank H. Knight Papers, University of Chicago Archives.

1921 * "The Religion of a Skeptic." Philosophical Club, University of Iowa, 10 May.

1922 "The Limits of Liberalism" (announced as "The Conflict between the Religious and the Scientific Attitude towards Life"). Young Peoples Religious Union, Iowa City Unitarian Church, 10 December. Manuscript, box 55, folder 10 (and box 36, folder 19), 2 pp.

1923 * "Science and the Religious World View." Discussion, Young People's Religious Union, Iowa City Unitarian Church, 18 February.

* "The Science of Society." Presentation, Young People's Religious Union, Iowa City Unitarian Church, 25 February.

Untitled notes. Discussion Group in Religion, Iowa City Unitarian Church, Sundays, 30 September—2 December, box 36, folder 21, 10 pp.

"The 'Concept' of Spirituality." Closing Address, Iowa and Nebraska Association of Unitarians, Iowa City, 17 October, box 4, folder 23 (and box 55, folder 21), 10 pp.

* "Liberalism and Religion." Young Peoples Religious Union, Fireside Hour, Iowa City Unitarian Church, 3 November.

"Liberalism and Religion. II: The Content of Liberal Religion." Presentation outline, Young Peoples Religious Union, Fireside Hour, Iowa City Unitarian Church, 10 November, box 20, folder 9, 10 pp.

1924 "Love and Force." Lecture, Philosophical Club, University of Iowa, 11 November, box 21, folder 18, 28 pp.

1925 Review of *The Christian Outlook: Being the Sermons of an Economist*, by Sir W. J. Ashley. *Political Science Quarterly* 40 (December): 624–26.

"Science and Human Values." Summary. Presentation, Iowa City Unitarian Church Men's Club, 8 December, FHK B55 F23, 2 pp.

1926 "Some Notes on Value." Notes, Iowa City Unitarian Church Men's Club, 17 March, box 55, folder 23, 1 p.

"On Force." Notes. Presentation, B-H group, 7 April, box 55, folder 23, 1 p.

1927 "On Personal and Impersonal Association: On the Interrelation of Forms of Association" (announced as "Types of Personal Relations"). Notes for presentation, Fireside Club, Iowa City Unitarian Church, 13 February. Manuscript, box 55, folder 1 (also box 36, folder 19), 5 pp.

1928 Iowa City Unitarian Church Men's Club, 20 February.

Undated "On Power: The Invincible Logic of Asceticism." Box 36, folder 21 (also in box 55, folder 15), 9 pp.

Appendix 2: Value Theory in Frank H. Knight's Work during the Iowa Years

The list below includes published essays and unpublished manuscripts, lecture notes, and other material from Knight's years at the University of Iowa. Presentations that have no surviving materials are also included, marked by an initial asterisk. The list is culled from Emmett 1999a, 1999b; more details are available there. Box and folder identifications are from the Frank H. Knight Papers, University of Chicago Archives.

1920 "Social Organization: A Survey of Its Problems and Forms from the Standpoint of the Present Crisis." Box 31, folders 6–7, 36 pp.

* "The Logic of Human Conduct." Philosophical Club, University of Iowa, 9 March.

Review of *The Place of Science in Modern Civilization*, by Thorstein Veblen. *Journal of Political Economy* 28 (June): 518–20.

1921 "Cassel's *Theoretische Sozialökonomie*." *Quarterly Journal of Economics* 36 (November): 145–53.

1922 "The Ethics of Competition." Lecture series, Harvard University, Department of Economics, January. Box 44, folder 2, 6 pp. Published as "Ethics and the Economic Interpretation," *Quarterly Journal of Economics* 36 (May 1922): 454–81, and "The Ethics of Competition," *Quarterly Journal of Economics* 37 (August 1923): 579–624.

"Individualism (or Economism) and Ethics." Lecture notes for Philosophical Club, University of Iowa, 14 February. Box 36, folder 19, 5 pp.

"Round Table Conference on the Relation between Economics and Ethics." *American Economic Review* 12 (March supplement): 192–93.

* "Logical Method in the Social Sciences." Political Science Club, University of Iowa, 16 October.

1923 * "Conscription of Wealth for War Purposes." Political Science Club, University of Iowa, 16 December.

1924 "The Limitations of Scientific Method in Economics." In *The Trend of Economics*, edited by R. G. Tugwell, 229–67. New York: Knopf.

"Economic Psychology and the Value Problem." Political Science Club, University of Iowa, 4 February. Published in the *Quarterly Journal of Economics* 39 (May 1925): 372–409.

"Society." Freshman lecture, University of Iowa, March. Box 44, folder 16, 3 pp.

"Some Fallacies in the Interpretation of Social Cost." *Quarterly Journal of Economics* 38 (August): 582–606.

Review of *Economics and Ethics*, by J. A. R. Marriot. *Journal of Social Forces* 2 (September): 757–58.

1925 "Utility as Fact, Force, End, Value: Science and Criticism in Economic Theory." Box 54, folder 8, 3 pp.

"Social Interpretation and Criticism." Box 54, folder 12, 33 pp.

"Limitations of Competitive Individualism, A: Mechanical Limitations." Box 54, folder 8, 14 pp.

"Limitations of Competitive Individualism, B: Ethical Considerations." Outline, box 54, folder 8, 2 pp.

"Energy, Human Energy, and Value." Box 13, folder 14, 35 pp.

Review of *Ethics and Some Modern World Problems*, by W. McDougall. *Political Science Quarterly* 40 (March): 138–40.

"Fact and Metaphysics in Economic Psychology." *American Economic Review* 15 (June): 247–66.

"Efficiency and the Social Ideal." Lecture, WSUI radio, Extension Division, University of Iowa, 8 October. Box 13, folder 6 (and box 55, folder 4), 6 pp.

"Some Explorations in the 'Twilight Zone' between Economics and Ethics." Lecture, Political Science Club, University of Iowa, 26 October. Box 35, folder 5, 22 pp.

Review of *Common Wealth*, by C. G. Campbell. Carbon copy, box 39, folder 23, 3 pp.

1926 "Economics at Its Best" [review of A. C. Pigou's *The Economics of Welfare*, 2nd ed.]. *American Economic Review* 16 (March): 51–58.

"What We Want (An Attempt to List Primary Wishes or Elements in Motivation)." Outline, October. Box 36, folder 18, 1 pp. An untitled addendum is in box 55, folder 22, 1 p.

"Some Observations on the Why of Human Behavior." Presentation, Political Science Club, University of Iowa, 10 January, and University of Chicago, 14 April. Box 47, folder 9, 4 pp. (also box 4, folder 25, 4 pp.).

"Science and Efficiency in Physics and Politics." Notes. Lecture, Baconian Club, University of Iowa, 18 February. Box 44, folder 13, 13 pp.

Review of *Social Progress*, by Ulysses G. Weatherly. *American Economic Review* 17 (September): 487–88.

1929 "Freedom as Fact and Criterion." *International Journal of Ethics* 39 (January): 129–47.

1932 "Das Wertproblem in der Wirtschaftstheorie." In *Die Wirtschaftstheorie der Gegenwart* (*Festschrift* for Friedrich von Wieser), vol. 2, *Wert, Preis, Produktion, Geld und Kredit*, edited by Hans Mayer with assistance from Frank A. Fetter and Richard Reisch. Vienna: Julius Springer.

Undated "Being and Doing." Box 55, folder 23, 2 pp.

"A Better List of Fundamental Wishes." Box 36, folder 18, 2 pp.

"A Discussion of Value Theory." Box 36, folder 17, 13 pp.

"Dismal Science." Box 55, folder 4, 18 pp.

"Economic Justice." Lecture notes, box 55, folder 26, 7 pp.

"An Ethical Social-Economic Order." Outline, box 36, folder 19 (and box 55, folder 22), 2 pp.

"The Evolution of Economics toward the Character of a Science." Box 36, folder 17, 9 pp.

"Further Notes on Power." Box 36, folder 18, 3 pp.

"Non-Economistic Conceptions of Value." Box 24, folder 12, 24 pp.; or "Non-Economistic Value." Box 24, folder 11, 30 pp. [Two drafts of same material.]

"Note for Possible Preface to a Treatise on Value." Box 55, folder 23, 3 pp.

"Outline of Ethics." Box 36, folder 22, 16 pp.

"Play, Art, and Work: A Little Book on the Value Problem for Students of the Social Science." Outline, box 36, folder 20, 7 pp.

"Science Is Mechanistic, [. . .], Civilization in Predicament." Lecture notes, box 55, folder 27, 9 pp.

References

Ames, E. S. 1910. *Psychology of Religious Experience*. Boston: Houghton Mifflin.

Boyd, R. 1997. Frank H. Knight and Ethical Pluralism. *Critical Review* 11.4:519–36.

Buchanan, J. M. 1982. Foreword to *Freedom and Reform: Essays in Economics and Social Philosophy*, edited by F. H. Knight. Indianapolis: Liberty Fund.

Dewey, D. 1990. Frank Knight before Cornell: Some Light on the Dark Years. *Research in the History of Economic Thought and Methodology* 8:1–38.

Doan, F. C. 1909. *Religion and the Modern Mind*. Boston: Sherman, French.

Emmett, R. B. 1992. Frank H. Knight on the Conflict of Values in Economic Life. *Research in the History of Economic Thought and Methodology* 9:87–103.

———. 1994. Frank Knight: Economics versus Religion. In *Economics and Religion: Are They Distinct?* edited by H. G. Brennan and A. M. C. Waterman. Boston: Kluwer Academic.

———. 1997. "What Is Truth" in Capital Theory? Five Stories Relevant to the Evaluation of Frank H. Knight's Contributions to the Capital Controversy. In *New Economics and Its History*, edited by John B. Davis. *HOPE* 29 (supplement):231–50.

———. 1999a. Frank Hyneman Knight (1885–1972): A Bibliography of His Writings. *Research in the History of Economic Thought and Methodology* (archival supplement) 9:1–100.

———. 1999b. Frank Hyneman Knight Papers 1910–1972: Finding Guide. *Research in the History of Economic Thought and Methodology* (archival supplement) 9:101–273.

Greer, W. B. 2001. *Ethics and Uncertainty: The Economics of John Maynard Keynes and Frank H. Knight*. Cheltenham, U.K.: Elgar.

Hammond, J. D. 1991. Frank Knight's Antipositivism. *HOPE* 23.3:335–81.

Kern, W. S. 1988. Frank Knight on Preachers and Economic Policy: A 19th Century Liberal Anti-religionist, He Thought Religion Should Support the Status Quo. *American Journal of Economics and Sociology* 47.1:61–69.

Kershner, F. D. n.d. Frederick Kershner Papers, Christian Theological Seminary, Indianapolis.
———. 1916. Knight to Kershner, 19 September, box 12, folder 9. In Kershner n.d.
———. 1921. Knight to Kershner, 27 November, box 15, folder 27. In Kershner n.d.
———. 1922a. Kershner to Knight, 5 July, box 15, folder 27. In Kershner n.d.
———. 1922b. Kershner to Knight, 1 November, box 15, folder 27. In Kershner n.d.
———. 1922c. Kershner to Knight, 20 November, box 15, folder 27. In Kershner n.d.
———. 1922d. Knight to Kershner, 16 May, box 15, folder 27. In Kershner n.d.
———. 1922e. Knight to Kershner, 30 October, box 15, folder 27. In Kershner n.d.
———. 1922f. Knight to Kershner, 15 November, box 15, folder 27. In Kershner n.d.
———. 1925a. Kershner to Knight, 17 March, box 22, folder 85. In Kershner n.d.
———. 1925b. Knight to Kershner, 12 March, box 22, folder 85. In Kershner n.d.
———. 1929. Knight to Kershner, 30 March, box 22, folder 86. In Kershner n.d.
———. 1938. *Those Gay Middle Ages*. Chicago: Willett, Clark.
Knight, B. W. 1936. *How to Run a War*. New York: Knopf.
Knight, F. H. n.d. Play, Art, and Work: A Little Book on the Value Problem for Students of the Social Science, box 36, folder 20. Frank H. Knight Papers, Special Collections Research Center, University of Chicago Library, Chicago.
———. 1921. *Risk, Uncertainty, and Profit*. Boston: Houghton Mifflin.
———. 1923a. The Concept of Spirituality, box 4, folder 23, and box 55, folder 21. Frank H. Knight Papers, Special Collections Research Center, University of Chicago Library, Chicago.
———. 1923b. Untitled notes, discussion group in religion, box 36, folder 21. Frank H. Knight Papers, Special Collections Research Center, University of Chicago Library, Chicago.
———. 1927. On Personal and Impersonal Association: On the Interrelation of Forms of Association, box 36, folder 19. Frank H. Knight Papers, Special Collections Research Center, University of Chicago Library, Chicago.
———. 1933. *The Economic Organization*. Chicago: University of Chicago.
———. 1949. Natural Law: Last Refuge of the Bigot. *Ethics* 59, no. 2, part 1, 127–35.
———. 1951. *The Economic Organization, with an Article "Notes on Cost and Utility."* New York: Kelley.
———. 1960. *Intelligence and Democratic Action*. Cambridge, Mass.: Harvard University Press.
———. 1963. Christian Ethics and Social Betterment, box 4, folder 6. Frank H. Knight Papers, Special Collections Research Center, University of Chicago Library, Chicago.
———. [1922] 1999. Ethics and the Economic Interpretation. In *Selected Essays by Frank H. Knight*, edited by R. B. Emmett. Chicago: University of Chicago Press.
———. [1923] 1999. The Ethics of Competition. In *Selected Essays by Frank H. Knight*, edited by R. B. Emmett. Chicago: University of Chicago Press.
———. [1924] 1999. The Limitations of Scientific Method in Economics. In *Selected Essays by Frank H. Knight*, edited by R. B. Emmett. Chicago: University of Chicago Press.

——. [1925] 1935. Economic Psychology and the Value Problem. In *The Ethics of Competition and Other Essays*. New York: Harper.
——. [1925] 1999. Fact and Metaphysics in Economic Psychology. In *Selected Essays by Frank H. Knight*, edited by R. B. Emmett. Chicago: University of Chicago Press.
——. [1928] 1999. Historical and Theoretical Issues in the Problem of Modern Capitalism. In *Selected Essays by Frank H. Knight*, edited by R. B. Emmett. Chicago: University of Chicago Press.
——. [1939] 1999. Ethics and Economic Reform. In *Selected Essays by Frank H. Knight*, edited by R. B. Emmett. Chicago: University of Chicago Press.
——. [1940] 1999. God and Professor Adler and Logic. In *Selected Essays by Frank H. Knight*, edited by R. B. Emmett. Chicago: University of Chicago Press.
——. [1951] 1999. The Role of Principles in Economics and Politics. In *Selected Essays by Frank H. Knight*, edited by R. B. Emmett. Chicago: University of Chicago Press.
Knight, F. H., and T. W. Merriam. 1945. *The Economic Order and Religion*. New York: Harper.
Marshall, Leon C. 1927. Marshall to Knight, 9 March, box 16, folder 1. Leon C. Marshall Files, Department of Economics Records, University of Chicago, Chicago.
Nelson, R. H. 2001. Frank Knight and Original Sin. *Independent Review* 6 (Summer): 5–25.
Nordquist, G. L. 1997. Frank Hyneman Knight: The Iowa Years. Paper presented at History of Economics Society, Charleston, South Carolina, June.
Raines, J. P., and C. R. Jung. 1986. Knight on Religion and Ethics as Agents of Social Change: An Essay to Commemorate the Centennial of Frank H. Knight's Birth. *American Journal of Economics and Sociology* 45.4:429–39.
Shils, E. 1981. Some Academics, Mainly at Chicago. *American Scholar* 50 (Spring): 179–96.
Stigler, G. J. 1987. Frank Hyneman Knight. In *The New Palgrave: A Dictionary of Economics*, edited by J. Eatwell, M. Milgate, and P. Newman. New York: Stockton Press.
Weber, M. 1927. *General Economic History*. Translated by F. H. Knight. London: Allen and Unwin.

Keeping Faith, Losing Faith: Conclusion to the Volume

Bradley Bateman and H. Spencer Banzhaf

As we noted in the introduction to the last section, there is a special irony in the fact that the last essay in our volume concerns the life and work of Frank Knight, a man known for his animosity toward religion. However, as Ross Emmett has shown, Knight thought deeply and seriously about religious belief, and these thoughts helped shape his work in the early development of neoclassical price theory. Knight was clearly one of the strong forces in disentangling religious belief from economic analysis, but he did so in part by *limiting* the role for economics rather than imperialistically extending it, so he actually plays a central role in both sides of the story we hope to address with this volume.

Another irony of ending the volume with an essay on Knight is that one of the earlier essays, by Daniela Parisi, involves Francesco Vito, who early in his career, while he was spending time in the United States in the 1930s, studied with Knight at the University of Chicago. Thus, while Knight held a particular animosity toward the Catholic Church, and was one of the giants of early-twentieth-century neoclassicism, his influence did not deter Vito from the pursuit of an economics that he hoped was consonant with his Catholic beliefs. As we said more than once in this volume's introduction, the story of the disentanglement of economics from religious belief was neither quick nor linear.

History of Political Economy 40 (annual suppl.) DOI 10.1215/00182702-2007-073

We also suggested that the disentanglement may not be complete or permanent. There is much contemporary evidence of an increase in work by economists who are interested in how religious beliefs might be brought into economic analysis. There is also much new work in economics that, while not of a religious provenance itself, nonetheless opens the door for the kind of ethical complexity that allows for the introduction of nonutilitarian (and explicitly religious) perspectives in evaluating economic behavior. We suspect that this last fact may make some people uneasy. There are still many in the academy who believe that good scholarship requires ignoring religious belief (one's own, as well as others'). For our own part, we cannot imagine how one could possibly ignore the influences, both good and bad, of religion in contemporary society. Nor can we imagine how one could ignore its influence in the history of ideas. That influence is sometimes direct and deliberate, sometimes an unintended consequence, but the essays in this volume make it clear that religion has a complex and important role to play in narrating the history of economic thought.

In fact, we would like to reiterate our suggestion from the introduction that the current trend toward a greater number of serious ethical discussions in economics and the inevitable movement beyond a simple framework of utility maximization as the sole descriptive and prescriptive ethical frame in economic analysis may actually make this an unusual moment for the history of economic thought. On the one hand, economists suddenly find themselves in need of a compelling narrative of how and why the discipline got stuck for so many decades on such an etiolated model of behavior and ethics. On the other hand, they will undoubtedly begin to wonder whether the past may hold any clear clues about alternative models and alternative ethical frameworks that could help them in their work.

To provide the answers to both of these two questions (How did economics become the way it was? Does the past hold any important ideas for us to develop?), the history that we have begun to tell in this volume must be much more fully developed. This work will require careful nurturing and patience not only from people who have a special passion for particular religious ideas but also from people who have a strong critical distance from the material and who may possess no religious belief. That is to say, like all good history, it will require many perspectives and many stories to paint a larger picture robust enough and detailed enough to provide the answers that our colleagues might find helpful and compelling. No one can deny that religion sometimes has a deleterious effect and that it can lead to destructive and undesirable behaviors. We hope that the community of scholars who pursue the history that is suggested by this volume can avoid those kinds of behaviors and that they aspire to the civility and grace that characterized the conference that led to this volume.

Contributors

António Almodovar is a professor of the history of economic thought at the University of Porto, Portugal. His current research involves the diffusion of classical economic thought and the history of Catholic economic thought. Recent publications include articles on Catholic economic thought (written with Pedro Teixeira) and on economics in Portugal (written with José Luís Cardoso) in the second edition of *The New Palgrave Dictionary of Economics* (2008).

Roger E. Backhouse is Professor of the History and Philosophy of Economics at the University of Birmingham, U.K. He is the author of *The Ordinary Business of Life/ The Penguin History of Economics* (2002) and is editor, with Bradley W. Bateman, of *The Cambridge Companion to Keynes* (2006).

H. Spencer Banzhaf is an associate professor of economics in the Andrew Young School of Policy Studies at Georgia State University. His work focuses on contemporary and historical applied welfare economics, with particular emphasis on the natural environment and other public goods. His research has been published in *HOPE*, the *American Economic Review*, the *International Economic Review*, the *Journal of Applied Econometrics*, and the *Journal of Environmental Economics and Management*, among others.

Bradley W. Bateman is the provost and executive vice-president of Denison University. He is the author of *Keynes's Uncertain Revolution* and coeditor (with Roger Backhouse) of *The Cambridge Companion to Keynes.* His work on the religious influences on American economics has appeared in many journals, including the *Journal of Economic Perspectives*, *HOPE*, and the *Journal of the History of Economic Thought.* He is working on a book on the religious influences in the formation of American economics in the late-nineteenth and early-twentieth century and how the discipline subsequently became secularized.

Stewart Davenport is an associate professor of American history at Pepperdine University and the author of *"Friends of the Unrighteous Mammon": Northern Christians and Market Capitalism, 1815–1860* (University of Chicago Press, 2008).

Ross B. Emmett is an associate professor of political economy and political theory and constitutional democracy and codirector of the Michigan Center for Innovation and Economic Prosperity, James Madison College, Michigan State University. His two-volume edited collection, *The Selected Essays of Frank H. Knight,* was published by the University of Chicago Press in 1999. *Frank Knight and the Chicago School in American Economics*, a collection of his essays, is forthcoming. He is the executive editor of *The Biographical Dictionary of American Economists* (Thoemmes/Continuum, 2006) and an editor of *Research in the History of Economic Thought and Methodology*. See his website at www.msu.edu/~emmettr/ for additional publications and information.

Gilbert Faccarello is a professor of economics at Panthéon-Assas University (Paris), cofounder and coeditor of the *European Journal of the History of Economic Thought*, and associate editor of the *Economics Bulletin*. He has published extensively on the history of political economy with special reference to classical and Marxian economics and to seventeenth- and eighteenth-century French political economy.

Donald Frey is professor of economics at Wake Forest University. He has research interests in the economics of education and the history of economic moral thought. He has published journal and encyclopedia articles on the Protestant ethic thesis, Daniel Raymond, Francis Wayland, eighteenth- and nineteenth-century American communes, Henry George, and Edward Bellamy. His book, *America's Economic Moralists: A History of Rival Ethics and Economics*, is scheduled to be published by the State University of New York Press in 2009.

Harro Maas is an associate professor at the University of Amsterdam. He has published widely on Victorian political economy and on Stanley Jevons in particular. His book *William Stanley Jevons and the Making of Modern Economics* (Cambridge University Press, 2005) won the Joseph J. Spengler best book award of the History of Economics Society in 2006. He is currently writing a history of observational practices in economics that is funded with a prestigious grant by the Netherlands Organisation for Scientific Research.

Stephen Meardon is an assistant professor of economics at Bowdoin College. His recent articles study the ideas and interests underlying the history of trade policy controversies in the United States and Latin America. In 2008 he was a Fulbright scholar and lecturer at the Universidad de los Andes in Bogotá, Colombia.

Steven G. Medema is a professor of economics at the University of Colorado Denver. He is the author of *The Hesitant Hand: Self-Interest, Market, and State in the History* *of Economic Thought*, *Economics and the Law: From Posner to Post Modernism and Beyond* (with Nicholas Mercuro), and *Ronald H. Coase*, and a coeditor (with Warren J. Samuels) of Lionel Robbins's *A History of Economic Thought: The LSE Lectures*. He served as editor of the *Journal of the History of Economic Thought* from 1999 to 2008.

Daniela Parisi is a full professor of the history of economic thought at the Universita' Cattolica del Sacro Cuore in Milan (Italy). Her main interests are to cross-analyze material preserved in Italian, foreign, and international archives and to verify the relationships among political economy and religious beliefs. Recent publications include "An Economist and His Books and Notes: The Case of Achille Loria's Library; Letters from Irving Fisher" (*Storia del pensiero economico*, 2005); "Overseas Pioneering in Economics in the 1920s" (in *Economics and Institutions: Contributions from the History of Economic Thought*, edited by F. Asso and L. Fiorito, 2007); and an edited volume, *The Crisis of the Economic System, Political Prices, and Autarky: Five Articles of the Young Franco Modigliani (Rome 1937–1938)* (2007).

Neil T. Skaggs is a professor of economics at Illinois State University. For the past twenty years he has been researching the development of monetary theory and policy, focusing primarily on the nineteenth-century British experience. In "Henry Thornton and the Development of Classical Monetary Economics" (*Canadian Journal of Economics*, 1995), he demonstrated that Thornton's monetary approach was picked up by writers in the banking school tradition, reversing the conventional wisdom that Thornton was a forerunner of the currency school. In other articles he has investigated the monetary economics of Thomas Tooke, John Fullarton, and John Stuart Mill, the main members of the banking school.

Philippe Steiner is a professor of sociology at Paris-Sorbonne University and a member of the Centre d'études sociologiques de la Sorbonne. His fields of interest are the history of the social sciences, specifically in France, economic sociology, and the sociology of organ transplants. He has recently coedited two volumes of J.-B. Say's *Œuvres complètes* (*Leçons d'économie politique*, 2003; and *Traité d'économie politique*, 2005), a study in the history of Durkheimian economic sociology (*L'école durkheimienne et l'économie: Sociologie, religion, et connaissance*, 2005). His *Traité de sociologie économique* (coedited with F. Vatin) and his study on organ transplants (*La transplantation d'organes: Un commerce entre les êtres humains*) are forthcoming in 2009.

Pedro Teixeira is a professor on the Faculty of Economics of the University of Porto and senior researcher at the Centre for Research in Higher Education Policies (CIPES) and the Centre for Macroeconomic and Forecasting Studies (CEMPRE). His research interests focus on the economics of higher education and on the history of economic thought, namely on the development of human capital theory. Recent publications include articles in several economic and higher education journals and his book *Jacob Mincer: A Founding Father of Modern Labour Economics* (Oxford University Press, 2007).

A. M. C. Waterman is Fellow of St. John's College, Winnipeg, and professor emeritus of economics at the University of Manitoba. His most recent book is *Political Economy and Christian Theology since the Enlightenment* (Palgrave Macmillan, 2005). In 2007 he was elected Distinguished Fellow of the History of Economics Society.

Index